Art

Imitates

Business

Art Imitates Business

Commercial and Political Influences in Elizabethan Theatre

James H. Forse

Bowling Green State University Popular Press
Bowling Green, OH 43403

All my offspring, and my spouse insisted,
A book should have a dedication in't.
And so to daughters Catherine Content,
And Constance Anne, and to son James Bruno,
And to spouse Lee, this book I dedicate.

Contents

ILLUSTRATIONS, TABLES, GRAPHS

i

Note on the Illustrations

Tables and graphs were compiled and designed by the author. Illustrations were chosen from sixteenth- and seventeenth-century engravings and drawings, with two exceptions. The map of London (p. 15) is reproduced from *The Riverside Shakespeare*, ed. G. Blakemore Evans, by permission of Houghton-Mifflin Company. The modern rendering of the interior of Blackfriars Theatre (p. 196) is reproduced from Irwin Smith's *Shakespeare's Blackfriars* Theatre, by permission of New York University Press. All illustrations were computerized, and computer enhanced, by Mr. Terry P. Morris, MA in Theatre, Western Illinois University, formerly a Technical Writer for Clarke-American Lincoln Company of Bowling Green, Ohio, and now residing in South Carolina.

Preface

Playscripts, plotbooks, *scenarii* comprise the largest body of original sources for the history of the theatre in the sixteenth century. Until recently, performance, artistic, ideological, and literary analyses of scripts have tended to dominate the study of theatre history. Yet purposes other than literary and artistic ones also motivated the theatre of Elizabethan England. Freeing itself from almost total dependence upon performances at Court, or in the houses of noble patrons, the theatre was becoming an autonomous entertainment business. Then, as now, that business was dominated by popular performers and by "money-men," those who financed the theatre facilities and the expenses of performance. Neither group was mutually exclusive. Philip Henslowe, the *impresario* of the Admiral's Men, might be classified as a "mere" investor, but his partner, and son-in-law, Edward Alleyn, was the most popular actor of his day. Shakespeare's acting company, the Chamberlain's Men, was a business partnership in which the senior actors also owned shares in the theatre buildings.

Since it was a *business*, commercial considerations played an underlying role in most aspects of the theatre. Playwrights were employees of the acting companies. They were commissioned to write plays specifically shaped to the physical resources and personnel available to those companies, and to provide material which brought audiences into the theatres. In that sense, playwrights needed to keep abreast of what we term "popular culture": current tastes, concerns, and preferences within the London audiences. By the same token, theatre companies had virtually no legal protection from arbitrary action by political authorities. To run afoul of the authorities meant the personal danger of being jailed, and the economic danger that the authorities would shut down the theatres. Not surprisingly, most of the time acting companies, though they paid attention to topical material, were cautious in their presentation of that material. At the same time, however, Elizabeth's Court was not dominated monolithically by any one person, or faction. Throughout the last two decades of the sixteenth century,

1

various aristocrats jockeyed for power, position, and prestige within the Court. Acting companies, therefore, were willing and expected to represent some of the interests of their aristocratic sponsors, whose own willingness to number the actors among their personal, liveried, servants, gave acting companies their only legal reason for existence. Business and political considerations, therefore, offer much in the way of explaining some of the "problems" and curiosities about sixteenth-century plays. Often those commercial and political interests, and their influences can only be discerned by studying plays within the context of the small slice of time in which they were written and initially performed.

Production and literary analyses cannot fully explain such influences, for until recently much that people think about Shakespeare's, and other Elizabethan playwrights', plays is based on attitudes formed long after they, and Shakespeare, died. For instance, *The Taming of the Shrew*, nowadays one of Shakespeare's most popular plays for performance, was not popular with *Shakespeare's* audience. *Shrew* became popular over forty years after Shakespeare died, and only in the form of *rewrites* of the script which stressed the story of Kate and Petruchio to such an extent that they deleted the sub-plots dealing with the drunken Christopher Sly, and with Kate's sister Bianca. From the Restoration until the second or third decade of this century, *King Lear* was unpopular. Critics and theatrical managers considered *Lear* too black, too tragic, too depressing, too huge for the stage. Nahum Tate's adaptation of 1681, with a happy ending in which Cordelia marries Edgar, and they, and Lear, all live happily ever-after, was what audiences saw throughout the late seventeenth, eighteenth, and into the first half of the nineteenth centuries. It was in the first half of the eighteenth century that Shylock in *The Merchant of Venice* became portrayed as a sympathetic, or at least human, character who represented the injustices perpetrated upon his race. That was done by Charles Macklin, till then a minor actor, who seized upon a new acting interpretation to make a name for himself.

Thus, when "traditionalists" talk about doing plays "like Shakespeare did it," or analyzing plays as "Shakespeare meant it," often they may mean like *adaptors* of Shakespeare did it, and meant it, in the eighteenth and nineteenth centuries to please their elite, wealthy audience. Really to do it "like Shakespeare did it" probably would discomfort most people in a modern theatre. Only a very special modern audience could appreciate, for instance, a man, in woman's costume, playing Kate, another man, in woman's costume, playing her sister Bianca, and both of them doing romantic scenes with other men.

Shakespeare, and his contemporaries in the theatre, "did it," and "meant it," to make money by pleasing not only the political, economic, and educational elite of their time, but the popular *mass* audience of London shop-keepers, skilled workers, their wives, and their apprentices, who made up the majority of their audiences. They also "did it," on occasion, to please the tastes and necessities for good publicity of their aristocratic patrons and those patrons' circles of friends and clients. Their scripts and performances were not designed consciously "for all time"; they were designed to fit the necessities of the moment. No one until Ben Jonson viewed plays, or playing, as ever-lasting art. When viewed as men trying to succeed in a new entertainment business, Shakespeare and his contemporary dramatists, cease to be *POETS*, or *SHAKESPEARE* (capital letters, trumpets, veneration, and all that), and instead look like much like any other script-writers who write for a fixed group of actors, and seek to please, and keep, a large, mixed audience—in other words, like writers for the movie studio system of contract actors of the 1930s and 1940s, or for on-going television shows like soap operas or situation comedies and weekly dramatic series.

Therefore, those essays herein that are concerned with plays *per se*, try to assess the historical spirit and motive behind how they did it—that is, to present a play that would: 1) help gain the acting partnership publicity, 2) pass the censorship of the authorities, 3) perhaps pay-back a patron with some veiled favorable publicity, and 4) appeal sufficiently to a *popular* audience that it would pay the price of admission, and come back again the next time the play was presented. Other essays attempt to assess various aspects of business and profit motives and activities, and political influences, upon Elizabethan theatre, in order to shed some further light on the *business* of theatre, and on theatre's place within the general milieu of Shakespeare's time. All of the essays hinge around ways in which, at particular moments in time, the pursuit of money, and the desire to continue in business, may have affected events and episodes in the theatre of the sixteenth century. None profess to be the final answer, nor the only approach, to interpretations of the plays, or the theatrical milieu of sixteenth-century London. Rather they proffer themselves simply as a few more *tesserae* to the historical mosaic we term Elizabethan England.

Some of these essays have been published previously in shorter form: "Mole," "Isle of Dogs," "(wo)Men," respectively, in volumes 13, 14, 15 of *Shakespeare and Renaissance Association of West Virginia: Selected Papers.* "Art Imitates Business" first appeared in the *Journal of Popular Culture*, volume 24, and "Extortion" in *Theatre Survey*, volume 31. These essays have been expanded and revised for inclusion in this book. The other essays have not appeared anywhere in print.

Acknowledgments are due to many. On a general level, one must recognize the exhaustive and valuable work done by numerous scholars over the years, beginning with Sir Edmund Chambers, and continuing to the present day in works by Muriel Bradbrook, Samuel Schoenbaum, Alfred Harbage, Herbert Berry, Glynne Wickham, Andrew Gurr, Gerald Bentley, William Ingram, E.J.A. Honigmann, Walter Cohen, and many, many, many others. All have made contributions which take the study of theatre far beyond the mere study of texts and themes, or romantic and antiquarian interests, which motivated many scholars until the twentieth century. Without their meticulous research and inspiration, no work could gather the facts to offer some modest re-analyses of aspects of sixteenth-century theatre. Anyone studying Elizabethan drama must give thanks to all of them.

Thanks are due on a more personal level. Five of these essays originally were presented at meetings of the Shakespeare and Renaissance Association of West Virginia. Scholars at those meetings gave me many useful suggestions, valuable criticism, and encouragement. Particularly kind and helpful over the years have been Professors Sophie Blaydes of West Virginia University, Trevor Owen of Potomac State College, Paul Orr of Wheeling Jesuit College and Edmund Taft of Marshall University. Participation at an NEH Institute on Renaissance Drama, organized by Dr. Lena Cowen Orlin, and directed by Professor Jean E. Howard of Columbia University, and sponsored and housed at the Folger Shakespeare Library in 1992, gave me much food for thought, especially in just how valuable the insights of literary-trained scholars can be in the reading and interpreting of texts within their historic content, and in discovering some of the underlying cultural assumptions in those texts.

Over the years, my wife Lee patiently and valiantly listened as I thrashed out, aloud, this twist, and that turn, in my research, and offered many valuable, common-sense suggestions. My colleagues Professors Thomas Knox and David Weinberg were helpful with bibliographic suggestions. My friend and mentor, Professor Deno J. Geanakoplos of Yale University often has shown me ways to link seemingly disparate persons and things. My editors, Ray and Pat Browne, were thoughtful and patient. Since my interest in Shakespeare and sixteenth-century theatre arose from directing Shakespearean productions for my community theatre, I must thank Bowling Green's Black Swamp Players for opportunities which triggered ideas leading to some of the conclusions arrived at in these pages. My friend and assistant Ms. Sherry Naselsky Leybovich carefully checked some of my research, and diligently proofread, and proofread, and proofread, the manuscript. Finally, I must thank two good friends, both knowledgeable about theatre, and Shakespeare "buffs": Mr. Kirk R. Wray, who helped me "walk" through some of these essays in their initial stages, and especially, Mr. Terry P. Morris. Mr. Morris put his considerable talents in computer graphics at my disposal. His encouragement when I was discouraged, and his suggestions, both as critic and "sounding-board" when I was developing these studies, have given me many valuable ideas, and forced me to explore areas I might not have considered on my own.

J.H.F.
Bowling Green, Ohio

July 1, 1993

Chapter 1

Art Imitates Business:
Profit and Business Practices in Elizabethan Theatre

Scholars have done much valuable work concerning commercial aspects of the Elizabethan theatre, but few have attempted synthesizing those aspects to suggest the full impact of commercialism upon those we credit with the creation of English drama. Sometimes scholars deal with the *business* of Elizabethan theatre reluctantly, or depreciatively. For instance, Alfred Harbage, describing the King's Men shaping its repertory to the new popularity of the private theatres like Blackfriars, calls "practical adaptability" an "ethical capitulation. There hovers a dubiety about the situation which might occasion a resigned pursing of lips on our part if we were dealing with a mere group of business associates, but these associates were also artists." William Ingram, distinguishing between what he calls "mere" theatrical speculators, John Brayne and Robert Keysar, and "actor-investors," Edward Alleyn, and Christopher Beeston (he might have added Richard Burbage and William Shakespeare) who were involved in producing theatre, says of the latter: "We diminish the breadth of their involvement if we suggest that they were in it only, or even primarily, for the money."[1]

Yet the "artists" too were, in many ways, "a mere group of business associates," and they too were in it "for the money," just like the "mere speculators" Keysar, or Henslowe, or Langley. Ingram himself convincingly argues for the attempt of James Burbage to monopolize profits from his own Theatre, and through a leasing-buy-out arrangement, from Henry Lanman's Curtain. Both groups sprang from commercialized classes, and employed commercialized motives and methods which distinguished their theatre from the amateur, or semi-amateur, types which preceded them. They entered into the *business* of theatre to make money as much as to create art. Oft quoted, Cuthbert Burbage's remark concerning his father James: that he was "by occupation a joiner, and reaping but small living by the same, gave it over and became a common Player in plays,"[2] seems to have been overlooked in its full import. Although sparse, information about occupational and social backgrounds, suggests some of those most venerated in the Elizabethan theatre did just as did James Burbage; they left traditional occupational backgrounds to increase their income in this new trade. The following table helps demonstrate the varied backgrounds of those closely associated with the history of the Elizabethan stage.[3]

Table 1 Selected List of Theatrical Wage-Earners, C. 1530-1630, and Occupational Backgrounds		
Theatrical Wage-Earner	**Prior Occupation**	**Father's Occupation**
Alleyn, Edward: Admiral's		Innkeeper
*Alleyn, John: part owner, Admiral's goods	Innkeeper	Innkeeper
Armin, Robert: King's Men	Goldsmith	Tailor
Arthur, Thomas: Court Interluder, 1528	Tailor	
Beaumont, Francis: Playwright		Lawyer
*Brayne, John: Partner in The Theatre	Grocer	
Burbage, Cuthbert: Housekeeper		Joiner & Carpenter
Burbage, James: Housekeeper		Joiner & Carpenter
Burbage, Richard: King's Men		Joiner & Carpenter
Chapman, George: Playwright	Soldier	
Chettle, Henry: Playwright	Printer	Dyer
"''Combs, William: Children of Windsor		Carpenter
Condell, Henry: King's Men, Housekeeper	Printer (?)	Fishmonger (?)
*Crane, Ralph: Copier, King's Men	Scrivener	Merchant-Taylor
Davenant, William: King's Men, Playwright	Page, Duke of Lennox	Vintner
Day, John: Playwright, Admiral's		Husbandman
Dekker, Thomas: Playwright, Admiral's	Sailor (?)	
Drayton, Michael, Playwright, Admiral's		Butcher & Tanner
Evans, Henry: Manager, Blackfriars Boys	Scrivener	
Ferrant, Richard: Manager, Blackfriars Boys	Choir Master	
#Field, Nathan: Blackfriars Boys, King's	Apprentice Printer	Clergy
Fletcher, John: Playwright, King's		Clergy, BP of London
Ford, John: Playwright, Henrietta's	Trained as Lawyer	Lower Landed Gentry
"''Grymes, Thomas: Queen's Chapel Boys	Apprentice	
#Hart, Charles: King's	Queen's Chapel Boys	Hatter

Heminges, John: King's, Housekeeper	Grocer (?)	
Henslowe, Philip: Housekeeper	Dyer	Game Warden
Heywood, Thomas: Queen's, Playwright		Clergy
Hudson, Richard: Player (1612)	Weaver	
*Islipp, Adam: Housekeeper	Printer	
*Jarman, Anthony: Housekeeper	Carpenter	
Jeffes, Anthony: Admiral's	Brewer	
*Johnson, Henry: Money-taker	Silk-Weaver	
Johnson, William: Leicester's	Vintner (?)	
Jonson, Ben; Playwright	Bricklayer/Soldier	Stpfather, Bricklayer
*Kendall, Thomas: Lessee, Blackfriars	Haberdasher	
*Keysar, Robert: Lessee, Blackfriars	Goldsmith	
*Kirkham, Edward: Lessee, Blackfriars	Innkeeper	
Kyd, Thomas: Playwright	Scrivener	Scrivener
*Langley, Francis: Housekeeper	Goldsmith	
Linster, Edward: Player	Weaver	
Lowin, John: King's	Goldsmith	
*Lyly, John: Playwright	Sec., Earl of Oxford	Clergy
Marlowe, Christopher: Playwright		Shoemaker
Marston, John: Playwright, Admiral's	Lawyer	Lawyer
Massinger, Philip: Playwright, King's	Page	Steward
Mayler, George: Court Interluder	Glazier	
Meade, Jacob: Housekeeper	Bear-Keeper	
Middleton, Thomas: Playwright, King's		Bricklayer
Munday, Anthony: Playwright, Admiral's	Apprentice Printer	Draper
*Nashe, Thomas: Playwright	Pamphleteer	Clergy
#Ostler, William: King's	Queen's Chapel Boys	
Pant, Thomas: Player	Shoemaker	
Peele, George: Playwright, Admiral's	Pamphleteer	Schoolmaster
*Rastall, William: Lessee, Blackfriars	Merchant	
Rosseter, Philip: Mgr, Whitefriars Boys	Choirmaster	
Shakespeare, Edmund: Player		Glover, Landlord
Shakespeare, William: King's, Housekeeper	Schoolmaster (?)	Glover, Landlord
Shank, John: King's, Housekeeper	Chandler (?)	
Shirley, James: Playwright, Henrietta's	Schoolmaster	Merchant-Taylor
Simpson, Christopher: Player	Shoemaker	
Simpson, Robert: Player	Shoemaker	
Slater, Martin: Admiral's	Iron Monger (?)	
Tarleton, Richard: Queen's	Swineherd (?)	Swineherd (?)
Tourneur, Cyril: Playwright, Blackfriars		Lawyer
#Underwood, John: King's	Queen's Chapel Boys	
Webster, John: Playwright, Admiral's	Tailor	Tailor
Young, John: Court Interluder	Mercer	

*Alleyn, Brayne, Crane, Islipp, Jarman, Johnson, Kendall, Kirkham, Keysar, Langley, Lyly, Nashe did not derive their primary incomes from the theatre business.
""Combs and Grymes do not appear later as actors in adult companies.
Field, Hart, Ostler, Underwood are about the only pre-1610 child-actors documented as continuing in the theatre business as adults.

The 68 people listed in Table 1 represent only about ten percent of the over 600 figures scholars have identified from theatrical records of the sixteenth and early seventeenth centuries, but the majority of those 68 were leading lights of the Elizabethan and Jacobean stage. None of these figures have any known links to the traditional entertainer groups of jugglers, tumblers, minstrels, and the like; nor do most come from the ranks of the Gentry or professional classes. Most, and among these the greatest names of the Elizabethan theatre, Alleyn, Burbage, Marlowe, Jonson, Heywood, Shakespeare, derive from the artisan/tradesman ranks of Elizabethan society, or as members of those ranks are called by some social historians, the yeoman class.

Though generally associated with agriculture, the term yeoman, at the beginning of the sixteenth century, was applied specifically to agriculturists who had become commercialized in their values and means of earning a living. Saving their money, these yeomen invested in land in such a way that they owned shares of communally-controlled properties. Expenses and harvest income were divided among these yeomen shareholders in relationship to the shares, or partial shares, each held. They practiced thrift, and closely watched after their personal and professional financial affairs.[4]

The term yeoman also began to be applied to those who invested in commerce, becoming merchants, artisans, tradesmen, innkeepers, vintners. The authorities tended to be a bit suspicious of the physical and social mobility of this new group,[5] but whether or not these yeomen types remained in rural areas and followed agricultural pursuits, or moved to the cities to pursue commercial livelihoods, *all* measured their social and financial security by the size of their income in *money*. In turn, money yielded from this profit-oriented approach to trade or agriculture, was reinvested, usually in land, whether urban or rural properties, still considered the most secure of investments. These lands generally were not developed or cultivated by the yeomen themselves; they supervised paid laborers, or collected rents, and managed properties with an eye towards increasing annual incomes in money, for wealth began to equal status.[6]

Such men also tended to aspire to membership in the upper-class of merchants or the landed Gentry. They became churchwardens, parish or municipal officers, lived in respectable neighborhoods with the mercantile or Gentry classes, gave money to the Church and the poor. In short, they became "pillars of the community." Some even applied for, and received, Coats-of-Arms from the Colleges of Heralds. Wealth offered possibilities of the status of the Gentry.[7]

The parallels to the "pillars" of the *theatrical* community are obvious. Henslowe's records reveal a careful accounting of his theatrical expenditures and income, as well as outlay and income from other properties and for personal and family expenditures. Letters exchanged between Philip Henslowe and his son-in-law Edward Alleyn reveal that Alleyn, already wealthy, and renowned as England's greatest actor, was very concerned about his garden and the maintenance of his horse, when touring the provinces with Strange's Men in 1593. Shakespeare seems to have had a reputation as somewhat of a skinflint, a man who drove shrewd and sharp deals with those who borrowed money from him. He sued at least two men for debt. All of these men, the Burbages, Condell, Heminges, Henslowe, Alleyn, Bryan, Pope, Shakespeare, invested in theatre properties as soon as opportunity presented itself, and rented or purchased London homes in The Strand, in Aldermanbury, in Blackfriars—all prime residential districts populated by successful merchants and government officers.[8] The Strand was the site of the London Royal Exchange, the chief financial center for rich merchants; Aldermanbury was the location of the London Guildhall, the seat of city government; and Blackfriars district, because of its proximity to Westminster, was home to many a lawyer and aspiring courtier and government officer.[9]

All these men invested in lands, whether London properties or rural farmlands. Shakespeare's investments in and around Stratford were valued at £300 a year (at least) in annual income. Richard Burbage's investments in London properties yielded about the same per year. Both Heminges and Condell received enough income from houses, tenements and lands in Blackfriars and other London districts to be described as men "of great lyveinge, wealth, and power." An income of £300 per year made a man prominent in the countryside, but to be called "wealthy" in status-conscious Elizabethan London, meant an income of over £1000 per year. Edward Alleyn's investments enabled him to buy a manor and found a college.[10] Alleyn's two retirements from the stage, Shakespeare's virtual retirement from the theatre after 1611, Heminges' probable retirement from acting at about the same date, when viewed within the yeoman success cycle become much clearer. Though perhaps not the only reason, their landed investments may have now demanded supervision which cut too deeply into the great amounts of time they had spent in theatrical activities. In Heminges' case, though he did remain active within the theatrical world, the reasons are much the same. His function as financial manager of the two theatrical facilities, the Globe and Blackfriars, and of the acting company, left him little time to continue as an active Player. His own syndicate seems to have recognized this. Though he owned a home in Aldermanbury, the acting company purchased him a second home near the Globe. Obviously, his duties had become so time-consuming that even a trip across the river and across town was inconvenient.

Just as the typical Elizabethan yeoman sought respectability, so too did these "yeoman" of the theatre. Pope, Phillips, Cowley, Heminges, Armin, Shakespeare, Henslowe, Alleyn, purchased or assumed Coats-of-Arms. Henslowe sought, and received, royal appointment as Groom of the Privy Chamber; Bryan sought, and received, royal appointment as a Yeoman of the Wardrobe; Shakespeare behaved like a country squire in Stratford; Heminges may have begun as a grocer, but his deathbed identification with the Grocer's Guild probably was because its members were prominent in the London City Council, and it was one of the most influential groups in the political and social life of London. Edward Alleyn, wealthiest of them all, may have aspired to knighthood. Perhaps Shakespeare did too. Most of them, once they became financially prominent, served as church wardens, parish officers, and other official capacities in their communities; most were known as philanthropists to the Church and the poor, naming both in their wills. Alleyn founded three almshouses for the poor in London, and a school and hospital at Dulwich.[11]

London, and the other developing cities, attracted yeoman tradesmen and artisans from more rural areas. Theatre "yeomen" also moved to London from smaller towns. Shakespeare, Marlowe, Tarleton, James Burbage, Henslowe, Heywood, and many others listed in Table 1, were not native Londoners, but immigrants to the city.[12] What motivated these schoolmasters, grocers, goldsmiths and the like to leave the security of their home towns and occupations must have been just as Cuthbert Burbage said of his father: "reaping but small living by the same [they] gave it over" to become Players.

As artisans and tradesmen, these men found that their traditional occupations offered little opportunity to increase income. The great Guilds, like the Merchant-Taylors, Grocers, Goldsmiths and the like, restricted the small practitioners' profits. Guilds were dominated by a small group of masters called liveried members, who oversaw production, limited the number of apprentices and journeymen per practitioner, levied fines for infractions of guild rules, and set prices and wages for the freemen or, as they were called, "yeomen," members of the guilds. These yeomen guildsmen were the actual producers of goods, unable to rise to the rank of liveried master without substantial capital investment, and unable to acquire the capital investment because their prices, standards, and wages were rigidly controlled by the masters. To cite examples: Philip Henslowe only gained fame and fortune because his master died, and left a widow and two orphaned daughters. Henslowe, his apprentice, married his former employer's widow, and thus gained control of substantial capital assets. Interestingly, he did not continue in his apprenticed trade as a Dyer, nor did he continue his former master's business; he quickly invested in rent-producing properties, a bearbaiting arena, money-lending, and the Rose Theatre. Francis Langley was apprenticed as a Draper; he invested in real estate, money-lending, and the Swan Theatre. Robert Keysar, who invested in the second Blackfriars Boys' Company, quit goldsmithing after six years of consistent fines, reprimands, and destruction of his finished goods by liveried masters of the Goldsmiths' Guild. Perhaps he was, as one scholar suggested, of dubious honesty and mediocre ability, but the continual interference of the liveried masters, coupled with their control over his prices and wages, gives clear evidence of the stringent management liveried masters of the guilds exercised over the yeomen craftsmen. For any man with entrepreneurial aspirations, the traditional guild system was a treadmill, a closed loop.[13]

The business of Playing, the theatre and its adjunct activities, on the other hand, was one of the few trades which "fell through the cracks" of the Elizabethan economic system. No Players' Guild existed to fix prices and wages; no class of "Master Players" existed to keep an enterprising actor from rising above his station. To be sure, these tradesmen turned theatre businessmen adopted many of the features of the guild system into their own organization, and clear distinctions emerged between "Sharers" (full partners) who owned the acting companies, and "Hired-men," who were salaried or paid by the day. Even the buy-in price of Sharer status was the same as the price charged a journeyman for full status in an artisan guild. Yet Hired-men, like Henry Condell and Alexander Cooke, were able to rise more easily to the ranks of Sharer than any yeoman guild member could rise to the ranks of liveried master. The fact that as early as the 1580s successful Players were prospering far beyond those who remained fixed in the tradesman and artisan classes,[14] certainly explains why clothworkers, grocers, joiners and carpenters, goldsmiths, scriveners, and the like, tried their hands a playing.

The Authorities characterized Players as "masterless men and vagabonds," who, because of that status, were exempt even from the restrictions placed upon minstrels, jugglers, tumblers by the Act of Apparel (1463).[15] Being "masterless" is just the point. The theatre business represented one of the few avenues of free enterprise open to an Elizabethan of modest means. Acting took small capital investment, and, at least until after the turn of the century, there was no long period of apprenticeship required of one who entered the Players' profession. Success depended solely upon one's own effort, talent, craft and thrift. We shall never know why some of these tradesmen's sons thought they could succeed in the theatre, but it is obvious why they tried. Distinctions between the "actor-investor" and the "mere" speculator do not hold up. Both were attracted to the theatre because it offered them business opportunities with potentially large profits, and few regulations and restrictions imposed from above.

Legal records of rental agreements, other records concerning wills, litigation, and the account books of Philip Henslowe provide relative good estimates of costs, investments, incomes, and other financial aspects of the Elizabethan theatre business. One thing stands out clearly in all these records—*it was business* in the minds of those Elizabethans whose names are intimately associated with sixteenth- and seventeenth-century London drama.

Just as other artisans realized that prosperity lay in the cities, James Burbage turned to London to launch the theatre business. By the mid-sixteenth century, London, with at least 150,000, and perhaps 200,000, inhabitants, dominated England's commerce. London alone accounted for 86 percent of all the Crown's custom revenues. The year that Burbage built The Theatre (1576), Parliamentary assessments for London were four times the total for all other English municipalities combined. It's largest class was composed of craftsmen and shopkeepers, with their wives, journeymen and apprentices. On a seasonal basis, depending upon the presence of the Royal Court, there also were numbers of "middle-income" lawyers and lower-ranked Court officers.[16]

About the only comparable European city in terms of size and composition was Venice, and just as there began to be entertainment geared to the public audience in that city in the 1560s and 1570s,[17] James Burbage realized London's potential as a market for popular entertainment. He risked his own money and, significantly, convinced his shrewd brother-in-law, John Brayne, a grocer, to risk substantial sums of his own to build The Theatre—London's first permanent theatrical enterprise truly free of aristocratic patronage and the vagaries of performing at inns. Brayne sold his grocery business, and its stock, to put up some of the £666 13s 4d that it cost to construct The Theatre.

Burbage already knew that London's City Council often blocked performances at the large inns and taverns. His distrust of noble patronage was justified with the collapse of Leicester's Men at the death of the Earl. He also knew that a Court Interluder had no chance for advancement. Security, room and board, were guaranteed, but the income had remained fixed since the reign of Henry VIII.

Admission prices at The Theatre (adopted by later theatres) reveal Burbage's plan to target the untouched mass market. There were more costly "lords' rooms," where aristocrats could maintain privacy, but the basic one-, two-, and three-penny admissions represented one-sixth to one-half the average daily income of an artisan, and placed costs easily within their reach, and that of their wives, journeymen, and apprentices. Burbage, and subsequently Henslowe, and their respective resident acting companies, clearly sought to offer affordable entertainment to a broad spectrum of London society—male and female, aristocrats, artisans and tradesmen, apprentices.

Very few other forms of entertainment were so designed, either in terms of price or broad appeal. Dining out cost from three to 12 pence per person. Contemporary writings like Thomas Nashe's *Pierce*

Penilesse (1592) indicate that these prices were within the budgets of money lenders, merchants, lawyers, and courtiers, but not the tradesman or artisan. Stopping by a tavern for a drink or two could cost at least as much as the basic admission to the theatre, and, of course, "good" women would not be accompanying their husbands to taverns. Nor would many of them be included to trips to the archery butts, bowling greens, tennis matches, cockfights, or bearbaitings. Aside from their undesirable location too close to the "stews" in Bankside, and reputations for rough-and-tumble behavior, these pastimes usually involved gambling, which, like card playing and dicing, pushed their actual costs far above what an afternoon of theatre would cost. Whoring (the minimum charge seems to have been six pence) cost an artisan a full day's pay. A penny would admit one to a puppet show, a fencing exhibition, an animal act, or tours of private gardens, Westminster Abbey, or St. Paul's, but how could these complete with the two or three hours of drama, music, spectacle, costumes, and the like to be had for the same price at the theatre.[18] Obviously Burbage's, and Henslowe's theatres were the London citizens' best entertainment bargain.

The capacities of The Theatre, the Rose, and subsequent public theatres, reveal this same target. Theaters built to accommodate 2,000 to 3,000 spectators are not designed for exclusivity.[19] The Theatre, and subsequent theatres, were erected quickly, for like other Renaissance entrepreneurs, "the patron was now building for himself."[20] In the case of the theatres, "building for himself" also meant getting customers in the doors as fast as possible.

Construction costs for The Theatre are estimated at £666. The annual rent for the land upon which The Theatre stood was £14. When these sums are placed in comparison to other Elizabethan figures concerning money, the capitalization for The Theatre was substantial indeed. The estimated yearly income of an English artisan of 1600 is about £15; land rent alone was almost equal to the annual income of an Elizabethan artisan. Construction costs represent a sum 44 times greater. At the other end of the social scale, annual household expenses for that year for a member of the peerage, Lord Cobham, were £875. Thus the total outlay for The Theater (£680) amounted to 77 percent of the expenses spent by a wealthy peer of the realm, and more than equaled the annual income of the lesser Gentry who averaged £300 to £750.[21]

James Burbage's success in providing permanent theatre in London must have inspired Richard Ferrant, Master of the Windsor Chapel and Royal Chapel boys' choirs. Ferrant, later in 1576, rented space in Blackfriars at £14 a year to provide a permanent locale for "rehearsals"—open to the public for a fee—for his choirboys (who seemed in need of continual practice before presenting plays for the Queen). Even though income seems to have been about half that of the public theatres, it still looked profitable enough that Ferrant's widow had no trouble sub-letting the property to Ferrant's successor choirmaster, William Hunnis at a price £6, 13s., 4d. above her £14 per year rent. Hunnis convinced a scriviner, Henry Evans, to assume the lease in 1583. When Evans became embroiled in litigation with Blackfriars' primary landlord, Sir William More, he sought outside help to keep the Boys' Company operating, bringing in John Lyly as playwright and joint-lessee. Lyly, secretary to the Earl of Oxford, must have seemed to Evans a man whose influence Evans could use. In 1584, Evans lost his legal battles, but he went down fighting.[22] The whole episode—Hunnis' sale to Evans, Evans co-opting John Lyly—looks more like the maneuvers of modern corporate executives trying to avoid a hostile takeover than esthetic concern for the arts.

Timely imitation shows the success of James Burbage's mass market theatre. The Curtain was built in 1577, a year after The Theatre, and virtually next door. Burbage's partner John Brayne sought to invest in another theatre planned at St. George's Inn in the 1580s. The Rose followed in less than ten years, financed by John Chomley, a grocer, and Philip Henslowe, a dyer, who had his wealthy new wife's money to invest. Francis Langley invested in the Swan and the Boar's Head theatres. The Rose cost £816. Costs for other theatres reveal the same substantial outlays: the first Globe (1599) cost £600, Henslowe's Fortune (1600), an almost identical sum.[23] The average construction cost was £673—in comparative terms equal to the upper income range of the Gentry, and 45 times greater than the annual income of the artisan.[24] How clearly success produced imitation is revealed in Philip Henslowe's contract detailing the construction of The Fortune Theater, erected in 1600 to rival The Globe, built the year before. Henslowe hired Peter Street, the same carpenter who had supervised The Globe's construction, and specified no less than four times in the contract how features at The Globe were to be copied at The Fortune. Furthermore, descriptions of the interiors of the theatres, like those of Thomas Platter, the Duke of

Stettin-Pomerania, and Johannes De Witt, indicate they were decorated lavishly. Pillars and posts were painted to look like marble columns. No doubt much of the rest of the interior was painted with vivid colors, as were the interiors of wealthy Elizabethan residences.[25] No wonder there were few scenic pieces in public theatres. The decoration of the theatre itself would have been scenery enough.

Attention to, and money spent on, decoration is yet another indication of theatre owners' attempts to attract a mass audience. The total effect must have seemed dazzling to the average playgoer, who not only could be entertained, but entertained in splendid surroundings, and witness costly "special effects:" a throne in the heavens, which cost £7 (half an artisan's annual income), or a gilded chariot; and see actors bedecked in velvet gowns costing £3, cloth-of-gold doublets costing £7, gilt crowns imbedded with glass jewels. All of these, and more, are mentioned in Henslowe's *Diary*. Foreign visitors like Johannes De Witt, the Duke of Stettin-Pomerania, and Thomas Platter, indicate there was little in their own countries to match it; plays themselves speak of players in lavish costumes; Thomas Heywood's *Apology for Actors* brags about how English theatres were a wonder to foreign visitors. Contemporary sketches of theatres only reveal what must be a pale reflection of their real glamour.

The very location of the various theatres further shows the concern of the owners for profit. To be sure, legal considerations played their part. The hostility of the London Council to all theatres was well-known. Much of that hostility was based on Puritanical values, and jealousy about theatres cutting into legitimate businesses' work-day and profits. To be fair to the authorities, some of that concern may have been justified. Though a metropolis by sixteenth-century standards, London, by modern standards of organization, was a "small town." There was no police force, no fire department. In a city in which law enforcement essentially was swearing out a posse, and riot control essentially was the citizen band described by Shakespeare in *Romeo and Juliet*—"Clubs, bills, and partisans! Strike! Beat them down!"—daily gatherings at theatres of groups of people whose numbers approached one percent of the total population must have seemed overwhelmingly frightening.

To be fair to the playgoers, on the other hand, their decorum seems to have been much better than the Puritan denunciations of rowdiness,

Fig. 1. Sketch of *Titus Andronicus* attributed to Henry Peacham (1594). Title page: *The Spanish Tragedy* (1615).

Fig. 2. Title page: *Roxana*.

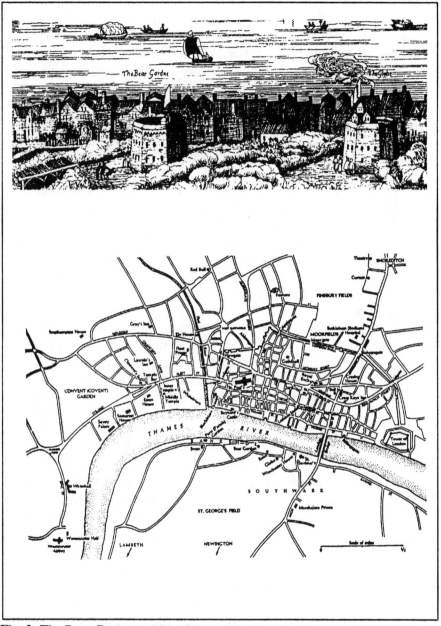

Fig. 3. The Bear Garden and The Globe Theatre: Visscher's *Panorama of London* (1616) Map of London.

wholesale immorality and thievery depict. To be sure, there were some courtesans in the crowd, but, at least from one foreigner's account, their dress and demeanor was no different than that of respectable women. Cut-purses were dealt with on the spot, tied to the stage posts. Various accounts mention the rapt and sober attention of the audiences, and the fact that the only casualties from the Globe fire were "a few forsaken cloaks; only one man had his breeches set on fire, that, a provident wit put it out with bottle ale," testifies that even under threatening conditions, playgoers seem to have been relatively disciplined in their behavior.[26]

To avoid the London Council's interference the theatres were all located in suburbs outside its jurisdiction, or, as in the case of Blackfriars, in areas exempted from its authority. The sites chosen also reflect a desire to reach all geographic areas of the metropolitan district. The Swan, the Hope, the Rose, the Globe, were to the south, across the Thames at Bankside. The Phoenix (or Cockpit) was located to the west of the city; the Red Bull was to the north, and The Curtain and The Fortune to the northeast.[27]

The famous story of the relocation and renaming of the Theatre as the Globe reveals the determination of the Burbage brothers, Cuthbert and Richard, to hold fast to their father's investment. With the land-lease for the Theatre about to expire, with the need for capital investment to move its components to a new location, the Burbages sold a half-interest in the facility to members of Richard's acting company—Pope, Phillips, Heminges, Kempe, and Shakespeare. The speed at which Philip Henslowe built a new and rival theatre, the Fortune, in an area which the now relocated Globe had vacated when it moved across the Thames (built there to compete with Henslowe's Rose), further attests to the competition which motivated the dominant characters of the London stage. After the Admiral's Men had relocated at the Fortune, the Globe syndicate sought to gain possession of the Rose, but offered less than Henslowe would accept.[28]

Not only capital outlay, but on-going theatrical costs were substantial. Litigation contained in the famous "Sharer Papers" of 1635, indicates annual outlays of approximately £1000 per year. Upkeep on the two theatres owned and operated by the Globe-Blackfriars syndicate (building maintenance, licensing fees, etc.) was approximately £100 per year. Henslowe's *Diary* listed costs for refurbishing the Rose in 1595 which totaled over £108. Owners also legally were required to make sure the streets fronting their properties were cleaned every week before Saturday evening; Henslowe recorded an expense of ten shillings for dung removal. Owners of London properties also were responsible for some street repairs.

Costs for play-production, costumes, properties, lighting, fees for musicians and playwrights, Hired-men's salaries, averaged about £900 per year. Just transportation of costumes and properties for a private performance could cost as much as 30 shillings (two months labor to the artisan). Sometimes on those jaunts, costumes and properties were lost or purloined, another expense to the company.[29] These annual expenses of £900 are higher than those expended by a Lord Cobham, a Lord of the Privy Council; they almost match the average income of an Elizabethan knight, and they equal what the artisan would have to work 67 years to amass.

Special "favors" also seem to have been expected by the authorities under whose jurisdiction the theatres fell. Henslowe recorded loans to Grooms of the Privy Chamber, and employees of the Lord Admiral, the Lord Chamberlain, and the Master of Revels. Some of the loans were as high as £10. He once was required by the Master of Revels to post a bond of £100. Around 1598, along with seven shillings per new play required by the Master for its licensing, a monthly stipend of £3 paid to the Master became the norm. John Heminges paid a substantial fee to the Master of the Revels to prohibit performances of Shakespeare's plays at the Red Bull, and also seems to have bestowed annual New Year's "gifts" upon the Master of the Revels. Christopher Beeston paid him an extra £60 per year on top of the usual fees, and, at least once, gave the Master's wife a pair of gloves whose price was almost a month's labor to the artisan.[30] Table 2, derived from seven years of expenses listed by Henslowe, gives an idea of the magnitude of some of those theatrical costs.

Figures for Spring, Summer 1597, and Fall, Winter 1600 are lower because part of the time the Rose was closed. In 1597, all playhouses closed from end of July until October by the Privy Council perhaps because of the *Isle of Dogs* affair. In 1600 the Admiral's Men moved to the Fortune. Figures for 1602 are larger because they are combined expenses for the Admiral's Men and Worcester's Men, playing, respectively, at the Fortune and the Rose.

Table 2
Production Expense, Henslowe's *Diary*,
Compared to Years (Months, Weeks) Income to Artisan
Total Plays Listed, 270

Time Period	Total Play Expenses	Years (Mns, Wks) Incm Artisan
Spring/Summer 1596	£32 3s 4d	2 years, 2 months
Fall/Winter 1596-97	£37 27s 8d	2 years, 7 months
*Spring/Summer 1597	£14 5s	11 months
Fall/Winter 1597-98	£75 27s 3d	5 years, 1 month
Spring/Summer 1598	£193 4d	12 years, 10 months
Fall/Winter 1598-99	£424 32s	28 years, 4 months
Spring/Summer 1599	£172 59s 14d	11 years, 8 months
Fall/Winter 1599-1600	£181 39s 6d	12 years, 2 months
Spring/Summer 1600	£153 26s	10 years, 3 months
*Fall/Winter 1600-01	£72 31s 6d	4 years, 11 months
Spring/Summer 1601	£106 13s 11d	7 years, 1 month
Fall/Winter 1601-02	£262 36s 11d	17 years, 7 months
*Fall/Winter 1602-03	£332 26s 12d	22 years, 3 months
Upkeep (£100/yr)	£700	46 years 8 months
Grand Total	£2769 10s 7d	184 years, 7 months
Yearly average (7 years)	£395 12s 11d	26 years, 5 months
Average per play (270 titles)	£7 15s 4d	6 months
Playwright Expenses	£747 5s	49 years, 10 months
Yearly average (7 years)	£106 15s	7 years, 1 month
Average per play (270 titles)	£2 15s 4d	2 months
Costume Expenses	£232 12s 14d	15 years, 6 months
Yearly average (7 years)	£33 4s 9d	2 years, 2 months
Average per play (270 titles)	17s 2d	3 weeks
Props, Salaries, Misc.	£1089 10s	72 years, 8 months
Yearly average (7 years)	£155 12s 9d	10 years, 4 months
Average per play (270 titles)	£4 7d	3 months

Table 2 shows that the financial claims and counter-claims in the Sharer Papers may not have been as inflated as some cautious scholars have warned. Claims that production expenses for both theatres averaged £2 per performance seem reasonable when compared to Henslowe's average of over £1 per performance at one theatre only. Though his total yearly production costs averaged a little more than £395, as compared to the £900 claimed in the Sharer Papers, it again must be pointed out that these are costs only for one theatre, and costs that are 35 years older than those given in the Sharer Papers (shortly after 1602 England went through a period of great inflation), and costs expended when only two companies, instead of five or six, were competing for the theatre-goers, and costs that included little in the way of extra musicians and special effects like those demanded by the repertories and clientele of the private theatres. While not all of Henslowe's costs are specified, it is clear that just those expenses specified for costumes, properties, and playwrights' fees were no little sums. Playwrights may have complained about their rewards, but their fees still amounted to over one-fourth of Henslowe's budget. This little glimpse we have of how Henslowe's figures reflect those given by the Globe/Blackfriars syndicate seem to indicate a relatively equal division of the theatre market between the Admiral's and Chamberlain's Men.

With these kinds of costs, what were the returns? From Henslowe's accounts, again, we can estimate the daily return for the public theatres tenanted by the Admiral's and King's Men at approximately £8.5 to £10 per theatre. The profit margin here is substantial. At an average production cost £1 and one-half, the net profit per day is £7 to £8.5, or over 466 percent profit. When the gross income per performance is multiplied by an average of 230 performances per year, average gross receipts brought in yearly by each of the two major companies must have approached £1955 to £2300. If Henslowe's yearly production costs

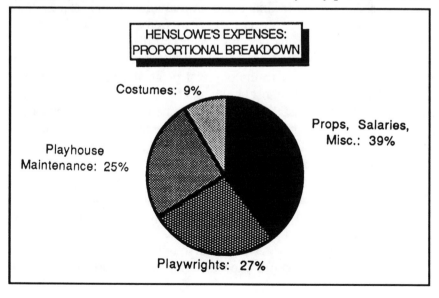

of about £300 is combined with the average £100 upkeep, for total expenses of £400, the yearly profit margin is still about 488 to 575 percent. To place these gross income figures within a comparative framework: the mean gross income of the 58 titled English peers in 1602 was £3360.[31] Hence the combined receipts of the two theatres at the lower daily figure (£3910) was greater than the Elizabethan peer's average income; individually, each theatre still averaged between 58 percent to 68 percent of the average income of a peer. In terms of the average tradesman, the combined incomes equaled almost 367 years labor, the individual 173 years of labor. In short, at an average of £10 per day the Globe or the Rose earned in one day what the artisan labored eight months to achieve.

Though receipts at The Globe declined to about £8.5 by 1610, those at the new theatre occupied also by the King's Men, Blackfriars, were £15.75 per day.[32] The total receipts for both theatres under their control averaged £23.8 per day, or £6545 per year. Thus the gross income of Blackfriars and The Globe in the year before Shakespeare retired was almost twice the average income of the titled nobility, was six times greater than that of the Gentry, was over 436 times greater than that of the average artisan. Another £20 to £30 per year income is added to the theatres from revenues generated by tap-houses, gardens, tenements, and food-concessions attached to the theatre properties.

What kind of an income could an individual Sharer expect from these receipts. From the "Sharer Papers" we find a sum of £180 given by the defendant John Shank, and undisputed by the plaintiff-actors, who were suing for the right to buy shares in the theatre facilities.[33] Hence even without an interest in the physical plant, the full partner in the acting company earned almost two-thirds the income of a member of the Elizabethan Gentry, and 12 times the income of the artisan. Even the buy-in share paid by an actor to achieve Sharer status (or the same buy-out share paid to the actor upon retirement, or to his heirs should he die), was at £70 to £90, almost five times the average artisan's income. A playwright received about £6 for a finished play, and probably a "benefit" performance upon its presentation for another £8.5,[34] a total, in other words £14.5, but still per play, almost equal to the average annual wage of an artisan.

The actor who was shrewd enough to invest his money from acting in the theatre facility could expect to earn much more, like Alleyn,

Burbage, Heminges, Condell, and Shakespeare. Richard Burbage, for example, owned a one-fourth share in the Globe, and a one-seventh share in Blackfriars. His other acting partners each owned one-eighth shares in the Globe and one-seventh shares in Blackfriars.

Using just The Globe receipts to begin with, Burbage, or Heminges, or Shakespeare, as a Sharer with seven other partners, were each entitled to one-eighth of half the gallery receipts, and one-eighth of all the "groundling" receipts. Groundling receipts, according to Henslowe's accounts, amounted to 32 percent of the total, or (based on an average of £8.5 per performance)[35] £2.72. Burbage's, or Heminges, or Shakespeare's one-eighth would be about £0.5. Gallery receipts accounted for 68 percent of the total receipts, or £5.9. The Sharer was entitled to one-eighth of half of the gallery receipts (totaling about £2.9), or £0.36. A Sharer in the Chamberlain's Men would earn per performance about £0.86. At about 200 pence per performance, therefore, the Sharer earned in a day what the artisan labored a month to achieve. Those of the company, like Burbage, who had become Housekeepers in the Globe syndicate would receive also a share of the gallery receipts. Burbage, with a one-fourth share would be entitled to another £0.72, about the same amount as his income as Sharer. His daily income from both sources would approximate £1.6. From this single theatre, then, Richard Burbage earned more in one day than the artisan or tradesman earned in two months. His total annual income as Sharer/Housekeeper at the Globe was about £368, equal to the average income of the country Gentry. Using the same formula for those with smaller Housekeeper shares, like Heminges, Condell, Shakespeare, their annual income still approximates £245.

Actor income at the Globe shrank after four partners were added (1603). A one-twelfth share would average £108 per year. Sharer income at the new Blackfriars facility, however, yielded perhaps another £180. A one-seventh Housekeeper share in the building produced another £135 or so, yielding the Sharer/Housekeeper there an income of about of £315. The combined Sharer/Housekeeper percentage of total receipts at Blackfriars (about £3208) was therefore about ten percent; at the Globe, the individual Sharer/Housekeeper percentage was about the same.

Pocket-money was generated through Housekeeper shares of the attached tap-houses, tenements, etc., earning the individual Housekeeper an additional £4 or so. A member of the Globe/Blackfriars

Housekeepers' syndicate, who was also a Sharer in the acting company, thus averaged a grand total (after 1609) of at least £560 per year. From theatrical income alone, therefore, the premier members of the Chamberlain's Men earned individual incomes equal to the middle ranks of the lower Gentry (£300-£750), and more than the average artisan could hope to earn in a lifetime. That income placed them in the income bracket of the top five percent of Elizabethans.[36]

Other figures connected to the activities of Shakespeare and his partners reveal men of substantial means in Elizabethan terms. Many of them invested in real estate, which increased their incomes beyond that yielded through theatrical activities. Shakespeare's lands in and around Stratford were valued at over £300 in income per year, a figure which by itself ranks him equal to many of the lower Gentry. He purchased a house in Blackfriars at a cost of £140 (over nine years labor to the artisan), paying £60 down and the remaining £80 in less than a year. In his will he left cash bequests totaling over £387.[37] Similar sums appear in papers concerning his confederates. Richard Burbage, whose Housekeeper shares were larger than Shakespeare's and whose investments in London real estate were also estimated at £300 a year, was believed to be slightly less well-off than Shakespeare; Condell and Heminges, who acquired larger and larger Housekeeper shares as members of the syndicate retired or died, were generally believed to be wealthier than Shakespeare. Condell, in the later years of his life, bought a substantial country-house at Fulham. Each of them had substantial investments in London real estate. To reiterate an earlier point: based on attitudes in London concerning relative wealth, to have been called men of "greate lyveinge, wealth, and power," by contemporaries, they must have earned over £1000 per year. William Ostler's widow valued her inheritance of her husband's Housekeeper shares at £600. Lawsuits brought against Henry Evans (of Blackfriars) by his three partners, listed £300, £400, £600 respectively as the amounts each had advanced him to buy into the venture. Alexander Cooke bequeathed over £150 in cash to his three children; Thomas Pope bequeathed £160 in cash to his heirs. And Edward Alleyn, by far the richest of these Elizabethan "yeomen" of the theatre, spent £10,000 for his manor and college at Dulwich, and £1,700 annually for their upkeep.[38]

Most of these sums, in comparative framework with other Elizabethans, rank with the average income of the Gentry, and about 20 times the income of the average artisan. In the case of Alleyn, the sums are stupendous. As the only other partner of his father-in-law Philip Henslowe in the theatre facilities both owned, Alleyn earned at least double that of Richard Burbage, or at least £331 per year from the Rose alone. His gross income as a Sharer in the Admiral's Men was also his net income. Unlike Burbage and other partners in both companies, who shared expenses as well as receipts, Alleyn was exempted from the Admiral's Men's production expenses. With shares in the Fortune, the Rose, and as Henslowe's partner in the bear-and bull-baiting business, his income must have tripled, at least, that of Burbage or any of the other actors in sixteenth-century London. As Henslowe's primary heir, he acquired full ownership of these entertainment businesses at Henslowe's death. This enabled him to buy Dulwich manor at a purchase price of £10,000, a sum three times greater than the average income of England's 58 titled peers, and equal to over 667 years of labor to the average artisan. Alleyn's household expenses alone, at £1,700 per year, equal the average income of England's 500 knights, and rival the household expenses of many peers of the realm. At the other end of the social scale, they represent 113 years labor to an artisan.

Lest these sums of money seem inflated, it must be remembered that conservative estimates state that 15,000 people per week attended the performances of the Admiral's and Chamberlain's Men. Vintners and victuallers complained because potential customers were at plays. City Fathers and merchants complained that attendance at Blackfriars clogged the streets with carriages and pedestrians, and drew pedestrian traffic away from shopping areas. When The Globe closed because of fire (1613), the ferrymen complained about a drop in business of "three or four thousand people, that were used to spend their monies by water."[39]

Since the penny represented the minimum admission price, the theatres reaped at least 15,000 pennies per week, or £62.5. The figure must have been much higher. One penny admissions accounted for only 32 percent of the gross receipts.[40] Thus the total weekly receipts for both Bankside theatres would be about 46,875 pennies, or £195.3. One other set of figures should suffice to display the huge sums generated by the London theatres. When, in 1628, the City Council attempted to buy out Blackfriars, the King's Men valued the property at £21,000. The commissioners appointed by the Council set a much lower value, £3,000, but even this sum was beyond what Council was willing to pay.[41]

Such large sums reveal that the principal figures of Elizabethan drama were far beyond the usual appellation "prosperous." Capital outlay, ongoing costs, receipts, incomes, indicate men who harnessed and managed the Elizabethan equivalent of a modern multi-million dollar business. Only those who practiced business skills, who, like other Elizabethan yeomen, were thrifty, used their income to increase their share of the business, who viewed and shaped their artistic talents as if they were business commodities, made such sums. Entertainment then, as now, offered the opportunity to earn enormous amounts of money compared to the average person's wages. Table 3 gives some comparisons of selected theatrical monies and compares these sums with the amount of time an average tradesman or artisan would have to labor in order to earn them.

Table 3
Comparison of Selected Theatre-Related Monies
to Number of Years' Wages to Artisan

Item	Pounds Ster.	No. Years' Wgs.
Construction Costs: Burbage's "Theatre"	£666	44.4 Years
Construction Costs: Henslowe's "Rose"	£816	54.4 Years
Construction Csts: "The Globe"	£600	40 Years
Construction Costs: Henslowe's "Fortune"	£600	40 Years
Average Constructions Costs (4 Theatres)	£673	45 Years
Land Rent, Annual: Burbage's "Theatre"	£14	11 Months
Average Play Production Costs: Annually	£900	60 Years
Average Building Maintenance Costs: Annual	£100	6.7 Years
Average Daily Receipts: "Globe" or "Rose"	£8.5	7 Months
Annual Receipts: "Globe" or "Rose"	£1955	130.33 Years
Average Daily Receipts: "Blackfriars"	£15.75	1 Year
Average Daily Receipts: Globe/Blackfriars	£23.25	1.6 Years
Annual Receipts: Globe/Blackfriars	£6545	436.3 Years
Costumes/Properties: "The Swan"	£300	20 Years
Buy-in, Buy-Out Share: Acting Companies	£70-£90	4.6 Years
Sharer's Annual Salary	£180	12 Years
Playwright's Fee + "Benefit" Performance	£14.5	1 Year
Heminges' Minimum Income (1623)	£1000	66.7 Years
Henslowe's Theatre Expenses (1593-1603)	£2399	160 Years
Shakespeare's Cash Bequests (in Will)	£387	25.8 Years
Cooke's Cash Bequests (in Will)	£150	10 Years
Alleyn's Upkeep Costs: Dulwich Manor	£1700	113.3 Years
Purchase Price of Dulwich Manor	£10,000	666.7 Years

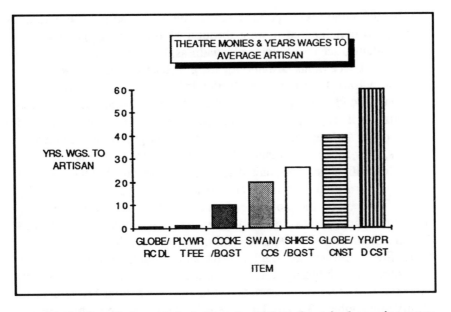

YRS. WGS. TO ARTISAN

THEATRE MONIES & YEARS WAGES TO AVERAGE ARTISAN

ITEM

Table 3 and the graph demonstrate that theatrical monies were astronomical when compared to the average Elizabethan artisan's income. Figures like Heminges' landed income or Alleyn's purchase price for Dulwich Manor would not even plot on a graph without making the scale in hundreds of years of labor. Such stupendous costs when compared to artisan income show why Henslowe and his rivals used gate-receipts, not artistic merit, to determine a play's stage life. A popular old war-horse like *Spanish Tragedy* was revived, and revived, and revived; a play which saw drastic reductions in gate-receipts after the first few performances was removed from the repertory, never to be reintroduced. Henslowe backed no "sleepers." In the same fashion *Titus Andronicus* and *Hamlet* played again and again at Shakespeare's Globe,[42] but other plays, even those by the Globe's premier playwright, such as *Taming of the Shrew*, *Love's Labors' Won*, and *Cardenio*, became figuratively, and sometimes literally, lost, or perhaps recycled under a new name.[43] From Henslowe, the "hardheaded capitalist" we expect such ruthless disposal of plays with limited popularity. It seems that Shakespeare, a shareholder in the acting company, a Housekeeper in The Globe—a man, in other words, with a prominent voice in the company's operations—was just as ruthless, even with his own creations.

By the same token, popular plays invited imitation. The *Spanish Tragedy*, so popular that it went through 11 printings in just over 21 years, contained scenes of "feigned" madness. Even the fastidious Greene copied that device in his *Orlando Furioso*. Shakespeare used it almost ad nauseam in *Titus Andronicus*, in *Hamlet*, in *Lear*, even in *The Taming of the Shrew*. Blood and gore were another feature of *Spanish Tragedy*, and one certainly finds the plays of Shakespeare and other dramatists littered with corpses and replete with scenes of almost gratuitous violence—beatings, slow, theatrical strangulations, throat-cuttings, eye-gougings.

"Box-office" success meant giving the popular audience what it wanted. Literary and dramatic criticism over the years has carefully isolated the themes, the plots, the dramatic devices tailored to the tastes of Elizabethan artisans and tradesmen and courtiers. Yet where did Dekker, Chapman, Shakespeare, and other playwrights learn of these tastes? Sheer instinct, nor trial and error alone could not have been their only sources. Producing plays was expensive even by Elizabethan standards. No good businessman would risk substantial investment to intuitive intangibles. Theatre businessmen—and recent research stresses even Shakespeare's hardheadedness as a businessman in the eyes of his contemporaries—must have done some kind of market research. The book trade offered an indication of what was of interest to the various classes of sixteenth-century London.[44]

Many have underestimated literacy among the artisan classes of sixteenth-century England.[45] Sir Thomas More's boast in the first quarter of the sixteenth century that 60 percent of all Londoners were literate, should be accepted, if not increased for the London of Shakespeare's day. By that time each county in England averaged ten grammar schools, most subsidized by the Gentry, the guilds, or the Church. Proximity and cost kept schooling within the reach of all but the poorest boys and girls. Education was a matter of concern to Elizabethans, as evidenced by a number of treatises written about schooling, and the government's periodic check-ups on the quality of schoolmasters through episcopal visitations and written inquiries. Even some servant girls could read and write. The emphasis on reading and writing was so strong that each and every guild required literacy of anyone admitted to apprenticeship. The sheer number of university and grammar school trained men jostling for patronship in Elizabethan London demonstrates that schools produced more "scholars" than there were jobs for them.[46]

Neither should one assume that the popular classes "did not read much." Plays, like *Westward Ho*, assume literacy even for shopkeepers' wives. In the last half of the sixteenth century, London supported an average of 25 printing establishments. Though the Stationers' Guild limited the printing per edition to 1,250 to 1,500 copies, the yearly average of new titles printed was about 200; each printer averaged about 9,600 copies per year. Hence 200,000 to 300,000 pieces were printed annually.

Considerable numbers such as these indicate a brisk market. Sales to the aristocracy, to the Gentry, to church libraries, and to the provinces could not have amounted to more than one-third of the total copies produced. Writers and their publishers clearly catered to a less well-off, and less well-educated, clientele. Most books sold in unbound copies costing from two to four pennies, no more than half the disposable income available per week to an artisan. Grafton's and Stowe's *Chronicles* competed with one another, periodically reissued in simpler, shorter, cheaper editions. Between 1564 and 1600 there were 16 separate editions of Grafton and 15 editions of Stowe. Philamon Holland flatly stated that his translations of Greek and Latin classical literature specifically were designed to make the classics available to "the husbandman, the mason, the carpenter, goldsmith, painter, lapidary, and engraver, with other artificers."[47]

It was simplified history books about England like Grafton's and Stowe's *Chronicles*, Greek and Latin classics in translation, and geography and travel books which were among the most popular titles selected by the working classes. And as regards playwrights like those working for Henslowe, or like Shakespeare, it seems to have been the appearance and popularity of these simple history books and the classics in translation which helped trigger their muse. Scholars have identified the sources (and probable sources) of Shakespeare's plots. What also is intriguing, as seen in the following table, is the chronological relationship between the appearance of printed copies of those sources and the subsequent production of Shakespearean plays drawing upon those sources.[48] Since the precise dating of the plays is the subject of scholarly debate (especially concerning the earlier plays), dates are not meant as absolutes. For convenience, they follow the traditional dating system merely as a chronological framework,[49] with a plus or minus variable of a year or so.

Table 4
Approximate Chronologies of Selected Sources and Plays

A. Histories (No Direct Year-by-Year Relationship)

History/Travel Book	Pub. Year	History Play	Trad. Dates
Foxe's *Martyrs*	1570	1 Henry VI	1589-90
Stowe's *Chronicles*	1580	2 Henry VI	1589-90
Anon. *Henry V*	1586	3 Henry VI	1590-91
Holingshed's *Chronicles*	1587	Richard III	1592-93
Mirror for Magistrates	1587	Collaborator, Thomas More	1594-95
Anon. *Reign of John*	1591	King John	1594-95
rev. Stowe's *Chronicles*	1592	Richard II	1595
Daniel's *Civil Wars*	1595	1 Henry IV	1595
rev. Foxe's *Martyrs*	1595	2 Henry IV	1596-97
Stowe's *London*	1598	Henry V	1599

B. Greco-Roman (No Direct Year-by-Year Relationship)

English Translations	Pub. Year	Greco-Roman Play	Trad. Dates
Appian's *Civil Wars*	1578		
Plutarch's *Lives*	1579	Titus Andronicus	1593-94
Lefevre's *Troy*	1595		
Homer's *Iliad*	1598		
Tacitus' *Annals*	1598		
Daniel's *Cleopatra*	1599	Julius Caesar	1599
Livy's *History*	1600		
rev. Plutarch's *Lives*	1600	Troilus & Cressida	1601-02
Pliny's *History*	1601	Anthony & Cleopatra	1606-07
rev. Plutarch's *Lives*	1603	Coriolanus	1607-08
Suetonius' *Lives*	1606	Timon of Athens	1607-08

C. Comedies-Tragedies (Near Year-by-Year Relationship)

Book	Pub. Year	Play	Trad. Dates
trans. Plautus' *Memaechmi*	1594		
trans. Plautus' *Amphitruo*	1594	Comedy of Errors	1593-94
trans. *Gesta Romanorum*	1595	Merchant of Venice	1596-97
Gerard's *Herbal* (songs)	1597	rev. Love's Labors' Lost	1597
trans. Contarini's *Venice*	1599	Othello	1604
Jones' *Songs & Airs*	1600	Twelfth Night	1601-02
Hall's *Popish Imposters*	1603		
trans. Montaigne's *Essays*	1603	King Lear	1604
Twine's *Painful Adventures*	1607	Pericles Prince of Tyre	1607-08
Jourdain's *Bermudas*	1610		
Virginia Council's *Virginia*	1610	The Tempest	1611
trans. Cervantes' *Quixote*	1612	Cardenio	1612-13

Fig. 4. Woodcut: Elizabethan School.

Table 4 indicates that Shakespeare may have operated on a principle much like: "You've read the book; now see the play." The relationship between the publication of a popular work and Shakespeare's subsequent and speedy use of that work seems quite clear in Part C, as, for example, Jones' *Songs and Airs* in 1600 and Shakespeare's use of some of those songs in *Twelfth Night* a year or so later, or the publication of Jourdain's *Bermuda* in 1610 and the performance of *The Tempest* in 1611, just as the earlier popularity of Brooke's poem *Romeaus and Juliet* with the Inns of Court gallants led to the play *Romeo and Juliet*. Such a close relationship is not as obvious in parts A and B until the books and plays in each category are examined as groups.

Whether one adopts the traditional dating of Shakespeare's first plays, or adopts the newer view which dates them earlier, the writing of comedy-romances, and to a lesser extent tragedies, is distributed somewhat evenly throughout his theatrical career. The writing of English history plays, and the writing of plays on Greco-Roman themes, are concentrated primarily into two separate periods: English histories up to 1599, Greco-Roman plays from 1599 to 1608. In each of these ten-year periods the London book trade produced several publications whose genre, content, or theme parallel the pattern of Shakespeare's plays.

A strong interest in history and geography, especially English history and famous English landmarks, was prevalent in England during the latter half of the sixteenth century. Between 1550 and 1600 about 110 travel and history books were published, some, like Holingshed's, Grafton's, and Stowe's *Chronicles*, and *The Mirror for Magistrates* going through multiple printings. The surge of national concern and feeling produced by the threat of, and "defeat" of, the Spanish Armada quickened that historical interest in the late 1580s and early 1590s, about the time Shakespeare himself went to London. Specifically, in 1587 Holingshed's popular *Chronicles* as well as the widely read *Mirror for Magistrates*, both used heavily by Shakespeare in his history plays, were revised, expanded, and reprinted. From that date on, until the end of the century, over 39 books dealing with travel or England's history were printed, an average of three new ones per year.[50]

Many historians have noted how Shakespeare's history plays reflected this surge of English nationalism, becoming, as A.L. Rowse put it, "the very voice of England in those years.... He caught the mood and made himself the mouthpiece; hence his earliest success."[51] Yet reflecting the spirit of the time is insufficient to explain why Shakespeare, who had written nine history plays—an average of one a year—abruptly stopped writing them in 1599. Obviously English nationalism did not drop off in 1599, but the publication of books about English history did. Only one new English history book appeared in 1599; none in 1600 or 1601.

About the same time, around 1598-99, for whatever reasons, printers began to issue new types of titles. One new trend in printing became translations of Greco-Roman sources, which, though a few had appeared in the late 1570s, now seemed to gain in popularity rather rapidly. At least 21 different translations of Livy, Ovid, Sallust, Homer, and other Greco-Roman writers, were printed between 1598 and 1610— at least one, sometimes two or more, new editions printed each year. London printers, and writers knew their patrons, and sought to make money; they produced books they knew would sell.[52] Shakespeare and his partners seem to have followed their lead, from 1599 until 1607, Shakespeare wrote, and his company staged plays based on Greco-Roman stories or themes, an average of one every 18 months. His *Julius Caesar* and *Anthony and Cleopatra* read like virtual dramatizations, down to the some of the minutest of details of selected Plutarch' *Lives*.

One might attribute Shakespeare's shift in theme around the turn of the seventeenth century to mere coincidence, or boredom concerning English history plays, or a change in his, and his acting company's, artistic tastes, if he, and his acting company, were alone in following the pattern described above. They were not. The following tables reveal that the Admiral's Men, seem to have followed the same trends. Table 5 demonstrates that the Admiral's Men almost seems to match Shakespeare's company in their own repertory, history play for history play right up until 1599.

As Table 6 shows, however, after 1600, several playwrights, working for several different companies began, like Shakespeare, to turn their attentions to Greco-Roman themes and plotlines.[53] When the repertories are graphed, the trend shows a startling synchronization between the types of books printed by the book trade and the types of plays produced for the rival repertories.

Table 5	
Chronology, Selected History Plays in Admiral's Men Repertory	
History Plays Listed in Admiral's Men Repertory	**Probable Date**
The Wounds of Civil War	1588
Famous Victories of Henry 5	1588
Battle of Alcazar	1589
Sir John Mandeville	1591
Harry of Cornwall	1591
Harry 6	1591
Edward 2	1592
Buckingham	1593
Richard the Confessor	1593
King Leare	1593
William the Conqueror	1594
The Siege of London	1594
Longshanke	1594
Captain Thomas Stuckey	1596
Pendragon	1597
Henry 1	1597
The Life and Death of Martin Swarte	1597
Hardicanute	1597
Robert Eearl of Huntington	1598
Sir John Oldcastle	1599

Table 6			
Chronology of Selected Greco-Roman Plays in Various Repertories			
Play	**Author**	**Company**	**Date**
Sapho & Phao	Lyly	Paul's Boys	1584
Galathea	Lyly	Paul's Boys	1584 (88?)
Endymion	Lyly	Paul's Boys	1588
Midas	Lyly	Paul's Boys	1589
Sejanus	Jonson	King's Men	1603
Philotas	Daniel	Queen's Revels Children	1604
Rape of Lucrece	Heywood	Queen Anne's Men	1607
Cupid's Revenge	Beaumont & Fletcher	Queen's Revels Children	1608
Philaster	Beaumont & Fletcher	Queen's Revels Children	1609
Valentinian	Fletcher	King's Men	1610 (14?)
Cataline	Jonson	King's Men	1611
The Queen of Corinth	Fletcher (&?)	King's Men	1616 (18?)

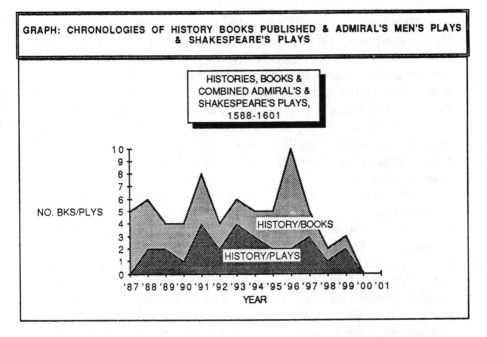

GRAPH: CHRONOLOGIES OF HISTORY BOOKS PUBLISHED & ADMIRAL'S MEN'S PLAYS & SHAKESPEARE'S PLAYS

HISTORIES, BOOKS & COMBINED ADMIRAL'S & SHAKESPEARE'S PLAYS, 1588-1601

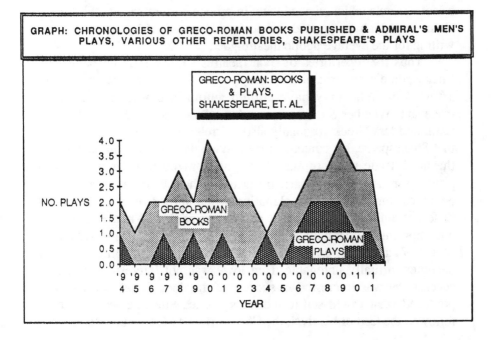

GRAPH: CHRONOLOGIES OF GRECO-ROMAN BOOKS PUBLISHED & ADMIRAL'S MEN'S PLAYS, VARIOUS OTHER REPERTORIES, SHAKESPEARE'S PLAYS

GRECO-ROMAN: BOOKS & PLAYS, SHAKESPEARE, ET. AL.

Henslowe's accounts and other theatrical records reveal that, like Shakespeare, the playwrights for the Admiral's Men produced new comedy-romances at a relatively consistent pace, tragedies playing a lesser role in the repertory until after 1599. Table 5, on the other hand, shows that new English history plays were added at an average of two per year from the year of the Armada until 1599. From that date on, throughout the same period in which Shakespeare continued to write, virtually no new histories were commissioned by the Admiral's (later Prince Henry's) Men or Worcester's (later Queen Anne's) Men.

After 1600, however, as Table 6 suggests, playwrights other than Shakespeare, whether writing for his company or its competitors, produced Greco-Roman plays at a rate approximating that of Shakespeare. The fact that none of the companies produced Greco-Roman plays with the same alacrity as they had history plays is not too surprising. The book trade was far less vigorous in publishing the classics, probably reflecting less avid demand for such works within the mass market. John Lyly's earlier plays in the 1580s really do not affect this pattern. Lyly, known for his "school" plays, and writing for the select clientele which viewed them in private performance at the Inns of Court, or which frequented the performances of Paul's Boys, was not writing for the average public theatre-goer.

Thus the repertories of rival theatres show a striking parallel to Shakespeare's pattern: history plays until 1599, Greco-Roman plays after 1599. Who may have copied whom is moot, and probably irrelevant. Whether Shakespeare or his fellow playwrights "knew little Latin and less Greek" probably also is irrelevant. What is significant is that Shakespeare, his contemporary playwrights in rival companies, and the book trade seem remarkably synchronized in their patterns of production. A change in artistic taste on the part of the playwrights becomes tenuous as an explanation when spread over a number of different authors and different acting companies. When Henslowe's uncompromising capitalism concerning the repertory of the Admiral's Men is factored in, an explanation based solely on changing tastes becomes virtually untenable. Henslowe was not interested in artistic success; he was interested in success at the door. Henslowe's writers produced what would sell to the mass market. Since he seems to have followed the lead of his rival, the Chamberlain's Men, in other areas, can one expect that his demands on his writers were different than the demands they placed on theirs?

There was even a certain synchronization between the book trade's popular targets and certain character types who appear in plays. In the 1590s and continuing into the seventeenth century, English travelers who took the so-called "Grand Tour" became the butt of jokes and the subject of criticism in pamphlets by writers like Nashe and Greene. They were attacked as foolish fops, or malcontents, or subject to sentimental melancholy, or spinners of false tales. Similar characters show up in the plays of Shakespeare (Jaques in *As You Like It*), Jonson (Amorphus in *Cynthia's Revels*), Chapman (Antonio in *Two Wise Men*), and others.[54]

The chronological relationship between the publication of popular books and the appearance of Shakespeare's and others' plays reflecting the themes of those books makes a strong case for profit motive as a factor in shaping the artistic expression of Elizabethan playwrights. The book trade offered these playwrights a vehicle for market research. Scholars have remarked on the London theatre's adaptability to changing popular tastes, and its exploitation of topical material in its offerings.[55] Book sales presented Elizabethan theatre entrepreneurs a tangible index of topicality and tastes. As much as Shakespeare's manipulation and adaptation of the sources for his plays may reveal his artistic genius, they also reflect his, and his fellow playwrights' opportunistic genius at cashing-in on sure-fire hits. When a particular literary genre proved popular, he, along with other writers, duplicated that genre in his plays; when its popularity had run its course, he, along with the others, ceased utilizing that genre. Just as a "docu-drama" on the Civil War or a mini-series based on a best-seller is almost guaranteed strong Nielson ratings today, Shakespeare and other members of the Elizabethan theatre community realized that the best-sellers of his day guaranteed many pennies at the doors of the Globe or the Rose or the Fortune or Blackfriars. Just as the one, two, and three-penny admission was designed to fit the pocketbooks of the popular classes, playwrights tailored their plays to its already expressed tastes as evidenced in the "best-sellers" of the day. Political reasons also may have influenced the rather abrupt halt to the publication of English history books and the staging of English history plays. That complication will be examined later.

Just as political prudence and good business practice seems to have shaped the writing and production of plays, the business practices of the individual companies seem to be reflected in their structure and format. The Elizabethan acting company was a firm, like a legal firm today—a partnership which bonded together, set clear terms for the sharing of expenses and profits, divided labor relatively evenly among its experts, provided for buy-outs of shares if a member wished to leave the firm. At least that is how most adult companies began.[56]

As for the children's companies, they project a picture almost Dickensian in the exploitation of child-labor. Housing, food, education, were furnished to the child-actor, since the companies also were a kind of boarding school, but child actors were paid no wages. Failure to learn parts speedily resulted in beatings or withholding of food. All of the profits went to the managers, who, armed with royal patents of privilege, had the legal right, as Masters of the Queen's royal chapels, to jerk promising young boys right off the street, and impress them into the company, with or without their guardians' consent.[57]

Children's Companies' repertories reflect their organization out of the choirs. Music was used extensively. Court records, and spectator accounts mention special songs and musical interludes. The Duke of Stettin-Pomerania saw a performance which was preceded by over an hour of musical numbers. Because of the school house nature of the organization, and the youth of the actors, generally only two performances were held per week. Though expenses probably smaller than for the adult companies, the smaller audiences, and fewer performances meant smaller returns. Law suits suggest the companies often skirted on the edge of insolvency. Therefore playwrights hired to provide novel plays for the novel performers, seem to have been expected to produce plays which stirred controversy so as to attract the elite patrons. The Boys' Companies were shut down in the 1580s because of their involvement in the religious Marprelate controversy; they were enjoined in the early 1600s because of their fostering of the so-called "War of the Theatres;" and they were dissolved permanently in 1608-09 because of their satirical attacks on the Court of James I. Since actors were not paid, most of plays in the repertories of the Boys' Companies called for larger casts than the average play at the adult theatres. Most plays called for the use of 15 to 20 actors. Since the playwright did not have to write for specific partners, roles could be tailored to the playwright's tastes (assuming he took into account his audience). Roles were constructed to show how cleverly boy-actors could portray young women or old men. Ben Jonson praised the thirteen year old Blackfriars Boy Salmon Pavey for his impersonation of extreme age. The masses could be sneered at, because the masses would not pay the six-penny admission.[58]

In time, certain aspects of the Admiral's Men came to deviate from the ideal partnership of adult Sharers sketched above. The combination of Philip Henslowe (father-in-law) and Edward Alleyn (son-in-law) came to dominate the company much like the combination of Goldwyn and Mayer dominated the activities of MGM. Henslowe and Alleyn began by owning the theatres, and in short order, through loans and advances to the playwrights and the Sharers, ended up owning the costumes and properties, owning the repertory of playbooks, and virtually owning the Players and the playwrights.

The bald facts of Henslowe's accounts have led some scholars to depict him as some sort of grasping spider. Yet, those same records indicate that the Admiral's Men Sharers themselves seem to have surrendered most financial aspects of the company to Henslowe. Whatever the reasons, there seems to have been no Sharer who emerged among the Admiral's Men to act as a financial manager as John Heminges seems to have done for the Chamberlain's Men. Henslowe's Diary reveals no consistent payee. The Admiral's Men Sharers allowed, or depended upon, Henslowe to pay the company's costume expenses, its transportation costs, its licensing fees to the Master of the Revels, its special costs for mounting a new production, its fees for commissioning new plays or revising old ones. At one point the accounts suggest Henslowe took over management of all the income, and paid the Sharers after deducting certain expenses. As one might expect, having surrendered control over finances, the Sharers surrendered control over other aspects of the theatre. Litigations show Players and playwrights associated with Henslowe protesting exploitation, over-work, low pay, restrictive contracts and impossible deadlines; playwrights and actors come and go.[59]

The repertory of plays presented by the Admiral's Men seems to match this business organization. Edward Alleyn's power as a "super-star" gave him such leverage within the Admiral's Men that his status as "senior" Sharer exempted him from all the company's on-going expenses.[60] Unlike any of the other Sharers, therefore, his share of the gross receipts was also his net share, and, until his retirement, the plays of the Admiral's Men tend to emphasize a single character—they are star-vehicles for Edward Alleyn. Subsidiary roles are just that. Cast size tends to be large, reflecting the use of cheap Hired-men and actors under heavy obligations. Plays often are hastily written, and the collaborative or serial work of two, three, four, or more writers shifted from this script to that to meet Henslowe's demands for a new play a week.[61]

By contrast, the Chamberlain's (King's) Men functioned more like the partnership of Players described earlier. Profits, responsibilities, and expenses, were shared among the eight to ten Sharers. The firm was remarkably stable. Of the original founders of 1594, all but two seem to have maintained connections with the firm until their deaths. Of the two who left the company completely, only Will Kempe left to continue a career in the theatre, and only Kempe, among the Sharers, clashed with the interests of the firm's overall business. When he did, he was expelled from the firm. Interestingly enough, Kempe's origins are unknown, but in terms of his reputation as a tumbler and performer of jigs, his lack of stable family life, his lack of a sense of business, all these suggest a background like the traveling troupes of minstrels, rather than the yeoman background of his partners. As for those remaining with the firm, they replaced their comedic expert immediately with Robert Armin, a man whose yeoman background as a goldsmith, and, judging by his early writings, whose conservatism was in tune with their own. Like most successful partnership firms, these men brought in new talent to expand the company, and, it seems, to replace themselves as they aged. Beaumont and Fletcher were hired away from rival troupes to write exclusively to the King's Men as Shakespeare became less active; Field, Ostler, and Shank were brought in as partners when Burbage, Heminges and Armin died or retired. Harmony and cooperative effort seem to be the key to this firm's operation.

Shakespeare's plays seem structured to this type of business organization and method of operation. With a few notable exceptions, most of his plays are not star-vehicles but composed so as to create a balance of roles for seven or eight principal actors. Shakespeare, after all, was writing specific roles for specific members of his firm, himself included, and tailoring most of those roles to their specialties.[62]

Bearing this in mind, modern criticism and production of Shakespeare might profit much from role-analyses focused upon which roles are vital to the plot itself, and which were probably constructed to provide suitable and sizeable roles for, say, Heminges, or Condell, or whoever. Using this approach, for example, it is amazingly simple to delete the popular role of Escalus from *Measure for Measure*, assigning his speeches to other characters such as the Provost, without losing hardly a word from the text, losing none of the irony or humor, losing little of the complexities of plot in the play. In short, we should ask the question how was a role tailored to the needs of Shakespeare's firm just as often as we ask how it was tailored to the esthetic and dramatic needs of the play. Similarly, many soliloquies might be analyzed as to which speeches are vital to characterization and plot, and which are providing audiences with the verbal arias they expect to hear.

Sound for the sake of sound in Shakespeare's plays has not been emphasized fully enough. Shaw recognized its importance, writing, "the ear is the sure cue to him," and calling Shakespeare a master in "word-music." The Elizabethans came to hear as well as watch a play. Sixteenth-century descriptions of acting place heavy emphasis upon the actor's ability to deliver "sweete words, equally balanced," and to "tye his [the playgoer's] eare to his melody." Diaries recorded synopses of public sermons because they were so effective to the ear. Significantly, most playwrights referred to playgoers as "auditors." Quoting popular speeches from popular plays seems to have been wide-spread among London theatre-goers. Granted the involvement in the action of the play which is attributed to Elizabethan audiences,[63] certain speeches must have become much like the "show-stoppers" of a Broadway musical. Perhaps the audience even "sang along" with the actor as he delivered a speech it had learned to quote, and which it awaited with anticipation. In short, many of the speeches we term memorable—"To be or not to be," "The quality of mercy is not strained," "Blow winds and crack your sheets," "Tomorrow and tomorrow and tomorrow"—may well have been written as much to provide Shakespeare's audience with brilliant solos for its favorite performers as to further the structure of the play. Certainly many of the less profound but poetically rich speeches found in his plays make fuller sense when viewed in this light.

Yet another aspect of business sense appears in the structure of Shakespeare's plays—economy of cast size. Doubling of roles by actors is easily done even in the most popular of plays. Scholars agree that Shakespeare's actors played double and triple roles; some suggest that the plays were designed in a two part structure so as to allow "virtuoso" character actors in the troupe to play doubled, middle-level roles in the first and second half of the play. Analyses by character and scene reveal that most plays can be performed with a cast of 12 to 15 actors. Providing roles for his character-role "specialists" is, of course, one factor, but good business sense is another.[64] Just as the agricultural and commercial yeomen kept their labor-costs as low as possible, this firm of theatrical "yeomen" would have little desire to spend their shares of the daily receipts on a large group of Hired-men.

If this seems to treat the English-speaking world's greatest dramatic works as commercial commodities, consider the Elizabethan world's own assessment of plays. Playwrights like Lyly, Greene, Marlowe, who considered themselves author-artists, viewed play-writing as a means to earn quick cash to support their "serious" writing efforts. Henslowe, of course viewed plays in terms of gate-receipts. New plays were always introduced on days guaranteed to yield maximum return. Here also, as in other of his practices, he simply paralleled his rivals, Shakespeare's company.

Scholars have noted how shrewdly Shakespeare himself seems to have managed his plays; perhaps he limited his output to two a year to avoid glutting the market; perhaps as a Sharer two a year was about all he could fit into his spare time. As to his concern for his place within the ranks of the *literati*, in the manner of a Ben Jonson, there is virtually no evidence to suggest that he had any. Nor does he seem to have had a burning desire to write. Unlike Thomas Heywood or George Chapman, among others, who wrote non-dramatic works throughout their lives; Shakespeare wrote only two serious narrative poems, *Venus and Adonis* and *The Rape of Lucrece*. Both were published when the theatres were closed in 1592-93, and Shakespeare's theatrical income was curtailed. Except for these two instances, he never seriously turned his pen to poems, or novels, or treatises again.

As for his plays, except to blunt the effect of pirated editions, he did not seek their publication. The *First Folio* appeared seven years after his death, and there are no indications he had any hand in preparing the edition. Jonson, on the other hand, scrupulously oversaw the editing of all his works, and, at least for his non-dramatic works, so did Marlowe. Except for *Venus* and *Lucrece*, Shakespeare did not. Most other playwrights, like Dekker, Chapman, Marston, seem to have paid little attention to the printing of their plays. It would seem that they, and

Shakespeare, viewed them as did Thomas Heywood. Plays were company assets, meant to generate profits for the acting company; they were not meant to be vehicles designed to propel their author into respectability within the literary circle.[65] Jonson wrote for posterity; Shakespeare wrote for prosperity.

In sum, then, the glory of the Elizabethan stage may have been as much the product of the spirit of Elizabethan capitalism as it was the spirit of artistry. Virtually every aspect of play-making was shaped by the demands of profit and business management. Realizing the potential market for their commodity in London, breaking free of the bonds of aristocratic patronship—just as agricultural capitalists broke free of the bonds of manorialism, and tradesmen broke free of the guilds—theatrical entrepreneurs, like James Burbage and Philip Henslowe, employed the methods and values of their middling class, yeoman, backgrounds to the creation of a new business, the theatre-business. As early as 1598, the pursuit of wealth, and its ability to raise the status even of "the Countrey Boore," was praised with faint damning by Richard Barnfield. These theatrical businessmen seem to be part of what Keith Wrightson calls "a swelling army of middle men who specialized in the supply of particular markets."[66] It was those who copied such capitalistic approaches, actors like Edward Alleyn and Richard Burbage, investors like James Burbage and Philip Henslowe, and playwrights like Thomas Heywood and William Shakespeare—men who shaped artistic skills as commodities subject to the demands of profit—whom we remember as the founders and greatest figures of the Elizabethan theatre.

The Court Interluder had security of place, and received room and board, but earned only £3, 6s, 8d in actual wages. Playwrights employed by Henslowe who viewed themselves as "poets" received only their £6 per play; no wonder they churned out an average of six plays per year. The Hired-man received a wage equal to the average artisan, though some were retained on a permanent basis at higher wages than the average. Even a celebrity like Will Kempe, if he relied upon his talents alone, and lacked business sense, found himself losing influence, position, and finally even place, in an endeavor which, like the Grocers' Guild forming the East India Company in 1599,[67] had become dominated by commercially minded syndicates of entrepreneurs, who were exploiting a new service-industry, and who could expect individual incomes approaching at least that of the country Gentry, £300 a year.

A Thomas Greene or a Christopher Marlowe, who scorned such practices, a John Lyly or a Ben Jonson, who could never cut loose from dependence upon aristocratic patrons, sought reputations as poets and intellectuals, and gentility instead of profit. Not for them the yeoman pursuit of income as a measure of success. Even though playwriting paid far more than broadsides, pamphlets, and other more "respectable" forms of literature, they viewed these efforts as their true vocations. Yet they seem to have overlooked one aspect of that gentility to which they aspired. Elizabethan peers, as well as the Gentry, merchants, and yeomen, ruthlessly pursued profits, and in so doing led England to glory in the commercial and imperial worlds. Sir Francis Drake sought to plunder the Spanish Main, and led England to glory on the seas. James and Richard Burbage, Edward Alleyn, Philip Henslowe, William Shakespeare, pursued their own "prises," seized control of the "Theatre Main," and in so doing led England to glory in the dramatic world.

Obviously there was money to be made in the theatre business. Just as obviously, that money did not come from the profession of writing for the theatre. The money to be made came from investing in theatrical properties and from acting, as a Sharer, in one of the successful troupes permanently housed in a London theatre. It is in that light that William Shakespeare's over-all career should be viewed. When viewed in terms of actor-income, as we shall see, Shakespeare looks less and less like a man who sought to establish himself as an artist or poet, and more and more like a man who found acting, and the entertainment business, a means to raise himself into the income bracket of Elizabethan society's elite.

Chapter 2

Have We Allowed His 'Tales' to Wag the Man?
What Was Shakespeare's Primary Occupation?

"In accordance with the Elizabethan scale of values Shakespeare's dearest wish was to be, and to be taken for, a poet." So writes A.L. Rowse, and so do many other literary and dramatic critics. To wit: Shakespeare was a poet, one that is, who channeled his poetry into plays, and who did some acting to give him the financial security to pursue his career as a writer.[1] Since our primary record of Shakespeare's activities is his playscripts, and since even in his own lifetime he was acknowledged as a master of dramatic writing, such a view is understandable. Despite his masterful characters, rich poetry, deft hand at telling a dramatic tale, however, Shakespeare's 20-year-long career *in toto* seems remarkably lacking in those things which mark contemporaries whose "dearest wish was to be taken for a poet," and who spent their energies to achieve the status of successful author.

If one excepts Shakespeare's plays, his published literary output is extremely slim—two narrative poems on classical themes (*Venus and Adonis* and *Rape of Lucrece*), 154 sonnets, and two shorter poems in "anthologies" (*The Lover's Complaint* and *The Phoenix and the Turtle*). There are no pamphlets or tracts dealing with philosophical, topical, historical, or artistic themes, no essays, no translations of classical works which can be, or were, attributed to his authorship, as one can find for George Chapman, John Lyly, Robert Greene, men who thought of themselves as poets who happened to write some dramatic works in order to meet living expenses. Thomas Heywood, who wrote plays during his career as fast as did Shakespeare, and who, like Shakespeare, was an actor-Sharer and a playwright, wrote several pamphlets, a history of the childhood of Queen Elizabeth, and numerous other non-dramatic works throughout his life. He considered these types of works his real efforts as an author; his plays, he believed, really belonged to the actors.

49

Indeed, Heywood chided Ben Jonson for publishing his plays as literary works: "My Playes are not exposed unto the world in Volumes, to beare the title of Works, as others," wrote Heywood.

Unlike Heywood, however, who wrote non-dramatic literature throughout his life, most of Shakespeare's non-dramatic works were written within the first five or six years of his 22-year-long career in the London theatre. No non-dramatic writings can be dated later than 1600.[2] Based on that pattern, if Shakespeare's "dearest wish was to be taken for a poet," he must have despaired of his literary abilities about 1594, and lived out the rest of his life seething with frustration.

Perhaps this explains his seeming indifference towards the publication of his works. Aside from the two long narrative poems, Shakespeare seems to have had no hand in the publication of his works: the sonnets obviously were published without his editing, and some years after the vogue for such poems had passed. There is little or no evidence that the other two short poems received any editorial attention from their author.[3] His collected plays, unlike Jonson's, were published without his supervision, seven years after his death, the editing done by his former associates John Heminges and Henry Condell. As for editions of specific plays published during his lifetime, Shakespeare seems to have insisted only upon his authorship being noted after 1598 in the "Good" Quartos of his plays, and that insistence probably was to quash sales of the pirated editions. Few of Heywood's 200 plays were published, and an examination of Henslowe's accounts shows that of the 280 plays he recorded over the ten-year period from 1592-93 to 1603, only 27, less than 10 percent, have survived.[4] Ben Johnson was, perhaps, the first of the Elizabethan-Jacobean playwrights to consider his plays as serious literature worthy of careful publication. Indeed we might thank Jonson for establishing playscripts as literary creations, else at least half (those not published until their appearance in the *First Folio*) of Shakespeare's plays might have perished altogether.

Even during the so-called "War of the Theatres," when Jonson lambasted Chapman, Marston, Dekker, and they in turn lambasted him, and each tweaked rival companies in their playscripts, Shakespeare took little part in these literary rivalries, save, perhaps, his famous lines between Hamlet and Rosencrantz and Guildenstern concerning the "little eyases," his glancing blow in *Twelfth Night* at Jonson's reliance on the comedy of humors, and his ridicule of Jonson as a person through the character of Slender in *Merry Wives of Windsor*.[5]

Jonson, Chapman, and the other poet/playwrights usually focused their criticisms of each others works on bad writing—the use of stale and inaccurate sources, the lack of classical "unities," the creation of exotic new words, the reliance upon sentimentality instead of intellect. Shakespeare, on the other hand, almost never criticized such literary concerns when he commented in his plays about contemporary theatre. Though his earlier works (until about 1596) may have taken some jibes at poorly constructed, collaborative playscripts, the thrust of his satire about theatre always remained criticism of bad performance by actors. Jonson satirized bad writing: Shakespeare satirized bad acting! Further, Jonson, in his epigrams, makes it clear he considers himself a poet. Shakespeare, on the other hand, when he does make a rare allusion to his career, as in sonnets 110, 111, 112, clearly refers to himself (if disparagingly) as an actor.

Officialdom in London, and certain *literati*, viewed him as an actor. In 1594, his name is included as a payee for court performances, and later, in 1602, the York Herald complained of the granting of a Coat of Arms to "Shakespear ye Player." The cryptic *Willobie His Advisa*, dated 1594, alludes to Shakespeare as a player. As late as 1605, the anonymous author of *Ratseis Ghost* refers to Shakespeare as a player. Even our first sure reference to Shakespeare's theatrical career, Robert Greene's celebrated death bed "Blast," clearly designates Shakespeare as an actor.[6] In 1592 then, despite the success of his Henry VI plays, the *literati* clearly did not view Shakespeare as one of their circle. Chettle's famous "apology" for printing Greene's attack hardly addresses Shakespeare's literary reputation. It simply states that important people have vouchsafed to Shakespeare's good character. Of course, the appearance in 1593-94 of his narrative poems *Venus and Adonis* and *The Rape of Lucrece* did establish his credit as a poet among those Inns of Court gallants who considered themselves part of the educated elite,[7] but was it that credit which enabled him to become a founding partner in the Chamberlain's Men?

Shakespeare's acceptance into full partnership in the newly organized Chamberlain's Men in 1594 is often assumed to be the result of the company's desire to utilize his already growing reputation as the author of popular plays. A good case can be made that he used his already written plays as his "buy-in." We know that the "buy-in, buy-out" share was about £70 to £90.[8] Recognizing the problems concerning the chronology of his early plays, it still seems that Shakespeare could offer six or seven plays to his new company. At the usual playwrights' fees of £6 to £10 per completed play, that equals a value of £36 to £70 that his plays would contribute to the partnership, close to the usual "buy-in" price.

If his fellow Sharers expected from Shakespeare what we know acting companies expected of other writers, these circumstances would suggest that he was contracted primarily to be the company's chief playwright. Yet the Sharers did not seem to lay those expectations upon him. Henslowe, for instance, pushed his writers to produce new plays at a fast rate, sometime one a week. Thomas Heywood may have averaged as many as five plays a year. George Chapman averaged at least three plays a year for the Blackfriars Boys' Company between 1600 and 1605; John Fletcher, hired by Shakespeare's own company, was at work on perhaps five to eight plays in the seasons between 1611 to 1613. Yet Shakespeare's average for his company was only two plays per year,[9] a remarkably low output for someone granted the enormous potential for income that Sharer status conferred. Shakespeare's average production is far below that mark. Nor, in the period from 1590 to 1600, was there any other acting company which granted Sharer status to any other playwright. All, save Shakespeare, were hirelings paid by the play.

Those tantalizingly few documents concerning Shakespeare' monies reveal some of that potential. In 1596 he probably laid out sufficient sums to insure the granting of a Coat of Arms to his father. In 1597,[10] a scant three years after the formation of the Chamberlain's Men, Shakespeare purchased a little over 120 acres of farmland near Stratford for £327, a sum 22 times larger than the London artisan's average income. A year later, 1598, he purchased the "New Place," one of the showplace homes in Stratford, at a cost of £60, a sum equal to four years' labor to the artisan. A year after that, in 1599, he purchased, again at a cost of about £60, a one-eighth share in the Globe Theatre. Given the typical £14 to £16 Henslowe's accounts tell us was the total amount an author received for a play, Shakespeare would have had to have written 35 plays to have raised the £447 he invested in land between 1597 and 1599. Table 7 shows Shakespeare's quick upward mobility, from son of a Stratford land owner and glover, who stayed away from church to avoid process-servers in 1592,[11] to a prominent and prosperous citizen in 1598, an upward mobility coinciding with Shakespeare's gaining status as Sharer in the Chamberlain's Men.

Table 7 Shakespeare's Rise to Riches		
Year	Theatre Career	Personal Life
1578		Father mortgages some lands
1582		Marries Anne Hathaway
1583		Daughter Susannah born
1585		Twins, Hamnet & Judith, born
1586		Father removed as alderman
1589	Goes to London (?)	Father sued for debt
1590	Reference as minor actor	Father sued for debt
1592	Reference to prominence	Father fined as recusant
1594	Partner, Chamberlain's Men	
1596	Partner, Chamberlain's Men	Buys Coat of Arms
1597	Partner, Chamberlain's Men	Buys land, £327
1598	Partner, Chamberlain's Men	Buys house, £60
1599	Partner, Chamberlain's Men	Buys Globe share, £60
Comparative sums: Average annual income of artisan/tradesman=£15 Average annual income of actor/partner=£198 Average annual income of Gentry=£300		

Sharer status also meant liabilities, sharing the expenses of the acting company. An analysis of expenses over the three-year period between Shakespeare's admittance to Sharer status and his purchase of Stratford farmlands gives some indication of the amount of profit he must have earned. Henslowe's accounts and the so-called "Sharer Papers" indicate the average cost of a performance was about £2.[12] At 230 performances per year, the three-year total (1594-97) for the Chamberlain's Men is approximately £1380. As one of eight Sharers, Shakespeare's share of those expenses is £172. He also had a wife and three children to support. Let us assume he was extremely frugal, spending only the artisan's £15 per year for living expenses those three years. All in all, then, a conservative estimate of his expenses in that period is £544 (a sum equal to 36 years' labor to the artisan). If he were living only on monies generated by writing plays, he would have needed to have written 37 of them to meet that figure—his total career output.

Shakespere
non sanz droict

Fig. 5. Shakespeare's Coat of Arms (Granted 1596).

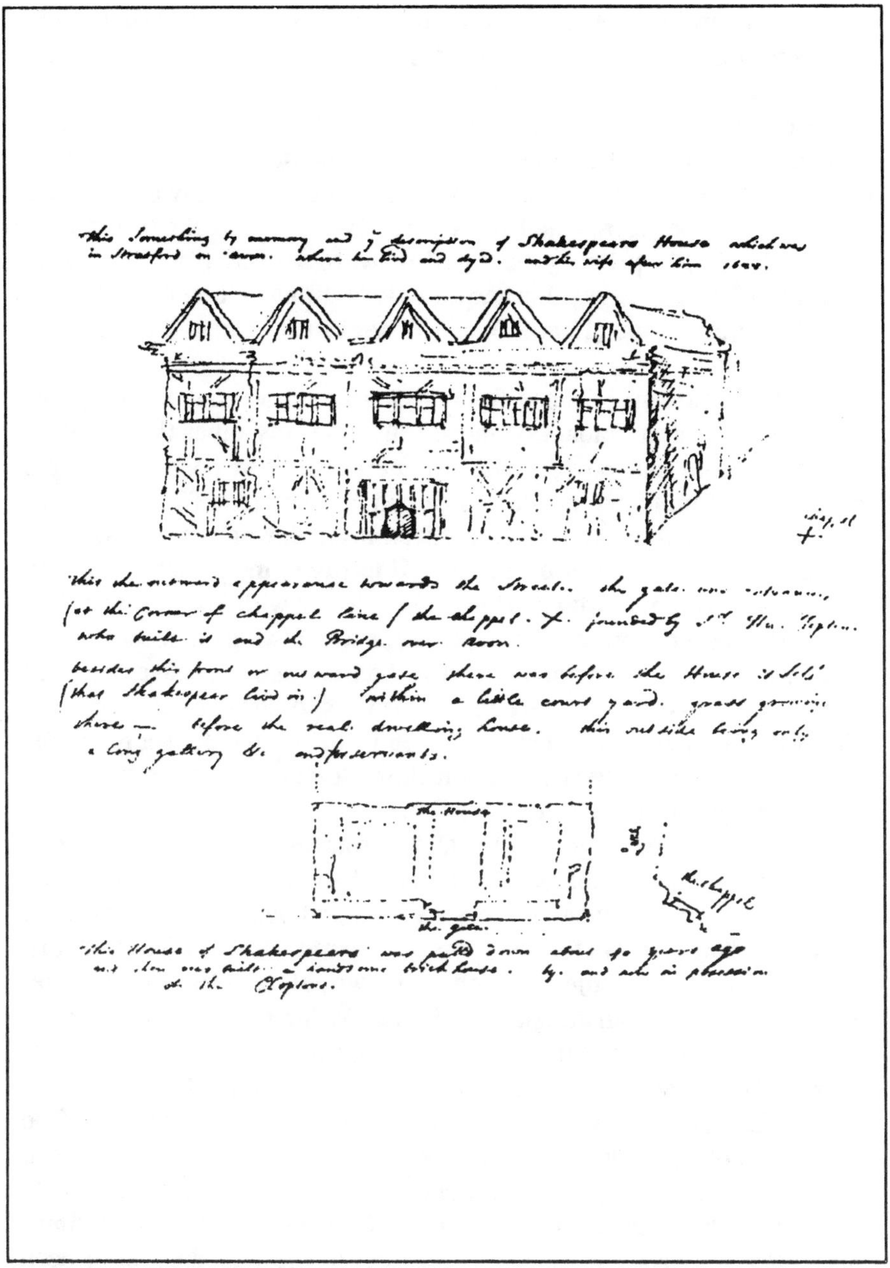

Fig. 6. Sketch of Newplace.

We know he wrote eight plays then, an output worth £116, leaving him another £428 to raise elsewhere. No matter, one might say, he worked as collaborator and reviser of other plays. Yet at the £3 (at most) a collaborator/reviser received, he would have had to total 142 collaborations to meet the remainder of his expenses. From Ben Jonson's writings and Henslowe's accounts we know it took about two weeks for collaboration on, or revision of, a play, five to six weeks to write an original.[13] If his primary occupation were writer, given the time necessary for that activity, Shakespeare was writing at least 466 weeks in that three-year period (1594-97), or 155 weeks per year, or 25 and a half hours per day.

The absurdity of these figures clearly shows that Shakespeare earned his greatest amount of money in some way other than writing. Camden wrote that poverty was a "fate peculiar to poets." Jonson's remarks to Drummond that he had earned no more than £200 for all his plays, his constant state of indebtedness, the paltry £8, 8s, 10d evaluation of his estate at his death,[14] all testify to the paucity of money to be made by a man who tried to make a living with his quill-pen. The only other occupation for Shakespeare for which we have record is that of an actor. E.J.A. Honigmann suggests Shakespeare may have practiced some money-lending; Greene's famous death-bed "Blast" at Shakespeare hints at as much,[15] but even if that be another source of his income, it still presupposes that somehow, somewhere, he earned sums of money sufficient to loan out.

It is clear, from almost all available sources about the theatre, that Elizabethan theatre companies expected their partners to act. Ben Jonson, George Chapman, Thomas Dekker, and other playwrights hired only as writers of plays for the actors were never accorded Sharer status. Thomas Heywood is the only other playwright, besides Shakespeare, who we know had Sharer status. His own writings, and other sources, indicate he spent much time on stage.[16] Shakespeare's partners must have expected the same of him in granting him the plum of a full shareholder.

G.E. Bentley describes a heavy schedule for an actor-Sharer. The acting companies averaged 230 performances a year, a six-day per week performance schedule, which repeated, at most, only one play per week. The demands of rehearsing, staging, performing four, five, sometimes six, different plays for 35 to 40 weeks out of the year must have been grueling. Bentley notes that it was "the most distinguished and popular performers in the troupe" who achieved Sharer status.[17] Shakespeare's own plays suggest that all the partners were expected to put in time on stage consistently. Aside from "starring" roles, like Richard III or Hamlet, there is a relatively constant size (eight percent or more of total lines, 30 percent or more of total scenes) for seven to nine "supporting" roles in most of Shakespeare's playscripts. Plays written for the company by other playwrights, like Ben Jonson's *Every Man in His Humour* or *Sejanus* or *Volpone*, display a similar balance of roles.[18] Thus, although Sharers like Heminges, Phillips, and Shakespeare never achieved the star status of a Kempe or a Burbage or an Alleyn, we should not dismiss their talents as of "no special distinction." John Aubrey, eagerly gathering whatever information he could about the past generation, averred that Shakespeare's reputation as an actor was that he "did acte exceedingly well."[19] Indeed, John Davies of Hereford (who echoed Robert Greene's view that actors were no more than puppets) linked Shakespeare's name with that of Burbage, as actors who, unlike most, were skillful in their use of voice, and who were outstanding in their portrayals of the parts written by the "poets." Davies, a scrivener with literary pretensions, was writing of Shakespeare, the actor, in 1603, a date by which scholars assume Shakespeare was a giant on the literary scene, and a date many aver marks his retirement from the stage to the status of full-time playwright. Perhaps, then, the several references to Shakespeare's "honied words" do not all pertain exclusively to his writings.[20]

Along with the hectic acting schedule expected of Sharers, Henslowe's *Diary* reveals that they were also expected to participate in selecting plays for the repertory, recruiting and dismissing players, purchasing properties, costumes, and other items necessary to performance. All in all, a full Sharer like Shakespeare had to be the "*Johannes Fac Totum*" Greene accused him of being. Seven other men, especially hard-headed businessmen like Heminges, Burbage, Phillips, Pope, Bryan, Cowley, would not exempt one partner from most of the grueling tasks of acting and adjunct activities necessary to the operation of the company, so that he could produce a mere two or three playscripts a year, especially since some of them, like Heminges, Phillips, and Burbage, wrote a play or two on occasion themselves.[21] In short, all the evidence we possess concerning the running of an acting company suggests that Shakespeare's partners viewed Shakespeare as a Sharer whose peculiar contribution to the firm was a couple of popular scripts a year on top of the other duties expected of them all, just as Heminges seems to have handled the accounting, and Burbage contributed his "super-star" status, and perhaps his talents as a decorative painter. Dwelling on the words he wrote, and most of the dedicatory pieces in the *First Folio* which write of him as a poet, we tend to gloss over James Mabbe's commendatory poem to Shakespeare the actor, and the fact that his name *heads the list* of "The Names of the Principall Actors in all these Playes."

One other aspect concerning Shakespeare's literary output *vis-a-vis* his acting career needs be discussed—how much energy or attention did he expend in his playwriting activity. Tradition has it he produced the first version of *The Merry Wives of Windsor* in a mere two weeks. Heminges and Condell implied in the *First Folio* dedications that he was such a quick and facile writer that little revision was needed on his first drafts. Jonson complained that Shakespeare should have taken the energy and time to revise some of his scripts, that he left in sloppy loose-ends in plot and overly bombastic speeches. Such statements seem to suggest that Shakespeare did not expend a great amount of energy in writing plays. For that matter, he did not seem to expend much energy in any kind of writing when compared to George Chapman or Thomas Heywood. Chapman not only wrote plays, but published translations of Greco-Roman classics. Heywood, like Shakespeare, worked as a Sharer in an acting company, and still averaged as many as five plays a year, and wrote numerous other non-dramatic works besides. Another measure of that energy Shakespeare spent on playwriting would be to view playwright-income within the framework of his total income. If he, and his associates, viewed his main occupation to be that of playwright, then that concentration of energy should be somewhat reflected in the percentage of his income earned through the writing of plays.

Recognizing all the problems of estimating income in such a volatile business as the theatre, Henslowe's accounts and the "Sharer Papers" still yield enough information to give some indication of income for the theatres and theatre companies. Even factoring in such vagaries as theatre closings because of plague or official censure, Henslowe's accounts, when averaged over a number of seasons, present relatively consistent figures. Allowing for minor variation in admission totals based on location, popularity of plays, and type of clientele, there is little reason to suppose that Henslowe's theatre and the Admiral's Men did significantly better or worse than the Chamberlain's Men. No contemporary records suggest anything other than parity between the two companies.

Bearing all that in mind, when one applies the known standard formula for dividing the daily take, it is possible to derive what must be reasonable estimates of Shakespeare's income as Sharer, his income as Housekeeper at the Globe and Blackfriars, and his income as a playwright. Total precision is, of course, impossible, and so in some cases, I have rounded off to the next highest number. In other cases, especially the playwrights' fees, I have retained decimals because, in view of the enormous value of the Elizabethan pound sterling, to do otherwise would inflate the figure beyond conservative estimates.

Playwrights received a flat price for their finished scripts which averaged £6. In addition, there usually was a so-called "benefit" performance in which a certain day's proceeds were to be paid to the playwright as a bonus. Of course that "benefit" day was not the first day of performance, when attendance was at its peak. The playwright received an average day's receipts, about £8.5. The total a playwright received for his play, therefore, was approximately £14.5 to £15. Around 1610 that fee seems to have risen to £20 for established and popular playwrights. Fees would be shared proportionately among playwrights who collaborated on a script.[22] At his usual of two plays per year, then, Shakespeare earned a yearly average of £29 from his work as a playwright. What did he earn as a partner in the Chamberlain's Men, a Sharer?

Sharers divided the daily take according to the following formula: all receipts for the "Groundlings" (standing room) were turned over to the acting company, and in addition it was entitled to one-half of all gallery receipts. Average daily take was £8.5. Only 32 percent of playgoers chose standing room (amounting to £2.7); 68 percent chose the gallery seats (amounting to £5.8).[23] Daily receipts for the acting company, then, were approximately £5.6. Henslowe's *Diary* indicates that as a Sharer in the Admiral's Men, Gabriel Spencer received, as his portion of the gallery receipts, at least five to seven shillings daily. If that is added to the probable receipts from the "Groundlings," Shakespeare's one-eighth share as a full partner would be about 14 to 17 shillings daily. At an average of 230 performances per year, Shakespeare's annual income from acting would amount to about £161 to £195, a sum not too far from the £180 per year listed as the usual income of an actor-Sharer in the 1635 "Sharer Papers," and a sum equal from 10 to 13 years' labor to the average artisan. After 1603, when the partnership expanded from eight to 12 men,[24] his annual share probably decreased slightly in proportion.

As seen above in Table 7, before 1599, when he bought into the Globe Syndicate, Shakespeare already must have used some of the substantial monies earned as an actor to invest in Stratford property. His name occurs in local documents concerning land investments after 1597; his 100+ acres of farmland were estimated by his contemporaries to yield at least £300 per year in income; his "New Place," purchased at a price of £60, and extensively renovated at further costs of which we have no knowledge, was a house comparable to the lodgings of the Warwickshire Gentry. Its street frontage alone was 60 feet in length. That was just the gate-house and servants' quarters, within was a courtyard and the actual dwelling for the master of the house. In 1605 he invested over £400 in tithe receipts, which yielded a tidy £60 a year, and sometime before his death he bought The Maidenhead and Swan Inn with adjoining houses in Stratford. His will mentions orchards, stables, and barns—always in the plural. Receipts from playwriting could hardly have given him those sums to invest. Perhaps the Restoration rumor that he was worth at least £1000 per year was correct after all (especially since he was his father's principal heir), but for the wrong reasons. That rumor maintained his acting company paid him that to write plays, but by the Restoration Shakespeare already was enshrined as a "poet," not as an actor and local landlord.[25]

Despite those substantial early investments between 1594 and 1598, in 1599, Shakespeare still had enough money left over to purchase a one-eighth share in the new Globe Theatre. As an one-eighth Housekeeper, he was entitled to that fraction of the Housekeepers' share of the daily take: to wit, one-eighth of 50 percent of the total gallery receipts (as seen above £5.8). That one-eighth share (1/8 x £2.9 x 230 performances) must have yielded about £83 per year.

After 1609 his Housekeeper income rose when he purchased a one-seventh share in Blackfriars, which his acting company now tenanted along with the Globe. Based on the 1635 "Sharer Papers," the Blackfriars share must have added at least another £135 per year to his income from theatre investments. Admission was significantly higher there, the six pence basic price was double the most expensive seats at the Globe. Finally, the "Sharer Papers" also indicate that acting at Blackfriars yielded another source of actor-income.[26] For the 1610-11 theatre season, the season after which he retired from the stage, a conservative estimate of Shakespeare's income is as follows: acting-income £289 (Globe and Blackfriars), theatre investments £218 (Globe and Blackfriars), Stratford investments £300, playwright income (£14.5 x 2 new plays) £29, for a grand total of £836, a sum equivalent to almost 56 years' labor for the average artisan, and placing him well within the income bracket which comprised the top five percent of Elizabethan society.

When those categories are examined in terms of percentages of total income we find: actor-income is about 35 percent, Housekeeper income is about 26 percent, Stratford investment income is about 36 percent, playwright income is a mere three or four percent.

The following tables attempt to represent the changing patterns to Shakespeare's income. Table 8 breaks down these sources of income over the 22-year period of Shakespeare's active association with the Chamberlain's/King's Men. Years are grouped according to changes in these sources of income. Table 9 ventures a view at three selected theatre seasons, one from the beginning of his partnership, one from the middle period of his career, one from the end of his active career in the London theatre. Both tables compare those totals with equivalent years an average artisan would have to labor to earn such sums.

If there be truth to the old cliché "money talks," these figures fairly scream that Shakespeare was not a playwright who acted and invested in land to gain the financial security necessary to his literary career, but rather that he was an actor who invested in property and wrote some plays on the side. At no time during his partnership in the Chamberlain's/King's Men could the percentage of his income derived from playwriting ever amount to more than 18 percent. The career average is only four percent. Actor-income, on the other hand, probably reached as high as 82 percent, and averaged no less than 24 percent as long as his theatre career continued. Further, it must have been his income as an actor in those first five years as Sharer in the Chamberlain's Men which was the source of the monies he invested in farm lands and theatres to produce his fortune.

Table 8
Shakespeare's Estimated Income
Sources of Income & Percentage of Total Income

Income Event	Thea Seas	Actr Shr	% Tot	Glbe Shr	% Tot	Blfr Shr	% Tot	Stfd Land	% Tot	Plwt	% Tot	Tot Incm	Yrs Arsn
Sharer, 1/8 share	1594-99	£805	82%							£174	18%	£979	65
Globe 1/8, buys Stfd lands	1599-1603	£644	24%	£417	16%			£1500	56%	£106	4%	£2667	178
Sharers now 12	1603-09	£322	12%	£500	18%			£1800	66%	£116	4%	£2738	183
Blckfrs 1/7	1609-11	£682	39%	£169	9%	£270	15%	£600	34%	£44	3%	£1785	119
Leaves stage, col 2 plays	1611-13			£169	16%	£270	25%	£600	57%	£22	2%	£1061	71
Sold Glbe 1/8, dies	1613-16					£405	31%	£900	69%			£1305	87
Grand Totals		£2453	23%	£1251	13%	£945	9%	£5400	51%	£462	4%	£10511	701
Av. Totl 22 Seasons	1594-1613	£112	23%	£57	12%	£43	9%	£245	51%	£21	4%	£478	32
Av. Actor 17 Seasons	1594-1611	£144	24%	£74	12%	£56	9%	£318	51%	£27	4%	£619	41

Table 9
Shakespeare's Estimated Income:
Three Selected Seasons

Income Event	Thea Seas	Actr Shr	% Tot	Glbe Shr	% Tot	Blfr Shr	% Tot	Stfd Land	% Tot	Plwt	% Tot	Tot Incm	Yrs Arsn
Rich2/R&J/ Midsummer	1595-96	£161	79%							£44	21%	£205	14
HnrV/Caes HamIt/AYL	1599-1600	£161	28%	£83	14%			£300	51%	£44	7%	£589	39
Cymbeline/ Winter's	1610-11	£287	35%	£83	10%	£135	16%	£300	36%	£29	3%	£834	56

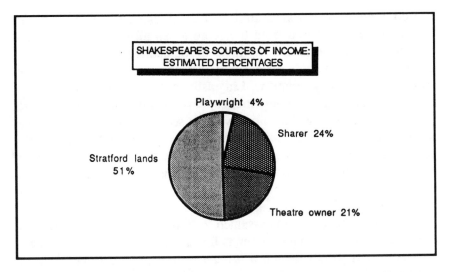

SHAKESPEARE'S SOURCES OF INCOME:
ESTIMATED PERCENTAGES

Playwright 4%

Sharer 24%

Stratford lands
51%

Theatre owner 21%

Finally, when Shakespeare stopped acting, for all intents and purposes he stopped writing. Many hold he quit the stage after 1603, but given his continued presence in London, and the sworn testimony of Cuthbert Burbage that names him as one of the players who expanded the King's Men's activities to Blackfriars in 1609, it seems unlikely that his partners tolerated his total absence from the stage. His output in this period averaged only of one play per year.[27]

The Tempest (1611) is considered to have been Shakespeare's last solo work as a dramatist. This play seems to mark the end of his active association with the acting company. The increasing number of references in local documents indicates his primary residence was Stratford.[28] As for his continued work as a dramatist, the only plays in which it is known he had a hand were collaborations, in which most assume he contributed while remaining at Stratford, expanding, or "doctoring," basic plots and story-lines sent to him by John Fletcher.

Neil Carson's recent article, "Collaborative Playwriting," shows that Elizabethan dramatists often worked separately, that dramatists turned over half finished scripts to others to move on to another project, that most were not contractually attached to a specific acting company, and that most were not actors, nor took any part, or interest, in the staging of their plays.[29] Some of this description certainly fits the Fletcher and Shakespeare collaborations which produced *Henry VIII* (1612), the lost *Cardenio* (1612), and *The Two Noble Kinsmen* (1613).

Fletcher never was listed among the actors of the King's Men; Shakespeare had retired from the stage to Stratford, and there is no evidence to suggest he had any hand in the actual production of these plays.[30] Unlike Carson's playwrights, Fletcher and Shakespeare were attached to an acting company. Linguistic and philological analyses of the two surviving Fletcher/Shakespeare collaborative plays have attempted to ascribe authorship to various scenes. Debate exists among scholars as to which scenes should be ascribed to whom, but that debate still suggests these plays match the pattern Carson sketched wherein playwrights worked independently, each on his own sections. Table 10 depicts one widely-held view of the division of labor between Fletcher and Shakespeare.[31]

Though Shakespeare is assumed to have been the guiding-hand in *Henry VIII*, his share in authorship is five and a half scenes to Fletcher's ten and a half. In *Two Noble Kinsmen*, Shakespeare's share is seven scenes to Fletcher's 16. In both plays Fletcher's ratio of scenes to Shakespeare's is two-to-one, or about two-thirds of each play. When we remember Carson's description of collaboration, it seems almost as if Fletcher may have begun these projects, sent them off to Shakespeare for fleshing out while he began new plays, and then put finishing touches on them when they were returned from Stratford.

When the probable chronology of these two plays, and the lost *Cardenio* (1611-13), is juxtaposed against Fletcher's other works in the same period—he was at work on at least three and perhaps five other plays in the same years—the probability of such a reconstruction of the Fletcher/Shakespeare collaboration seems likely. Fletcher may have been writing/revising/planning a total of eight plays within those two seasons, all for the King's Men, all produced by that company at the Globe or Blackfriars. It also must be remembered that *Cardenio* was no doubt commissioned for a command performance at court—a performance which therefore could not be delayed. Clearly, then, Fletcher was over-extended during this period which immediately followed Shakespeare's retirement from the stage and from London. Francis Beaumont, also hired as a playwright by the King's Men at about the same time as Fletcher, and with whom Fletcher had collaborated successfully before, quit playwriting about the same time that Shakespeare retired.[32]

From then on, until at least 1616, Fletcher worked alone, the only exception being the three plays in which he collaborated with

Table 10 Henry VIII & Two Noble Kinsmen Scenes Probably by Shakespeare, Probably by Fletcher		
Play & Scene	**Shakespeare**	**Fletcher**
Henry VIII		
Prologue		XXXXX
I, 1 XXXXX		
I, 2 XXXXX		
I, 3	XXXXX	
I, 4	XXXXX	
II, 1	XXXXX	
II, 2	XXXXX	
II, 3 XXXXX		
II, 4 XXXXX		
III, 1	XXXXX	
III, 1 (1-203)	XXXXX	XXXXX
III, 2 (204 on)		XXXXX
IV, 1	XXXXX	
IV, 2	XXXXX	
V, 1 XXXXX		
V, 2	XXXXX	
V, 3	XXXXX	
V, 4	XXXXX	
Epilogue		XXXXX
Two Noble Kinsmen		
Prologue		XXXXX
I, 1 (song)		XXXXX
I, 1 XXXXX		
I, 2 XXXXX		
I, 3 XXXXX		
I, 4	XXXXX	
I, 5	XXXXX	
II, 1 XXXXX		
II, 2	XXXXX	
II, 3	XXXXX	
II, 4	XXXXX	
II, 5	XXXXX	
II, 6	XXXXX	
III, 1 XXXXX		
III, 2 XXXXX		
III, 3 XXXXX		
III, 4 XXXXX		

III, 5 XXXXX		
III, 6 XXXXX		
IV, 1	XXXXX	
IV, 2	XXXXX	
IV, 3	XXXXX	
V, 1 (1-33)		XXXXX
V, 1 (33 on)	XXXXX	
V, 2	XXXXX	
V, 3 XXXXX		
V, 4 XXXXX		
Epilogue		XXXXX

Shakespeare. What we may see here is Shakespeare, like the old firehorse, putting on the harness in an emergency to help out his old partners in the King's Men, and help guarantee audiences at playhouses in which he still held financial interests. These collaborations probably are not evidence of Shakespeare the poet continuing his art. Robert Greene quit writing when he quit the Earth (and even spoke beyond the grave in the case of his *Groat's Worth of Wit*). Ben Jonson quit writing when he quit the Earth. Shakespeare quit writing when he quit the stage. The man hailed as England's greatest dramatic poet seems to have lost interest in drama and poetry once his creations would have no relevance to his personal acting career.

Such a perspective, I believe, can enhance analyses of Shakespeare's plays. It shifts focus away from the text and towards performance of that text. It helps explain why scholars have more trouble finding Shakespeare's auctorial voice than that of his contemporaries. He was writing for many voices, those of his partners as well as himself. It also helps explain Shakespeare's continuing popularity within today's theatrical profession. Comparisons of Shakespeare's versification with that of other playwrights, like Jonson, or Ford, who considered themselves first as poets, reveals that some of the "irregularities" of his verse may well be stage-directions built into the script. Shakespeare, for instance, does not seem to continue a line merely for the sake of metric integrity. If the stage situation is an aside, or an actor's entrance, when the character supposedly has not heard the line, acting circumstances make metrical continuation of the first character's lines absurd. Shakespeare often simply has the second character start a fresh line. Jonson, Webster, Ford, however, more concerned with poetic than performance values, often force that character to continue the metrical cadence, despite its contrived appearance for performance. As one scholar put it, unlike Jonson, Shakespeare "did not write for book and posterity, but for the next production."[33]

Actors love to play Shakespearean roles. They express that love in terms of "challenge," or "depth of characterization," or "stretching one's talents," and they do not just mean the huge roles like Hamlet or Othello. Actors would almost kill for roles like Antonio in *Merchant of Venice*, like the Fool in *Lear*, or like Mistress Quickly in *Merry Wives*.[34] Laying aside all the character-analyses, sub-texts, and the like, which have been written concerning these and other roles, what they all hold in common is an opportunity to the actor to dominate the stage, to "shine" before an audience. In *A Midsummer Night's Dream*, for example, while the characters Bottom and Puck may seem to overshadow many of the others, the other supporting roles garner about the same percentage of scenes and lines. I am not suggesting that modern playwrights do not script good roles, but few of them script play after play with eight or nine supporting roles consistently designed to give each role an equal number of lines, scenes, and "solos" so that the special talents of each are displayed. Few modern playwrights are actors. So too were few of Shakespeare's contemporary playwrights, and although they accommodated the acting companies for which they wrote, few created the number of supporting roles which excite an actor's ego as much as do Shakespeare's.

These supporting roles generally give the actor at least one opportunity in the limelight. Most have their own soliloquy with sounds and lines memorable to the audience. Hamlet has his "To be or not to be," but Polonius has his "Neither a borrower nor a lender be." Macbeth has (among many) his "Is this a dagger which I see before me," but Banquo has his "Thou hast it now: King, Cawdor, Glamis, all." Not just the leading role, but most of the supporting roles—those which must have been taken by partners—have their own verbal arias.

All roles, including the back-breakers like Hamlet (1422 lines), Richard III (1124 lines), Iago (1097 lines, and incidentally, the secondary male role), give an actor a chance to catch breath—a time when the actor is off stage. Even Hamlet does not have to face the audience from the beginning of the play to its end, without relief, as do

Neil Simon's George in *Chapter Two*, or Noel Coward's Charles in *Blithe Spirit*, or Jean Anouilh's Joan in *The Lark*.[35]

Roles are easy to learn, and to rehearse. Most plays written in the 1590s used striking imagery, more rhythmically structured poetry, more rhyme: all techniques useful in memorization.[36] The sub-plotting for which Shakespeare is so famed serves an actor's purpose in limiting both time on stage and reaction to shifts in tone from scene to scene. Excepting the histories, comedies and tragedies alike tend to group three or four major characters over and over again in scenes largely independent of one another, until the last scene "wraps it up." Actors are thus spared the necessity of reacting to several different types of characters at once, and can rehearse most of their scenes independent of the others. Two sets of scenes thus can run lines, establish movement and business, work out problems of characterization, simultaneously. Minor roles (attendants, soldiers, messengers, etc.) may have to sit around and wait, or shift in and out of scenes, but the major supporting roles do not. Hired men, after all, were just that—employees, paid by the day, only for the days they worked. Partners' times, however, were precious, their roles designed to display their distinctive skills; thus their scenes were designed to facilitate that display.

Though obviously versatile actors, bits of evidence do suggest that Shakespeare's partners did have specialties. Burbage and Heminges seem to have been best known for dramatic roles; Kempe, Bryan, Pope for comedic ones. Shakespeare's plots and sub-plots seem to reflect those specialties. Most plays group clowns with clowns, straight-actors with straight-actors, and as noted above, these character-types could rehearse and perform their scenes without the problems of shift in mood of scene, or problems of on stage relationships to dissimilar character-types.

Let us briefly take a look at two of Shakespeare's plays keeping these factors in mind—*The Tempest*, since it is considered his last play, and *The Taming of the Shrew*, which I believe was the first play he wrote (or rewrote) for the newly-formed Chamberlain's Men. Both plays, though of different tone, do affect that balance of groups of characters, and in both, the sub-plots involve the more boisterous comedic roles. One could hardly call scenes in *Shrew* involving Petruchio, Kate, and Grumio "tame" comedy, but the sub-plot concentrates the activities of the clowns in the Elizabethan and Italian sense of the word, Tranio and

Biondello. In *The Tempest* there is an almost monotonous alternation of scenes between the "serious" characters (Antonio, Sebastian, Alonzo, Gonzalo) and slap-stick roles (Caliban, Trinculo, Stephano). In both plays these sub-plots could be greatly abbreviated without doing much damage to the main theme or plot of the action. In the case of seventeenth- and eighteenth-century adaptations of *Shrew*, the sub-plots often were deleted. In both plays, as in most of his others, these disparate types of scenes can be rehearsed with little or no connection to each other.

In both plays verbal arias are given to supporting roles. In *Tempest*, Gonzalo has his "Had I plantation of this isle," Caliban his "All the infection that the sea sucks up." In *Shrew*, Grumio has his delightful prose speech "Tell thou the tale," and Gremio has his hilarious description of the wedding of Kate and Petruchio. True bit-parts in both plays are just that—servants, haberdasher, sprites, who drift in and out of scenes. These roles demand little time, little memorization of lines, little reaction to characters. Actors talk of ensemble in a play, and of how difficult that is to achieve within a cast. In Shakespeare, however, it is difficult not to achieve, not on a grand scale, perhaps, but within those groups of characters whose main function is to appear together again and again in similar scenes. Finally, in *Shrew* and in *Tempest*, as in many other of Shakespeare's plays, there is that final scene, when all major characters are brought together. That scene too serves an actor's purpose as much as it does a dramatist's. At the end of the play, ready for the applause, stand most of the major characters, each ready to receive equal due.

In short, it seems clear that Shakespeare's interests as an actor-Sharer permeate the construction of his playscripts. We still possess the playscripts; we've canonized them, and we analyze the words, speeches, characters, and scenes as indication of Shakespeare's poetic, philosophical, and literary intent. In so doing, however, we sometimes seem to turn the character Hamlet into a real person, the playscript *Macbeth* into a philosophical treatise on evil, usurpation, and tyranny, the story of Celtic King Lear into a dramatization of abuse of the elderly. All of these approaches offer legitimate analyses of the texts and their possible relationship to their society. Yet it may cause us to lose sight of the fact that Shakespeare's primary occupation was acting, and that he was creating roles for himself and for fellow actors who were close associates, business partners, and long-time friends. We allow his "tales" to wag the man.

One characteristic of Shakespeare's plays seems out of joint with this perspective, that is, that he wrote plays around a relatively stable partnership of actors. He is also known for the consistent use in his plays of "juicy" female roles equal to those probably assigned to full Sharers. In the view of most scholars, those roles were taken by boy actors, who, of course, periodically would need to be replaced as they matured. Perhaps it is time to reassess that view.

Chapter 3
Why Boys for (wo)Men's Roles?
or, Pardon the Delay, "the Queen was shaving"

"Why Did the English Stage Take Boys for Women?" This subtitle to Stephen Orgel's article ("Nobody's Perfect"), asserting certain homoerotic, and misogynistic aspects in the psychology of the Elizabethan theatre,[1] reflects a common scholarly presupposition that major female roles in the age of Shakespeare almost always were taken by boy actors. To cite a few examples: one scholar asserts that when writing *1, 2, 3 Henry VI* Shakespeare had "a leading boy of unusual range." Another remarks that when scripting *Midsummer Night's Dream* Shakespeare must have been able to draw upon "an unusually large number of boy actors." Yet another scholar writes, "the relatively few female roles" in Shakespeare's plays shows that "in his company at any given period only a very limited number of boy actors were capable of playing major roles."[2]

Compared to contemporary playwrights, however, Shakespeare scripted an unusual number of substantial female roles. In most cases these female roles equal, in lines and scenes, major supporting male roles assumed to have been designed for the Sharers in his company. Beyond mere size of role, Shakespeare's prominent female characters also surpass in depth of characterization, in dominance of scene and plot, the roles found in the plays of his contemporaries.[3] Furthermore, as Table 11 (comparing percentages of lines and scenes for primary and secondary female roles with those for a supporting male role) illustrates, these meaty roles show up in every genre of play he wrote, history, comedy, or tragedy. The plays cited are those to which Shakespeare is ascribed sole authorship. Dates and sequences listed are, of course, only approximate, and, for sake of convenience, based on the more traditional dating consensus. Percentages of lines, and classification according to genre follows that given in Marvin Spevack's *Concordance to the Works of William Shakespeare*. Percentages of scenes is derived from scene divisions given in *The Riverside Shakespeare*.[4]

71

	Table 11										
	Approximate Chronology & Comparison,										
	1st & 2nd Female Role with Supporting Male Role										
Year	Play	GNR	1 Fem	%In	%sc	2 Fem	%In	%sc	Male	%In	%sc
1590	*1HnVI*	Hist	Joan	9%	38%	C.Avn	2%	4%	Plant	7%	31%
1591	*2HnVI*	Hist	Mrgt	10%	50%	D.Glo	4%	20%	York	12%	31%
1592	*3HnVI*	Hist	Mrgt	10%	28%	L.Gry	3%	16%	York	6%	7%
1593	*RchIII*	Hist	Eliz	7%	24%	Mrgt	6%	8%	Buck	10%	32%
1593	*Errors*	Com	Adrna	15%	54%	Lucna	5%	54%	DroE	9%	55%
1593	*Titus*	Trag	Tmora	10%	31%	Lavna	2%	46%	Satrn	8%	23%
1594	*Shrew*	Com	Kate	8%	57%	Bianca	3%	50%	Tranio	11%	62%
1594	*2Gent*	Com	Julia	14%	39%	Silvia	7%	33%	Lanc	10%	22%
1594	*John*	Hist	Cnst	19%	10%	Elinor	2%	25%	Hubrt	8%	30%
1595	*Rich II*	Hist	Quen	4%	24%	D.York	3%	12%	York	10%	29%
1595	*LLL*	Com	Prncs	10%	33%	Rsline	6%	33%	Ferdn	11%	50%
1596	*R & J*	Trag	Juliet	17%	54%	Nurse	9%	50%	Caplt	9%	42%
1596	*Midsm*	Com	Helen	10%	55%	Hrmia	8%	55%	Bott	10%	56%
1596	*Merch*	Com	Portia	21%	44%	Nrissa	4%	44%	Shylk	13%	28%
1597	*1HnIV*	Hist	L.Prcy	2%	11%	M.Qck	2%	11%	K.Hnr	11%	26%
1597	*Wives*	Com	M.Pge	12%	39%	M.Qck	10%	39%	Shall	4%	35%
1598	*2HnIV*	Hist	M.Qck	5%	17%	Doll	3%	11%	Shall	6%	24%
1598	*M Ado*	Com	Brtce	11%	41%	Hero	5%	35%	Claud	10%	47%
1599	*Henr V*	Hist	Kthrn	2%	9%	M.Qck	1%	9%	Flull	9%	30%
1599	*Caesar*	Trag	Portia	4%	11%	Calpur	1%	11%	Anth	13%	44%
1599	*AYLike*	Com	Rsline	26%	45%	Celia	10%	36%	Jacq	8%	32%
1600	*Hamlt*	Trag	Ophla	4%	25%	Gertr	4%	50%	Horat	7%	40%
1601	*12 Ngt*	Com	Viola	13%	39%	Olivia	12%	33%	Belch	14%	56%
1602	*Troils*	Trag	Crssd	9%	26%	Cassd	9%	4%	Theri	8%	22%
1603	*Alls W*	Com	Helen	16%	55%	C.Ros	12%	35%	Parol	13%	55%
1604	*Msure*	Com	Isobel	15%	47%	Marian	2%	18%	Ange	11%	30%
1604	*Othello*	Trag	Dsdm	11%	60%	Emilia	7%	60%	Cassi	8%	67%
1605	*Lear*	Trag	Regan	6%	31%	Goner	5%	31%	Edmd	9%	35%
1606	*Macbth*	Trag	L.Mcb	11%	29%	1 Wtc	3%	14%	Macd	8%	32%
1607	*Ant/Cl*	Trag	Cleo	19%	38%	Charm	3%	33%	Enobr	10%	31%
1607	*Corio*	Trag	Volm	8%	21%	Virgla	1%	17%	Mene	16%	46%
1608	*Timon*	Trag	Tmnda	0.2%	6%	Phryn	0.2%	6%	Flavs	8%	40%
1608	*Pericl*	Trag	Marin	8%	15%	Bawd	5%	11%	Simn	6%	20%
1609	*Cymbl*	Trag	Imogn	16%	37%	Quen	5%	19%	Clotn	7%	26%
1610	*Winter*	Com	Paula	10%	33%	Herm	6%	27%	Leon	20%	40%
1611	*Tempst*	Com	Mrand	7%	44%	Iris	2%	11%	Calib	8%	44%

Whether one adopts the traditional chronology of Shakespeare's plays, or the newer criticism which pushes the dates of his first efforts back into the late 1580s,[5] there still appears a tendency to script at least one, and often two, meaty female roles in his very first plays, and that tendency continued throughout most of his theatrical career. Percentages of lines gives one indication of the consistency with which Shakespeare populated his plays with significant women's roles. Percentages of scenes confirms that fact. Spevack's *Concordance* is geared to literary analysis (words and speeches). It does not provide information concerning scenes, that is the frequency and amount of time characters spend on stage. The character Gower in *Pericles*, for example, gives 12 percent of the lines, but that character's time on stage is limited to some prologues and an epilogue. However, when percentages of lines are coupled with percentages of scenes—in other words number of lines *and* number of appearances on stage—there emerges a pattern of at least one significant female role in 30 out of 36 plays. In 15 of those plays there is also a significantly meaty secondary female role, which, though the percentage of lines may look somewhat small, the number of appearances on stage indicates that the role goes beyond the "scriviner," "messenger," "attendant" roles probably played by "hired men."[6] Interestingly, the scenes often ascribed to Shakespeare in his collaborations with Fletcher on *Henry VIII* and *Two Noble Kinsmen* are the best scenes for the major female characters, respectively, Queen Catherine and Anne Boleyn, and Hippolyta and Emelia.

Only six of Shakespeare's plays lack a woman's role comparable to a supporting male role: *Richard II, 1* and *2 Henry IV, Henry V, Julius Caesar,* and *Timon of Athens.* Most of those plays are plays in which historical sources gave Shakespeare few women around whom to build a part. Most are what one might term "war plays," where emphasis is placed on battle spectacles, clearly plots in which females could play only limited roles.

Chronology also reveals an interesting consistency of a particular type of female character stretching over most of Shakespeare's theatrical career. Over and over again there appears what we might term a "shrew." This is a woman who, in comic or serious vein, displays some form of assertiveness or aggressiveness, sometimes plays a role which dominates story development as much as a male character (Queen Margaret or Lady Macbeth for example), and interacts with the male characters in other than traditional female responses. Table 12 traces those roles. It does not, however list the crossdressing roles of Julia, Portia, Rosaline, and Viola. While much that is interesting has been, and continues to be, written about this phenomenon in Shakespeare's middle comedies,[7] these roles show females becoming assertive by donning male guise. They do not display what I would term the "shrew" character, that is a "woman" as a woman displaying assertive behavior.

<table>
<tr><td colspan="4" align="center">**Table 12**
Chronology of Assertive Female Roles</td></tr>
</table>

Year	Play	Genre	Character
1590	*1 Henry VI*	History	Joan la Pucelle
1591	*2 Henry VI*	History	Queen Margaret
1592	*3 Henry VI*	History	Queen Margaret
1593	*Richard III*	History	Queen Margaret
1593	*Comedy of Errors*	Comedy	Adriana
1593	*Titus Andronicus*	Tragedy	Tamora
1594	*Taming the Shrew*	Comedy	Katherina
1594	*King John*	History	Constance
1595	*Love's Labour's Lost*	Comedy	Princess of France
1596	*Romeo & Juliet*	Tragedy	Nurse
1596	*Midsummer*	Comedy	Hermia
1596	*Merchant of Venice*	Comedy	Nerissa
1597	*Merry Wives*	Comedy	Ms Page/Ford/Quickly
1598	*Much Ado*	Comedy	Beatrice
1599	*As You Like It*	Comedy	Audrey
1600	*Hamlet*	Tragedy	Gertrude
1601	*Twelfth Night*	Comedy	Maria
1602	*Troilus & Cressida*	Tragedy	Cressida
1603	*All's Well*	Comedy	Countess
1604	*Measure for Measure*	Comedy	Mistress Overdone
1604	*Othello*	Tragedy	Desdemona & Emilia
1605	*King Lear*	Tragedy	Regan & Goneril
1606	*Macbeth*	Tragedy	Lady Macbeth
1607	*Anthony & Cleopatra*	Tragedy	Cleopatra
1607	*Coriolanus*	Tragedy	Volumnia
1608	*Pericles*	Tragedy	Bawd
1608	*Cymbeline*	Tragedy	Queen
1610	*Winter's Tale*	Comedy	Paulina

Mistress Quickly is a special case. Though her role in the *Henry IV* and *Henry V* plays seemed too small to include her character in the table above, she appears in all three of them. All in all, then, Quickly is scripted into no less than four plays, a record matched by only one other Shakespearean character, Queen Margaret. The Quickly character spans five years, and if *Merry Wives of Windsor* were written to show Falstaff "in love," its author took the opportunity to script large scenes for Mistress Quickly too. She has the second largest female role in the play, yet in terms of plot development she has little to do except bear messages back and forth. Her bawdy, bossy, working woman type appears earlier as the tavern hostess in *Taming of the Shrew*, and later in the guises of the Nurse (*Romeo and Juliet*), Maria (*Twelfth Night*), Mrs. Overdone (*Measure for Measure*), and the Bawd (*Pericles*), giving her character type a longevity stretching throughout most of Shakespeare's career.

The scheming, manipulative, and sometimes violent virago is another consistent variation on the shrew. First created in the guise of Joan la Pucelle (*1 Henry VI*) she reappears four times in the person of Queen Margaret. Margaret's appearance in *Richard III* is an historical anachronism of which Shakespeare would have been aware. It is an appearance as peculiar as that of Mrs. Quickly in *Merry Wives*, who suddenly is transformed from the hostess of an Eastcheap tavern in London into the housekeeper of Dr. Caius in Windsor. Obviously these two characters had made a hit with the theatre goers. The Margaret type shrew also appears as Tamora (*Titus*), Constance (*John*), and the Duchess of York (*Richard II*), and after a lapse of some years, resurfaces in somewhat quieter vein as Gertrude (*Hamlet*), Lady Macbeth, (*Macbeth*), Volumnia (*Coriolanus*), and the Queen in *Cymbeline*.

There is even a curious consistency in the relationship of the first and secondary female roles scripted for the plays containing the crossdressing roles of Julia, Portia, Rosaline, and Viola (excluded from the table). This consistency is echoed in the characters of Helena and Hermia from *Midsummer Night's Dream*. In each of these scripts there is a line or two which indicates that the leading female role is taller than the secondary one. Yet the scripts cover a time span of over seven years.[8]

Given the presupposition that "at any given period only a very limited number of boy actors were capable of playing major roles," Shakespeare serendipitously must have been blessed with a string of extremely talented boy actors from the beginning to the end of his career. Regardless of the time in which he wrote, and regardless of whatever company with which he was affiliated before 1594, and afterwards when he became a member of the Chamberlain's Men, he had available to him a boy of "unusual range." With such a stable from which to choose, it would seem logical that Shakespeare would have scripted several plays in which children would have substantial speaking roles integral to the plot, so as to give them experience on stage working with the adult members of the company. Table 13 details those plays which specifically require speaking parts for children, or, as with the fairies in *Midsummer Night's Dream*, generally are assumed to have been played by children.

What a startling difference here between these 11 plays, grouped basically into three, three-year periods, and the 30 plays with one (often (two) partner-sized, women's roles which stretch throughout Shakespeare's dramatic career. There seems a paradox here. Obviously Shakespeare did not break in his boy actors gradually. The normal procedure, if we suppose he used boy actors for these parts, was to start them right off on equal footing with himself and his partners in a juicy role like Portia or Rosaline. Further, given the fact that a consistent

Table 13
Chronology, Specified Children's Roles, % Lines & Scenes

Year	Play	Genre	Role(s)	%Lines	%Scenes
1590	*1 Henry VI*	History	Rutland	0.8%	4%
1593	*Titus*	Tragedy	Lucius' son,	2%	38%
			Blackamoor child	0%	23%
1593	*Richard III*	History	Son, Clarence	0.5%	4%
			Daughter, Clarence	.2%	8%
1596	*R & J*	Tragedy	Page	0.1%	4%
1596	*Midsummer*	Comedy	4 Fairies (ex Puck)	3%	56%
1597	*Merry Wives*	Comedy	Robin	0.3%	13%
			William	0.4%	4%
			Schoolboys/Fairies	0%	13%
1598	*1 Henry IV*	History	Page	0.7%	11%
1599	*Much Ado*	Comedy	Boy	0.7%	6%
1604	*Measure*	Comedy	Boy	0.2%	6%
1607	*Macbeth*	Tragedy	Son of Macduff	0.8%	4%
1608	*Timon*	Tragedy	Page	0.3%	7%

character type, the comic or vitriolic shrew, also is woven throughout his repertory—year after year, as their voices and bodies changed (or as Cuthbert Burbage put it "the boys wearing out daily")[9] he must have found anew yet another boy of that "unusual range" necessary to play shrew roles he scripted beginning with Joan la Pucelle and continuing through the years to Cymbeline's Queen. Finally, if we can believe his comments scripted in *Hamlet* (II, 2), there seems yet another paradox. Shakespeare did not care for boy actors. Nonetheless, throughout his career, he wrote some of the most memorable roles in English dramatic literature for these same "little eyases," who, as Cuthbert Burbage put it were "wearing out daily," and whose shrill little voices Shakespeare disparaged, sometimes out of their own mouths on stage.

Perhaps it is time to apply Occam's Razor to this doubled paradox. It may be more logical to assume that from the beginning of his career, Shakespeare was associated with one, probably two, actors who were extraordinarily good at female characterizations. Yet because they project backwards from Caroline and Restoration sources (sources which themselves admit to ignorance about the theatre of Elizabeth's day),[10] and because to nineteenth- and twentieth-century minds female impersonation conjures up visions of drag-queens in garter belts and fishnet stockings, perhaps scholars subconsciously blinded themselves to the possibility that Shakespeare wrote his great female roles for adult partners in his company.

The logic of the Elizabethan theatre business suggests that possibility as strongly as does the logic of chronology. In the first place, as the company's premier playwright, and one who was an acting partner to boot, we must assume that Shakespeare's plays reflect the types of plays and roles commissioned of other playwrights by the Chamberlain's Men. Neither Shakespeare, nor Chapman, nor Dekker, nor any other Elizabethan and Jacobean playwright scripted plays, and then looked for actors to fit the roles; they all wrote plays and parts to fit the actors within the company which paid them.[11]

Year after year, Elizabethan acting companies gave six performances a week, presenting at least four, five, sometimes six, different plays. Given this hectic schedule, there must have been little time for long rehearsal periods. Only actors who were accustomed to certain types of roles for themselves, and to one another's performance techniques, could function smoothly under such a strain. Scholars like

Andrew Gurr and Gerald Bentley have pointed out that the repetition year after year of similar male character types: Dromio to Launcelot Gobbo to Dogberry to Polonius, Saturninus to Shylock to Iago to Claudius, Hotspur to Laertes to Macduff, demonstrates as much. Male roles tend to become more mature the later the date at which scripts were written. Hamlet is obviously older than Romeo; Macbeth's maturity suggests an age older than Hamlet's.

The tables above demonstrate there is a similar consistency in female roles. A Margaret, a Mistress Quickly, a Portia, a Viola, a Gertrude, a Lady Macbeth, was a staple of the repertory. Moreover, Shakespeare's female characters seem to age over the length of his writing career just as do his male characters. Ages are rarely specified in the scripts anyway; one exception is the insistence that Juliet is not quite 14, but that insistence probably is to make it clear to the audience she is not the typical, mature, youngish aristocratic female, like Rosaline, usually portrayed in Shakespeare's plays written prior to 1600. It is interesting to note that when Cleopatra (scripted 1606-07), herself known to have been in her 30s at the time period encompassed by the play, asks the age of her rival Octavia, she is told "thirty."

If the androgynous qualities of pre-pubescent boys were necessary to these female roles, there must have been a tremendous turnover, but there is no evidence regarding recruitment of boys. Scholars logically point out that hired men, or apprentices, only could be brought in to play roles which demanded little preparation or only minimal interaction with the main characters,[12] such as attendants, or devils, or messengers, or an Anne Page. Blinded by the presupposition that only a boy could play women's roles, they thereby seem to imply that the Chamberlain's Men molded its *male* repertory to its existing partners, but shaped its *female* repertory to the prospect of cycling a boy into a partner-sized role every few days, and cycling a new boy into the company every couple of years. Or they write of "boys playing women's roles until the age of 21 or beyond."

Further, in one way or another, loss of money to the company as a whole, and to individual actor-partners, would be involved in such a practice. Henslowe's *Diary* occasionally lists large sums of money spent on costumes, and on tailors and materials to make costumes. Certain of his figures specified expenditures for women's gowns, farthingales, bodices, etc. Based solely on those figures, figures which do not include hidden costs such as tailors' fees, yards of cloths for unspecified costume items, lace trims, and the like, Henslowe laid out over £87 in a six-year period (1597-1603), an average of almost £15 a year—the average tradesman's salary. Such sums make no sense if laid out for a string of boy actors. Plays, and the costumes for them, were meant to repeat themselves in the repertory. No hardheaded businessman like Henslowe would expend that kind of money on women's costumes which would have to be altered substantially or replaced, as boy actors grew, or new boys were brought in to replace those who moved on. Those sums argue a consistent group of actors among the Admiral's Men playing the women's roles. There is nothing in the sources to suggest the makeup of Shakespeare's company was radically different.

By the same token, Henslowe's accounts indicate that an actor-partner earned from gallery receipts alone between five to seven shillings per performance. When that sum is added to the probable receipts from the "Pit," the total daily income for a Sharer was about 198 pence per day, a sum equal to two weeks labor for a *skilled* craftsman. Henslowe also indicates that he charged the Admiral's Men three shillings a week (six pence a day) for the use of his apprentice James Bristow, though what use was made of him is not specified.[13] Therefore, if the boy or his master were paid even that minimum of six pence a day, that expense cut into the partners' daily profits. If, on the other hand, we accept the supposition that the boy was the apprentice of one of the partners, the other partners would be giving that partner his 198 pence share for *not* working while they toiled on stage. And if the partner with the apprentice were *not* paid his usual share on those days his apprentice appeared in a major role, but only the six pence Henslowe's accounts indicate, *he* was losing 198 pence that day, a goodly sum considering it equalled about 20 days labor to the average artisan. Yet Henslowe's accounts, and the fortunes earned by Shakespeare and his partners testify to the financial acumen of the successful theater businessmen. Shakespeare himself seems to have had the reputation of a skinflint.[14] All of them look like a group of men who squeezed pennies tightly.

Another aspect of Elizabethan theatre business militates against using boys in major roles; it is, in effect, an aspect which pertains to the exclusion of women from the stage as well, and one which traditional historians, new historicists, and neo-Freudians alike perhaps have overlooked. Many of the founders of the theatre business derived from the artisan and commercial classes—Philip Henslowe the dyer, James Burbage the carpenter, Robert Armin the goldsmith, and so on.[15] Though they may have chosen this new "masterless" profession as a means to circumvent the guild system's restrictions, should we expect them to organize themselves any differently than the guild system in which they grew up?

Actor-Sharers, like masters of the traditional guilds, achieved that status only after significant financial outlay. Acting companies required £70 to £90 as a "buy-in" share; guilds required proof of stock worth £70 before allowing a man to set up a shop. Like guild masters controlled the guilds, "master-players" (Sharers), controlled all aspects of the companies' operations, and reaped all the profits. Like the journeymen of the guild, actors who were "hired men," worked for wages fixed by the partners, and hoped to achieve partner status some day.[16] Within the guild system, women and children could inherit a business, like that of a goldsmith, but they were not given the status of practicing members of the guild. Membership reverted to the guild, to be granted out when, and to whom, the guild masters saw fit.[17] Theatrical heirs and heiresses could inherit a share in the theatre building, but never a share in the acting company. After an appropriate "buy-out" price was paid to the heirs, that share reverted to the company, to be granted out as the partners saw fit.[18] Within the traditional guild system, apprentices learned their craft working under the direction of master carpenters, or goldsmiths, or whatever, but they never were allowed access to the master's major assets, and never could produce a "masterpiece" until after long years of apprenticeship, when the masters were willing to grant them full status in the guild. Since the "master-player's" "masterpieces" and his major assets were his performances in a major role, can we expect that apprentice actors routinely were allowed a freedom *denied* apprentices in traditional guilds?

As a quick aside, I think that overt misogynistic or homoerotic tendencies among Elizabethan males have little to do with the absence of women from the English stage. Contemporary Italian acting troupes employed women, but the typical Italian business organization was a *family* business, which utilized the contributions of wives, children, cousins, in-laws and the like. Typical of Shakespeare's London, however, was the joint-stock company dominated by guilds which excluded, even in the case of the weavers, women from membership.[19]

Rather than a conscious choice by Elizabethan actors to exclude females from the stage, their masculine, artisan backgrounds may have blinded them, and their artisan-tradesman audiences, to the possibility of women as Sharers or employees. Is it only coincidence that it took the English Civil War and the closing of the public theaters, an almost total upheaval of the English society and the English theatrical world, before women were accepted on the English stage? Female costume had become more revealing of feminine shape, and interestingly, like actors in the Elizabethan era, most actresses were recruited from the middle classes.

One argument for the use of boys for women in plays centers upon the preference for "realism" expressed in Elizabethan documents. Only boys, this argument holds, have the "freshness" of face, and suppleness necessary for subtleties of feminine movement. Yet no matter how close to the stage an Elizabethan playgoer may have been, "close-ups," like we expect in television and movies was, and still is, impossible when it comes to the stage. Broad movements suggesting femininity are the best one can achieve, and further, we cannot know exactly what Elizabethans meant by "realism."[20]

Elizabethan feminine costume was not revealing. Dressed as a woman, noble or any other class, an actor was swathed in cloth from neck to toe. Skirts for all classes were full; in addition noblewomen wore farthingales, obliterating any hip line. Bosoms often were covered, and even were there *decolletage*, breast outlines were smashed flat by whalebone, wooden, or steel stomachers slid down the gown's front. Much the same can be said for male garb. Doublets ballooned at the chest, gathered only at the waist, and most had at least short skirts, which together with varieties of ballooned trousers hid the hips. The exaggerated codpieces of the reign of Henry VIII were no longer in fashion. Illustrations of Elizabethan garb show[21] that hardly any gender distinguishing female physical characteristics would be revealed whether the actor played in woman's garb, or a crossdressed woman's role like Rosaline. The first set of illustrations shows how much of the anatomy was disguised by Elizabethan male and female clothing. In particular, the wood-cut of the infamous Elizabethan transvestite Moll Cut-purse illustrates the ease with which she was able to frequent theatres, alehouses, taverns, and tobacco shops without detection. It was only when she told someone she was a woman that she was discovered. Femininity of movement hardly would show in the voluminous gowns with puffed out sleeves and farthingales worn by actors in female dress. In crossdressed roles, femininity of movement, if needed, would be easy to actors who often observed courtiers at taverns, and the theatre (and who probably aped them in roles like the foppish courtier Moth from *Love's Labour's Lost*). Courtiers' movements often are referred to snidely in Elizabethan sources as "prancing" and "mincing."

As for facial features, about all an actor needed was a clean-shaven face. Heavy lines, wrinkles, jowls, usually do not show up on men or women until after the age of 40. An actor playing a working-class female, like Juliet's Nurse, would be expected to look a bit coarse and shop-worn, a bit "horsey" so to speak. As for playing noblewomen, aristocratic women in Shakespeare's day used make-up conventions mimicking those of the Queen, make-up designed to hide Elizabeth's age. Private dispatches by foreign diplomats described the layers of "paint" applied to Elizabeth's face. Many women aped her *coiffure*— plucking their foreheads bald and donning elaborate wigs.[22] Shakespeare's aristocratic female characters, like Portia, probably appeared on stage with faces painted in a white base, relieved by red blush on cheeks and lips, and in wigs. They would look like any aristocratic woman at Court, and no doubt not much different than adult, *male* Japanese *Kabuki* actors who play female roles.

The *Kabuki* parallel probably extends to attitudes Elizabethan audiences had towards those actors who portrayed females. Rather than female impersonators in the modern sense of the word, they probably viewed them as do modern Japanese audiences. Crossdressing probably was little more than a tried-and-true stage convention in which some actors were known for specialization in female parts.

Acceptance of that convention probably means there was little awareness of the "masculinity" of actors portraying females. Contemporary portraits show none. A description of Desdemona at Oxford (1610) always referred to the character as "she." In other words, the *triple entendre* concerning a crossdressed role like Viola (a man playing a woman, playing a man) may not have been as obvious to Elizabethans as it seems to us today. They expected females to be portrayed by males. To keep the illusion that it was women that the audience was watching, Shakespeare, and others, scripted male characters to make allusions to the femininity of female characters, much in the same way they scripted allusions to time or place to cue audiences into passage of time or changes of locale.

Unlike a modern crossdressed character, like Julie Andrews' role in the movie *Victor-Victoria*, in which the gist of the plot is that both the audience, and some of the on-screen characters are aware that a woman is playing a man, who is supposed to be a female impersonator, that type of joke is absent in most Elizabethan scripts. A pageboy disguised as a Lady is scripted specifically to make Christopher Sly the butt of a joke in *Taming of the Shrew*. The character Celia knows the character Rosalind is a woman playing a man; she is not scripted to know that it is a man playing a woman, playing a man.

Rarely do Elizabethan playwrights "play" upon the audience's awareness that it is a man in a woman's role, except perhaps for a "one-liner" or two, and for Rosalind's obvious joke, and that only in the epilogue of *As You Like It*, that men would refuse the actor's offer of a kiss. Such certainly is not the case with a Japanese audience viewing a male *Kabuki* actor portraying a female. Be that as it may, the last set of illustrations reveals how easy it would be for an Elizabethan actor (in this case a rather famous one) to disguise his sex by shaving, applying heavy make-up, and donning a woman's gown and wig.[23]

Nonetheless, the "proof" of my "pudding," so to speak, must rest in the "reading" of contemporary sources. Restoration sources wrote of boys "brought up at Blackfriars" who played women's parts, but even these are vague about what age these boys were when they began to play, and continued to play female roles. John Honeyman, called "Gentleman" in an epitaph written after his death (an appellation never given to a boy by Elizabethans), played female roles for a span of seven years; John Thompson seems to have played female roles for as many as 17 years; Robert Pallant, Richard Sharpe, and William Trigge, played female roles over spans of four or five years. They may have begun their acting careers in female parts as "boys," but they were still playing those roles when they had reached at least the age of 18, and maybe still were doing so at 28 or 30. Evidence suggests that many apprentices (except, of course, choirboys) were hardly "little eyases," and perhaps already young men, when they began apprenticeships. Most young Englishmen entered apprenticeship between the ages of 17 and their early 20s, Venetians 14 to 20. English law stipulated apprentice status lasted until the age of 24. Philip Henslowe himself was at least a 19-year-old, and more likely a 29-year-old, apprentice when he married his master's

Fig. 7. Woodcuts: *Roxburgh Ballads*.

Fig. 8. Woodcuts: *Roxburgh Ballads* and various Tradesmen.

Fig. 9. Title Page: *The Roaring Girl.*

Fig. 10. Shakespeare: *First Folio* engraving, two views.

Fig. 11. Queen Elizabeth. Shakespeare in Elizabeth's costume.

widow. Almost none of the boy-actors seem to have crossed over to the adult companies. In three cases for which documentation shows that cross-over, Nathan Field, William Ostler, and John Underwood, none seem to have moved into female roles. Field, for instance, assumed Burbage's roles after Burbage's death.[24]

What did Shakespeare's contemporaries say about the use of boys in women's roles? They said surprisingly little. Shakespeare did script a remark by Cleopatra that someday a "squeaking" boy may act her part,[25] but that may say more about Shakespeare's attitude towards Boys' Companies, and the *vocal qualities* of boy-actors, than it does his use of boy actors on a regular basis. No internal, textual evidence suggests he shaped roles to boy-actors. Thomas Heywood's *Apology for Actors* replied to criticism about "youths" wearing feminine garb on stage,[26] but "youths" is a relative term which does not necessarily imply boys. Rare records concerning boys acting with the *adult* companies indicate minor parts such as page-boys, fairies, devils, and children. A few references exist concerning the Children's Companies which remark upon the charming novelty of boys who were expert at portraying young women and old men, but that may just be the point, the *novelty* of it all. When the Boys' Companies tried plays, like *Spanish Tragedy*, that were staples of the adult company, their efforts appear to have been laughed off the stage.[27] Perhaps the best modern analogy to their effect and appeal would be a trained dog act in which the dogs are anthropomorphized in costumes, as their trainers put them through the motions to act out a skit.

There exist no correspondingly complimentary remarks about the boy (or boys) "of unusual range" who portrayed Shakespeare's Portia (*Merchant of Venice*), or Rosaline (*As You Like It*), or Thomas Kyd's Bel-Imperia (*Spanish Tragedy*), or any other of the substantial female roles in the repertories of the adult companies. Spectators commenting on the adult companies did not mention boys. They wrote about *actors* dressed as men and women dancing at the conclusion of performances; they wrote about the lavish costumes and the lavish decoration of the theatre buildings; they wrote about the plots of plays they had attended; they praised the performances of the Elizabethan super-stars Edward Alleyn, Richard Tarlton, Will Kempe, and Richard Burbage.[28] They did not comment on the actors who played Buckingham to Burbage's Richard III, Claudius to his Hamlet, or Iago to his Othello. Obviously there appeared nothing to them out of the ordinary there. They also did not comment on who played Margaret to Burbage's Richard, Gertrude to his Hamlet, or Desdemona to his Othello (except for one reference to how effective an actor had been in portraying Desdemona's death scene), and therefore I think we can assume that, unlike the novelty of the Children's Companies in which boys charmingly portrayed women, there appeared nothing out of the ordinary there either.

Puritan pamphlets attacking the immorality of the theater abound. These roar and thunder at the practice of crossdressing, at males dancing with, and kissing, males, at such practices enticing people to sodomy, but they almost never specify that boys are cross-dressing, dancing and kissing. It is the "immorality," "unnaturalness" and "ungodliness" of men pretending to be women that the Puritan authors most often attack.

The position of his name in the cast list given by Ben Jonson when he published *Sejanus* (1603) and *Volpone* (1605) suggests that Shakespeare's partner Alexander Cooke may have played the roles of Agrippina and Fine-madam Would-be. The cast list of *Sir John van Olden Barnavelt* (1619) clearly states that Nicholas Tooley, for a time perhaps with the Admiral's men, but after 1605 with the King's, at the age of *44* (hardly a boy), played the role of Barnavelt's wife. Some scholars believe that the "Nick" and "Sander," named in the 1590 cast list of *Seven Deadly Sins* as playing women's roles probably are these same two men.[29] Tooley, then 15, might possibly fit the description of boy, but Cooke, at two or three years older, certainly cannot. Finally, lines in the poetic prologue to a performance of some form of *Othello*, Sir William Davenant's royal patent to organize an acting company (both dating from 1660),[30] and a chance remark in the town records of Reading, dating from the turn of the sixteenth century,[31] seem to belie that it was general practice to use boys for major female roles. The poetic epilogue was given to soften the impact of the first time a woman appeared on the English stage. It states, in part:

> But to the point: - In this reforming age
> We have intents to civilize the stage.
> Our women are defective, and so siz'd
> You'd think they were some of the guard disguis'd:
> For, to speak truth, men act, that are between
> Forty and fifty, wenches of fifteen;
> With bone so large and nerve so incompliant,
> When you call Desdemona, enter Giant. -

Davenant certainly knew the usual practices of pre-Restoration theatre. He became Governor of the company at the Cockpit in 1640, and continued in that capacity until the closing of the theatres in 1642. He himself obtained the clause in his patent which specifies "That, whereas the women's parts in plays have hitherto been acted by men in the habits of women, of which some have taken offence, we permit and give leave for the time to come, that all women's parts be acted by women." The Reading document relates that an actor apologized to a select audience composed of the mayor and aldermen for a delay in beginning the performance because, "the Queen was shaving."

Who then were these partners of Shakespeare who took the large female roles? Unless some heretofore hidden document surfaces, we will never know for sure. But many scholars are convinced by the circumstantial evidence sketched above that Nicholas Tooley and Alexander Cooke may well have been specialists in female roles. There was yet another actor assigned a female role in the cast list of *The Seven Deadly Sins*, a certain "Will." Malone, noting that so many of the others listed in that cast as members of Lord Strange's Men ended up as Chamberlain's Men, asserted that it was Will Shakespeare. Later scholarship, noting the ambivalence of the names, has dismissed Malone's speculation. Honigmann, on the other hand, recently has reasserted Malone's identification, making a strong circumstantial case for Shakespeare's association with Strange's Men perhaps as early as 1588.[32]

If that "Will" be our Will, what female roles did he play? It should be remembered that his primary occupation was that of *actor*, one who wrote a couple of plays per year on the side as a special contribution to his company. Logic would seem to say that an actor would script parts designed to make his appearances on stage as memorable for himself as for any he wrote for his partners. Somehow roles often ascribed to him by tradition, Old Adam and Hamlet's Ghost,[33] just do not seem to fit that description. Logic would also seem to say that one should look for a character type which appears in his earliest plays, and continues throughout his career. Table 12 demonstrates there is such a role—the "shrew," and there is little doubt that Queen Margaret, the Nurse, and Mistress Quickly do dominate scenes in which they appear. In fact, in Shakespeare's earliest plays, *1 Henry VI*, and its two sequels, the "shrew" role is the only female role with much substance. Clearly at the beginning of his career as an actor and a playwright he must have been associated with someone who was good at those kinds of roles.

Nicholas Tooley's full association with Shakespeare and his partners can be dated only after 1603. At least for a few years before and after the turn of the seventeenth century he seems to have had some association with the Admiral's Men. Cooke probably worked with Shakespeare earlier, but the first sure reference to him only appears from Jonson's cast lists.[34] The only actor clearly associated with William Shakespeare from the beginning to the end of his theatrical career, was William Shakespeare.

The beginning of that career needs some examination. Except for the possible reference to Shakespeare as "Will" in the cast list of *Seven Deadly Sins*, there is precious little about him before he suddenly appears as a full partner in the Chamberlain's Men in 1594. All the other full partners, Richard Burbage, John Heminges, Will Kempe, Thomas Pope, George Bryan, Richard Cowley, William Slye, and Augustine Phillips had long-established reputations as actors dating back at least to 1590. Even Henry Condell, who only gained partner status much later, also had long-term experience before joining the Chamberlain's Men. What was it that a William Shakespeare, with short experience on stage in roles that gained no recorded notice, had to offer these seasoned actors? One answer might be his already written five or six plays including his popular *Henry VI* cycle. Yet no Elizabethan playwright was given the potentially lucrative position of Sharer on the basis of his playwriting. Thomas Heywood is the only other example from Shakespeare's age of an actor-playwright partner, and it is obvious that he appeared on stage often. It only stands to reason that Shakespeare must have had some special acting talent. Yet what did this new company need in the way of specialities? In Burbage, and probably Heminges, it already had seasoned serious actors. In Cowley and Phillips it had veteran character actors. In Bryan and Pope it had popular, widely-travelled, and proven clowns. In Kempe it had the most renowned comedian of the times. One speciality never associated with these actors, however, is the speciality of playing women's roles, and that speciality may well have been the one that Shakespeare already had demonstrated when working for Strange's and/or Pembroke's Men.

Some of the strength, determination, and lack of passivity attributed to Shakespeare's female characters show remarkable similarities to women from his own surroundings. Many of his cousin's households and possessions were run by widowed aunts. His mother's aged step-mother was sharp enough of mind and purpose to ensure by deposition her nephew's inheritance, even though she was too enfeebled to appear personally in court. His sister, his two daughters, and his own wife, seem to have had the determination and will to have at least some part in choosing their mates and arranging their own marriages. His daughter's mother-in-law had long owned and managed a tavern in Stratford. In short, he had numerous examples from his own life to script, and to portray, of determined and assertive wives and mothers, and bossy (and probably bawdy) working women[35] like his fictional Mistress Quickly.

What tantalizing little evidence concerning Shakespeare's appearance may suggest it would not be difficult for him to have portrayed women. John Aubrey, close to the age of Shakespeare, and eagerly gathering all the information he could from anyone who could remember pre-Restoration theatre, wrote that his sources described Shakespeare as "a handsome, well-shap't man." Caroline Spurgeon, exhaustively analyzing the imagery in Shakespeare's works, wrote that at least some sort of a self-portrait of Shakespeare emerges in his writings: "The figure of Shakespeare which emerges is of a compactly well-built man, probably on the slight side." Schoenbaum, usually extremely cautious, even when examining the painted likenesses attributed as Shakespeare portraits, nonetheless, wrote Spurgeon "may well be right." Scholars have remarked upon the seeming "femininity" of the Droeshout engraving from the *First Folio*, and it, and the only other easily authenticated portrait we possess, the memorial bust in Stratford's Holy Trinity Church, portray a man with very little facial hair and an extremely high forehead. Shakespeare's lack of facial hair is in stark contrast to portraits of merchants, courtiers, and even of his fellow actors Tarlton, Alleyn, Kempe, Armin, and Burbage, all of whom sport the full beards seemingly in fashion among Elizabethan men. Slightness of build and lack of facial hair would be an asset to an actor portraying women; delays because "the Queen was shaving" would be infrequent. So too would the high, receding forehead; it matched that of the Queen and other Elizabethan ladies of the court, who in imitation of the Queen's semi-baldness, plucked their forehead and donned wigs.[36]

Brooke Ld Cobham.

Fig. 12. William Brooke, Lord Cobham.

Fig. 13. Robert Armin: Title page *Two Maids of Morclack* (1609)/Richard Tarlton. Richard Burbage: Engraving of portrait at Dulwich.

Recently, computer analysis of clusters of so-called "rare" words seems to confirm that whoever played Old Adam probably also played Hamlet's Ghost; a significant number of "rare" words in Adam's vocabulary reappear in speeches given by the Ghost. Identifying other clusters of "rare" words, and relating them backwards and forwards chronologically to *As You Like It*, seems to suggest a progression of roles comprising a number of minor, elderly, royal, or noble, parts, such as Bedford (*1 Henry VI*), Egeon (*Errors*), King Philip (*John*), Old Adam (*As You Like It*), the Ghost (*Hamlet*), and Brabantio (*Othello*), in plays dating from *1 Henry VI* to *Pericles*. The study asserts that "when Shakespeare memorized a role for a particular play, the memorized lines strongly influenced his subsequent lexicon as a writer."[37]

The assertion that this stylometric analysis, linking Old Adam to Hamlet's Ghost, identifies Shakepeare's roles is based on the traditions that Shakepeare was an indifferent actor, and played only tertiary roles like Old Adam and Hamlet's Ghost, and therein lies its problem. The traditions concerning Shakespeare's specialities in portraying old men, like Old Adam, and kings, like Hamlet's Ghost, are based on very, very, broad interpretations of very, very slim evidence.

The Old Adam tradition stems from third- and forth-hand, post-Restoration anecdotes. One states that a brother of Shakespeare, when that brother was a very old man, told old Mr. Bowman (the Restoration actor), who then told, Mr. Oldys, that he once saw his brother William play an old man who was carried on stage to the dinner table, and then someone sang a song, but he could give no other particulars about the play. Another version tells substantially the same tale, but its provenance is even further removed. Thomas Jones, an old man from a village 18 miles from Stratford, told Thomas Wilkes, that he heard the story from an elderly, but unspecified, relative of Shakespeare. The details sound like a scene from *As You Like It*, but the play is not named. From this reference about all one can say is that one time, in one play, Shakespeare may have portrayed an old man.

The probability of the source of first Old Adam story is further clouded when it is remembered that none of Shakespeare's brothers survived him (unless there was a bastard Shakespeare about whom we have no other reference), and the source of the second, Thomas Jones, is called to question when it is remembered that he is the source of the "deer poaching" anecdote, the probability of which Schoenbaum, among others, has punctured.[38] The Hamlet's Ghost tradition, and assumptions that he played kingly roles, are based on Nicholas Rowe's (1709) report of an anecdote related to him by Thomas Betterton (the Restoration actor), and a cryptic epigram by John Davies of Hereford, who wrote (1610):

> *To our English Terence Mr. Will: Shake-speare.*
>
> Some Say good *Will* (which I, in sport, do sing)
>   Had'st thou not plaid some Kingly parts in sport,
> Thou hadst bin a companion for a *King*;
> And, beene a King among the meaner sort.
> Some others raile; but raile as they thinke fit,
> Thou hast no rayling, but a raigning Wit:
>   *And* honesty *thou sow'st, which they do reape*;
>   *So, to increase their* Stocke *which they do keepe.*[39]

Stylometric computer analysis, therefore, may well have identified an Actor X, and no doubt will identify Actors Y, Z and others, but there is no way to tell how much twenty years of possible revision or actors' interpolations may have been influenced the final printed copies of Shakespeare's plays, especially since *As You Like It* was not printed until its inclusion in the *First Folio*, seven years after Shakespeare's death. In view of the relatively minor characters ascribed to the Old Adam actor, coupled with the remarkable stability of Shakespeare's company, Actor X perhaps was a senior Hired-man who remained with the Chamberlain's/King's Men for years, but never achieved Shakespeare's Sharer status.

Unlike the post-Restoration traditions, there probably is a clearer identification of one of Shakespeare's roles, *in one of his own plays*, dating from nearly the beginning of his career. Robert Greene's famous *Groat's Worth of Wit*[40] creates a pun on Shakespeare's line in *3 Henry VI*, "O tyger's heart wrapt in a woman's hide" by rewriting it as "his Tyger's heart wrapt in a Player's hide." Greene's allusion, written shortly before his death in 1592, is one of the first we possess concerning Shakespeare in the theatre. His allusion to Shakespeare as "an upstart Crow, beautified with our feathers," also seems to echo lines from *2 Henry VI*, when Queen Margaret says of the Duke of Gloucester, "Seems he a dove? his feathers are but borrow'd/For he's disposed as the hateful raven." The *Henry VI* plays, as Thomas Nashe's allusion in *Pierce Penilesse* points out, had become extremely popular by 1592. Yet as an author, Shakespeare's reputation probably had not spread very far. Playwrights, in the early 1590s, were rarely identified with their plays; neither George Peele, nor Thomas Kyd, nor Christopher Marlowe, nor William Shakespeare are named as authors on the title pages of the earliest printings of *Arraignment of Paris*, *The Spanish Tragedy*, *Tamburlaine*, and *Titus Andronicus*. Nashe's reference to *1 Henry VI* is to audience reaction to a particular scene, Talbot's death; the allusion names neither the play nor the playwright. Nor were great numbers of plays published in the early 1590s. Henslowe's *Diary* tells us that over 90 percent of the repertory of the Admiral's Men did not survive in printed copy.[41] Nor had Shakespeare's narrative poems (*Venus and Adonis* and *The Rape of Lucrece*), which established his reputation with the gentlemen of the Inns of Court, yet been penned.

The "Tyger's heart" line in Greene's pamphlet, as scholars have pointed out time and time again, clearly alludes to *3 Henry 6*. But for some reason scholars have not paid much attention to the context of the line within the play. The line, "O tiger's heart wrapt in a woman's hide!" is delivered by Richard of York, a man who knows he is about to die. It is a curse, and description of, his greatest nemesis. When he wrote *Groat's Worth of Wit*, Robert Greene was dying, and, like York, Greene knew "himselfe be dying." Like York too, he took this last opportunity to strike out at someone he considered his greatest nemesis, "an upstart Crow, beautified with our feathers," a "*Johannes Fac Totum.*" Greene obviously denied Shakespeare a place among the "poets"; he was, in Greene's words, just another one of "those Apes, rude grooms, peasants," one of those parasitic "Puppits, (I meane) that speake from our mouths, those Anticks garnisht in our colours." Greene sneers that this "upstart Crow, beautified with our feathers...supposes he is as well able to bumbast out a blanke verse as the best" of the real poets. Why should we suppose Greene's reworking of lines from *2 Henry VI*, and pun on a line from *3 Henry VI* was meant to give any recognition to Shakespeare as an author? His allusions to those plays always center upon the character of Margaret. He may well have punned "Tyger's heart wrapt in a Player's hide" not to identify Shakespeare the poet, but to identify him among the many of "these painted monsters," as the "Shake-scene" *actor*, whose *public recognition* to date was derived from his portrayal of a "Kingly" (or at least royal) part, the "she-wolf of France," Queen Margaret.

Viewing Shakespeare as an up-and-coming actor writing for other up-and-coming actors may cast some light on one of his earlier plays, *The Taming of the Shrew*. Tantalizingly, in view of Shakespeare's sonnets numbers 37 and 89, with what some scholars think may be possible allusions to Shakespeare's lameness: "So I, made lame by Fortune's dearest spite/...So then I am not lame, poor, nor despis'd" (37), and "Speak of my lameness, and I straight will halt" (89), there is a joking reference in that play to reports of a character's lameness. Petruchio (II, 2) says: "Why does the world report that Kate doth limp?" And later in the same speech he reiterates: "Oh let me see thee walk. Thou dost not halt." Be that as it may, for years *The Taming of the Shrew* has been viewed by literary critics, performers, and directors as a so-called "problem play." Perhaps, however, many of those problems disappear if the play is viewed from perspectives relating to the probable circumstances surrounding the play's composition, and its first known performance, as we shall now do.

Chapter 4

Shakespeare's Dramatic Joke:
The Taming of the Shrew

Though successful adaptations of Shakespeare's *The Taming of the Shrew* were produced after the Restoration, it was not until 1844 that an attempt was made to perform the original script as published in the *First Folio*. All of the adaptations previous to this time had stressed the relationship of Petruchio and Katherine. Of all the seventeenth-, eighteenth-, and nineteenth-century adaptations, only John Lacey's *Sauny the Scott* (1698) included scenes from the Bianca sub-plot; nor did many adaptations include Christopher Sly.[1] Thus critics, directors, actors, and audiences had been conditioned firmly for 200 years to believe that the major purpose of the play was to tell the story of the peculiar love affair of Petruchio and Katherine as it unfolded through Petruchio's attempts to tame his shrewish wife.

When confronted with a staging of the original script in 1844, critics, reviewers, directors, actors and audiences now had to puzzle over seemingly extraneous or intrusive elements in the play, particularly the so-called Induction with its drunken clown Christopher Sly, the complex sub-plot of the wooing of Kate's sister Bianca, and the seeming brutality of Petruchio's actions towards Kate, coupled with her abject capitulation in the last scene. All of this stood in the way of a clear portrayal of Kate and Petruchio's story. A survey of literary and dramatic criticism, and performance techniques, reveals how critics, directors, actors, have grappled with these problems over the past 150 years.[2]

Christopher Sly's explosive appearance and subsequent disappearance after only two scenes and an interlude at the end of Act 1, scene 1, always has perplexed literary critics. Some maintain that subsequent Sly scenes, such as those found in the parallel script *The Taming of A Shrew*, believed by many to be a pirated version of Shakespeare's script, were somehow omitted in the *First Folio*. Others assert that Shakespeare intentionally wrote the character out of the play to avoid inordinate clowning, which would detract from the story of Kate and Petruchio. Margaret Webster thinks that Shakespeare just lost interest in the Sly plot.[3] All critics agree that as printed in the *First Folio*, the Sly episodes present difficulties for the story line unless properly explained and handled.

Directors and theater critics have adapted similar viewpoints as to the validity of the Sly scenes to the script as a whole. Productions by E.A. Sothern in 1906, and a Stratford, Ontario production of 1973 omitted the Sly material. Drama critics praised them because "the Induction has no bearing on the story of Petruchio and Kate," and its deletion allowed the Kate/Petruchio plot to "move at a pleasant pace." Reviews of other productions, however, have insisted that without some reminder that the Shrew-taming is but a play, the process becomes mere stage-brutality. Hence, many productions have emphasized the device of strolling players while omitting the Sly scenes. William Ball's American Conservatory Theater production in San Francisco (1973) utilized the venue of a troupe of *Commedia dell'Arte* performers. In the same year Jean Gascon at Stratford, Ontario, placed minor cast members on stage as actor-spectators making sound effects and comments. These productions, praised for excising Sly scenes, were criticized, nonetheless, for allowing the strolling players device to emphasize "mechanics of the performance" rather than the Kate/Petruchio story.[4]

Another strategy used to fill in the gap in Shakespeare's script caused by Sly's disappearance in Act I, is to graft on the interludes and epilogue from the 1594 anonymous *The Taming of A Shrew*. Directors who used this approach have found reviewers taking them to task for adhering too slavishly to the concept of play-within-a-play. Reviews complain that the Sly episodes "intrude on the action of the play proper," and that this approach suffers from the director's "insistence on Sly and the mechanics of the troupers' performance." Naturally, when the play is produced exactly as found in the *First Folio*, the disappearance of Sly at the end of Act I, scene 1 is described as awkward and incomplete.[5] Thus, the problem of Christopher Sly and the Induction present performances with a classic "Catch-22" situation—damned if included, damned if not included, damned if expanded upon, damned if limited to the *First Folio* script.

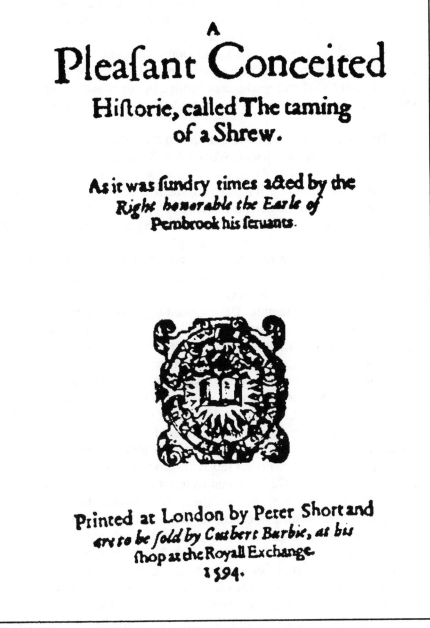

Fig. 14. Title page: *The Taming of a Shrew* (1594).

Similar controversy exists concerning the so-called sub-plot of Katherine's sister Bianca and her suitors. Though the suggestion of some scholars that Shakespeare did not script these scenes is no longer widely held, some scholars such as Mark Van Doren complain that in language and dramatic action the Bianca scenes are dull. Yet E.M.W. Tillyard heads another list of critics who are charmed by the Bianca sub-plot and who stress its integral part in the unfolding of the story of Kate and Petruchio.[6]

Theater reviewers too have questioned the value of the sub-plot of Bianca and her suitors. Richard Watts (*New York Post*, 26 April 1951), commenting on Margaret Webster's *Shrew* wrote: "This has always been one of the most obscure and mystifying subplots in the annals of classic comedy." A review of Clifford Williams' production at the Royal Shakespeare Theatre (1973) asked: "Is anything more tedious than the parallel subplot scenes of Bianca's wooing?"[7]

In answer to these objections directors and actors have applied a variety of approaches to the sub-plot and its characters. In the late nineteenth and early twentieth centuries, abridgements such as Augustin Daly's (1881) were common. Daly spliced together scenes 2 and 4 of Act IV—Hortensio's discovery of Bianca's preference for Cambio/Lucentio, and the agreement to Bianca's marriage reached by Baptista, Tranio and the Pedant—and then connected scenes 1, 3, 5 of Act IV to make the story-line of the "taming school" continuous with the scene depicting Kate and Petruchio *en route* to Padua. Daly also reduced the tutoring scene (III, 1) to only 75 percent of its original length. The famous Lunt-Fontaine production followed this rearrangement, and moved the scene when Tranio and Hortensio forswear Bianca into the wedding scene (III, 2). Fritz Lieber, in productions for the Chicago Shakespeare Society (1929-32), completely excised Act V, scene 1, the scene which completes the sub-plot. Yet, despite their seeming impatience with Bianca's scenes, theater critics have been quick to condemn such rearrangements and deletions. Such approaches, they lament, make the sub-plot even more confusing, and, what is worse, make the Kate/Petruchio plot proceed too quickly to be believable.[8] Apparently, then the sub-plot scenes are necessary to make up for Shakespeare's failure to provide sufficient scripting in the "main plot" to account for the transformation of Kate and Petruchio into a loving couple.

Since the Bianca scenes are considered so dull, and yet are so vital, and since Bianca's character is so necessary,[9] on-stage interpretations of Bianca have varied in order to answer one or more of these problems. She has been portrayed as a simple-minded, libidinous sex-kitten, or as a duplicitous sex-kitten who connives against her sister Kate, her father, and her suitors in the guise of feigned docility and sweetness. She has been portrayed as a ninny who shows preference for Lucentio at the start, or as a sweet Bo-Peep or as a "silly Lolita." But nothing satisfies the reviewers. Bianca as a conniver, we are told, detracts from the character change Kate is supposed to undergo, because it is evident that Kate's shrewishness is justified, and it is clear "who the real shrew will be." Bianca as a docile beauty is dull, only "a lovely white cow of a girl," and such a portrayal turns Kate into a vicious, unprovoked persecutor. Bianca as a single-minded "sex kitten," destroys the contrast between Kate's honesty and Bianca's deceptive role-playing.[10] The composite we have here then is that a portrayal of Bianca must display enough docility to emphasize Kate's shrewishness, enough duplicity to counterpoint Kate's honesty, enough simplicity to emphasize Kate's complexity, enough subtlety to emphasize Kate's directness. If such a contradictory characterization be possible, one wonders why, rather than Katherine, *Bianca* is not considered the leading female role.

But, as Margaret Webster writes, "Katherine and Petruchio are what we came to see."[11] Here at least, then, there should be little controversy among critics, or in performances. Yet disagreement exists about the natures of Kate and Petruchio. Some critics call Petruchio a tyrant, a bully, a fortune-hunter, a "woman-hater." Others view him as perceptive and humane, genuinely in love with his Katherine, and seeking only to tame her willfulness. Katherine has been depicted as an indomitable spirit of independence who will never give in to male domination, or as truly kind, and humorous underneath, and longing for a mate virile enough to match her spirit. Virtually all agree, however, that whatever the case, the characters fall in love, even those who have earlier characterized Kate as defiant of male pretensions to dominance, or Petruchio as a "woman-hater."[12]

Where in the script itself do we read their mutual declarations of love? In *Much Ado About Nothing* it is abundantly clear, textually, that Benedick and Beatrice, strong-willed counterparts to Kate and Petruchio, continually talk about one another. There is no such underpinning in line or plot for Kate and Petruchio, though that "oversight" is taken care of in the parallel *Taming of A Shrew*, and in all the post-Restoration adaptations of Shakespeare's script.[13]

No wonder, then, that critics take refuge for their opinions in "theatrical realization as opposed to mere reading." Clever staging and acting will show "what is legible between the lines of the play—that Katherine has fallen in love with Petruchio at first sight." A survey of production strategies proves that seemingly firm ground for criticism is quicksand. Attempts to present Kate as a formidable opponent worthy of taming, such as that of the Lunts' (1940), or the *Commedia dell'Arte* approach of William Ball (1973) invariably have brought forth criticisms of brutality, exaggerated slap-stick and lack of character development for Kate and Petruchio. Productions such as Jean Gascon's (1973), which attempt to show Petruchio as pretending the bully to tame Kate, are criticized for presenting weak-livered heroes. If Katherine is portrayed as clever enough to be aware of the game, her taming is criticized as a mockery. If she truly portrays repentance in her final speech, the reviewers complain of abject submission. If the two characters display love at first sight, reviewers believe the taming becomes mere formality; if they do not display an early attraction to one another, the taming of Katherine is characterized as a crass triumph of brute force.[14]

All of this stage business necessary to a fully developed Kate and Petruchio story—falling in love, character development, gradual appreciation of one another—depends upon the impression of a lapse of time, given by the "tedious" Bianca scenes, and upon the "reminders" that we are not witnessing reality, as the Sly scenes or *Commedia* approach emphasize. Yet these scenes are characterized invariably as "irrelevant," or "intrusive," or "tedious," because we really want to note "the stages by which both Petruchio and Katherine—both of them for in spite of everything the business is mutual—surrender to the fact of their affection."[15]

What coil is this? "Katherine and Petruchio are what we came to see,"[16] but neither performance techniques nor literary analyses seem to solve the stumbling blocks to a clear exposition of their story in Shakespeare's *The Taming of the Shrew*. Perhaps, then, Katherine and Petruchio are not what we ought to see. Perhaps another approach is needed—one which attempts to treat this script from a viewpoint other than a play, the goal of which is to tell the story of Petruchio's taming of Kate the Shrew.

The Taming of the Shrew has received a good deal of attention as an historical document for the study of gender problems and relationships in early modern Europe, but dramatic and literary critics have been relatively loathe to discuss this script within the context of comedic analysis of Shakespeare's plays, except to note the internal problems inherent in telling the Kate/Petruchio story. J. Dennis Huston notes the almost complete lack of reference to *Shrew* in many studies dealing with common characteristics of Shakespeare's comedies.[17] Northrup Frye, for example, makes use of virtually all of the Shakespearean comedies except *Troilus and Cressida* and *The Taming of The Shrew*.[18] Nor do critics often cite the characters of Kate and Petruchio as examples of Shakespeare's comedic heroes and heroines. Even if the problems of the Induction are ignored, it seems this script is out of joint with the other comedies.

Critics tell us that Shakespeare's comedic heroines overshadow their male counterparts. In Shakespearean comedy it is the women who solve love's crises—Rosalind rather than Orlando, Viola rather than Orsino. Compared to Shakespeare's comedic heroines "their male counterparts pale into insignificance."[19] Yet in Shakespeare's *Shrew*, from the first Kate is practically silent and impotent in the face of Petruchio. It is he who initiates and carries out the solution to their romantic problem. What *female* character is it in Shakespeare's *Shrew* who manipulates plot and characters alike to solve a lovers' problem? It is not Kate; it is *Bianca*.

Critics contend that Shakespeare's genius shines forth in his fully developed characterizations.[20] Yet look at the incomplete characters in *Shrew*. Christopher Sly is given definition, and then dumped before the end of the first act; Hortensio, who looks as if he will play a major role in the unfolding of the strolling players' play, fades out as a minor suitor; Gremio, given the early promise of a classic Pantaloon, all but disappears after Baptista's attempt to auction Bianca off to the richest suitor.

Critics tell us that Shakespeare was a master craftsman in blending all aspects of his play together. All the elements of *Comedy of Errors* (an earlier play), of *Love's Labor Lost*, of *Midsummer Night's Dream* (to name comedies not far removed in time from the composition of *Shrew*) are resolved. Yet in *Shrew* we see an introductory series of scenes with immense comedic potential given no resolution; we see Tranio aware of

Hortensio's intention to go to the "taming school" without any mention in the script of this intention, or of Petruchio's "taming school," prior to Tranio's announcement; we see Petruchio aware of Bianca's marriage to Lucentio before he arrives in Padua, indeed *before* he and the rest of the play's characters are apprised of the "true" Lucentio. All in all, if one were to describe this script without reference to title and author, I believe we would classify it as a poorly crafted work. It certainly falls far short of the standards attributed to Shakespeare's works composed both before and after *Shrew*.[21]

What then can account for the appearance of this "thorn" amid a bed of early-blooming "roses?" I contend that there is evidence, admittedly inferential and circumstantial (though is that not true of most Shakespearean criticism?), which suggests that the script of *The Taming of the Shrew* is not a vehicle to present a theme of wife-taming and male/female relationships, but is rather a well-crafted and subtle parody of bad scripting and bad acting. In other words *The Taming of the Shrew* may well be Shakespeare's equivalent of Mozart's *A Musical Joke*.

Critics have always noted Shakespeare's consistent, almost self-conscious, use of allusions to the theater even in the most serious of his works. Shakespeare could, and did, poke fun at his profession, his colleagues, and his contemporary playwrights. The mechanicals' scenes in *Midsummer Night's Dream* display his ability to satirize the theater. Snug the joiner, for instance, may well be an allusion to James Burbage, a carpenter and joiner before he entered the theatrical world. The plot-line of a group of tradesmen who band together to become "players" in order to better their position reflects the reality of the origins of many Shakespearean actors: Ben Jonson the bricklayer, Henslowe the dyer, Alleyn, son of an inn-keeper, Condell, son of a fishmonger, Shakespeare himself, son of a glover.[22] The characters of these mechanicals parody recognizable theater types: Quince, the "manager" unable to manage his company, Bottom, the egotistical lead-actor who believes he can play all parts, Flute, who says all his part "cues and all." The characters are comical—but doubly so to anyone who has participated in theatrical activity. And what a masterpiece of bad scripting is "Pyramus and Thisby": a prologue which drifts from point to point and gives the entire plot away, trite speeches given by almost every character which are full of malapropisms, bombast, and over-done alliteration, and a cast of actors who cannot stay in character.

Shakespeare here clearly shows he has the craft and sense of humor necessary to compose a good "bad" play.

There are other instances of "bad" plays in Shakespeare's work. "The Murder of Gonzago" within *Hamlet* is not meant to be an excellent piece of theater; the "Masque of the Russians" in *Love's Labour's Lost* is followed by an even worse play, "The Nine Worthies." Note that in all these cases the "bad" plays are plays-within-plays, poorly conceived, and poorly acted. Further, among the "professionals" in the theatre of the late sixteenth century, strolling players, like those who supposedly are presenting the story of Katherine and Petruchio, were considered inferior theatrical fare—"the people of the worst memories," to quote Dekker's *The Roaring Girl* (Act II, 2).

How does all this relate to *The Taming of the Shrew*? Considering the craftsmanship and brilliance with which the so-called "Induction" is written, and the subsequent device of introducing strolling players, it seems obvious that Shakespeare intended to make clear that *The Taming of the Shrew* was a play-within-a-play. The fact that in the *First Folio* these "Induction" scenes are labeled Act I, scenes 1, and 2, seems especially significant. Later editors created the distinction between Sly scenes and the play proper, not the editors of the *First Folio*, among whom were Shakespeare's former colleagues John Heminges and Henry Condell. Indeed, Heminges' association with Shakespeare, and probably Condell's too, dates back to the time of the first recorded performance of what probably was *The Shrew* by the Chamberlain's Men.[23] Putting aside the debate over whether there was originally a dramatic epilogue, it seems clear that the Sly scenes were considered to be an integral part of the play. Shakespeare's other works certainly make a clear distinction between prologue, epilogue and play proper.

For the nonce let us return to "Pyramus and Thisby." Beyond the obvious clowning, Shakespeare subtly spoofs careless and hurried playwriting. In the first mechanicals' scene Quince is to play Thisby's father, Starveling, Thisby's mother, Snout, Pyramus' father. In the rehearsal in the woods no mention of these characters is made. Instead, Quince now will be the Prologue, Starveling the Man-in-the-Moon, Snout the Wall—new characters created to account for developments in the story-line not considered in Quince's first draft. Nor are the speeches given by Bottom and Flute at the rehearsal in the woods recreated in the performance before Duke Theseus. Here we see shifts in situation, plot, character, and script—not so subtle gibes against sloppy play construction.

Consider certain parallels in *Shrew*. A series of introductory scenes concerning Sly and a lord shift to another scenario created by the arrival of the strolling players. In turn, once the strolling players begin to perform, we find a plot which seems to promise a series of characters and events all revolving around the wooing of a pretty young girl guarded by a protective father and a shrewish sister. But then these characters and situation give way to yet another: a braggart fortune-hunter and his oafish servant, and their adventures while cowing the shrewish elder sister. Shakespeare begins his play with the explosive quarrel between Sly and the Hostess, re-begins it with the elaborate trick engineered by the lord, re-begins again with a group of strolling players who perform a play which seems to promise the wooing of a beautiful younger sister, which in turn re-begins with the slapstick confrontation of Kate and Petruchio.[24]

Remember, in the first scene of *Shrew* proper, it is clearly Bianca who is the center of attention and promised comic machinations. It is not until Act III, 2 that the total number of lines devoted to the so-called main plot surpasses the total number of lines devoted to Bianca's wooing. In terms of scenes devoted exclusively to one or the other plots, Bianca has six to Kate's four. Even in total lines devoted to the development of the two plots, the Bianca plot is shorter only by approximately 166 lines. As the play progresses seemingly major characters such as Hortensio and Gremio wither, new characters such as the Pedant and the Widow suddenly are created, and characters suddenly know things before they happen.

Remember too, that nowhere in the script is the play done by the strolling players identified. Indeed, contradictory descriptions are given to Sly. At one point he is told he will watch "a pleasant comedy," and only eleven lines later he is told it "is a kind of history."[25] Within a few minutes after the strolling players began to perform, the *Elizabethan* audience probably would have assumed they were about to view a reworking of an older play, George Gascoigne's *Supposes*. Modern critics agree on that script as the source for the Bianca plot, indeed, certain scenes and lines are close enough to Gascoigne's play as to smack of plagiarism in the modern sense of the word, something which cannot be said of the 1594 parallel script *Taming of A Shrew*.

Many in Shakespeare's audience must have been aware of Gascoigne's script. Though it dated from 1573, Gascoigne's *Whole Woorkes* were printed in two separate editions in 1587. Most theatre goers also were used to contemporary playwrights "borrowing" from one another, and from older plays.[26] Imagine the impact on that audience when the plotline it had been led to believe would be that of *Supposes* was suddenly sidetracked by a "taming plot," and then later resumed as if nothing had interrupted. The literate among the spectators might also have noticed that the hero of this "taming plot" is named for a character who appears in *Supposes*. But in *Supposes* the character Petruchio is a servant to the equivalent of *Shrew's* Pedant, has no lines, and appears only in the list of characters and in the stage directions to one scene ("enter Scenese attended by Paquetto and Petruchio, his servants"). Shakespeare borrowed one other name from *Supposes*, Litio. In *Shrew* the name is assigned to Hortensio in his disguise as a music-master, but in *Supposes* Litio is a servant to that play's equivalent of Vincentio, Lucentio's father.[27] Since Shakespeare utilized none of the other character names from *Supposes*, does it not seem plausible that he was making a wry comment on confused re-workings of older plays: assigning the names of minor characters from *Supposes* to major characters in his supposed revision?

Finally, our playwright praised for his skillful resolution of all elements of a multifaceted play, fails to wrap-up the situation with which he began the play. The Sly scenes, called by Bullough "among the riches pieces of comedy ever written by Shakespeare," are left hanging. Even more curious, *Shrew* is the only occasion in which Shakespeare scripted an induction or frame. The device was common to comedies written by his contemporaries in the 1580s and early 1590s, and oft as not served to comment on the action of the play proper. Usually there was a dramatic epilogue at the end to complete the play.[28] Yet Shakespeare, who seems to have adopted this convention just this once, leaves it unfinished. Some scholars hold that other scenes depicting Sly were lost or missing from the so-called "foul papers" used to prepare the *First Folio* version. Perhaps instead, Shakespeare purposefully dropped Sly mid-way into the first act, and not because he was "bored," or found that Sly "intruded," or because he wished to get rid of a mugging clown. To the contrary he scripted *four* clowns, Sly, Tranio, Biondello, Grumio (five, if Petruchio is viewed as a typical braggart-soldier type). Perhaps he dropped Sly because he saw such an omission as the perfect way to craft a supposedly sloppy ending to a supposedly sloppy play.

The Taming of the Shrew abounds with speeches designed to be played "stalking and roaring," as well as scenes which carry on exaggerated clowning. Both were targets of scorn in many of Shakespeare's other plays. Hamlet's advice to the Players is generally taken as a gibe against bombastic acting. Falstaff's parody of *King Cambyses* and Pistol's mouthings (*1 Henry IV*, 2, 4 and *2 Henry IV*, 5) are passages believed to be satires of rival companies. The lines in the latter passages are taken from plays in rival repertories. There are similar snide remarks concerning overblown acting in *Troilus and Cressida*, and *Richard III*, the latter probably close to *Shrew* in time of composition. Yet there is plenty of "tear-throat" material in *Shrew*. Petruchio's speeches are almost always harangues, full of bombast, verbose, rich in sound, poor in content.[29] Is there much more to his "Have I not heard lions roar" speech than "sound and fury?" And do not his rages at the wedding guests, at his servants, at the haberdasher at the tailor, offer splendid opportunities for "stalking and roaring" like a Herod from an old-fashioned cycle play?

Who was famous for "stalking and roaring"? It was Edmund Alleyn,[30] premier actor of the Admiral's Men, Shakespeare's company's chief rivals. Playwrights for that company were noted for hasty and loosely written scripts. Henslowe, the Admiral's guiding force, employed about half-a-dozen writers to insure a large turn-over in the repertory. Henslowe's records show that a new play was added about every two weeks. Up to speed, Dekker and Heywood, among other of Henslowe's dramatists, produced one play each per month. By contrast, Shakespeare produced two or three plays per year. It is no wonder then that many of the Admiral's Men's plays are full of confusions of names and places, curiously repeated actions, sudden and easy satisfaction of problems at the resolution of the play. There is only one script in the Shakespeare canon in which critics puzzle over these same short-comings, *The Taming of the Shrew*,[31] which looks surprisingly like a bad play from the Admiral's repertory.

The probable circumstances of *Shrew's* first performance by the Chamberlain's Men may well explain why it can be viewed as reflecting the style and composition of an Edmund Alleyn play. The first recorded instance of its probable performance was in June 1594, at Newington Butts, when the newly formed Chamberlain's Men (many of whose members had come over from Alleyn's company and were thus familiar with its style of performance and repertory), was sharing the theater with the already well-established Admiral's Men, probably performing on alternate days. What better way for an up-and-coming playwright to display his prowess than by doing a reworking of an older "wife-taming" play, folded into a reworking of Gascoigne's *Supposes*, all of which served as a parody of what the audience had seen a day or two before—Marlowe's *The Jew of Malta*, or the lost *Hester and Ashwerus* with Alleyn "stalking and roaring," followed by *Shrew* with Burbage doing the same actions in a comic context. Shakespeare later used this type of parallelism in *1 Henry IV* to set up certain Falstaff scenes and lines as a parodies to more serious ones which preceded them.

Such a view may also serve to reconcile some of the recent controversy surrounding the date of the play and its relationship to the parallel *Taming of A Shrew*. Much of that controversy revolves around whether *A Shrew* is a pirated version of Shakespeare's script, and around the probable use of phrases in the *First Folio* from the anonymous *A Knack to Know a Knave* (*ca.* 1592), and from some version of John Fletcher's *Women Pleas'd* (*ca.* 1603-05). The allusion to *Women Pleas'd* seems to substantiate a date of *ca.* 1604 for the *First Folio* version of *Shrew*, and suggests that it was *A Shrew* which was performed at Newington Butts in 1594. Yet the allusions to *Knack to Know a Knave*, in both *A Shrew* and *The Shrew*, seem to point to the earlier date for the composition of Shakespeare's script. Both views may be correct. Perhaps it is time to return to the older scholarly opinion that Shakespeare either reworked *A Shrew*, or rewrote a lost, older version of a "wife-taming" play, which may have been the basis for both scripts. That view may provide some of the answers to the controversy over the dating of the play, and help to explain the publication of *A Shrew* before the Newington Butts performance. The allusions to *Knack to Know* may represent Shakespeare's earlier 1594 version, written for the Newington Butts performances, especially when those allusions are coupled to Shakespeare's slavish use of the rather recently printed version of Gascoigne's *Supposes*, a play long out of print by the first years of the seventeenth century. The allusions to *Women Pleas'd*, on the other hand, may represent a later attempt to revise the script and place it back into active use in his company's repertory. After all, from 1599 to 1605 or so Shakespeare, and his contemporary playwrights, were adding new plays to company repertories at a rapid pace, and revising old plays. Revisions of *Spanish Tragedy* and *Doctor Faustus* were commissioned for the Admiral's Men. Shakespeare himself seems to have revised an earlier version of his own *Merry Wives of Windsor*, and reworked a lost *Hamlet* and the old Queen's Men comedy of *King Leir*.[32] Shakespeare was capable of revising and reworking plays in the later stages of his career; he certainly must have been not only capable of the same, but even more prone to do so in 1594, when beginning his association with the Chamberlain's Men, who, after all, needed to build both a repertory and a reputation.

Other plays in the repertory of the Admiral's Men's from the early 1590s are echoed in *The Taming of the Shrew*. Most critics have noted the obvious ridicule of notorious bombastic passages from Kyd's *Spanish Tragedy* in *Shrew*, but the style and language of the wooing scene in *Shrew* also seems comically reminiscent of that play's tragic love scene between Horatio and Bel-Imperia, just before Horatio is murdered.[33] At very least, it is a more than obvious parody of the conventional Elizabethan love scene in which the male pursues and the female demurs. It is only matched in its ironic twisting of that dramatic convention by Shakespeare himself, in his macabre scene in which Richard III woos Anne around the coffin of the father-in-law he has killed, and which dates from a similar phase in his writing career. Furthermore, do not Petruchio's lines

> Have I not heard great ordinance in the field,
> And heaven's artillery thunder in the skies?
> Have I not in a pitched battle heard
> Loud 'larums, neighing steeds, and trumpets clang?[34]

ring subtly similar to sections of a speech from Alleyn's most famous role as Marlowe's *Tamburlaine the Great*?

> Hast thou beheld a peal of ordnance strike
> A ring of pikes, mingled with shot and horse?
> Hast thou not seen my horsemen charge the foe,
> Shot through the arms, cut overthwart the hands?[35]

Fig. 15. Edward Alleyn as Tamburiaine.

Even Petruchio's behavior at his wedding, described as the ravings of a mad-clad madman seems to suggest borrowings from other plays. Feigned madness was first popularized by Kyd's Heironimo in *Spanish Tragedy*, and carried on, and copied, in Robert Greene's popular *Orlando Furioso*.[36] Both plays were staples in the permanent repertory of the Admiral's Men. It looks suspiciously like Shakespeare was resetting revenge-tragedy stage conventions from popular Admiral's Men's plays in comic form.

We know Shakespeare was often subtle in his gibes at fellow playwrights and actors. Ben Jonson, so the *Parnassus Plays* tell us, was "purged" by Shakespeare—but it is only by analyzing Jonson's reputation in the contemporary context of the late 1590s that T.P. Morris has identified Shakespeare's "purge" as the character Abraham Slender in *The Merry Wives of Windsor*.[37] We also know that about the same time as the earlier version of *Shrew* may have been written, Shakespeare successfully had played a sort of "can you top this" game in two earlier plays: outdoing Plautus' *Menaechmi* by adding another set of identical twins in *Comedy of Errors*, and outdoing the blood and gore of Kyd's *Spanish Tragedy* with his own *Titus Andronicus*. (For instance, Kyd's Bel-Imperia is sworn to a vow of silence, but Shakespeare's Lavinia has her tongue torn out and her hands cut off, and the serving up Tamora's sons' heads to their mother in meat pies surpasses anything in Kyd's or Marlowe's repertory of the macabre.) If we give Greene's famous diatribe in *Groat's Worth of Wit* some due, Shakespeare appears to have been rather cocky about his accomplishments.[38] Just as a young Mozart could wryly poke fun at the cobbled together, poorly performed efforts of his critics and rivals, so too a young Shakespeare could satirize rival playwrights and companies through a play which seemed an innocuous comedy on the surface, but just happened to expose all the flaws to be found in his rivals' repertories and performances.

The most obvious example we have of this kind of play-long, theatrical satire comes later with Beaumont's and Fletcher's *The Knight of the Burning Pestle*, but writers of plays connected with the so-called "War of the Theatres" also took pot-shots at each other, and each other's companies. From 1599 to 1602, plays such as Marston's *Histriomastix*, Jonson's *Poetaster*, Dekker's *Satiro-mastix*, abound with references to shoddy play construction, implausible plot-lines, and overblown acting. *Satiro-mastix* actually reworked characters and scenes from Jonson's own *Poetaster* to lampoon Jonson and his pretensions.[39]

Most of these plays had short lives on stage. *The Knight of the Burning Pestle* was not successful with audiences; the satire was too subtle, too "in-house." Similarly, it does not appear that *Shrew* held a prominent role in Shakespeare's repertory. Except for the possibly pirated version, or version Shakespeare himself pirated, the parallel script *Taming of A Shrew*, published shortly before the Newington Butts performance in 1594, the first published version of Shakespeare's *Shrew* is that of the *First Folio*. Popular plays often found their way into publication, either in pirated or semi-authorized versions. *The Spanish Tragedy*, for example, went through many editions between 1587 and 1602, and numerous versions of Shakespeare's own plays found their way into print. Nor is there evidence to suggest that *The Shrew* was performed often by the Chamberlain's Men. It is not mentioned in Meres' list of titles ascribed to Shakespeare as of 1598. There are no clear allusions to the play, or its characters, in contemporary Elizabethan documents, and possible allusions to a post-1604 staging are problematic. After 1594, the first sure reference to a production of Shakespeare's *Shrew* is one listed as performed before Charles I in 1633, 17 years after Shakespeare's death. It seems likely that the play was not popular as were most of his other comedies. What we may have in the *First Folio* is a revision of *The Shrew* that Shakespeare never finished, as he never seems to have finished *Timon of Athens*. Like *Timon of Athens*, and *Troilus and Cressida*, it may have never been performed on the London public stage, or at very least failed there.[40] Outside the context of immediate comparison to the Admiral's Men provided at Newington Butts, the play-long joke of *Shrew* would be confusing, too subtle, too professionally-oriented.

Why then is the "joke" obscured? In 1861 Hector Berlioz turned *Much Ado About Nothing* into the opera *Beatrice et Benedict*. In so doing, he down-played what is, strictly speaking, the main plot of Shakespeare's comedy in favor of the lively and comic relationship between Beatrice and Benedict. Just as actors, audiences, and readers follow Berlioz's lead as regards *Much Ado*—remembering the colorful Benedick and Beatrice, not Hero and Claudio—so too we remember the rowdiness of Kate and Petruchio, chafe at Christopher Sly's intrusion, and groan at sitting "through Bianca for the sake of Kate and Petruchio." So too, when Shakespeare's *Shrew* was revived following the

Restoration, it was in adaptations which stressed the story of Kate and Petruchio. It was probably David Garrick's 1754 adaptation, *Catherine and Petruchio*, which fixed the notion that Kate and Petruchio were the focus of *The Taming of the Shrew*. Garrick's adaptation was played in Britain and America for the next hundred years. Even after the revival of Shakespeare's original script in 1844 (200 years after its last recorded performance), Garrick's adaptation continued its popularity until well into the nineteenth century.[41] By then the idea that the play was the love story of Kate and Petruchio was etched in granite. And happily ever after, critics, reviewers and performers have sought to alleviate the apparent weaknesses of Shakespeare's script.

Interestingly, the anonymous *Taming of A Shrew* is a better script, technically speaking. *A Shrew* subordinates the sub-plot of wooing the younger sister; it adds a third sister for the Hortensio character; it continues the Sly episodes with interludes in which he comments on the action, and scripts a dramatic epilogue which tidies up the ending, making Sly think he has dreamed it all; it scripts asides which profess mutual attraction between Kate and Petruchio at their first meeting. In terms of dramatic cohesion, it is a "tighter" play. It does all those things critics, actors, and directors believe need to be done in order to tie the script together, and still bring out the story of Kate and Petruchio. Yet with all its garbling up of plot line, characters, and scenes, Shakespeare's version of the "wife-taming" story is still a script which gives a better play in performance.

Here, perhaps, is Shakespeare's greatest joke; his "dramatic joke" was so subtle and so well-crafted that its popularity grew the further away it got from the circumstances of its composition. Perhaps the "joke" was misunderstood even then. Irving Ribner believes that *The Taming of A Shrew* is a pirated version of *The Shrew*, composed "by a hack dramatist attempting to capture the salient features and at the same time improve on it."[42] Perhaps it is; or perhaps, in view of its publication date earlier than Henslowe's record of the Newington Butts performance, it is a play Shakespeare intentionally garbled to bring attention to the talents of his new company, and to himself as a playwright. Yet in garbling it, or a common source play, Shakespeare created for himself and his fellow actors (and for actors even since) not a unified play, but certainly a series of brilliantly crafted, comedic scenes designed to give full reign to their comedic talents.

So we wrack our brains to make this series of scenes fit our insistence that, somehow, because of our infatuation with the Shrew and her Tamer, it must all fit together. But just imagine the impact on Shakespeare's audience at Newington Butts, when there was no tradition of Garrick-like adaptations, when the repertories of rival companies were fresh in its mind, and when the most recognizable plotline was that Gascoigne's *Supposes*, clearly reflected in the story line of the wooing of Bianca. Would that audience not have wondered at the intrusion of the slap-stick Kate and Petruchio upon the subtler story-line of Lucentio and Bianca? Would that audience not have recognized the parodies of dramatic conventions and plots, just an American movie audience today can recognize those same parodies in Woody Allen's *Play It Again Sam*, or Mel Brooke's *Young Frankenstein*, or Neil Simon's *The Cheap Detective*? And what would critics, and directors be writing, or playing, today if Shakespeare had named his parody *The Wooing of Bianca* instead of *The Taming of the Shrew*?

If *The Taming of A Shrew* be a pirated version of Shakespeare's script, it was just one of many which were printed in cheap, pirated, so-called "Bad" Quartos, as his plays became more popular with London playgoers. Almost half of Shakespeare's plays appeared in unauthorized editions. Some printers even put his name on works he did not write, hoping to cash in on his reputation and popularity. Around the turn of the seventeenth century, however, pirated editions of Shakespeare's own plays stopped. It appears that the Chamberlain's Men found a "leak" within their own ranks, and took steps to plug it.

Chapter 5

The "Mole" in Shakespeare's Company: "Industrial Espionage" in Elizabethan Theatre

The *First Folio* was the first "official" edition of all of Shakespeare's plays, carefully compiled, and lavishly published under the direction of his former partners John Heminges and Henry Condell. Between the year 1594 and the appearance of the *First Folio* in 1623, approximately 20 other versions of some of his most popular plays were printed in Quarto form. At least one-half of these earlier Quarto editions are so-called "Bad" Quartos, versions of plays which differ so radically from the *First Folio* that they may have been pirated and printed without the authorization of the playwright or, more importantly, the Chamberlain's Men, the acting company which owned them, and to which Shakespeare belonged. Playbooks were the most valuable asset of an acting company. They were the basis for the individual repertories which set each company apart from the others. An Elizabethan acting company's plays would be, in modern terms, like a modern rock-group's special musical arrangements. In view of the fierce competition among the rival companies to lure audiences to their theaters,[1] these "Bad" Quartos represent a "leak" of supposedly closely guarded company secrets as serious as a modern corporate executive leaking news of an impending merger, or a member of a rock group giving a rival recording company pirated tapes of the group's latest recording session.

Textual evidence based on various scholars' careful and laborious comparisons of "Bad" to "Good" Quartos and to the *First Folio*, suggests that a prime source of these "leaks" was someone within the Chamberlain's Men itself who was quite familiar with the scripts. In other words, there was what the world of espionage calls a "mole" within the acting company. About 1600 it appears that the "mole" was uncovered; few unauthorized versions of Shakespeare's plays appear after that date. Who was this mole? A multitude of clues point to none

121

other than Will Kempe, the company's most popular comedian, and one of its original founders. Kempe seems best to fulfill three prime categories used by prosecutors for bringing charges—opportunity, method, motive.

Although the dates when Shakespeare wrote his plays are not entirely certain,[2] nonetheless a chronology of the "Good" and "Bad" Quartos based on printers' dates can be established. That chronology,[3] when coupled with the selection of plays pirated, bears much on the identification of Will Kempe as the source of the leaks.

So-called "Good" Quartos of *Richard III, Romeo and Juliet,* and *Love's Labour Lost* were printed in 1598-99. "Good" Quartos of *1* and *2 Henry IV, Much Ado About Nothing, A Midsummer Night's Dream,* and *The Merchant of Venice* appeared shortly after the pirated editions of 1600. A "Good" Quarto of *Hamlet* was printed in 1604. The "Good" Quartos are versions probably authorized by the acting company. Most "Bad" Quartos are believed to be memorial reconstructions—that is, versions cobbled together from the recollections of actors familiar with lines from other plays, and with many of the scenes and lines in the Shakespearean script which was pirated.

Interesting coincidences emerge when Will Kempe's acting career is compared to these "Bad" Quartos. Since Shakespeare's company was a repertory company in which members took a role in almost every play,

Table 14
Chronology, "Bad" Quartos and Corresponding Theatre Events

Date	"Bad" Quarto	Shakespeare's Play	Theatre Events
1594	*Lancaster and York*	*2 Henry VI*	Theatres closed—plague
1594	*Taming of a Shrew* (?)	*The Taming of the Shrew*	Theatres closed—plague
1595	*Richard of York*	*3 Henry VI*	Theatres reopen—Mar.
1597	*Richard III*	*Richard III*	Theatres closed, July—censor
1597	*Romeo & Juliet*	*Romeo & Juliet*	Theatres closed—censor
1597	*Love's Labour Lost*	*Love's Labour Lost*	Theatres reopen—Oct.
1600	*Sir John Oldcastle*	*1 & 2 Henry IV*	Kempe leaves the company
1600	*Victories of Henry V*	*Henry V*	Kempe trying to raise money
1602	*Merry Wives*	*Merry Wives*	Kempe starting new firm
1603	*Hamlet*	*Hamlet*	Kempe dead

scholars have attempted to pinpoint roles probably assigned to certain senior members of the company. References in certain Elizabethan writings establish some of those roles. Richard Burbage, for example, probably played Richard III, Hamlet, King Lear, and Othello. References within printed versions of the plays sometimes give the actor's name instead of the character's. Using those methods, consensus assigns the following roles to Kempe.[4]

Table 15
Chronology of "Kempean" Roles

Date	Kempe's Probable Role	Shakespeare's Play
1594	Christopher Sly	*The Taming of the Shrew*
1597	Peter	*Romeo & Juliet*
1597	Falstaff	*1 Henry IV*
1597	Falstaff	*The Merry Wives of Windsor*
1597	Bottom	*A Midsummer Night's Dream*
1597	Launcelot Gobbo	*The Merchant of Venice*
1598	Falstaff	*2 Henry IV*
1598	Costard	*Love's Labour Lost*
1599	Dogberry	*Much Ado About Nothing*
Revised 1599	Falstaff	*The Merry Wives of Windsor*
1599	First Gravedigger	*Hamlet*
1599	Polonius (?)	*Hamlet*

Note the coincidences between plays in which Kempe played key supporting roles and pirate editions of these same plays. Of the 11 plays listed above, 7 were pirated. In those plays Kempe played Peter, and probably played Sly, Falstaff, Costard, Polonius, and First Gravedigger, roles which witness much of the action of the plays. Although not pirated, it seems that authorized versions of *Much Ado*, *Merchant*, and *Midsummer*, were rushed into print—all in the same year, 1600—to preempt their being pirated. In those plays Kempe is known to have played played Gobbo and Dogberry, and probably Bottom, also roles which stretched across the action of the plays.

An ordinance of 1583 gave the Stationers' Company the right to punish printers who brought out works already registered with the Company. Since there was no copyright protection as we know it, except for a Royal command, the only way to prevent a written work from unauthorized printings was to have one's own printer be the first formally to present, and register, a printed work with the Stationers' Company, or, as was done at least once by Philip Henslowe, pay the printer *not* to publish the play. *Merchant of Venice* was registered with the Stationers' as not to be printed "without lycence first had from the Right honorable the lord chamberlene." In those ways other printings could be blocked.[5] Authorized versions of *Romeo and Juliet*, and *Love's Labour's Lost* (1598-99), *Richard III* (1599), *1* and *2 Henry IV* (1600) and *Hamlet* (1604) probably were released to counteract the pirate editions published, respectively, less than a year before each of the "Good" Quartos of those plays. Most of these "Good" Quarto editions specify Shakespeare's authorship, or that they are "newly augmented," or "corrected." In sum, there is a total of 11 plays—7 of them printed in pirate editions, and 3 plays hastily printed in authorized editions, in every one of which Will Kempe played important comedic character parts.

Such a striking coincidence between assigned role and pirated play cannot be made for the pirate editions of *2* and *3 Henry VI* and *Richard III*, yet certain circumstances link these "Bad" Quartos to that of *Romeo and Juliet*, and point to Kempe's probable connection with these pirated editions. A.S. Cairncross has pointed out that analysis of passages and scenes within these pirated versions reveals that they were pieced together by a pirate or pirates familiar with the following repertory: not only *2* and *3 Henry VI* and *Romeo and Juliet*, but also Shakespeare's *Titus Andronicus*, Kyd's *Spanish Tragedy*, and Marlowe's *Edward II*. Snatches from all of these plays appear in garbled form within the pirate editions (*Contention*, *True Tragedy*, and *Richard III*). Cairncross further asserts that these snatches, used to fill in for lines where it was obvious the pirates' memories of the actual text of Shakespeare's plays were dim, appear to be drawn from the memory of actors who had actually given those lines in the other plays, not in other words, a cut-and-paste job from printed texts. Cairncross concludes that these pirate reconstructions resulted from collusion among members of the troubled, then defunct, then briefly revived, Pembroke's Men, and that at least one so called "reporter" was familiar with the entire repertory listed above, and was a contributor to all four piracies.

Glimmerings of information suggest that Shakespeare may have begun his theatrical career connected in some way to Lord Strange's Men and slightly later to Lord Pembroke's Men, since *1, 2,* and *3*

Henry VI and *Richard III* are listed by printers as having been performed by that company. In 1592-93, shortly before it disintegrated, Pembroke's Men was part of a trio of amalgamated companies which included Lord Strange's Men and the Admiral's Men. Elizabethan superstar Edward Alleyn, of the Admiral's Men (the Paul Newman of his day) seems to be the bridge between Strange's and the Admiral's companies. Will Kempe was a member of Strange's Men, and thus, through its association with Alleyn, would have been acquainted with the Admiral's Men's repertory, which included Marlowe and Kyd. Shakespeare, whose plays mentioned above were originally in Pembroke's repertory, joined with seven or so other actors including Bryan, Heminges, Burbage, and *Will Kempe* to found the new company known as the Chamberlain's Men.[6] Here are circumstances which link Kempe to the repertories of the Admiral's Men and the early Shakespeare histories, and to those actors of the revived Pembroke's Men who had not affiliated themselves with Alleyn's or Shakespeare's companies. Cairncross[7] points out that the reemergence of the revived Pembroke's Men ensconced in London at the new Swan Theater by 1597, clearly coincides with the printing of pirate editions of *Richard III* and *Romeo and Juliet* in that same year, just as the earlier pirated versions of *2* and *3 Henry VI* clearly coincide with the period in which Strange's and Pembroke's Men dissolved.

Moving in and out of this confusing alignment and realignment of players was Will Kempe. In 1588, he was in search of a company when Leicester's Men broke up. He was soon associated with Strange's Men, which then amalgamated for a couple of years with the Admiral's and Pembroke's Men, and finally he joined with Shakespeare, Burbage and the others to form the Chamberlain's Men.[8] When these circumstances are linked to those surrounding the pirating of plays in which he played major roles for the Chamberlain's Men, a chain of circumstantial evidence links Will Kempe to every single pirated version of a Shakespeare play.

Kempe's opportunity, then, to leak pirated editions of the Chamberlain's Men's repertory seems clear. What of his method? In the cases of *Shrew*, the two *Henry IV* plays, *Merry Wives*, and *Love's Labour*, he probably played characters which carry throughout most of the action of the plays, or at least which make those characters witness to most of the action. Since most of Shakespeare's plays were written to give seven or eight of the senior partners in the acting company prominent exposure on stage, and since doubling-up on roles was quite commonplace,[9] even a smaller role would not have precluded Kempe from witnessing most of the action of plays in the repertory of the Chamberlain's Men.

The *Taming of A Shrew* is generally believed to be a pirated, or perhaps earlier, version of Shakespeare's *The Taming of the Shrew*. *A Shrew* considerably beefs up the role of Christopher Sly, Kempe's role. In a sense that may be how the play was scripted originally, or at least those extras for Sly in *A Shrew* may have been Kempe's *extemporare* additions to a bare-bones script. The *First Folio* version of *the Shrew* gives indications of a cobbled together version; some scholars believe that sections were lost before the play was edited for the *Folio's* publication. It may have been the first play Shakespeare wrote, or more to the point *rewrote*, for his new partners, and wrote as a parody of the Admiral's Men with whom the brand new company was sharing a theater in June 1594. All of that may account for the confusing elements of the subplot, characters coming out of nowhere, and other loose ends found in the *Folio* version of *Shrew*. Those defects are "tidied-up" in the parallel *A Shrew*; they are so clearly addressed that Irving Ribner maintains *A Shrew* looks as if a hack-writer tried to "improve" on the original.[10] Scholars of the piracies have also pointed out that *A Shrew* (1594), if it be a pirated play, and the pirated versions of *Henry V* (1600) are likely the work of the same pirates[11] despite a six-year gap between the two.

Henry Gray's article, "The Roles of William Kempe," argues that the pirated version of *Merry Wives* was pieced together through collusion of two actors, one who had played Falstaff (Kempe), and the other who had played the Host of the Garter, whom Gray identifies as young Ben Jonson, who was working for the Chamberlain's men in 1598-99 before he ended up working for the new Boys' Company at Blackfriars.[12] The method of reconstructing *2* and *3 Henry VI*, *Richard III*, and *Romeo and Juliet*, both from memory and from bits and pieces of *Titus*, *Spanish Tragedy* and *Edward II*, already has been sketched above. Though the pirated editions of *1* and *2 Henry IV*, *Henry V* and *Hamlet* do date after Kempe had left the Chamberlain's Men, the *Henry IV* plays and *Hamlet* had been on stage before the middle to end of 1599. Many scholars believe Kempe played Falstaff, the premier comedic role of the plays for the company's premier clown. Some believe he also played Polonius and the First Gravedigger in

Hamlet. Though it was not the focus of his article, J.M. Nosworthy's article attempting to identify the pirate of *Hamlet*, frequently notes that those sections of the "Bad" Quarto often most accurate are those in which appear Polonius and the Gravedigger, and that "our pirate seems, in general, to have remembered the comic speeches far more accurately than the rest." *Henry V* probably was being composed before 1599 as well only to have Falstaff removed from the script despite the promise in *2 Henry IV* that he would return because Kempe had left the acting troupe. Scholars' arguments that the 1600 edition of *Henry V* is a "Bad Quarto"[13] make sense when set against a notion that accurate reconstruction of a play in which Kempe had not yet acted, and which was unfinished when he left the Chamberlain's Men, would be impossible.

So much for method; what then of motive? Most obvious of all motives is financial gain, and here, as with the circumstances of opportunity and method, there are striking coincidences of events. Kempe once remarked that acting brought good revenue to the most popular players.[14] He himself certainly fit that category. But from 1588-95 Kempe was shifting from the defunct Leicester's Men, to the short-lived amalgamated Strange's Men, to the yet unproved Chamberlain's Men, and for much of the time between 1592-94 London theaters were closed because of plague in the city. Normal revenue from acting must have been scant. Pembroke's Men, for example, sold itself into extinction in order to raise money, disposing first of its properties and costumes, and then of its most important asset, its repertory of playbooks.[15] Despite bad times for acting, however, the demand for printed copies of popular plays was making itself felt. Quick money to tide oneself over the dry period could be made by selling a play to a printer for a fast £6 or £7 (about one-third to one-half the yearly wage of an average Elizabethan artisan). That probably accounts for the printing of 20 plays in 1594.[16] In that period (between 1594 and 1595) three pirated editions of Shakespeare's plays appeared, but only three; there would be no others for three years. From mid 1595, The Chamberlain's Men, Kempe's new company, and one in which he was a senior partner, was firmly established in its own theater in London, and was growing rapidly in popularity.

In 1597, however, acting revenues were threatened. Famine prices probably reduced attendance. A third acting company, the new

Pembroke's Men was performing at Langley's Swan Theatre. That would have reduced daily receipts further, and Pembroke's Men probably were desperate for plays. Finally, in July of 1597, all theatre revenues in London came to an abrupt halt. The theaters in London were closed by the Privy Council, perhaps in retaliation for an apparent satire of the Court and of some high-placed lord of the Privy Council contained in *The Isle of Dogs*, a play by Thomas Nashe and Ben Jonson then appearing at the Swan Theater. The Privy Council ordered playing banned within a three-mile radius of London, and even called for the demolition of all playhouses, including The Theatre and the Curtain, the playhouses used by the Chamberlain's Men. Jonson, along with two of the principal actors in the play, were jailed. The Chamberlain's Men, one must notice, hastily left London on tour as soon as the Privy Council orders were published. Queen Elizabeth's wrath, when aroused, was known to be ferocious; for instance, she wished to have an obviously insane man, who attempted an attack on Sir John Hawkins, tried and executed according to martial law because civil courts might excuse him of the crime.[17] The theaters were allowed to reopen only three months later, in October,[18] but who in July and August would have known that would happen? In 1597, there appeared three new pirated editions of Shakespeare's plays, but only three; there would be no others for three more years.

Kempe abruptly left the Chamberlain's men in mid to late 1599, apparently under stormy circumstances. His name does not appear in connection with any other acting company at that time, yet without his position with the Chamberlain's Men he must have needed to seek income somewhere. London was full of free-lance clowns, dancers, acrobats, ballad singers, and the like; so Kempe must have seen the need to do something spectacular in order to earn money. Early in 1600, he made his famous Morris dance from London to Norwich and wrote his account of that adventure, *Nine Days' Wonder*.

The Morris dance demonstrates he was attempting to appeal to the popular audience rather than seeking an aristocratic patron. Morris dances appealed to the Commons, not the aristocracy. Soon after his dance, he rather hurriedly left the country for the Continent hoping to make a lucrative tour in France and Italy. His hopes on that score were unfulfilled. Accounts of his meeting in Italy with Sir Thomas Shirley's reveal he found Kempe in dire financial straits in Italy. The entertainment scene in Europe had changed since his last stint as a Court entertainer in Denmark and Germany almost 15 years before. By 1600 the *Commedia dell'Arte* troupes were immensely popular in Italy, Germany, and France and were touring the various princely Courts. There would be no room for a Will Kempe in one of those close-knit, family-oriented, highly specialized and disciplined companies; and there would be little opportunity to perform profitably elsewhere. His opportunities would have been limited to stunts like his Morris Dance to Norwich. He does seem to have offered to Morris dance over the Alps, but received no financial backing for the idea.

Kempe returned to England in 1602 having failed in his hopes for financial success on the Continent. He joined with some other actors probably including actor-playwright Thomas Heywood, who shortly afterwards is listed as a Sharer, to form a new acting company, Worcester's Men. Typically, Kempe needed money. Loans from Philip Henslowe to Kempe for "start-up" costs to begin playing, and for personal use to buy clothing for himself and his "boy," mark our last record of the man. Presumably he died later in that same year. Burial records in 1602 note the interment of "Kempe, a man."[19] Coincidentally, in 1600, shortly after he left the Chamberlain's Men, there were two new pirated versions of Shakespeare's plays. In 1602, after Kempe's return from the Continent, another new pirated edition appeared, and early in 1603, less than a year after notice of his burial, yet another. There would be no more ever, save for, much later, some editions of *Pericles*.

There emerges, then, a pattern to the piracies of Shakespeare's plays. They do not appear in a steady trickle stretching over many years; they appear in spurts concentrated in the short space of one year. In each case that one year period corresponds to times in which Kempe's income as an actor would have been reduced drastically, or cut off completely. It would seem too, that Kempe's grip on money was not firm. His partners in the Chamberlain's Men were already men of means by 1599. Kempe may have received the usual "buy-out" sum of £70 to £90 (four to five years' labor to the artisan) when he left the company. Perhaps, however, he was thrust out without receiving that payment. Yet, he must have received back his probable investment of something in the neighborhood of £60 (over three years' labor to the artisan) in return for his Housekeeper's share in the new Globe Theater. As litigious as was the Elizabethan theater business, a law suit would have occurred over that

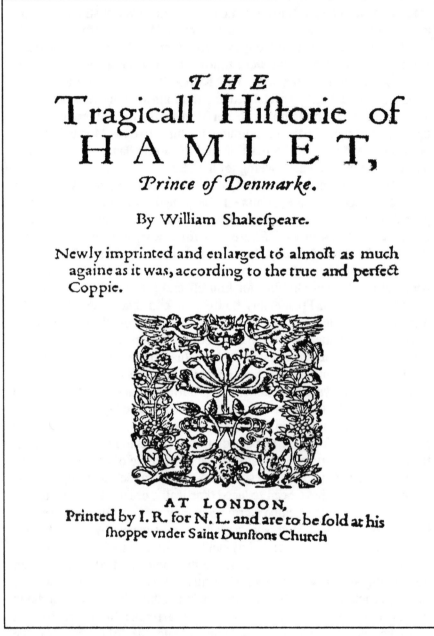

Fig. 16. Title page: "GOOD" Quarto, *Hamlet.*

Kemps nine daies vvonder.

Performed in a daunce from
London to Norwich.

Containing the pleaſure, paines and kinde entertainment
of *William Kemp* betweene *London* and that Citty
in his late Morrice.

Wherein is ſomewhat ſet downe worth note; to reprooue
the ſlaunders ſpred of him: many things merry,
nothing hurtfull.

Written by himſelfe to ſatisfie his friends.

LONDON
Printed by *E. A.* for *Nicholas Ling*, **and are to be**
ſolde at his ſhop at the weſt doore of Saint
Paules Church.   1 6 0 0.

Fig. 17. Title page: Kempe's *Nine Days Wonder*.

matter if he were not paid. Nevertheless, Kempe's *Nine Days' Wonder* makes it clear that he was anxious about his finances less than a year after receiving these sums. His return to London is signalled by a personal loan from Henslowe, and the last record of his existence is yet another personal loan.[20]

The status of Sharer (senior partner) in the Chamberlain's Men had made Shakespeare and his fellow partners substantial sums by 1599. That income had enabled them to invest in real estate, use the legal title of "gentleman," and buy coats of arms. Their incomes ranked in the top five percent of Elizabethan society. The potential income to be gained from a "Housekeeper's" share in the theater building was even greater. How great that potential was needs to be emphasized. Kempe's one-tenth share in the Globe would bring him about 79 or 80 pence a day. In one day Kempe could earn what an artisan would earn in a week.

James Burbage's financial success as owner of The Theatre, was clear. At the time of its construction he was valued at less than £100; by 1596 he was able to buy Blackfriars outright, and spend substantial sums on its renovation. Philip Henslowe's success as owner of the Rose Theater was equally obvious; his account books show him making loan after loan and laying out expenditure after expenditure for the Admiral's men in sums which Elizabethan artisans would need to work years to earn. Given the average daily income an Housekeeper like Henslowe (who had only one partner) could expect, his annual income, at 230 performances per year, had to be in the neighborhood of the £700, over twice the income of the lower Gentry and representing 46 years' labor to the artisan. Kempe, Shakespeare, and their three other partners who each owned a tenth-share of the Globe, would receive less, about 79 or 80 pence per day. Nonetheless, each of their shares would still amount to a yearly sum nearing £76 or £77. That represented over four years' wages to most London artisans. Yet seemingly almost as soon as he achieved it, Kempe relinquished a potential source of income which would have increased his actor income by almost half again.

Just his actor income as Sharer in the Chamberlain's Men should have amassed Kempe a tidy sum. Kempe as a senior partner could expect to average £160 to £190 per year, over ten times the yearly artisan wage. In the four-year period between 1594 and 1598 Kempe probably grossed at least £640. Shakespeare, after all, was able to invest over £500 in real estate in the same period. Yet Kempe, almost immediately upon leaving the Chamberlain's Men was worried about money. He needed loans for clothing upon his return from the Continent in 1602. There is no record he invested in real estate, no record he was supporting a family, and unlike his former associates (Burbage, Heminges, Shakespeare and the others), he does not seem to have had enough assets to bother making a will. Only one conclusion seems plausible: Will Kempe lacked financial judgment, must have lived right up to the edge and beyond the limits of his income and, therefore, was hard pressed for cash whenever he was not employed as an actor. What other assets did he possess—his inside knowledge of popular plays staged by one of London's most popular acting companies and written by one of London's most popular playwrights.

Still another motive besides quick cash suggests itself. When the Chamberlain's Men was formed in 1594, Kempe was the company's biggest star. Shakespeare's earlier plays reflect this. Parts which play upon Kempe's talents as a clown and extemporaneous comic such as Dromio in *The Comedy of Errors* are numerous. By 1597, however, Richard Burbage was beginning to challenge the superstar status of the Admiral's Men's Edward Alleyn. Shakespeare began to write better and better parts for Richard Burbage; Will Kempe's roles began to shrink. No longer were the scripts evenly balanced between Kempe and Burbage as they had been in the earlier years of the acting partnership.[21] Whether or not this meant anything financially is fascinating but probably unanswerable. There are no records which inform us if Sharers received a smaller percentage of income for smaller roles. Yet certainly this turn of events would have offended Kempe's ego as a performer. He was an acclaimed and popular comedic celebrity whose roles were dwindling; in a modern soap opera we would term it being "written out." If, as seems plausible, he played Polonius in *Hamlet*, Hamlet's jibe about Polonius—"he's for a jig or a tale of bawdry, or he sleeps"—is especially pregnant and smacks of a cruel on-stage joke about Kempe's limited talents.

Kempe himself seems to have resented the preeminence that Burbage was achieving. He rather pointedly styled himself the equal of Burbage in honor.[22] Perhaps the fact that Hamlet's most famous speech, "To be or not to be," is horribly garbled—almost to the point of comic nonsense in the pirated version of *Hamlet*—is because it is Kempe's parting shot at Burbage and Shakespeare rather than just a poor piece of memorial reconstruction. Be that as it may, financial need coupled with professional resentment proffer themselves as powerful motives for this founding member of the Chamberlain's men to sell its "secrets." Need and greed coupled with resentment have led many a modern corporate executive into company betrayal.

It may well be that the Chamberlain's Men reached these same conclusions in 1599. Perhaps the group of pirate editions in 1594-95 aroused few concerns or suspicions; these plays had been performed by Pembroke's Men and in conjunction with Strange's Men. Affairs were as yet somewhat unsettled for the new Chamberlain's Men; who could pinpoint any individual from that former group of shifting companies? Perhaps Shakespeare himself may have been involved in "leaking" flawed versions of his plays. Career and financial matters were shaky enough for any of the members of the new troupe. Anyone in those circumstances might seek a quick £6 or £7 that a printer would pay for a play-script.[23] The appearance in 1597 of new pirated editions, however, must have alerted and alarmed the troupe. By this time the Chamberlain's Men had become settled and was challenging the primacy of the Admiral's Men. The company could expect, on average, an income of at least 755 pence per performance. A popular play, and Shakespeare's plays were popular, could expect to be cycled in the annual repertory about 30 times, earning at least £94-95 per year. If printed, however, one of the less established and less reputable companies might perform it, or, more likely, people might simply read the play rather than attend performances. Evidence suggests that Elizabethans often read aloud to one other. Therefore not only could some of the atmosphere of performance be achieved but, also, *one* printed copy would mean that *more than one person* might be deterred from attending performances. The relative pittance made by the Chamberlain's Men from the sale of the "Good" Quartos to printers in 1598-99 cannot have been the company's motive. The title pages of these "Good" Quartos stress Shakespeare's authorship, their new and accurate revisions, and that they are here printed in the true versions as acted by the Chamberlain's Men. The company and its playwright must have been trying to prevent, or at least blunt the impact, of the leaked pirated editions by registering the "official versions" of printed playbooks with the Stationer's Company before any other printer beat them to it.[24]

About the time Kempe left the Chamberlain's Men, Shakespeare was in the midst of revising *The Merry Wives of Windsor*, perhaps for a performance before Queen Elizabeth. Several scholars assert that Kempe's abrupt departure from the company in mid rehearsal for *Merry Wives* can only be explained by the fact the other members of the troupe learned he had leaked a version of it to the newly revived Queen's Chapel Children, a company of child-actors starting up again at Blackfriars. Beyond the evidence which suggest close acquaintanceship among the professional theatre people, Kempe would have had some direct contact with Henry Evans and Nathaniel Giles, the masters of the boys' company; they were in the process of leasing Blackfriars Theatre from Richard Burbage.

Up to the time of Kempe's abrupt departure from the company, and beyond, the Chamberlain's Men was a remarkably stable acting company. Of the eight or ten men who formed the company in 1594, only two left the company before they reached late middle age. One of them, George Bryan, left the theater to become a servant of the Queen; only Will Kempe left to pursue an acting career elsewhere. Hence scholars have concluded that Kempe did not resign from the company; he was expelled! Rumors of his role as pirate of *Merry Wives*, they assert, explain Kempe's peculiar defensiveness in his *Nine Days' Wonder* concerning some unnamed "gifts" to the Queen.[25]

What a broil that must have created within the Chamberlain's Men. Plays including the Falstaff character had proven popular. Audiences liked the character so much that Shakespeare had already scripted Falstaff into three plays and promised to bring him back in a fourth. Leaking a potentially popular play was bad enough, but leaking it before it had been performed and to a hated children's company would have been adding insult to injury. The leak would be especially harmful in 1599 when the Chamberlain's Men were scrabbling for additions to the repertory because the political situation concerning Essex had made history plays controversial. We have no way of knowing how many history plays by other playwrights are involved, but at least *nine* plays by Shakespeare alone probably now became moribund within the repertory, including the two (*1* and *2 Henry IV*) which contained the Falstaff character.

Certain aspects of the *First Folio* version of *Merry Wives*, which probably was re-revised after 1600, help substantiate the argument that

Kempe and Ben Jonson pirated the play for the Chapel Children. Comparisons of Jonson's *Every Man In His Humour* and *Merry Wives* reveal that Jonson seems to have been familiar with Shakespeare's play. Both the manager of the boys' company, Henry Evans, and Ben Jonson are burlesqued in the *First Folio* version through characters substantially changed from those appearing in the pirated "Bad" Quarto. The Welsh parson Hugh Evans, who also runs a school, is an obvious parody of Henry Evans, the Welsh scriviner who managed Blackfriars. Abraham Slender, the bookish buffoon of a suitor, just happens to be an assistant to Evans, and describes things about himself which are close allusions to gossip about Jonson. Slender's line in the last scene, when he complains that the boy he thought was Anne Page in disguise was a "postmaster's boy," no doubt was a joking reference to Evan's difficulties with the Privy Council resulting from Evan's attempt to impress the son of a Norfolk squire and probably a master of the post into the Blackfriars boys. Shakespeare's criticisms of the Boys' Companies are immortalized in *Hamlet*, and he needled Jonson's "Aristotelianism" in *Twelfth Night*. He even may have reiterated *Merry Wives'* personal burlesque of Jonson (the character of Slender) in *Twelfth Night* descriptions of Aguecheek as tall, pseudo-educated, quarrelsome, and overly fond of canary wine. Shakespeare obviously had some axe to grind with Evans and Jonson. Will Kempe himself, in his *Nine Days Wonder*, complains of "slanders" made against him by Jonson; he describes a tall youth called "Jansonius," who was "a little stooping in the shoulders," and who wrote a "story of Macdoel, or Macdobeth, or Macsomewhat," who had appeared "on a publique stage, in a merry Hoast of an Innes part." It has long been suspected that Jonson may well have played the Host of the Garter in some version of *Merry Wives*; he was described by rival playwrights as stoop-shouldered, and Henslowe's *Diary* records payments to Jonson for a tragedy about a Scottish king.[26]

With the leaking of *Merry Wives,* and Kempe's departure from the company, the finger of suspicion must have pointed clearly to him as the source of the earlier piracies. Once the "Bad" Quartos of *Henry IV* and *Henry V* appeared in 1600, the company's suspicions must have been confirmed and its worst fears aroused; now that Kempe was a free agent, he was beginning to release all the repertory to which he had been privy. One reason for the publication in 1600 of the "Good" Quartos of *Henry IV* and *Henry V* may be an attempt to make the best of a bad situation.

The rapid release of *Much Ado About Nothing, Midsummer Night's Dream,* and *Merchant of Venice* in the same year is not explained by this rationale. None of these scripts had been pirated; the Chamberlain's Men was not in need of money; but each of these plays contained prominent roles which had been played by Will Kempe. The company probably was acting quickly to forestall the possibility that Kempe would pirate these plays too. Indeed, as the following graph demonstrates, the company always seems to have reacted quickly to pirated versions, bringing out "authorized" printings within a year of the pirated editions.

Hindsight reveals that the "Bad" Quartos ceased with the publication of the pirated Hamlet in 1603, less than a year after Kempe's disappearance from the scene. It seems that the Chamberlain's Men already anticipated our hindsight. There were no more hurried publications of "Good" Quartos to preempt possible pirate editions during the rest of Shakespeare's lifetime. Shakespeare's fears of pirate editions seem to have been laid to rest along with Will Kempe.

Just as good business sense dictated the handling of play piracies, Shakespeare and his company sometimes catered to the interests of their powerful, high-placed patrons. A case in point is *The Merchant of Venice*. Sometimes labeled a "problem" play, when the script is examined within the framework of the time of its composition, some of those "problems" are solved.

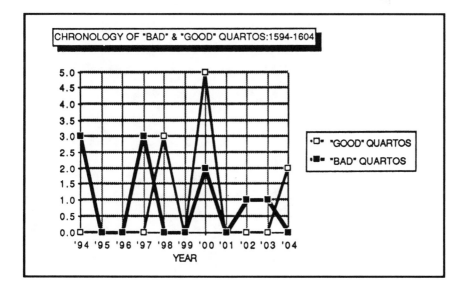

Chapter 6

The Very Human Shylock:
Court Intrigue, Propaganda, Patron Payback,
and *The Merchant of Venice*

Elizabethan theatre companies needed the patronage of a powerful lord in order to maintain the legal right to exist. Without putting themselves forward as the Lord Admiral's or Chamberlain's or Earl of Leicester's Men, those troupes of actors would be considered "masterless men" and vagabonds under the law. As such they would be subject to immediate arrest, impressment in the military and other forms of official harassment. By the same token, individuals also received favors and sometimes financial aid from lords. Shakespeare is a case in point. It is generally accepted that during the time when the London theatres were closed because of plague throughout much of 1593-94, Shakespeare received some sort of financial assistance from the Earl of Southampton. The dedication of his narrative poems *Venus and Adonis* and the *Rape of Lucrece* to the Earl are generally viewed as recognition of that assistance. Patrons expected more than that from a client. But what could they expect? There is no record of any financial payments made directly to a patron from theatre companies or individuals. Yet Lord Admiral Charles Howard often told his subordinates he expected them "to have a good care of such thinges as doe concerne me." Those interests were more than purely financial. They involved questions of prestige and favorable opinion, all of which abetted a lord's position within the intrigues of the Elizabethan court. What one could expect from a theatre company and an author were presentations which in one way or another presented the patron or his "interests" in a favorable light, and it appears that such may have been one goal Shakespeare was attempting to achieve when he wrote *The Merchant of Venice* with its memorable characterization of the Jewish money lender Shylock.

139

The role of Shylock in *The Merchant of Venice* has been interpreted as a comic villain, a tragic hero, a victim of his own hate and greed, a victim of social prejudice, and a variety of interpretations between these extremes. Yet whatever the interpretation, theatre historians, literary and dramatic critics, and performers alike have commented upon the complexities of the role.[1] Like many of his other characters, Shakespeare individualized Shylock's character by scripting speech patterns and little personal details which make Shylock seem like a real person, or, to quote one scholar, "a closely observed human being."

The chances are he truly was. To identify who was the very "human" Shylock, and why he was chosen as Shakespeare's model, is a story in two parts. The first part tells of a man whose downfall was caused by Court intrigue and the petty and determined malice of a high-placed lord; the second part tells of how that downfall was burlesqued as amusement for the London playgoer and political propaganda for a patron. Both parts are intricate, the intricacies of the one necessary to understand the intricacies of the other. Neither tale is a nice one.

Part the First. There is a good deal of mystery surrounding the life and death of Elizabeth's Chief Physician Dr. Lopez. Some scholars assume Dr. Roger Loppez, as he signed himself,[2] emigrated to England in 1559 from Portugal; others, noting the presence in London of a Portuguese Dr. Hernando Lopez during and after the reign of Henry VIII, suggest Roger Lopez was born in England a few years before Elizabeth. The State Papers note that his wife was named Sarah, and that his father-in-law was a certain Dunstan Ames (or Anes), a member of the Grocers' Guild. Baptismal records for Ames' children, however, list daughters named Mary, Rachel, Esther (obviously Judaic names), but do not list a Sarah.[3] Gabriel Harvey, in the 1580s, wrote that Lopez descended from Portuguese Jews but was himself a practicing Christian. After his trial, Sir Francis Bacon wrote he was "suspected to be in sect secretly a Jew though here he conformed to the rites of the Christian religion."[4]

He, or his progenitors, must have been among the many *Marranos* (Jewish converts) who fled Portugal in the first half of the sixteenth century as religious persecution there increased. Massacres of the so-called "new" Christians occurred in Lisbon. The Portuguese *Cortez* (parliament) attempted in 1525 and 1535 to bar the *Marranos* from the practice of medicine or pharmacy for fear they would use their arts to poison the "real" Christians. An Inquisitional Tribunal, modeled after the Spanish version, was instituted in Portugal. As a result of its activities several *Marranos* were burned for heresy.[5] Whether or not the *Marranos* were actually Christians, or only conforming to an outward Christianity while secretly practicing their ancient faith, was of no matter in the Iberian Peninsula. All *Marranos* were suspect. It appears from Bacon's quotation they were in England as well. During and after his trial popular opinion, as evidenced in William Camden's *Elizabeth*, considered Lopez a Jew; and, despite 35 years in England, popular opinion, as evidenced in Sir George Buck's *Richard the Third*, considered him a foreigner.[6]

Lopez's skills as a physician are shrouded by the same kind of contradictions in the sources as are his place of birth and religious practices. He is chastised for neglect of charity work; he is commended for his service to the poor; Gabriel Harvey sneers at his medical techniques; certain patients testify to his medical successes. Whether it was his skill, or, as Bacon put it "being a man very observant and officious, and of a pleasing and applicable behavior,"[7] he earned enough of a reputation to be listed in Stowe's *Annals* (1584) as one of London's most prominent physicians. He was admitted to the College of Physicians; he became House Physician of the Hospital of St. Bartholomew's; he numbered among his patients, and patrons, Sir Francis Walsingham and the Earl of Leicester. In 1581 he was named Chief Physician to the Queen.[8]

At least as early as 1586, he also seems to have worked within Walsingham's espionage network, no doubt gathering information from contacts among the *Marranos*' communities in Antwerp and in Portugal. Evidence of contacts among the *Marranos* throughout Europe is plentiful; the State Papers indicate Lopez maintained communication with Antwerp, Constantinople and Lisbon.[9] Spanish documents reveal that Lopez, and his Anglicized father-in-law Dunstan Ames, helped in the planning of Drake's attacks against the Azores and the Portuguese mainland, and a plan to seize Brazil. In 1591, after Walsingham's death, much of his network of agents passed to the Cecils, and Lopez himself seems to have been working under their patronage. In August of that year he was part of a commission assigned by Lord Burghley to question Emanuel Andrada, a servant to the Portuguese Pretender Don Antonio, and two other Portuguese suspected of being Spanish agents. Lopez was to translate all documents found on their person, and partly through his efforts, Andrada was enlisted as a double agent and sent back to Spain. Lopez was to be his English contact. Andrada returned to Spain, contacted the Spanish Court, relayed the fact that Lopez had prevented the hanging of 300 Spanish sailors captured after the Armada, and was told to continue cultivating his association with Dr. Lopez. He was given a "jewel," a diamond and ruby ring from King Philip's personal jewel collection, to take back to Lopez's daughter as proof of Spain's interest. Andrada too was given some jewels for his upkeep. Spanish papers reveal that the Spanish treasury was so near bankruptcy in 1591 that the only form of payment to Andrada possible was "old jewels" taken from Philip's private collection.[10]

All of this activity by a former agent of his father-in-law, Sir Francis Walsingham, must have made the Earl of Essex view Lopez as a desirable addition to an espionage network he was assembling to rival that of the Cecils.[11] Perhaps he hoped he was "turning" (to use modern espionage jargon) one of the Cecil's most trusted agents. Dr. Lopez was trusted by the Queen. He had been her personal physician for over 12 years; Spanish papers reveal he had ready access to her person, and that she had paid him the singular honor of visiting his home to dine with the Portuguese Pretender Don Antonio.[12] Essex himself lacked any clients with such potential influence. Though Elizabeth had pampered him personally, she seemed reluctant to give offices, grants of authority, or personal access to any of his known associates. Elizabeth held off appointing him to the Privy Council until 1593 and only after a long period in which she carefully watched his conduct. The Cecils, on the other hand, could count as allies and associates at Court, the Lords Admiral and Chamberlain, the Attorney and Solicitor Generals, several members of the Queen's Privy Household, and several lesser servants of the Privy Council. Essex could see that the Cecil faction at Court contained many people with strategic offices, extensive patronage, and ready access to the Queen's Person; the Essex faction was a faction of one.[13]

Whatever Essex's hopes, subsequent events prove that Lopez was not the trusting and devoted tool Essex sought. Some of Lopez's actions even suggest he may have been a Cecil "plant" in the Essex camp. When first approached by Essex with the suggestion he play double agent by pretending through his overseas contacts that he wished to return to Portugal, Lopez first consulted the Queen. When he began to receive information, he always gave it first to her and then to Essex. Elizabeth would then humiliate the Earl by laughing at his second-hand information in front of members of the Court. In private conversation Lopez mocked Essex, describing his treatment of the Earl's diseases. Many scholars assume the treatment was for syphilis. Court gossip hinted at some form of venereal disease.[14]

Furthermore, Spanish documents reveal that Lopez's avowed intentions were to act as a go-between for *peace* negotiations between England and Spain. Peace negotiations were not what the Earl of Essex had in mind. Almost certainly the Queen, as early as 1593, was interested in a truce with Spain. The Cecils, too, may have been leaning in that direction. Only three or four short years later (by 1597) we know they were. Essex, who dreamed of military glory and whose every avenue to riches and power save the military seemed blocked by the maneuvering of the Cecil faction, remained steadfastly opposed to any rapprochement with Spain until his downfall.[15] Lopez certainly was not playing the Earl's game. He may not have been playing the Cecils' game. Some scholars suggest the 69-year-old doctor was acting on his own for greed, or for a desire to emigrate to Constantinople in order to practice Judaism openly, or for some other unspecified reasons and unspecified gains.[16]

Bishop Goodman, writing in the reign of James I, however, suggests something even deeper. Goodman wrote that throughout his interrogations, his trial, and his imprisonment, Lopez never revealed the Queen's secret business. When the courier Stephen da Gama was first arrested, Lopez went straight to the Queen asking her to release da Gama so as to allow the two of them to continue the work towards a truce for which they had already laid the foundations. Elizabeth specifically commissioned Lopez to translate da Gama's letters after his arrest; and after Lopez's arrest by Essex, she summoned the Earl to Court where she berated him for his actions, avowing that she knew Lopez was innocent of wrong-doing. What these actions suggest is that Lopez may well have been playing the *Queen's* game. Elizabeth often sought the views and utilized the services of informed people outside the Privy Council and kept aloof from Privy Council deliberations to maintain independence from its manipulation, especially if she held a minority opinion there.

Further, she publicly curried her subjects' support and approval.[17] Hence, Elizabeth, because of popular opposition to peace with Spain and Privy Council divisions over that issue, may have wished to pursue peace overtures outside official organs (and the factionalism) of the Court.

Probably Essex did not get wind of Lopez's offer to negotiate for peace; and even if he did, his former favor had already turned to hatred. Lopez's espionage activities and his gossiping had humiliated Essex publicly and privately, and Lopez was preferred by the Cecils and the Queen as an espionage agent over Standen, an expatriate Catholic who had returned to England after several years in Spain, and a man whose cause Essex had determined to champion. Lopez was trusted with sensitive missions; Standen had difficulty even in being presented at Court. Every attempt by Essex to gain Standen a position within the Elizabethan espionage network was thwarted by the Cecils. Just before the Lopez matter, Essex, with great difficulty, had finally received his appointment as a Lord of the Privy Council. At the height of the Lopez matter Essex was striving unsuccessfully to force Elizabeth to install Francis Bacon as Attorney General. Elizabeth disliked Bacon, but he and Essex were convinced that it was the Cecils who were blocking the appointment. Essex vowed that any who stood in his way should feel the weight of his enmity. In that sense, Lopez may have been a pawn in Essex's attack upon the Cecil faction.[18] Any of these reasons were sufficient to Essex to prove that Lopez and the Cecils were out to destroy him. Essex simply displayed the paranoia he and other Elizabethan courtiers often displayed when faced with political failures.[19]

That paranoia fueled his campaign against Lopez. He seems to have convinced himself that Lopez truly was a Spanish agent and had been doing mischief for years. He is said to have suggested to Elizabeth that Lopez poisoned his father-in-law Sir Francis Walsingham.[20] When Essex got hold of the Portuguese emissary, Stephen da Gama (who was bearing messages for Lopez) he grilled the man for days.[21] Da Gama, a former servant of Don Antonio, admitted he had borne messages to and from Spanish agents and, under pressure and perhaps fear of the rack, "confessed" he was returning to England with a plot against Don Antonio and with instructions to win over Dr. Lopez. Later he added there also was some plot against the Queen.[22]

All of this has an ominous sound except when it is remembered Essex, like Walsingham earlier, had put Lopez in the role of a double agent. Subsequently da Gama wrote he was confused by Essex's leading questions and his own imperfect knowledge of French. Da Gama knew little or no English; Essex knew little Portuguese or Spanish; interrogations were carried out in French.[23] Essex arrested the old doctor, and whisked him off to Essex House where he held him in confinement. Lopez was then interrogated before Essex and William and Robert Cecil (both of whom sought to protect him from Essex by having the doctor transferred to the Tower, safely out of Essex's direct control);[24] his house was searched; his papers were examined. Nothing incriminating came to light. Robert Cecil bore that news to the Queen and, when Essex was summoned to Court, Elizabeth tongue-lashed him in front of Cecil and the Lord Admiral calling the Earl a "rash and temerarious youth" who was hounding the "poor old man" out of "personal malice."[25] Essex stormed out of the Court and shut himself up in his private chamber. After two days of brooding alone Essex burst forth to write to his client Anthony Bacon: "I have discovered a most dangerous and desperate treason. The point of the conspiracy was her Majesty's death. The executioner should have been Doctor Lopez; the manner poison. This I have so followed, as I will make it appear as clear as the noon-day."[26] This was the first mention anywhere of a plot by Lopez to murder the Queen.

From then on Essex doggedly pursued Lopez. He conducted numerous lengthy examinations of Lopez and his supposed fellow conspirators da Gama, and Emanuel Tinoco, another Portuguese whom Essex originally had sought to recruit for his own spy network and who had been lured back to England with promise of safe-conduct. Both da Gama and Tinoco were associates of Lopez; both had deserted the service of the Pretender Don Antonio; both had lodged in Lopez's house; and both, the Spanish papers reveal, had been recruited to aid Lopez in possible peace negotiations because Philip II himself, as well as the Spanish agents in The Netherlands, had become convinced that Andrada was unreliable, dangerous, and might initiate actions which would abort the attempted negotiations.[27]

Essex locked himself away with Lopez for two days scarcely taking time from his interrogations to eat (we do not know if Lopez was given any time to eat). Tinoco and da Gama were subjected to barrages of questions by Essex and other court figures such as William Waad, William Cecil's secretary. Both, and perhaps Lopez also, were threatened with the rack if not actually racked. The State Papers deny use of the rack; the courtier Philip Gawdy wrote that Lopez "hathe bene often examined and dyvers time uppon the racke, he confesseth all things very franckly." It came out during Tinoco's and da Gama's trial that they were promised immunity if they were willing to testify against Dr. Lopez.[28] The State Papers reveal that everyone's depositions changed and changed until each accused the other and reinforced answers Essex wanted to hear.[29]

Perhaps Essex had another motive beyond his hatred for Lopez in his determination to prove the old doctor guilty of treason. At about the same time as the arrest of Lopez and the other two Portuguese, a trio of Irish Catholics had also been arrested as Spanish agents. Under close interrogation conducted by Lord Admiral Howard, they told a tale that they had come to England to murder the Queen and had been instructed to win over the Earl of Essex to their plots. They had brought him a "jewel" as a token of friendship from the Spanish king. Over and over again in their interrogations they were asked if they had any connection with Dr. Lopez. They admitted to having met Tinoco in The Netherlands, denied any connections with Lopez but affirmed that they had brought a jewel to enlist the aid of the Earl of Essex. Essex, it was rumored, planned to join in a conspiracy with the Earl of Derby to overthrow the Queen and "have the crown himself."[30] Essex was aware of these accusations, and must have been acutely embarrassed and not a little frightened by them. This episode may help explain the repeated emphasis placed on Lopez's "jewel." Essex could shift focus away from the investigation of the Catholics and the jewel intended for him by proving that the "jewel" Lopez had received years earlier from Philip II was a down payment on a plot to poison the Queen.

Sources are unclear about this "jewel." All agree that Lopez offered it to the Queen; some maintain she refused it; Lopez maintained at his trial that the Queen possessed it. Other "evidence" against him is equally ambiguous. Certain "incriminating" papers were produced which Lopez explained as dating from the time he had worked for Walsingham. That argument was disallowed. It would appear that the espionage work Lopez had done for Walsingham as a double agent was now used as evidence against him. It was revealed that he had been in touch with

Spain for some years. That was true technically but London rumor, as revealed in Venetian dispatches, made no mention of his spying for Walsingham. Walsingham, of course, was dead and could not shed light on the matter. The interrogations of Lopez, Tinoco, and da Gama were intensified; their several "confessions" and mutual denunciations were "leaked" to Essex's source of popularity, the London gossip-mill. Anti-foreign sentiments were high in England. Riots over foreign laborers occurred in London in 1593; in that same year and again in 1594, petitions were made to Court requesting the registering of all foreigners. Once charged Lopez now became the "Portingale" and, especially in the writings of Essex supporters like Bacon, the "vile Jew," his foreign birth and his Jewish ancestry no doubt being stressed to paint a blacker picture of him. In the popular mind Jews were monsters, Christ-killers, ritual murderers of children, devious villains who sought clever ways to destroy Christians, usurers who profited from death and the misery of others. Public opinion, therefore, was inflamed against Lopez even before he was brought to trial. It was kept at a fever pitch afterwards through the circulation of numerous pamphlets like Thomas Nashe's *The Unfortunate Traveller or the Life of Jacke Wilton*, which, with its tale of a Roman *Jewish* doctor's plot to poison the pope, is obviously modeled after Lopez, and like Bacon's, *True report of the detestable treason intended by Doctor Roderigo Lopez*. Bacon's connection with the Essex faction in 1594 is famous, but Nashe's dedication of his work to the Earl of Southampton makes it clear he too perhaps was writing "on cue."

Even Lopez's former patrons like the Cecils quickly adopted the now "official" line, issuing public and semi-private statements concerning their belief in his guilt. Perhaps, as some scholars aver, they too became convinced of Lopez's guilt; perhaps, as others aver, they were willing to sacrifice a minor figure to alert the Queen to danger and force her to pursue a more vigorous anti-Catholic and anti-Spanish policy. Perhaps, however, as some documents suggest, the Cecils were pressured into public denunciation of Lopez by a desire to save face for the government now under pressure from the heat of popular opinion in London which demanded Lopez's death. A well-publicized, showy trial presided over by most of the prominent Lords of the Privy Council had just been held. In a sense Essex had managed to shift the focus of the Lopez matter from a question of his personal credibility to questions touching upon the credibility of the Queen's justice. Bishop Goodman asserted that the Queen told Lopez he would have to be patient about his release because the affair had become one which impinged on the honor of the state. The State Papers from the same time contain a letter from Sir Thomas Egerton: "Doctor Lopez has kept his bed for the most part, since his trial, and whether he practices anything by slow poison, to prevent his execution may be doubted. If this instant trial should be deferred [the trial of Tinoco and da Gama], and Lopez should die before execution, great dishonour and scandal might ensue."[31] Perhaps too, the Cecils feared that the Lopez matter was becoming an issue to stir up English Catholics; William Cecil received a report from an agent as far away as Durham that "our papists here do secretly whisper, that the stay of Lopus his execution may argue, that his condemnation is but to draw the king of Spain in odium with our nation; which indeed would be credited of too many, if he should not suffer [execution]."[32] Perhaps they feared the wrath of popular opinion should word of Lopez's attempts at peace negotiations reach the public. England in 1593-94 was in no mood to talk peace with the Spanish; the memory of the Armada was too fresh, and Drake and the other English privateers had been achieving spectacular, if not terribly profitable, privateering successes throughout Spanish waters in the Americas.[33]

Lopez was tried before a court presided over by Essex in the London Guildhall on February 28, 1594. As with most other aspects of the matter, smoke and fog surround the trial. No record of the trial appears in the State Trials; the State Papers list only summaries of the evidence and indictments against Lopez. Four letters written by Lopez concerning minor matters were preserved in the State Papers but not one of the "incriminating" letters referred to in the State Papers was preserved, only digests and summaries of the supposed letters. The result of the trial was a foregone conclusion. Elizabethan treason trials assumed the guilt of the person charged.[34] Lopez was convicted of treason and sentenced to be hanged, cut down while still alive, disemboweled and quartered, the body parts to be set about London. The courtroom packed with Londoners cheered and applauded the verdict. On June 7, 1594, that sentence was carried out at Tyburn Hill. No plays were performed on that day.[35]

Interlude. During the year or so encompassing Lopez's downfall, several points, some real, some mere gossip, concerning Lopez became fixed in the common perception of the man:

1. His Christianity only was a veneer; he secretly was a Jew; despite 35 years in England, he was considered a foreigner.
2. He was obsessed with amassing wealth.
3. He sought matches with wealthy Jews for his daughters.
4. He secretly despised the Portuguese Pretender Don Antonio.
5. He was a practiced poisoner.
6. He received a diamond and ruby ring from the King of Spain.
7. The Queen offered him every chance to exonerate himself.
8. His own confederates denounced his villainy.
9. The Queen delayed his execution for three months.
10. A portion of his fortune was restored to his widow, and children, within nine months of his execution.[36]

Keep these points in mind, for they have bearing on the second part of this story.

Part the Second. There is little doubt that the London theatre of Elizabeth's day cashed in on current events, or was used on occasion to promote certain individuals or ideas. Numerous examples exist of people, events, issues, which, in one way or another, found their way to the stages of London. *The Battle of Alcazar* was dramatized soon after it occurred. A lawsuit informs us of a suitor who hired the playwright and the players to present his side of the story in a disputed betrothal. Actors would wear "a Beard resembling his" when portraying a real person on stage. Masters of the Revels closed plays which on reading seemed harmless, but once on stage actors portrayed people of importance by assuming their characteristic dress, facial features, gestures and speech patterns. The Privy Council once threatened to shut down all theatres in London because of the "scandalous and seditious matter" contained in Nashe's and Jonson's *The Isle of Dogs.* The most famous example, of course, was the arranged staging of *Richard II* the day before the Earl of Essex's abortive attempt to seize the Court, and Essex himself, before the attempted coup wrote to Elizabeth complaining that the theatres "will play me in what forms they list upon the stage."[37]

Though treated as a minor incident by modern historians, the Lopez affair was a *cause celebre* in Elizabethan and Jacobean London. From the time of Lopez's arrest to that of his execution, Henslowe's company trotted out the old *The Jew of Malta,* and the even older (and now lost) *The Jewe* over and over again. As late as ten years after the events in question, Lopez was used as a personification of treachery in

Fig. 18. Cartoon of Dr. Lopez: *A Thankful Remembrance* (1624). Hanging and quartering: *Theatrum Crudelitatum Haeriticorum* (1592).

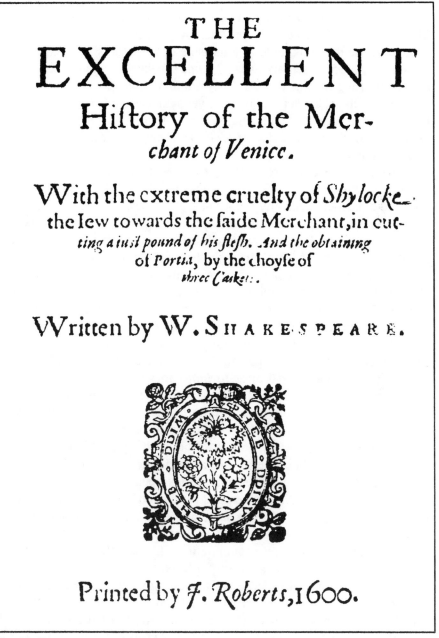

THE
EXCELLENT
History of the Mer-
chant of Venice.

With the extreme cruelty of *Shylocke*
the Iew towards the saide Merchant, in cutting a iust pound of his flesh. And the obtaining
of *Portia*, by the choyse of
three Caskets.

Written by W. SHAKESPEARE.

Printed by *J. Roberts*, 1600.

Fig. 19. Title page: *The Merchant of Venice.*

revisions of *Doctor Faustus*, in plays by Dekker, and in plays by Middleton. Would London's premier playwright, who was shrewd enough to use the book trade as a measure of Londoners' tastes, ignore such a juicy piece of sensationalism? Some scholars have tentatively and reluctantly suggested he did not. They admit to some possible allusions to Lopez in the character of Shylock, yet skitter away from that notion by noting the probable later composition of the play (1596-97), and assert that Marlowe's *The Jew of Malta* is of much greater influence on Shakespeare's Shylock.[38]

To deny Shakespeare's allusions to Marlowe's play and some parallels to his character Barrabas would be idiotic. Yet scholars who note these parallels generally point out that Shakespeare's Shylock is a more "realistic" Jewish villain. Attempts to relate Shylock with Lopez, however, have not been too successful. One reason may well be that scholars have looked for clear, extended and obvious references and have, therefore, cited passages such as Portia's and Bassanio's dialogue (III, 2) about "racking" forcing a man to admit anything or Gratiano's speech (IV, 1): "...thy currish spirit/Govern'd a wolf..," which has been interpreted as a triple, multi-lingual pun, Lopez to the Latin *lupus* to the English wolf. Other scholars rightfully point out that such remarks are too general to specify the Lopez affair, though interestingly, Dekker and Middleton did make the Lopez to *lupus* to wolf connection. Some scholars warn that almost any attempt to equate seeming allusions to actual Elizabethans is doomed to failure. Yet, as a recent paper has revealed, Shakespeare's method of allusion to people and events was subtler and more indirect than those of his fellow playwrights such as Thomas Dekker and Ben Jonson. Just as he developed his plotlines with clues scattered lines and scenes apart, Shakespeare used little clues— words, phrases, personal idiosyncrasies—scattered lines and scenes apart to develop the burlesque of a person he wished to plant in his audiences' minds. No one phrase or image is sufficient reference to the person by itself, but the layering and accumulation of those clues reduces the coincidence of "random-seeming" phrases concerning an actual contemporary, to no coincidence.[39] There are probably many references to Lopez and contemporary events in *The Merchant of Venice* about which we will never know. Our information about the details of Shakespeare's England and Lopez's life is 400 years old, not fresh in our minds as it was to Shakespeare's contemporaries. Yet in returning to our section entitled *Interlude*, we find not just one or two or three of those widely known aspects concerning Lopez are echoed in one way or another in *The Merchant of Venice*; all *ten* of them are.

1. Portia refers to Shylock as an "alien" (IV, 1) and there are several jokes concerning Shylock and Christianity. Jessica's plan to convert upon her marriage to Lorenzo brings forth from Launcelot Gobbo that so many conversions of Jews will raise the price of pork (III, 5). Antonio remarks of Shylock "The Hebrew will turn Christian, he grows kind" (I, 3). Shylock is forced to convert as terms of his sentence, and Gratiano quips that he would prefer 12 godfathers to bring Shylock "to the gallows not to the font" (IV, 1). Dr. Lopez's statement at the gallows that he "loved the Queen as much as he loved Jesus Christ" had been a source of merriment to the crowd gathered for his execution. As Harvey's remarks point out, Lopez's "Jewishness" and his "pretended" Christianity rarely surfaced until after he was accused by Essex; but by the turn of the century he had become "That Spanish-Iewish, Atheist, and Lop-heauie-headed Leach,/(Vnworthy a Physitions name) fowle Lopas, we impeach."[40]

2. Shylock, of course, is a money-lender, a miser, and considers himself broken when his goods are confiscated (IV, 1). Lopez was censured by St. Bartholomew's Hospital for neglecting charity cases, was criticized for toadying to the rich, sought and received royal grants of monopolies, and once petitioned the Privy Council on behalf of his business partner, an expatriate Genoese merchant, for the collection of debts owed by Henry Howard. Tinoco and da Gama continually stressed that Lopez kept asking Spanish agents when he would get his money. At his trial Lopez continually averred that all he sought to do was to "cosen the King of Spain and wipe him of his money."[41]

3. Shylock seeks to protect his daughter from prodigal Christian men and, hearing of her marriage to Lorenzo, remarks "Would any of the stock of Barrabas/Had been her husband, rather than a Christian" (IV, 1). Lopez is mentioned in Privy Council documents, Cecil papers, and Spanish dispatches as concerned with suitable matches for his daughters. One of those matches sought was with a wealthy *Marrano* money lender from France. Incidentally, as far as we know, Shakespeare actually coined the name Jessica for Shylock's daughter. He only used the name in this one play and *The Merchant of Venice* contains the first recorded use of the name.[42]

4. Shylock's hatred of Antonio for his prodigality and arrogant contempt of Jews crops up often in the play. He states that he will avail himself of Antonio's hospitality "yet I'll go in hate to feed upon the prodigal Christian" (II, 5). Lopez's fraternization with Don Antonio was well known as was his disillusionment with the Pretender because of Don Antonio's sloth and extravagance. In a letter to the Queen, Lopez had apologized for his support of Don Antonio's ill-fated and costly attempt to invade Portugal.[43]

5. In Shylock's most famous speech asks: "if you poison us, do we not die?" (III, 1). Since the passage is not verse but prose and, therefore not written for metrical purposes, why the reference to poison as a form of death, why not, for instance, "if you stab us" or "if you shoot us"? Jews were often accused of being poisoners, but more specifically, Dr. Lopez, it must be remembered, was not only convicted of plotting to poison the Queen, but common gossip held he had also furnished poisons to the Earl of Leicester who used them to do away with enemies.[44]

6. Shylock complains that his daughter not only fled with his ducats but with "two stones, two rich and precious stones" (II, 7). He later laments that there is "a diamond gone and other precious, precious jewels" (III, 1). One of the oft-mentioned "proofs" of Lopez's guilt was the precious jewel, a diamond and ruby ring sent him, for his daughter by the king of Spain. Salarino's lines (II, 8)—"Why all the boys in Venice follow him,/Crying, his stones, his daughter, his ducats"— obviously an Elizabethan double entendre, may be an entendre that worked on two levels. Then as now, "stones" was a sexual pun for testicles. Just as "all the boys in Venice" followed Shylock, all the boys (and men and women) in London probably followed Dr. Lopez as he was dragged on hurdles to Tyburn[45] and the first mutilation performed upon the condemned traitor after he was cut down from the gallows was castration.

7. Portia, posing as a doctor of law at the Venetian court (IV, 1), repeatedly tries to allow Shylock to slip out from under the penalties to which he is subject for "direct or indirect attempts" to contrive "against the very life" of the merchant Antonio. Shylock, until tripped up, demands the law and protests his willingness to abide by its application. "My deeds upon my head! I crave the law." Lopez, of course, was convicted of "imagining" and conspiring against the lives of both the

Queen and Don Antonio. Reports concerning his interrogations indicate he swore great oaths avowing his innocence and stated that, if the charges were proven, he deserved the rigors of the law. It was common knowledge that the Queen had refused to listen to Essex's first undocumented accusations against Lopez. Court gossip in the next reign asserted that Elizabeth assured Lopez he had no fear of anything he had done on her behalf, only those things which he might be liable for under the law. Some scholars have pondered the peculiar status Portia seems to have in the Venetian law-court. She seems neither Shylock's, nor Antonio's, nor Bassanio's attorney. Over and over again she is called a "judge."[46] To an Elizabethan, however, the Queen was, in a sense, chief judge of the realm, able to intervene to commute, or pardon, any offender's sentence.

8. Shylock is denounced often for his villainy by his servant Launcelot Gobbo: "Certainly my conscience will serve me to run from this Jew..." (II, 2). Both Tinoco and da Gama, the Portuguese Christians who denounced Lopez, claimed "pangs" of conscience had led them to turn against the Jewish Lopez; both had been his dependents, lodgers in his house, and both claimed to be his messengers to the agents of Spain.

9. Shylock not only continually asks when he will receive his ducats, as Lopez was supposed to have done, but he, Bassanio and Antonio mention the three month's term of the bond eight separate times in the short space of Act I, scene 3. It is repeated far more often than the sum owed, so often in fact that it almost seems a litany—three months, three months, three months. Lopez was convicted and sentenced the last day of February 1594. The Queen delayed his execution despite pressure from her advisors and the grumblings of the London populace until June 7th, just a week past three months. There is even some question whether she ever consented to his execution.[47] Three months until the execution of the bond in *The Merchant of Venice*, three months until the execution of the man in the real-life drama of Roger Lopez.

10. Antonio the merchant graciously offered one-half of the goods confiscated from Shylock to his daughter and son-in-law upon Shylock's death (IV, 1). A royal grant, issued less than nine months after Lopez's execution, restored Lopez's properties and his goods up to the value of £100 to his widow and children, save the ruby and diamond ring which the Queen retained and which tradition holds she wore ever after at her girdle. Scholars have remarked upon this uncharacteristic generosity on

the part of Elizabeth. Later, perhaps Lopez's ring, Shylock's ring and Portia's ring may have become garbled into the Restoration legend of Elizabeth's ring given to Essex with the understanding that should he ever need her pardon, he should send it to her. Perhaps the ring legend concerning Elizabeth and Essex crept into popular folklore from the lines in *The Merchant of Venice* and the connections people made between Portia, Bassanio, Elizabeth and Essex, just as the famous deer poaching legend about Shakespeare arose out of the lines in *The Merry Wives of Windsor* and the connections people made between young Shakespeare and Sir Thomas Lucy.[48]

Other passages from *Merchant* may well be allusions to Dr. Lopez. They are not humane ones, though on the surface they may seem so. Shylock complains of Antonio spitting on his "Jewish gabardine" (I, 3). According to the Oxford English Dictionary, a gabardine in Elizabethan usage was a long, smock-like outer garment made of coarse cloth, something that would resemble a doctor's gown. Shakespeare seems to be the first to use the word "gabardine" as peculiar to a Jewish robe. There may be some truth after all to the tradition that the first actor to play Shylock donned a beard in imitation of Lopez's and wore a doctor's gown. On other occasions actors copied the beard and dress of people they impersonated on stage.

One line of Shylock's concerning the ring Jessica has traded for a monkey has been interpreted as evidence of his familial tenderness: "It was my turkis, I had it of Leah when I was a bachelor" (III, 1). Dr. Lopez's wife was named Sarah, but a brother-in-law of Lopez, Don Solomon, was known to be a high official in the court of the Ottoman sultan, the "Grand Turk" as he was called. An interesting coincidence that Shylock's ring is a *turkis* (turquoise) given him by his future wife, when it was also known that Lopez's *Turkish* brother-in-law interceded on Lopez's behalf after his conviction. Leah, incidentally, means "cow," an etymology which would have been known to the Inns of Court gallants in Shakespeare's audience and generally was in use in the late sixteenth century only among the Puritans, a favorite target of those same gallants.[49]

Shylock's most famous speech "Hath not a Jew eyes?" (III, 1) may not be the high-minded plea for equality some have thought it to be. From his references in *Love's Labour's Lost* (I, 2) to the performing horse who was trained to count by tapping his hoof, and in *Merry Wives of Windsor* (I, 1) to the ferocious bear Sackerson of the Paris Garden arena, we know Shakespeare was aware of, and perhaps attended, the alternative entertainments in London. Among the most popular animal acts in London were those involving apes, such as those that rode ponies at Paris Garden. One of the most popular performing apes in London was a blind baboon named Gue. There are several allusions to "Blind Gue (or Gew)" in writings at the turn of the century. References to his act suggest he was prodded and pricked to make him dance, refuse to bow to an effigy of the pope, and "ape" other human gestures.[50] "If you prick us do we not bleed? If you tickle us, do we not laugh? If you poison us, do we not die?" says Shylock, which in three short sentences seems to equate an ape with a Jew with Dr. Lopez the poisoner. A scant 46 lines (or 17 speeches) later in the same scene Shylock and his co-religionist Tubal twice mention monkeys. Tubal: "One of them showed me a ring that he had of your daughter for a monkey." Shylock: "I would not have given it for a wilderness of monkeys." It is with these lines, seemingly coming out of nowhere and leading nowhere, that Shakespeare confirmed his baboon joke to his audience.

Lest this seem too cruelly outrageous, it must be remembered that contemporary Christian woodcuts showed Jewish women giving birth to piglets, and it also must be remembered that Shakespeare earned his living by pleasing the tastes and popular prejudices of his Christian audience. In the *First Folio*, designed for readers, it may not be printer's vagary that "Hath not a Jewe eyes?" is the only place in the speech that Jew is spelled with a final "e." That "e" would set up the pun making the sound of Jewe equals Gue abundantly clear to a reader. In the 1600 "Good Quarto" edition of Merchant, probably prepared from a prompt book, always uses the final "e," suggesting that the similarity of sound was hammered home in actual performance.[51] To draw a modern parallel: without stage directions specifying a woman in a gorilla suit wearing a yellow Star of David, would not the Emcee's song "If you could see her through my eyes" from *Cabaret* seem to be a tender love ballad. Probably "Hath not a Jew eyes" was designed as a verbal aria with the same mocking intent. The word "Jew" almost always is used with negative implications in *The Merchant of Venice*. Bellylaughs, not sympathy, was what Shakespeare hoped to elicit from his audience. It was not until Charles Macklin's performance of 14 February 1741 that

Shylock became interpreted as a "tragic" rather than a comic figure and, even then as the script itself so clearly indicates, he still was portrayed as the villain of the play.[52]

Lopez had been dead for almost three years when the version of *Merchant* we possess was staged, probably in early 1597. Some scholars suggest an earlier version was staged in August of 1594, assuming Henslowe's listing of a play called *Venesyon Comodie* indicates he had acquired Shakespeare's first draft of *Merchant*. Yet by August Shakespeare had been a full partner in the Chamberlain's Men for at least three months; it seems unlikely that he would have written a play for the rival company. One might therefore ask: "Why the guarded allusions, why a play so far removed from its immediacy?" The answer is that the immediacy does not center on the Lopez matter *per se* but on the recent Cadiz expedition led by the Earl of Essex and Lord Admiral Charles Howard. Scholars have used the reference in the play to the "Andrew" (I, 1), a Spanish galleon sunk in the sea battle outside Cadiz, as a means of dating the play's composition.

Venice, too, was "in the news" so to speak in 1596-97. A Venetian ambassador arrived in London in the summer of 1596. Word reached London from Venice that the Cadiz victory was so celebrated there that Venetians wanted pictures of Queen Elizabeth, and it was well known that Lopez's brother-in-law's family, the Mendez, had important banking interests in Venice. Another temporal association overlooked by scholars may be the two references (II, 8, and III, 1) to a Venetian ship lost in the "Narrow Seas" (English Channel). On 23 January 1597 a Venetian argosy filled with grain was detained at the Channel port of Portsmouth. The dispute between the Privy Council and the Venetian government over its detention dragged on for months.

There even was a Venetian Jewish merchant in London who was connected with Essex's Cadiz expedition. A certain Alonso Nuñez de Herrera from Venice had been taken hostage at Cadiz by the Earl of Essex and transported back to England along with other hostages. He protested that he was an emissary of the Sultan of Morocco and requested his release to the custody of friends in London. Not much else about his personality is known, save his release in 1600 was preceded by an apology (in 1599) regarding his capture from the Queen to the Sultan. Yet his presence and his connection with Essex and the Cadiz expedition must have been known in London in 1596-97.

Other allusions to the Cadiz expedition probably are references made throughout the play to the dangers of the sea in I, 3, in III, 1, for example. Though these references are couched in terms of mercantile sailing, the implicit praise of the bravery of those who fight on the sea seems obvious. Scholars have also noted the seeming parallel between Bassanio's friendship for Antonio and Essex's friendship and support for Don Antonio the Pretender and Antonio Perez the Spanish defector, both enemies and supposedly potential victims of Roger Lopez, as Antonio the merchant is the enemy and potential victim of Shylock.[53]

The intricacies of the politics at the Court before and during 1596-97 need to be addressed here. Those intricacies bear upon the intricacies of the Lopez/Shylock allusions. Essex had been unsuccessful in his suits for his clients since at least 1592 when his ally Sir John Popham became Lord Chief Justice of the Queen's Bench. There is no direct evidence that the Queen ever consented to Lopez's execution, and his transfer from the Tower to Queen's Bench and thence to Tyburn. Indeed, she seems to have been dealing with this matter as she often did with Essex (and with other peers); avoid direct confrontation, preserve the public dignity of the nobility, let Essex have his head at first, stall, and change things later when his attention was diverted elsewhere. No warrant for Lopez's release from the Tower for execution has survived; there exists only a third-hand reference to unnamed Privy Council Lords assuring the Lieutenant of the Tower that the Queen had finally consented to Lopez's execution. The weight given supposed orders from Lords of the Privy Council was enormous. A Privy Council Lord could, as Essex did with Lopez, arrest, detain and interrogate people on his own initiative. Several enterprising con-men took advantage of this power and, by posing as agents of Privy Council Lords, "arrested" citizens until they extorted "bail" from the unfortunate detainees. The entire matter concerning Lopez's execution was accomplished swiftly when Elizabeth was absent from London on Progress. He was transferred from the custody of the Tower to that of Queen's Bench (under Popham's jurisdiction) and immediately hauled off to execution. Bishop Goodman, writing in the next reign, asserted that Essex used his ally Popham, the Lord Chief Justice, to manipulate that absence and get round the Queen's aversion to carrying out Lopez's sentence.[54]

It is interesting to note that from 1594 until after Essex's execution, Elizabeth went on fewer progresses outside the near vicinity of London than she had in years before. Generally, from 1594 to 1601 she removed herself only to nearby Greenwich and Nonsuch Palaces. After Essex's death in 1601 until her own in 1603, however, she made progresses to Windsor, Wiltshire, Hampshire, Berkshire, Buckinghamshire, Bath, Bristol. One is tempted to think that the Lopez matter caused the Queen to mistrust and perhaps even to fear Essex a little. He had been too successful in manipulating the London populace. Francis Bacon warned Essex not to woo popularity with the people. Always anxious herself for public approval and acclaim, Elizabeth resented any rival for her subjects' affection. The public prayer sessions and bell-ringings Londoners gave Essex in honor of his exploits galled the Queen. Be that as it may, from 1594 on Essex placed virtually none of his clients in any post of importance. His own preferments always involved military activity which took him out of the country, such as the expedition to Cadiz (1596), the expedition to the Azores (1597) and the ill-fated expedition to Ireland (1599) which ultimately led to his downfall.[55]

As for the Cadiz expedition itself, Elizabeth had from the first worked to diminish any glory that Essex might obtain from its execution. The Queen insisted that Essex share command with the trusty old Lord Admiral. She had publicly acknowledged Lord Howard's part in the victory with a congratulatory letter stating that he had made her "famous, dreadful and renouwned, not more for your victory than for your courage," and in the royal patent creating him the Earl of Nottingham, a patent granted while Essex was absent at sea. On the other hand, she had intervened in the immediate aftermath of the expedition to stop celebrations in honor of the Cadiz victors, greeted Essex on his return with coldness, complained publically of the number of men Essex had knighted without her approval, the cost of the expedition and the pilfering of the loot from the expedition, and she forbade the publication of a pamphlet celebrating Essex's role in that victory.[56]

One of Essex's closest associates was the Earl of Southampton, who had planned to accompany him on the Cadiz expedition, who was co-defendant at Essex's trial for treason, and who, at one time at least, had been Shakespeare's personal patron when the theatres were closed and Shakespeare must have been in need of money. There are indications Shakespeare himself had some connection with the circle of *literati* around Lady Mary Sidney, Essex's step-cousin. Essex himself seemed to have some appreciation for the propaganda value of theatre; he once staged a little pageant for the Queen, transparent in its praise of his service and devotion to her. He, or his supporters, attempted to use the theatre in some fashion or another in his "Last Hurrah" to rally the crowd to his side. Given all that and the frustration of Essex and his followers in late 1596 and early 1597 that *he* was being denied all opportunity to tout *his* rightful place as the *true* hero of the Cadiz expedition, a word from his confederate Southampton to Southampton's former client, the actor-playwright William Shakespeare, that Essex needed some good publicity does not seem beyond logic.

At the time of the play's opening, one of the most influential groups in the audiences of the Chamberlain's Men were the Inns of Court gallants, among whose ranks was the Earl of Southampton. Those gallants always were extremely receptive to Essex's charms, and he often sought to curry their favor. There may even have been some money involved for *The Merchant of Venice*. Staging a play was not cheap in Elizabethan England. The average cost of a single production was £2; staging a new play could cost as much as £25 to £30, a sum almost double the average Elizabethan artisan's annual wage. The Essex faction did pay the Chamberlain's Men 40 shillings (£2) when it requested the company to stage *Richard II*. Monetary as well as patron pressure may well have played its role with Southampton's client.[57]

That client, nonetheless, would need to be very circumspect. The Master of the Revels, Edmund Tilney, or his deputy, in this case his kinsman George Buck, had to read and approve any script before it could be staged. Tilney and Buck were related to the Lord Admiral, and the Office of The Revels was under the jurisdiction of the Lord Chamberlain. Both the Lord Admiral and the Lord Chamberlain were related by marriage; both were allied to the Cecil faction; and both were enemies of Essex. Neither the Queen nor Essex's powerful enemies would tolerate an obvious paean to the Earl. The Queen's fury was notorious and the London City Council perpetually looked for any excuse to shut the theatres down. It would not take a clairvoyant to imagine the draconian measures the Privy Council did take with the acting company and the playwright over the affair of *The Isle of Dogs,* and its actions in 1599 when, believing that Sir John Hayward had seditious intent in the publishing of his *Life of Henry IV*, it confiscated and burned 1500 copies of the book and sent Hayward to the Tower. The actor-playwright Shakespeare could not risk personally, nor professionally, the ire of men who could deny him, and his partners, their means to make a living. Romantic allusions to the Queen and her most faithful and devoted suitors, however, might fly, especially, especially among the Inns of Court gallants who were part of the Essex-Southampton circle, and if those allusions fit the official propaganda of the 1590s—the Queen was caring, just, merciful, generous, virginal and beautiful.[58]

All those qualities fit Portia, and the plotline of Portia and her suitors seems an obvious romantic allusion to Elizabeth as Gloriana, and her suitors. Just as Whitehall, where Elizabeth held her court, was removed from the bustle of London, Belmont, a serene place where Portia holds court and dispenses favors, is a place removed from the bustle of Venice. Just as Elizabeth owed her throne to the provisions of the will of Henry VIII, Portia is given her position, and bound by its terms, by her father's will. Just as at various times Elizabeth was courted, among others, by Philip II of Spain, the Austrian Archdukes Ferdinand and Charles, the French prince the Duke of Alencon, the English Earl of Arundel, and the Scottish lord the Earl of Arran,[59] Portia is courted by a prince of *Aragon,* two *German* noblemen, a *French* lord, an *English* baron, and a *Scottish* lord. Though Elizabeth never was courted by a Prince of Morocco, as was Portia, it is an interesting coincidence that ships from *Moorish* Tripoli, allied with the English, fought at the battle of Cadiz, that Tinoco credited Elizabeth with his release from captivity in Morocco, and that Elizabeth was in some sort of contact with the Sultan of Morocco over the issue of Essex's capture of Alonzo Nuñez de Herrera.[60]

Regarding other important figures, a few vague hints to Court rivalries might be made. That may explain Portia's somewhat peculiar remark (I, 2) about "a hot temper leaps over a cold decree; such a hare is madness, the youth" skipping over "the meshes of good counsel, the cripple." One of Essex's heraldic devices displayed greyhounds and hares, and Robert Cecil, a hunchback, contemptuously in popular gossip, often was called "the cripple." That line might elicit a few chuckles but, beyond the vague parallel of Bassanio seeking his fortune by courting Portia, proving his steadfast love and devotion to her, petitioning her to come to the financial assistance of his friend Antonio, who was threatened with ruin and death by an evil Jew (as Essex actually did petition Elizabeth to favor Antonio Perez and to continue her subsidies to Don Antonio), one should not expect too obvious a parallel between the Earls of Essex and Southampton and the characters in *The Merchant of Venice*. Perhaps, after all, Bassanio's lines concerning "racking" forcing a man to admit to anything are allusions to Essex, but allusions any more obvious than that would not pass the censors. Yet, allusions to the machinations of a "vile Jew" could be used to bring to the audience's mind the Earl's brilliant success in "saving" the Queen's life a few short years ago. Aside from the Cadiz victory, Lopez's conviction for treason had been Essex's most recent and celebrated political success. Lopez's conviction had made him immensely popular with Londoners. By the next century the popular version of the story portrayed Elizabeth herself ordering Essex to begin his investigations. To the end of his life, Essex always sought that popular approval. His own contemporary, John Chamberlain observed, concerning Essex's demeanor at his trial: "a man might easilie perceive that as he had ever lived popularly, so his chiefe care was to leave a good opinion in the peoples mindes now at parting."[61]

But even the "vile Jew" must be handled delicately. Depersonalization would help. After his arrest, Lopez's name tended to be used less and less; he became "the Jew." Shylock also is addressed only 17 times in the play by name; most of the time he is called, or referred to, as "the Jew." Just as everybody in the play but Portia (perhaps) outwardly despised Shylock, everybody in London but the Queen outwardly despised Dr. Lopez. Whatever her reasons, the Queen had been remarkably reluctant to proceed against Lopez. Lord Burghley had drafted a speech for the Queen denouncing the plot; she never gave it. Londoners eagerly awaited the execution; the Queen ordered the Lieutenant of the Tower not to release Lopez for execution. Londoners, who were aware that Elizabeth had wanted an execution more brutal than hanging and disemboweling for Babington and his fellow conspirators against her life (1587),[62] must have been bewildered at the three-month delay in Lopez's execution. There even seems to have been a rumor that in mid March when the Queen fell ill, she had brought the convicted poisoner out of the Tower to treat her.[63] If, on the other hand, Portia (= Gloriana) could be shown to be determined to save Shylock (= Lopez), until he condemned himself by his own mouth, if all allusions to everyone and everything could be made ambiguous enough to pass the censor, anger no one who mattered and flatter anyone who did, then

Southampton's request could be granted. The Chamberlain's Men could present a wonderfully comic and romantic fairytale which just happened to evoke images of real events and real people on a visceral level *if* the audiences thought about it. Many scholars believe that is just what Shakespeare was doing in *Love's Labour's Lost*, using "a technique of hints and half-light" to present allusions to Lord Strange, Sir Walter Raleigh, and others of that circle, "not as straight portraits, however, but as general likenesses."[64]

It may be that here we see at least one instance which answers a perplexing question concerning the Elizabethan theatre. What did the patrons of the acting companies receive in exchange for the occasional use of the Lord's money, name, protection or acts of favoritism? We know Lords expected something from clients. Shakespeare's company received allotments of cloth to make new liveries to march in the funeral parade for Queen Elizabeth as part of the Lord Chamberlain's retinue and later another allotment of cloth from King James to march as his servants in his triumphal procession into London. Shakespeare's sonnets allude to carrying the canopy for a lord in parades. Yet his sonnets and the dedications to *Venus and Adonis* and *Rape of Lucrece*, also often speak of somewhat more intangible duty and obligation due to Southampton, and the Lord Admiral's letters to various of his clients often contained phrases like "once againe myndinge yow to be carefull of my buyssines." Clues to how his acting company was "myndinge" his "buyssines" are precious few, save we know that Henslowe built a special room in his theatre for the Lord Admiral, and lent money to his servants. On one of the Queen's visits to his country estate, the Lord Admiral once summoned his company there to entertain her. No payment for the performance is recorded.[65]

The Lord Admiral's Men were noted for presenting plays which reflected the conservative values of their patron like *Sir John Oldcastle*, which in 1599, with its confirmation of concepts of duty and obedience and protestant martyrdom correspond to values his faction at Court wished to stress at a time when there were fears of Catholic conspiracy, Spanish invasion, and the machinations of the Essex faction. It is likely that Shakespeare already had shaped aspects of *Romeo and Juliet* to gain public sympathy for the young Earl of Southamton and his two cronies Sirs Charles and Henry Danvers. Perhaps, too, *The Merchant of Venice* was something of the same—a piece of political propaganda designed to remind Londoners of the virtues of the Earl of Southampton and the triumphs of the Earl of Essex but cleverly disguised to slip by Shakespeare's censors, just as in our century Anouilh's *Antigone* reminded Frenchmen of their struggle against the Vichy regime and Giraudoux's *The Mad Woman of Chaillot* was cleverly designed to slip by the Nazi censors in occupied Paris.[66]

The Merchant of Venice often has been considered a so-called "problem play,"[67] in which the relationship between the two plots seems unclear, and its major theme (or themes) rather vague. It has been interpreted as a play displaying notions of Aristotelian justice; it has been interpreted as a play about social bonds; it has interpreted as a play about friendship or cultural differences. Perhaps it is all of these. It certainly is *not* a veiled condemnation of anti-Semitism, as it romantically was viewed in the eighteenth and nineteenth century, and the "tragic" Shylock first portrayed in 1741 by Charles Macklin was not, as Alexander Pope observed, "This is the Jew/That Shakespear drew."[68]

Though admittedly owing something to Marlowe's *Jew of Malta*, the time of *The Merchant of Venice's* composition comes too late for Shakespeare to have been cashing in on that play's popularity. *Jew of Malta's* heyday was in 1591-93 with a revival in 1594 paralleling the London citizens' interest in the Dr. Lopez incident. From late 1594 to 1597 Henslowe's records show that it was presented only four times. It is curious that at a time when the "vile Jew" has lost the interest of Henslowe's audiences, Shakespeare not only wrote a play around such a character but created a character far more "real" than Marlowe's Barabbas. The character of Shylock, which displays that individualization and seeming human reality we associate with Shakespeare's characters, perhaps is not entirely due to Shakespeare's genius at writing idiomatic speech patterns but to the fact that he reproduced and burlesqued on stage a model from real life—Dr. Roger Lopez, who along with the Cadiz expedition was Essex's other claim to popularity and fame with the London populace.

Shylock's speech patterns have been described as terse and unornamented. If the four letters we possess written by Dr. Lopez are any indication, Dr. Lopez's speech patterns were also terse and his language of preference was Italian just as Shylock was a resident of Italian Venice. Perhaps it was not Richard Burbage who, as tradition has it, first played Lopez, donned a doctor's robe, and made himself up to look like the ill-fated doctor, but it may well have been Heminges, or Condell or one of the other partners.[69] When Ann Barton, in her introduction to *The Merchant of Venice* wrote of the character of Shylock as "a closely observed human being,"[70] she may have hit closer to the mark than ever she suspected.

Shakespeare played safe when it came to controversy; even episodes of elicit love affairs rarely find their way into his scripts though his sources provided that information. In *Shrew*, for example, Bianca and Lucentio are "pure" lovers; in Gascoigne's *Supposes*, the source for the Bianca plot, Bianca's counterpart becomes pregnant before the lovers are married.[71] Plays like *Love's Labour's Lost, Romeo and Juliet,* and *The Merchant of Venice* did contain material shaped to give favorable airing to the image and interests of his personal patrons, but never did Shakespeare seem to produce clear and biting attacks upon political figures of his time. Ben Jonson, on the other hand, began his playwriting career with a play so blatant in its target that the Elizabethan authorities made sure that even the playscript did not survive. The tale of that play demands reenactment.

Chapter 7

Ben Jonson's *The Isle of Dogs*:
Politics and Playwriting in Elizabethan England

In July, 1597, the newly reconstituted Pembroke's Men, performing in the newly renovated Swan Theatre, performed a new play, *The Isle of Dogs*, by Thomas Nashe and a new playwright, Ben Jonson, in hopes of attracting attention to this new theatre. Attract attention they did, but not the pennies at the door they had hoped. Instead they may well have attracted the attention of the Privy Council. On 28 July it issued an order which shut down not only the Swan, but the two other theatres in London, and threatened to pull down every theatre building in the London area. A few days later it jailed the playwright Ben Jonson, and two of the principal actors, Robert Shaa and Gabriel Spencer, and hunted down and destroyed every copy of the script.[1] Public theatre had aroused official displeasure before this, and would again afterwards, but never before nor after, would official reaction be so violent and sweeping. Cautious scholars warn that the *The Isle of Dogs* and the Privy Council order may not be related, yet Henslowe seems to have recognized such a relationship in early August, and the *Isle of Dogs* affair remained a topic of popular gossip for years afterwards, frequently alluded to over the years by authors who wished to sting Ben Jonson.[2]

Several questions are raised by this incident. First, why would Francis Langley the new theatrical entrepreneur, and the newcomer company the Pembroke's Men, risk so much by performing this play? Despite Marchette Chute's assumption that its contents "would probably seem harmless enough to a modern reader,"[3] the company at the Swan must have realized it was flirting with a play which might (as it proved) be construed as "full of seditious and slanderous matter." Second, given the strict censorship of plays, pamphlets, even portraits in Elizabethan London, why did the Master of the Revels even allow the play to reach the stage? In another case, at about the same time, the then Master, Edmund

Tilney, was so scrupulous about revision of politically "dangerous" scenes in *Thomas More* that the writers seem to have abandoned the effort.[4] Third, what, or who, was the primary target of the play's satire? Finally, what, in general, was the probable form of the play, and what were some of the probable character-types, incidents, and scenes?

"Newness" is a key to many of these questions, and clearly provides an answer to the first—why take the risk? The answer is simple, and the answer is money. The financial success of Philip Henslowe, theatre owner, and his resident company the Admiral's Men, and of James Burbage, theatre owner and his resident company the Chamberlain's Men, was evident by 1595 when Francis Langley began a new, third theatre. At least 15,000 people attended the two established theatres weekly. Daily receipts per theatre averaged between £8.5 and £10, sums equal to seven to ten months' labor to an Elizabethan artisan; combined weekly receipts for both theatres reached perhaps £120—a sum equal to eight years' labor to the artisan, and about one-third the annual income of the Gentry.[5]

Francis Langley, goldsmith, wished to cash in on this new market in emulation of James Burbage, carpenter, and Philip Henslowe, dyer, who had already proven its potential. The tradesman origins of these theatrical investors is not to be underestimated. Burbage's son Cuthbert readily admitted that his father left carpentering to make money. Court depositions concerning disputes between Burbage and the heirs of James Brayne, his brother-in-law and "silent" partner in funding construction of the Theatre attest to the fact that Burbage was worth little money until after the Theatre began operations; neither Henslowe nor Langley even underwent the apprenticeship in theatre that Burbage had served as an actor in Leicester's Men. Avarice, not art, drove these men. Langley often was called a greedy man. They were not aristocratic patrons providing condescending sums to support amusing and artistic clients. Nor were they viewing theatre as a subsidiary business. It was expected to yield substantial returns on their not insubstantial investments. Burbage and Henslowe laid out an average of £650 (over 43 years' labor to an artisan) to erect theatre buildings to house already established acting companies.[6] Langley, faced with building a theatre and startup funds for a new company, needed to lay out even more.

Just to begin a new, third theatre involved substantial up-front investment. Permission from court to open a theatre must have required

Fig. 20. De Witt sketch of The Swan.

a "gift" or two placed in the right hands. Langley had connections at Court—his brother-in-law Sir Anthony Astley, a clerk of the Privy Council, and Astley's kinswoman Katherine Astley, a Gentlewoman of the Privy Chamber. Langley himself held a Court sinecure as Alnager and Searcher of Cloth.[7] How much actual money in "gifts" Langley dispersed is not known, but even though Elizabeth's Court was not quite as venal as that of her successor James I, favors and influence rarely came free. Lord Burghley, Robert Cecil, the Lord Admiral, and other influential members of the Court, regularly received "gratuities," and annual New Year's gifts, from clients, and prospective clients, all to secure their influence and continued good will. Henslowe lent money to servants of the Lords Chamberlain and Admiral, and the Master of the Revels; Heminges and Beeston regularly gave special gifts to the Master of the Revels. Based on other people's "gifts" we do know about, Langley must have invested a minimum of £100 or more distributed among those whose permission was vital to his undertaking.[8]

That sum is a pittance compared to amounts spent to open the new Swan. In February 1594 Langley mortgaged all his properties in Cheapside as collateral for a loan of £1,650, much of which must have gone into the purchase and renovation of Paris Garden, an old manor complex containing what would become the Swan. Langley spent at least £850 to purchase the property, which included gaming places, and the bearbaiting arena he converted into the Swan Theatre. His costs to convert the arena to a theatre must have at least equalled those of converting the Bear Garden into a theatre in 1616, which was £320. Probably his costs were in the neighborhood of £400 or more; contemporary accounts indicate the Swan was the most lavishly decorated of the existing theatres.

Other costs arose later. Perhaps Langley opened in the summer of 1595 with a third theatre company headed by George Attewell, but if so, that company does not seem to have put much of a dent into attendance at the other theatres; Henslowe's records show little drop in revenues. Perhaps in the Autumn of 1596, Shakespeare's company played the Swan, a period of time in which the company and James Burbage were arguing with Giles Allen over the land lease to The Theatre, and the company had lost its patron on the Privy Council with the death of Henry Carey, Lord Chamberlain. Henslowe's records do show a greater dip in that period, but by the Christmas Season of 1596-97, Lord

Hunsdon's Men (George Carey, second Lord Hunsdon, had taken over patronage of his father's acting troupe) was playing at Court and afterwards seem to have moved to the Curtain.

Langley, therefore, needed a permanent acting company at the Swan in 1597. To lure actors away from existing companies, he offered advances which probably totaled £150—£30 each to William Bird, Thomas Downton, Robert Shaa, Gabriel Spencer and Richard Jones, and required each to post a bond with him to the effect they would play only at the Swan for a year. It appears that he and this group of actors may have sought to reconstitute the Earl of Pembroke's Men. Richard Jones and Thomas Downton seem to have come over from the Admiral's Men, the former affiliations of Robert Shaa, William Bird and Gabriel Spencer are unknown. Perhaps they had retained affiliation with the old Pembroke's Men but there is no record of that company's activities after 1593. Perhaps they came over from Shakespeare's company. All of them had been affiliated with Strange's Men, many of whom ended up in the Chamberlain's Men after its formation in 1594; and, coincidentally, the pirating of three plays out of the Chamberlain's Men repertory, *Richard III, Romeo and Juliet*, and *Love's Labour's Lost* also coincide with the reappearance of a Pembroke's Men in London in 1597.

At any rate, the old Pembroke's Men, a troupe to which Shakespeare may have been attached, had gone broke in 1593, selling off its store of costumes, properties, and playbooks. To provide those necessities in 1596-97 Langley, so litigation tells us, spent at least £300, a cost not out of line when it is remembered he had to compete with the lavish costumes, like velvet gowns and gilt crowns and properties, like gilt chariots and thrones in the heavens of the already established theatres. By the first quarter of 1597, therefore, Langley's Swan had cost him at least £1800 (£100 "gifts," + £300 costumes and props, + £150 actor advances, + £850 Paris Garden, + £400 conversion of the bear pit), sums equivalent to 120 years' wages to an artisan. By July 1597 we must add perhaps another £1000—£100 per year for maintenance of the property and the streets around it and £900 in production costs to cover playwright's fees, licensing fees, salaries of musicians and hired men, and other miscellaneous costs.[9] Hence, by the first performance of *The Isle of Dogs*, Langley had invested at least £2800 on his theatre, double the average income of an Elizabethan knight and 186 years' wages to an artisan.

By 1597, the annual receipts for the two already established theatres (Admiral's Men at the Rose and Chamberlain's Men at the Theatre) totaled about £5500.[10] If Langley's Swan attracted one-third of the London audience, the Swan company could expect gross receipts of approximately £1833. Given that possibility, Langley would have been £967 *in the red* after his first year of operation.

His losses may have been worse. Henslowe's *Diary* shows average daily receipts of £8.5 to £10. Once can assume a similar average for the Chamberlain's Men, for a total of £17 to £20 brought in by both companies. If the Swan did draw one-third of the daily audience, each of the three theatres should average £5.7 to £6.7. Henslowe's records indicate a tiny decline in average daily receipts during the summer of 1595 when the Swan may have begun operations, but the decline was to a level of £7.5, a loss of less than £1.[11] One must assume that the Chamberlain's Men suffered no greater decline.

Perhaps Langley's receipts went up, if, as suspected by some scholars, Shakespeare's company played the Swan in the Autumn of 1596, but by February 1597 they no longer did. Thus Langley's daily take at the Swan in 1597 may have been as low as £2, only 12 percent instead of 33 percent of total London theatre receipts. If Langley was averaging only 12 percent of the theatre attendance, his annual return sinks to £660 and his loss grows to £1140.

Needless to say, the companies at the Rose and the Theatre must have intensified their efforts in order to minimize the impact of the new competition. Glimmerings of just such efforts emerge. Henslowe's *Diary* indicates a record number 34 new plays introduced between August 1596 and July 1597. Other plays staged were old favorites, such as Marlowe's *Tamburlaine*, *The Jew of Malta*, *Doctor Faustus* and the old work horse *Spanish Tragedy* by Kyd with London super-star Edward Alleyn in the starring roles. Other offerings such as *Nebuchadnezzer* and *Vortegern* (which cost over £10.5 to stage as against £8 in income), indicate emphasis on lavish spectacles—*Tamburlaine*, for instance, included a scene in which defeated kings pulled Tamburlaine in a gilded chariot across the stage, and *Doctor Faustus* is full of special effects using traps, Hellmouths and devils. Unfortunately we have no such details for the Chamberlain's Men, but Shakespeare, already becoming London's most popular playwright, produced four plays that season up two from his usual average.[12]

One other factor affecting theatre attendance was the disposable income of the tradesman classes. Records of prices and wages indicate that necessities—first food at 80 percent, then lodging at eight to ten percent—accounted for 88 to 90 percent of the income of most urban, Elizabethan wage earners, leaving only 10 to 12 percent available for clothes, luxuries such as entertainment, or for emergency expenses. In the best of times that translates into an average of £1.5 per year or seven pence per week. Over two-thirds of an average Elizabethan audience paid the extra one or two pence per person to sit in the galleries. Hence most people probably attended only *one* theatre *once* a week, when times were good. Times were not good in 1596-97. Three years of poor harvests had produced famine prices for food. The authorities feared food riots might erupt. In 1597, the government enacted a "Poor Law" to address the problem of starving people. Therefore, that disposable income of seven pence per week must have declined drastically. The theatres not only had to contend with one another, but with what must have been a shrinking audience.

Langley and the company at the Swan needed to fight, and to fight hard, to capture a share in the market large enough to make a profit. Recycled old plays would not do nor would standard theatre fare. Why would audiences leave performances of new plays such as Chapman's *Humorous Day's Mirth* or Shakespeare's *Midsummer Night's Dream* just to see yet another version of something like *Spanish Tragedy* done by the third-ranked new company? *Hardicanute*, the history play in the Pembroke's repertory, would seem to offer small challenge to the Admiral's *Uther Pendragon* or its *Life and Death of Henry I*, or to the Chamberlain's *1 Henry IV*.[13] Langley's Pembroke's Men needed a novelty, a bombshell, to stir up interest among London playgoers. Current politics, complaints about prices and taxes, gossip and rumors about powerful lords, and about Court intrigue, were favorite topics of conversation. A play which touched on all of these would be a probable hit. In view of the need for potential profits, "seditious and slanderous matter" would be worth the risk.

Yet, while Langley and his company might be willing to risk staging "seditious and slanderous matter," it was the responsibility of the Master of the Revels to prevent such plays. Under Edmund Tilney censorship had expanded greatly. By the 1590s he not only had the authority to license plays but also acting companies and playhouses as well. Tilney, or his deputy, was to read each play before staging and was empowered to imprison (duration at his pleasure) anyone staging a play over his objections. Tilney's commission as Master of the Revels specified his right to license or "put down" anything he believed "meet or unmeet unto himself or his said deputy in that behalf." Tilney himself vowed to purge plays of "all profaneness, oaths, ribaldry, and matters reflecting upon piety and the present government." His objections to parts of the play *Thomas More* probably caused the playwrights to abandon the project, and he insisted that the scene depicting the abdication and death of Richard II be excised from performances and printed versions of Shakespeare's play.[14] How, then, did *The Isle of Dogs* elude his watchful eye? In answering that question, we may be able to discern the play's probable target, and the probable sources of the so-called "seditious and slanderous matter" by threading our way through the complexities and intrigues of Elizabeth's Court.

As Master of the Revels, Tilney's post fell under the supervision of the Lord Chamberlain. In 1596-97 there were three who held the office. Henry Carey, first Lord Hunsdon, died in 1596. He was succeeded by William, Lord Cobham. After Cobham's death (March 1597), the second Lord Hunsdon, George Carey, assumed the office of Lord Chamberlain. Under the Lord Chamberlain's jurisdiction also were the Ladies and Gentlemen of the Privy Chamber who included Ladies Katherine Howard (daughter of Henry Carey and wife of the Lord Admiral Charles Howard), Lady Frances Cobham (wife of William Cobham, Lord Chamberlain 1596 to March 1597), and Katherine Astley, kin to Anthony Astley, clerk of the Privy Council who was brother-in-law of Francis Langley.

Edmund Tilney's kinsman, Sir George Buck, may have become Deputy Master of Revels in 1597. Buck, who had served under the Lord Admiral in the Cadiz expedition (1596), continued to serve the Lord Admiral as a courier. Both Buck and Tilney were distant cousins of Lord Howard as well as faithful supporters. Katherine Astley, as Gentlewoman of the Privy Chamber, also served Robert Cecil in his capacity as Privy Purse Treasurer. Lady Cobham, before and after her husband's death, was a supporter of Robert Cecil and his father Lord Burghley; her daughter, after all, was married to Robert Cecil. Another firm supporter of Robert and William Cecil was John Herbert, Secretary to the Privy Council, kin to Henry Herbert, Earl of Pembroke, who was patron of Francis Langley's theatre company.[15]

When all this is tied together we find that Langley's links to the Court, the Pembroke's Men's links to the Court (as well as the Admiral's and Chamberlain's companies'), and the playscript's links to Court, through the Master of the Revels and his Deputy, all lead back to people united through kinships and common purposes: Robert Cecil, Lord Admiral Charles Howard, the Lords Chamberlain Cobham and the Careys, and the Earl of Pembroke, who was squabbling with Essex over disputed estates in Wales, and with his own wife Mary Sidney, who was tied into the Essex circle. All of these Lords of the Privy Council were bitter enemies of, and political rivals of, Robert Devereaux, the Earl of Essex; all were men Essex repeatedly sought to humiliate and destroy; all, save Cobham (d. 1597) and Pembroke (d. 1601), ultimately united to destroy Essex.[16] The diagram below may help to sort out this complicated web.

Other "actors" in the saga of *The Isle of Dogs* are linked to Essex enemies, especially to Robert Cecil. Anthony Astley had been sent by Cecil to keep watch over Essex on the Cadiz expedition of 1596. He had fallen from favor with Cecil over his involvement with a purloined diamond, part of the loot captured off a Portuguese ship in 1592. His brother-in-law, Langley, was implicated too and Astley blamed Langley for his fall from favor and temporary imprisonment in the Fleet. Another

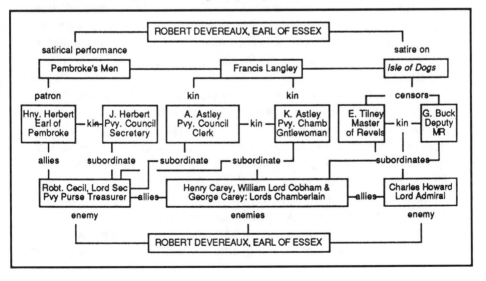

reason for Astley's temporary incarceration had been accusations levelled against him by Gelly Merrick, Essex's steward. Richard Topcliffe, who himself arrested, and who was named the chief inquisitor of, the offending playwright Jonson, and the actors Spencer and Shaa, was an agent of both Cecils, and at least once reported directly to Robert Cecil concerning the play and "our purposes." One of Topcliffe's deputies was Anthony Munday, sometime playwright for the Admiral's Men, whose "producer," Philip Henslowe, as Groom of the Privy Chamber, also had connections to the Cecils and the Lord Chamberlain. Closing the circle even tighter are other fascinating coincidences. Robert Cecil in 1588 was a member of the peace negotiation team sent to the Netherlands, headed by the Earl of Derby, Lord Strange. At that time, too, George Bryan and Will Kempe (in 1597 of the Chamberlain's Men), and Thomas Downton (in 1597 of the new Pembroke's Men) were all on the Continent, and may have sought Lord Strange's patronage. All are found as members of Lord Strange's Men less than a year later. Thomas Nashe, the senior playwright of *The Isle of Dogs*, who was conveniently absent from London when the Privy Council struck, just happened to have been a contemporary of Robert Cecil at Cambridge University. Ben Jonson, the junior playwright, later served as Robert Cecil's agent in investigations of the Gunpowder Plot (1604), and, when seeking release from prison after the scandal of *Eastward Ho*, wrote first to Cecil, reminding him of their longstanding relationship.[17]

The incident of *The Isle of Dogs* coincides with a period of time (1596-97) when the factional rivalry between Essex and his enemies had surfaced dramatically. Essex and Lord Admiral Howard were squabbling publicly over credit (and blame) for the Cadiz expedition in which they had shared command. Essex still fumed about defeats he had suffered (1594) when his candidate for Attorney General, Francis Bacon, lost out to a client of the Cecils, and again (1595) when Bacon was passed over in favor of another Cecil man for Solicitor General. He had returned from the Cadiz expedition to learn another of his clients had been denied appointment to the Secretaryship of State. Elizabeth had waited till he sailed, and appointed Robert Cecil. Cecil was beginning a policy of seeking peace with Spain, a policy the bellicose Essex opposed. Early in 1597 there was an appearance that Essex and Cecil had pasted over their differences, but by summer they were maneuvering to place their own candidates in Parliament in the up-coming elections. The competition was so blatant that Elizabeth herself intervened, insisting that local men be elected in order to thwart both men's attempts to pack the Parliament with their respective supporters. Though Essex remained popular with the London citizens, Cecil's maneuverings at Court were becoming so successful that courtiers seeking favors began to avoid Essex's endorsements. Francis Bacon began to distance himself from the Earl, and Sir Thomas Bodley felt constrained to quit Court for Oxford University because Essex's favor angered the Queen rather than brought advancement. The bitterness of the struggle was evident to courtiers, who warned favor-seekers "the factions never were more malicious." The French Ambassador reported on the vicious factional strife.[18]

Against the backdrop of the intense battling between the Cecil-Howard-Carey alliance and the Essex faction in 1596-97, such a convergence of clients of Essex's enemies in the affair of *The Isle of Dogs* seems a coincidence bordering on the contrived. Tilney, and perhaps also Buck (who, as a client of the Lord Admiral, had no reason to love Essex after the Cadiz expedition), may have failed to censor *The Isle of Dogs* because Essex was the butt of the "seditious and slanderous matter, and either they themselves wished to embarrass the Earl before his one source of support, the London populace, or they were told to do so by their superiors, the Lords Admiral, Chamberlain and Lord Secretary Robert Cecil.

Further, the links between members of the Court who were clients of Cecil, Cobham, Carey, and Pembroke and Langley's acting company, probably explain the sources of sensitive and embarrassing information concerning Essex. The careful circulation of Court gossip and rumor to undermine enemies was a tactic used by William and Robert Cecil. Essex and his supporters used it also, though, except perhaps in the case of Dr. Lopez, never with the discretion and impact of the Cecils. That Essex and his supporters seem to have believed the theatre could be used to influence popular opinion is demonstrated by the staging of Richard II, with the abdication scene, the day before Essex's attempted coup d'etat in 1601, and Essex himself, when under house arrest, complained he would be parodied on the stage. In short, perhaps the incident of *The Isle of Dogs* was the Elizabethan equivalent of selected "news leaks" for the purposes of "media manipulation." The Privy Council, under Cecil's leadership at the time, seems to have let the play continue until "officially" informed of the "slanders." The diarist John

Manningham wrote that Cecil always worked through "the hand of some other, on whom, if it fall out otherwise than was suggested or expected, the blame may be translated;" Astley, for instance, never received any written instructions concerning his role on the Cadiz expedition, and Ben Jonson himself later said that Robert Cecil "never cared for any man longer nor he could make use of him."[19] Perhaps, then, Langley and the Pembroke's Men may have been "set-up," though their own need and greed probably made them willing partners.

It is easy to see how such a "set-up" could come about. Langley's own relationship to the Astleys, both privy to goings-on at Court, would give him access to Court gossip. Beyond this, courtiers often frequented taverns, such as the famous Mermaid, where they talked more-or-less freely and began many a rumor. The illustrious Sir Walter Raleigh himself frequented the Mermaid, and Raleigh, another bitter enemy of Essex, was allied with Cecil and Howard—until, that is, Essex was beheaded. Henslowe's accounts, the writings of Ben Jonson and Francis Beaumont, all make it clear that taverns like the Mermaid also were favorite gathering places for the theatre companies—places where new plays were read and discussed, battles-of-wit were frequent, and exchanges of information occurred. How simple it would be for Anthony Astley to join his brother-in-law Francis Langley, and Langley's actor business associates over dinner or wine and relate, "in confidence," the latest Court gossip about the popular Earl of Essex. He had no love for Langley, whom he blamed for his disgrace over the diamond episode; he was begging Cecil for a chance to get back into favor, and it seems that Cecil was lying-in-wait for a chance to undermine Langley.[20] Raleigh could easily (and maliciously) drop a few remarks about Essex during one of his visits to a tavern; Anthony Munday, agent of Robert Cecil but also fellow playwright, could chuckle with his colleague Thomas Nashe about indiscretions at Court; and even Buck and Tilney, obviously on close working terms with the acting companies, could hint at a sympathetic reading of a satire play on Essex.

The newness of the Langley company looms large here too. The same gossip would be circulated to the members of the Admiral's and Chamberlain's Men, many of whom had ties with Pembroke's actors. These companies were established firmly, but the Admiral's Men were noted for their reflection of their patron's conservative attitudes, and George Carey's appointment to the office of Lord Chamberlain and the

Privy Council was very recent. Shakespeare himself seems to have had some connection to the Essex circle. His personal patron, the Earl of Southampton, was a firm supporter of Essex. The two established companies' success to that point, and afterwards, was based on their cautious conservatism regarding controversial topics. Henslowe's company would not rise to the bait, nor would Shakespeare's, nor, perhaps, would their legal patrons the Lords Admiral and Chamberlain wish them to do so. Hence the Admiral's Men and the Chamberlain's Men may have seen the need for political circumspection in their performances. But Langley's company, hungering for a larger share in the London audience, would snap at material for a possible "hit" show.

Events subsequent to the performance of this play full of "seditious and slanderous matter" suggest Essex as its target. The "over-kill" displayed by the Privy Council's actions reflect the usual hyperbole of Essex's words and deeds. After the attempted Essex coup d'etat in 1601, when it was known that members of the Essex faction had paid Shakespeare's company to stage a play about the deposition of a monarch (Richard II), the Chamberlain's Men merely were questioned for a seeming involvement in a far more sinister incident than *The Isle of Dogs* matter, but here Robert Cecil was in charge. Essex, however, always struck out at his rival's clients, just as the theatres of his rivals' client acting companies were closed along with the offending theatre. The insistence upon using Topcliffe, the Council's most vigorous inquisitor, the planting of informers in Jonson's cell, the search of Nashe's lodgings for incriminating papers, all suggest the actions of someone determined and desperate to uncover something damning about someone highly placed. These efforts most resemble Essex's handling of the Lopez incident in 1594, when he was determined to prove something incriminating about the unfortunate doctor. After all, the offending theatre had been closed, the offending scripts had been hunted down and destroyed—what need to question the playwright and actors so closely? Essex's, not Cecil's, influence at court was waning; he desperately needed to undermine the Cecil-Howard-Carey alliance.

After all this sound and fury, the aftermath of the affair was surprisingly mild. Neither Tilney, the Master of the Revels, nor his Deputy, George Buck, lost their places at Court. Yet later, in 1599, when Privy Council Lords believed John Haywood's *Life of Henry IV* was seditious material favoring Essex, they not only jailed the author, but interrogated Samuel Harsnet, the censor who had allowed the book's printing.[21] Topcliffe seems to have uncovered no plot in this case. Topcliffe, who seemingly could force most of the subjects of interrogation to admit almost anything, got no answers from this affair. Jonson later affirmed his judges could "get nothing from him to all their demands but I [aye] and No." Topcliffe kept a torture chamber in his own house to interrogate Jesuits, but he does not seem to have employed his usual brutality in this affair. Jonson never complained of torture, or any ill treatment, and also noted that he had been "advertised by his keeper" about the two informants placed in his cell. Francis Langley was not allowed to re-license the Swan as a theatre, but may have continued performances there until his venture petered out early in 1598. He lost his lawsuits against the players who jumped to Henslowe's Rose, but, though he suffered financial loss, he otherwise was left unscathed, and even attempted a new investment in the Boar's Head Theatre. Finally, Jonson, Shaa and Spencer were quietly released from prison, and the Admiral's and Chamberlain's Men quietly reopened their theatres in London in October, about one week after the Earl of Essex set sail on an expedition to the Azores. Many a time in the relationship of Essex to Elizabeth, the Queen, for whatever her reasons, allowed him his head, tolerated his excess actions, pampered his vanity, and then quietly undid his actions when he was absent from Court.[22]

Within that context of behavior *Isle of Dogs* affair seems but one further example of Elizabeth's indulgence of Essex's vanity. When he opposed Cecil's appointment as Secretary of State she let him bluster, and then appointed Cecil when Essex was absent; when he fumed about the Lord Admiral's role in the Cadiz expedition, she let him fume, and then rewarded Lord Howard with the earldom of Nottingham when Essex was absent; in like manner with *The Isle of Dogs* there was a flurry of seeming furious reprisal—the playwright and principal actors were jailed, the scripts destroyed, the theatres closed—and then the playwright and actors were released, and the theatres reopened, when Essex was absent.

Material for satire abounded in the England of the late 1590s, and much of it one way or another touched upon matters related to the Earl of Essex. Men claiming to be his agents extorted money by detaining citizens in his name. Essex, at various times, and for somewhat trivial reasons, had challenged Sir Walter Blount, Sir Walter Raleigh, Lord

Howard or any of his supporters to duels because of purported insults to his dignity. Scandal rocked the military, Essex's claim to fame. On the Netherlands campaigns, in which Ben Jonson had served, suppliers and officers shorted food and clothing, privately sold supplies meant for the army, furnished men in the field with shoddy and defective clothing and arms. Some commanders pocketed salaries sent to dead soldiers, and intentionally sent poorly armed and poorly clad men into battle under-strength to increase casualties so as to increase their graft. Coincident with Jonson's tour in the Netherlands, had been the comic-opera interlude of Essex's expedition to Normandy. Essex had left his well-equipped, large force to gallop off to visit King Henry IV of France. Then, finding his way back to his army blocked by Spanish forces, had called out the entire force to extricate him. He later sailed home achieving nothing. Essex's and Howard's expedition to Cadiz, still fresh in people's minds, was spectacular, but in-fighting among the commanders, and desires for personal glory had resulted in losing the main prize to be had, the Spanish merchant fleet. Essex, fearing that Lord Howard would capture the city without him, allowed the merchant fleet to escape while he landed his troops to rush to the attack of Cadiz. Profiteering on that expedition was rife; Langley's brother-in-law at Court, Anthony Astley, fell under a cloud at Court, and was jailed concerning some valuables that may have been part of the booty meant for the Queen, but purloined by members of the expedition. He was denounced by Essex's steward, and counter-charged that the Essex people had pilfered much from the loot of Cadiz. Back home, Essex quarreled with Lord Howard, insisting that he, Essex, should have credit for all the successes, and that Lord Howard should be blamed for all the failures.

Most of this was common gossip, and coincidentally, a mid-level courtier connected with *The Isle of Dogs*, Sir George Buck, Deputy Master of Revels, also had served under the Lord Admiral's command during the Cadiz expedition. In July 1597, before *The Isle of Dogs* opened, Essex faced another blow to his ego. He had sailed forth to attack the Spanish with flags waving and his usual grandiose promises, only to have his fleet dispersed by storms, and limp piece-meal back to port. Of course, continuous gossip circulated about Essex's tantrums, pouts, and intentional absences from Court, and the back-biting (and stabbing) polarization in the Privy Council.[23] No doubt, then, much of the "seditious and slanderous" matter of the play *The Isle of Dogs* incorporated thinly veiled allusions to these matters, and to Essex's behavior towards his enemies and the Queen.

Again we return to the newness of the company. Most playwrights already were employed by established companies. Chapman, Heywood, Dekker, Chettle, Marston, Munday, were all writing for the Admiral's Men; some also for the Chamberlain's Men. One of the few writers of reputation available to Pembroke's Men was Thomas Nashe. Nashe, one of the so-called "university wits," was noted for his controversial, biting satire, his irreverence for rank and position, but to date had written only one play, and had collaborated on Marlowe's *Dido, Queen of Corinth* for the first Blackfriars Company. To aid Nashe, Langley seems to have used a new man attached to the company, Ben Jonson. Jonson, new to the theatre, seeking to make a living for his family, also burned to make a reputation for himself in literary and theatrical circles.

Neither of these writers, then, had much experience with playwriting; neither had learned the caution of playwrights functioning within established companies. Nashe may have provided the overall idea and begun the project, but Jonson seems to have scripted most of the play. Nashe later claimed that the play was turned "from a commodie to a tragedie," and that his part in writing *The Isle of Dogs* was confined only to "the induction and first act of it, the other four acts without my consent, or the least guesse of my drift or scope, by the players were supplied." No doubt this was a self-serving claim, but it was a claim that Jonson never denied. Contemporary playwrights, when excoriating Jonson, always attributed authorship of *The Isle of Dogs* to him.[24]

What would these two plot out? Satirizing Essex and the Court would need some circumspection. Langley and the Pembroke's Men might take risks, but they hardly were fools. Lacking a surviving copy of the script, one can only speculate, but Nashe's and Jonson's educational backgrounds and pretensions may well give us clues. Both were well grounded in Latin and Greek classical authors. Nashe had been educated at Cambridge, and Jonson had been educated at Westminster School under William Camden. Later, Camden and Jonson complemented each other's learning. Both schools were among the few which taught Greek. Both schools were dominated by scholars descended from the Colet/More/Erasmus circle. Indeed, Erasmus taught Greek at Cambridge from 1511 to 1514, and Jonson's friend and mentor, Camden, held Erasmus in great esteem.

Fig. 21. Thomas Nashe.

Fig. 22. Ben Jonson.

Erasmus, the most influential figure in Greek studies in northern Europe, stressed that the study of Greek poetry should begin with interesting and lively material: to wit, the plays of Aristophanes. Camden, Jonson's mentor, stressed the study of Greek poetry, and probably instilled Jonson with his love of it. Jonson later claimed himself "better versed in Greek and Latin, than all the poets in England." Drummond, chronicler of Jonson's remarks, said of him: "He excelleth in a translation." Nashe and Jonson made allusions to Aristophanes' plays in their writings, Jonson in at least seven of his later plays and masques.[25] Both Nashe and Jonson were familiar with the plays of Aristophanes, were aware of the thinly disguised social satire in them, and imbued with Humanist notions of intellectual and moral lessons to be found in Latin and Greek classics.

Aristophanes had another appeal. His works had not been translated into English. Few, even among the educated, knew Greek well; his works certainly would be unknown to the public. Nashe and Jonson had low esteem for the intelligence of the average playgoer, and so may have thought that they could use Aristophanes' approach, and probably direct translations of his lines as well, to disguise their satire. Jonson's play, *The Case is Altered*, borrowed heavily from untranslated plays by Plautus. Drummond's remarks concerning Jonson's abilities as a translator must be remembered, as well as Jonson's own pedantry. To accusations by critics that he was a "plund'rer" of classic writers, Jonson responded that his everlasting desire was to produce English plays, modeled on classical forms, to "instruct" the masses. To prove his classical historicity and accuracy, Jonson insisted upon listing every one of the classical sources he had quoted, used, or consulted, in the printed version of *Sejanus*.[26]

Keeping all this in mind, let us turn to the somewhat peculiar title of the play itself. A peninsula on the north bank of the Thames, down river from London, was known in Jonson's day (and still is today) as the Isle of Dogs. Almost directly across the river stood the Palace of Greenwich, a favorite residence for summer, and hunting, of Elizabeth, and later James I. The Isle of Dogs derived its name from traditions it was the site of a large royal kennel.[27] To pedants like Nashe and Jonson, who had read *Birds, Frogs, Wasps*, with their rampant parodies of prominent Athenian politicians, an English play, modeled on Aristophanic classics, and perhaps using the symbolism of dogs fawning over their master, and yipping and snapping at each other for their place in the pack may well have seemed an obvious choice. Interestingly, in 1601, at Essex's trial for treason, Francis Bacon compared the contrived claims of danger from enemies of the Athenian tyrant Pisistratus, to the actions of the Earl of Essex.[28]

We can discern the play's probable matter: satires of political, economic and social problems, of Court gossip, of a pompous popinjay. Even lacking a script we can now see its plausible, possible form: an Aristophanic satire with scenes, lines, and character-types lifted from the Greek originals. Some of the characters and situations in Aristophanes' plays are hauntingly similar to the England of Ben Jonson's age, especially if scripted over a chorus whose function may have served a similar purpose as Aristophanes' choruses. Jonson's apologists defended him against attacks that he plagiarized the classics, asserting he "translated and improved" upon them, presenting them as modern lessons for his contemporaries.[29]

Throughout the plays of Aristophanes are constant references to prolonged war between Athens and Sparta, the costs of the war in taxes, profiteering from the war by suppliers, commanders, and politicians, and privations faced as a result of all this by the common soldiers and citizens. England, in 1597, had been involved in costly expeditions against Spain since the 1580s; scandals over military procurement and supply were rife; special assessments were levied to support expeditions to the Netherlands, France, and Cadiz; and three years of poor crops had produced food shortages. Jonson had enumerable choices from Aristophanes to parallel these situations—from *Knights*, from *Peace*, from *Wasps*, from *Archarnians*, from *Lysistrata*, from *Ecclesiazusae*. Most of these plays were alluded to by Jonson in later works.[30] Even more pointed, in view of the playwrights' choice of title for their play, are the "coincidences" that in *Knights* over 30 lines carry on an analogy between greedy naval commanders and dishonest canines; and in *Wasps*, there is an episode in which one dog prosecutes another for stealing cheese. The point, evident to any sixteenth-century scholar of Greek, was to reveal unscrupulous Athenian politicians using the courts for revenge on their enemies. The following table suggests interesting parallels between situations in two of Aristophanes' plays popular with sixteenth-century scholars, and gossip involving the Earl of Essex.[31]

Table 16
Aristophanic Scenes Compared with Essex Episodes

Aristophanes' *Knights*	Episodes Involving Essex
Bully Servant Seeks Clients: "He goes round among the servants dropping hints/That they'd be wise to purchase his protection."	Essex Seeks Clients: Lord Grey complained that Essex: "has forced me to declare myself either his only, or friend to Mr. Secretary [and his enemy]."
Bully Servant at War: "Forging, while the fires of war are hot,/A chain of graft for handling prisoners."	Essex Accused of Graft: Naval captains purloin the plunder from Cadiz, meeting London merchants at sea.
Bully Servant Grabs Credit: "What's more, the tidbits we prepare he steals/And gets credit for. The other day/When I'd cooked up a Spartan mess at Pylos/The scamp slipped by me, grabbed the dish and ran/And brought it to the master as his own!"	Essex Demands Credit for Cadiz? Essex rushes troops ashore to prevent the Lord Admiral from taking the city. He bridles at any credit given the Lord Admiral; absenting himself from Court when the Lord Admiral was made Earl of Nottingham.
Bully Servant's Tactics: "Bellowing? That is how you always floor the people you oppose." Bully servant replies, "I must be first or I shall burst."	Essex's Tactics: "the Attorneyship for Francis [Bacon] is that I must have, I will spend all my power, might, authority, and amity, and with tooth and nail defend and procure the same for him against whomsoever; and whosoever getteth this office out of my hands for any other, before he shall have it, it shall cost him the coming by."
Bully Servant Labels Rivals with Treason: "He'll crash the meeting, smear us all with lies,/And raise an everlasting hullabaloo."	Essex Acccuses Dr. Lopez of Treason: Essex accuses him of ploting to poison the Queen, hounds Lopez until he is convicted of treason.
Bully Servant's Military Extravagance: "Paphlagon [the Bully] is ever asking you/For ships to go around collecting tribute." In response the master complains about the costs of such expeditions.	Essex Presses for Expeditions: Essex, prime mover for the Cadiz expedition. After its lack of revenue, he pushes for another expedition to the Azores; Elizabeth is reluctant to spend on such ventures.
Aristophanes' *Frogs*	Episodes Involving Essex
Dionysus Dandies Himself Up: Heracles says: "A lion skin on top of yellow silk."	Essex Supporters Described: "green-headed youths, covered with feathers and gold and silver lace."
Dionysus' Bravado: At the gate to Pluto's palace Dionysus strikes a brave pose and calls himself "The valiant Heracles!" When challenged by the gatekeeper he faints, fouls himself, tries to protect himself by calling upon his servant to change clothes with him.	Essex's Bravado: Essex parades his forces at the siege of Rouen. Goes off to visit King Henry IV; becomes trapped away from his forces; calls out the entire army to get himself back to the English camp. The expedition achieved little, but cost to the Queen large sums of money.

If these parallels between episodes from Aristophanic plays and common lore about the Earl of Essex seem to offer sparse possibilities for plot, it must be remembered that intricacies of plot are not found in most of Jonson's comedies. Critics often observe that his forte was in characterization, and in the reactions of characters to one another in various groupings, set up by simple and transparent plot devices. Story took second place to Jonson. For him the ends of comedy and tragedy were, in his own words, to "delight and teach," to show "persons such as Comedie would chose, when she would shew an Image of the times," and, as stated before, Jonson knew these plays well enough to allude to them in other writings.[31] For instance, in Aristophanes' *Knights*, two dogs are put on trial for stealing cheese; in Jonson's *The Staple of News* (V, 4), Penniboy Senior holds a "trial" for the offenses of his two dogs Lollard and Block. Jonson's later plays often were referred to by *literati* as "like his great grandfather Aristophanes." For that matter, Aristophanes' plots, like many of Jonson's, are not complex. *Frogs* hangs on the journey of Dionysus to Hades to bring back a tragic poet to Athens; *Wasps* turns on the attempts of a son to prevent his father from running off to serve on juries; *Wealth* depends upon the notion that Blind Wealth will be given sight so that only the virtuous will reap rewards; *Knights* revolves around attempts to destroy the influence over his master of an obnoxious and dishonest servant. What drives these plays are the ludicrous posturing of cowardly and greedy characters, and the running commentary on contemporary social ills. Can much more be claimed for *Every Man in His Humor, Volpone* or *The Alchemist*?

Much of the satire in *The Isle of Dogs* must, of course, have been done through the actors' accents, mannerisms, and costuming. Even had the script survived, many of its allusions might not be clear to us because we have few records of the vocal qualities, speech patterns and mannerisms of the figures of the time. But to a skilled actor, then as now, mimicking a prominent contemporary figure while supposedly playing a fictional character would be easy, and easily recognizable to an audience. A letter sent to Sir Robert Sidney told of an actor portraying Sir Francis Vere: "he that plaid that Part gott a Beard resembling his." Aubrey described a time that an actor dressed "like Chief Justice Coke and cutt his beard like him and feigned his voyce." Other documents dating from the turn of the seventeenth century describe the impersonization of influential figures on stage. We have record from Jonson's own life of such an occurrence. At performances of *Eastward Ho* (another play in which Jonson's satire was so pointed that he was jailed) an actor, already performing in a play obviously pillorying the venality of King James' Scots courtiers, assumed a Scots' burr to say: "I ken him weel: he's one of my £30 knights." This bit of obvious satire followed on the heels of James' recent apology to Parliament for selling too many knighthoods.

Ironically (or perhaps intentionally) the setting for the scene in which this line occurs is on the Isle of Dogs, and the scene opens with the English knight Sir Petronell believing he has washed up on the French coast, when he spies two approaching gentlemen (one of whom later gives the "£30 knight" line). Sir Petronell says: "See! Here comes a coople of French gentlemen: dost thou think our Englishmen are so Frenchyfied, that a man knows not whether he be in France or England when he sees 'em." There were already observations, and grumblings, among Elizabeth's old servants about James' preference for French customs and manners, and his preferences for those courtiers who affected them. Coincidentally, the play opened shortly after Jonson served as Robert Cecil's agent in Gunpowder Plot investigations, and when Cecil was locked in competition with the new Scots courtiers brought to England by James. When the play was performed, James and the Court were ensconced in Greenwich Palace just across the river from the Isle of Dogs.[32]

Jonson's indiscretion about a reigning monarch in *Eastward Ho* suggests an Aristophanic scene which may have been incorporated into the earlier *Isle of Dogs*. Most popular of Aristophanes' plays with sixteenth-century *literati* was *Wealth*. In one episode an old woman complains about her deteriorating relationship with a young man. Her lines read: "I'd a lad who loved me well, poor, but so handsome and fair to see...; whate'er I wished he did...and what he wanted, I in turn supplied....And if, perchance, some gallant threw a glance my way, he'd beat me black and blue, so very jealous had the young man grown." She complains that the man has become inattentive, basking in wealth and position to which she raised him, whereas before: "He vowed my hands were passing fair and white."[33]

The parallel to Essex's relationship to Elizabeth is devastatingly clear. Essex's jealousy about the Queen's attentions to other courtiers was well known. He had been wounded in a duel with Sir Charles Blount, fought over a gift given Blount by the Queen. Only the intervention of the Privy Council prevented his proposed duel with Sir Walter Raleigh, and by 1596-97, Essex had quarreled openly with

Elizabeth over matters of government policy and government appointments, and intentionally absented himself from Court when balked by the Queen. The line referring to hands "passing fair and white," if given in *The Isle of Dogs*, might well have caused an Elizabethan audience to suck in its breath—it was well-known that the Queen had a fetish about her hands. The Venetian ambassador, reporting on Elizabeth when she was heir-presumptive to her sister Mary noted that "her hands, which she takes care not to conceal, are of superior beauty," and portrait after portrait of Elizabeth gives prominence to her ungloved hands.[34]

This scene, if Jonson adapted it for his *Isle of Dogs*, coupled with references to famine and military scandals, would have given Essex enough to persuade the Queen to strike out strongly. Could Jonson have been so foolishly indiscreet? His subsequent career suggests it. He was summoned before the Privy Council in 1603 because his tragedy *Sejanus* seemed to touch too closely upon the Essex rising. He was ejected from a Christmas masque at James' Court, in which Queen Anne herself played a role, because of vociferous comments on the poetry of its author. Dekker wrote that Jonson attacked "Court, citty, country, friends,/Foes, all must smart alike." In his prologue to *Every Man in His Humor*, Jonson scorned artistic temerity: "I fear no mood stamped in a private brow when I am pleased t'unmask a public vice. I fear no courtier's frown, should I applaud the easy flexture of his supple hams." As a seasoned dramatist he was jailed over *Eastward Ho*, when he scripted lines too close to a reigning monarch's sensitivities.[35] Surely, in *The Isle of Dogs*, one of his very first plays, when he was a newcomer to the theatre business, he may well have believed he could get by with allusions only the educated should know.

It is no wonder that the controversial Jonson went to work for Henry Evans at Blackfriars. The Boys' Companies stirred up controversy, not just through their repertory, but once, at least, through abuse of the powers granted by the Queen to those who supposedly were her Masters of the Chapel Choir. That story shows us clearly how the theatre business reflected the mores and practices of the Elizabethan age.

Chapter 8

Extortion in the Name of Art:
The Impressment of Thomas Clifton
into Blackfriars Boys

In 1599-1600, after a lapse of almost ten years, the Children's acting companies reappeared in London. The Paul's Children seem to have been the first to resume playing, quietly and modestly, no doubt testing the waters. After all, the Boys' Companies had one after another been officially suppressed between 1584 and 1590 because of their penchant for controversial material and the continual litigation among investors in the various earlier companies.[1] Seeing the growing success of the new Paul's Boys, one of these earlier investors, Henry Evans, a Welsh scriviner, worked to reconstitute a company of boy actors at Blackfriars.

Evans must have been attracted to the profitability of theatrical endeavors through his connections to Sebastian Westcote, Master of Paul's Boys. Westcote, who in 1551 seems to have been the first to use the choirboys as actors, amassed a tidy fortune before his death in 1582. Evans, named Westcote's "deere friende" and co-executor in his will, must have been impressed with the over £230 in cash bequests, and numerous valuable household goods, silverware, jewelry, violins and viols, Westcote left to family members, friends, servants, choirboys and former choirboys, and the poor in four separate parishes and nine prisons. Evans was left £6, 13 shillings, 4 pence, a sum equal to half a year's labor to the London artisan.

Since Westcote's successor Thomas Gyles, for whatever reasons, did not continue the playhouse activities of Westcote, Evans maneuvered himself into the Blackfriars lease held by William Hunnis, Master of the Queen's Chapel Children, who was producing plays there with choirboys. Various legal battles shut that playhouse down in 1583, but only after Evans had attempted to save the venture through enlisting the aid of the Earl of Oxford and his secretary, poet, and sometime playwright, John Lyly. His final attempts to maintain some involvement with the Children's Companies was squashed in 1590, when all the companies were suppressed because of their involvement in the politically explosive Marprelate controversy.[2]

Seeking to make good on his aborted 1582-83 attempt as theatrical entrepreneur with the first Blackfriars Boys' Company, Evans first formed a partnership with Nathaniel Giles, Master of the Queen's Chapel Children. The Chapel Children formed the nucleus of the company and gave it a legal reason to exist. Ostensibly the boys were to perform plays and interludes for the Queen. Their weekly "rehearsals" would be at Blackfriars, open to the public for fees starting at six pence, and rising up sharply depending upon one's choice of seating. Giles carried a royal warrant for the impressment of promising young singers into the Queen's choir, and no doubt he also possessed a court subsidy to defray costs of maintaining the living expenses of the boys. Evans probably contributed seed money to restart the company, and expertise he had gained from his connections with Westcote and in managing the first Blackfriars Boys'.

Next, he and Giles obtained a lease of the Blackfriars Theatre from Richard Burbage, who had inherited the property from his father, James. James had purchased Blackfriars in 1596, had spent considerable sums to convert it into a permanent indoor theatre, but had been stopped by a combination of city fathers and important neighboring citizens from putting it to use. Today we would say he was denied a zoning variance. The theatre had lain vacant for four years, and that, coupled with the fact that the semi-official status of the Children's Company technically made the facility a schoolhouse for the Queen's Chapel Choir, would allow it to slide past the prohibition against playing at Blackfriars (as the first Blackfriars Boys had done), is probably what convinced Evans and Burbage to conclude a lease. Evans took possession in September 1600.[3]

Yet after all this shrewd and careful preparation, Evans and Giles found themselves embroiled with the authorities in December, even before they had opened the doors. On 13 December 1600, their agent James Robinson used the commission of impressment to "haul, pull, drag, and carry away," Thomas Clifton, the 13-year-old, only son and heir of Henry Clifton, Esquire, from Toftrees in Norfolk. Clifton had taken a house in London to provide for, and supervise his heir's education. Thomas was waylaid on his way home from school by Robinson, and dragged off to Blackfriars.[4] Henry Clifton immediately went to Blackfriars to demand the return of his son. His demand arrogantly was refused by Giles and Evans.

Clifton was a member of the Norfolk upper Gentry. At this time the title "Esquire" was reserved to the descendant of younger sons of peers and knights. Henry Clifton descended from John Clyfton, knight, listed in the Commissioners' List of 1433 of the Gentry of Norfolk. The family possessed lordship of Buckenham Castle until the main branch died out. His Nottinghamshire cousins had achieved prominence for their branch of the family during the reigns of Henry VII and Henry VIII. The Cliftons had achieved enough status that William Cecil, Lord Burghley, personally drew up a Clifton genealogy for inclusion in his personal papers. Henry Clifton's right to a Coat-of-Arms was certified by the Clarenceaux King of Arms.[5] No record links Henry Clifton of Toftrees to the magistracy of Norfolk, but his grandson became a Justice of the Peace. He, himself, may have been a local Master of the Posts. Toftrees lies on a postal road; the manor is described as possessing large stables; and Henry's name is conspicuously missing from the Norfolk Muster Rolls. Only Justices of the Peace, clergy, and Masters of the Post were exempt from those rolls, and Clifton was neither Justice of the Peace nor clergyman.

If he were a local Master of the Post, he would have been acquainted with Sir John Stanhope, Master of the Royal Posts. Indeed, Clifton had indirect ties to Stanhope through his association with Sir Roger Townshend of Raynam who was married to Stanhope's sister. Stanhope was an intimate of Privy Council lords, and an especially close associate of Sir Robert Cecil, the Lord Secretary, and Lord Admiral Charles Howard. Henry Clifton's status within the Norfolk elite also would have brought contacts with the Lord Admiral Charles Howard, Attorney General Sir Edward Coke, and Sir Francis Bacon—all of whom were members of the Norfolk aristocracy. The Howards were the ducal family of Norfolk; Francis Bacon's father and uncle were Justices of the Peace there; and Coke still retained his Justiceship in Norfolk in 1600. Clifton's manor at Toftrees was located less than 12 miles from Stiffkey, primary manor of Francis Bacon's uncle Sir Nathaniel Bacon, less than three miles from Mileham, the primary Norfolk residence of

Attorney General Sir Edward Coke, who was chief patron of the parish church at Toftrees, and about the same distance from the manor of Sir Roger Townshend of Raynam, who was knighted for services during the Armada by Lord Admiral Charles Howard, and whose son John was married to Nathaniel Bacon's daughter, and co-heir Anne.[6]

These connections enabled Clifton to secure the intervention of the Privy Council through the person of Sir John Fortescue, Chancellor of the Exchequer. Young Thomas was released after "a day and a night," but Clifton did not let the matter rest there. A year later he introduced a complaint in the Star Chamber that resulted in Evans' censure by the Privy Council, forcing him to hide his investments in the company, withdraw from active participation, and leave London for the space of at least one year.

Neither Evans' careful preparation to start up the company in 1599, nor his behavior when involved in the first Blackfriars company, display such seeming stupidity. At that time, to preserve his investment, he had maneuvered in the courts and enlisted the services of John Lyly, secretary to the Earl of Oxford, in order to secure the protection of a powerful lord. Evans only had been pushed out by litigations among the various parties to the lease, combined with the desire of the influential Sir William More to repossess the property.[7] Having already been defeated by a member of the Gentry with connections at Court, what could have possessed Evans to dare the same situation again? Perhaps Robinson had acted on his own when he waylaid young Thomas Clifton, but that does not explain why Evans and Giles refused to release the boy when the angry Henry Clifton, Esquire, showed up to demand his son back. Indeed, the two men taunted Clifton and dared him to take his case "to whom he would." Such behavior seems to belie all the evidence that suggests Evans was a clever and hard-headed businessman.

But does it? Clifton testified that his son, and most of the others impressed, possessed no musical talent or training, though it appears that Evans and Giles did use their legal right of impressment to steal talent from the rival company. Alvery Trussell and Salmon Pavey, named in the suit, were apprenticed to the Choirmasters of St. Paul's; Nathan Field attended Paul's grammar school, which, along with Paul's choir, was involved in presenting masques and interludes at Court, and now plays at Paul's. Evans and Giles may have been in a hurry to augment the numbers of their troupe,[8] and Thomas Clifton may have been handsome, but there were plenty of handsome boys, without well-connected fathers, who could be impressed without fear of reprisal. Perhaps there are other business issues here beyond recruiting likely boys to swell the ranks of the new acting company. Perhaps instead of thinking about the Clifton affair from the viewpoint of "talent-scouting," we should instead think about it from the one indisputable concern of any business—making money.

Before Evans and Giles could begin performances, the new partnership was faced with considerable up-front expenses. Burbage struck a hard bargain on the lease of Blackfriars. The annual rent was set at £40, almost double the £20 13s 4d Evans had paid for the facility in 1583. Payments were due in quarterly installments of £10. Realizing the risk of theatrical endeavors (or perhaps hoping Evans would fail), Burbage insisted that Evans post a bond of £400. Since the average income of an Elizabethan artisan only was £15, the £400 bond was the equivalent of 27 years' wages to the man on the street. Further, all maintenance and repair costs to the property were to be borne by Evans. Henslowe's accounts and the "Sharer Papers" tell us that sum could amount to as much as £100 per year,[9] almost seven times an artisan's annual income.

How many costumes and properties Evans still retained from his earlier venture we do not know, but even if most of them were still in his possession, they would need some refurbishing and repairs. Giles could also draw upon costumes and properties from the Revels Office because of his position as Master of the Chapel Children.[10] We can assume, therefore, that Evans and Giles did not to lay out a sum like the £300 (20 years' labor to the artisan) Francis Langley had paid to start up his ill-fated theatre venture at the Swan in 1596. Yet a sum one-third that amount, £100, probably is not too far from the mark.

A smaller expense would be playwrights' fees for new plays. Though these need not be paid in full until scripts were completed, Henslowe's accounts tell us that a £2 advance was typical, especially to a Ben Jonson and George Chapman, who were in chronic states of penury. Jonson may even have been an under-master for the choir boys. His epigram to Salmon Pavy, and his later assertion that "Nid Field was his scholar," a statement reinforced by Field's description of Jonson as his "worthiest maister," suggest a closer relationship than just that of an author of plays in which they acted. He would earn perhaps £10 per year,

Fig. 23. Blackfriars: Imaginative reconstruction. From: Irwin Smith, *Shakespeare's Blackfriars Theatre*.

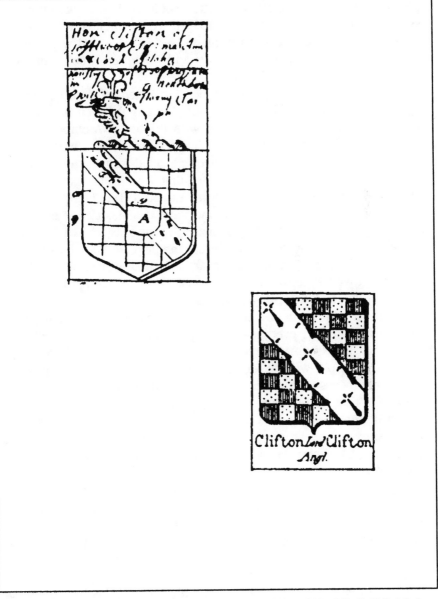

Fig. 24. Clifton Coat-of-Arms. Drawing from *Visitation of Norfolk* (1664). Modern rendering from *Illustrations to the Armorial General.*

plus housing, in such a capacity. That would help to explain how he supported himself in the period of 1599 to 1603, when he left working for the public theatres, published quartos of his plays, and was seeking patrons. Two plays, *Cynthia's Revels* and *Poetaster*, would not have yielded him much income.[11]

Finally, there would need to be distributed, discreetly, certain "gifts" to appropriate authorities at Court. Such "gifts" were an accepted practice to gain the favor of those with influence. Members of the nobility paid them, and so did theater businessmen. They too understood that certain unspecified "favors" were expected from time to time by those with authority. We have record that John Heminges gave the Master of the Revels £5 to prohibit the Red Bull company from performing Shakespeare's plays, and gave the Master annual "New Year's gifts." Christopher Beeston once gave the Master's wife a pair of gloves worth "at least twenty shillings," and paid the Master £60 a year above and beyond the usual fees charged by that office.[12] Evans must have bestowed at least that amount (£60) to secure permission to reactivate the Blackfriars Boys' Company.

Let us total up those expenses that Evans and Giles would have had to pay out before ever presenting a performance: £400 bond, £60 for Court "gifts," £100 for costumes and props, £4 to Jonson and Chapman, the first hired playwrights for the company, as advances (and perhaps £10 more to Jonson as under-master's wages). We need to add at least another £40 or £50 to clean and spruce up the facility at Blackfriars, which had lain vacant for four years, and to ready it for the use and occupancy of the boys. Evans later asserted he bore the cost of converting "the schoolhouse and the chamber over the same...to dine and sup in" and furnished it with "divers implements of household stuff."[13] Adding all these sums yield a total of at least £1168 (a sum nearly as large as the average income of a knight, and representing 78 years' labor to the artisan), a sum which Evans and Giles had to raise, somewhere, between September 1600, when they took possession of Blackfriars, and Christmas, when the quarterly installment on the rent came due.

The Evans-Giles partnership faced ongoing costs beyond those necessary to reopen Blackfriars as a theatre. For all intents and purposes, the Queen's Chapel Children was a boarding school as well as a choir. The boys were provided with lessons in Latin grammar, manners and music, with food and clothing, and with lodging. A petition to the Court in 1573 by the then Master of the Children William Hunnis, and certain household accounts and school records yield some indications as to what those ongoing costs might have been.

Hunnis wrote that his Court subsidy, including six pence per boy per day for food, and £40 per year for clothing and furniture, was insufficient to his responsibilities. The subsidy did little to defray the cost of salaries for his Usher (under-master) and for the male and female servant necessary to prepare food, tend to the premises and keep the boys' clothes (and the boys themselves) clean. Implied, as well, was the cost to him of food and lodging for the under-master and the two servants. Nor did his subsidy, he contended, extend to the boys who no longer sang in the choir because their voices had changed. These boys still remained Hunnis' responsibility until a place for them was found elsewhere[14]—usually an apprenticeship.

Records from the Merchant Taylors School, the Tonbridge, Sandwich, Shrewsbury, Westminster Schools, and King's (in Cambridge) School reveal that Hunnis' Court allowance was none too generous. Though qualifications varied, most under-masters were expected to be good Latinists and preferably versed in Greek as well. Many under-masters were at least Bachelors of Arts, some were Masters of Arts. All, obviously, had more than a minimal education. The average annual salary for under-masters was between £10 and £20, plus food and lodging, or an allowance for the same.[15]

Costs for meat, fish and eggs for 20 students listed in King's School accounts reveal an average meal for 20 students cost 44 pence. At the usual two meals a day, the average cost per day was at least 88 pence, an average of four and one-half pence per student. This average is quite close to Hunnis' allotment of six pence per day, especially considering that the King's School costs do not include items such as bread, beverages (usually cider and beer), vegetables, porridge, and other such items which rounded out the boys' diet.[16]

Account books for the Sidney, Rutland, and Ancaster households give glimpses at some clothing costs: seven pence for a pair of child's shoes, five pence for a pair of hose, 12 pence for a "ready-made" shirt.[17] Two of each of these items per the allotted 12 student-choirboys under Giles care (12 boys x 2 pairs of hose x 2 pair of shoes x 2 shirts) equals 576 pence (£2 4s 16d). King's school records list a payment of £5 for 20 bedsteads. While these expenditures look significantly less than Hunnis' £40 allotment for clothing and furniture, we need to assume further expenses for such items as doublets, coats, trousers, gloves, hats, chairs, tables, dishes, books and the like. The Queen's Chapel Children could hardly appear tatty in public, and boys notoriously are hard on furniture and dishes. The Elizabethan Court was noted for its stinginess, and thus the £40 allowed Hunnis per year probably was figured just as close to actual costs as was the six pence per day for food.[18] The Court did not respond officially to Hunnis' petition, but its subsequent actions seem to acknowledge its validity; his allowance was not increased, but he was granted estates in the countryside to supplement his income.

How many of these "school" costs were met by Giles' allowance from Court is not known. Given Hunnis' testimony in 1573 that his subsidy was "no whit less than her Majesty's father, of famous memory, therefore allowed"—a figure based on prices 26 years old—it seems unlikely that Giles' allowance was any more generous. If Giles' contribution to the partnership did cover all these costs, including expansion of the Chapel Children from 12 to the 20 or so more boys necessary for theatre presentations, there still existed the stupendous startup cost of £1168 or so. With no money coming in as yet, with the prospect of potential earnings only about half that of the adult companies,[19] Evans and Giles must have been strapped for ready cash by December 1600, and the quarter's rent would come due at Christmas.

Herein may lie the real reason that on 13 December 1600, Evans and Giles "did haul, pull, drag, and carry away" young Thomas Clifton, as earlier, according to Henry's deposition, they had done to "divers and several children from divers and sundry schools...and apprentices to men of trade...against the wills óf the said children, their parents, tutors, masters and governors, and to no small grief and oppressions of your Majesty's true and faithful subjects."[20] Faced with a money shortfall, haunted by the prospect of forfeiture of the £400 bond and the loss of all they had invested to date, Evans and Giles may have sought a way to turn Giles' royal commission into ready cash.

Elizabethans were accustomed to fees, bribes, and abuses of power by those in authority, or their representatives—so used to it, in fact, that several con-men posing as military captains, royal messengers, or servants of the Privy Council lords such as the Earl of Essex, extorted fees from subjects or "arrested" them until they paid for their release.

The Privy Council saw to it that some of these men were branded, or lost their ears, but the practice was not stamped out entirely. Those armed with genuine royal warrants or patents of privilege were hardly better. Acts of the Privy Council over a period of several years deplored widespread abuses. They cited misuses of power such as extorting sums of £1 and up to avoid impressment or to be discharged from military service after impressment; wardens of prisons sending out "sweeps" to arrest men from whom they could extort bail money; Justices of the Peace using impressment to harass enemies or impress political opponents' supporters at election times; and the Lord Mayor of London impressing men he had been forbidden to touch, such as gentlemen, serving-men, lawyers or clerks at Court. In an address to the Commons in 1601, the Queen acknowledged abuses, and promised reforms, saying: "That my grants shall be made grievances to my people, and oppressions be priviledged under colour of our patents, our princely dignity shall not suffer."[21]

Given this seemingly almost endemic use of royal warrants for personal gain—gain obviously substantial enough that some were willing to risk their ears, trusting that counterfeit warrants and faked liveries would intimidate most subjects—Evans would have had to be a paragon of virtue not to contemplate the potentials of his partner's royal commission. Giles possessed a commission issued under the Queen's Privy Seal, and was armed with a patent issued under the Great Seal, which commanded "every one of you to whom this our commission shall come, to be helping, aiding, and assisting to the uttermost of your powers, as you will answer at your uttermost perils."[22] Hence Giles, his associate Evans, and their deputy Robinson, lawfully could impress boys for the Queen's Chapel Choir. Even if there had been laws against kidnapping (which in Elizabethan England there were not), Giles and Evans were protected by a legal grant of authority. Many of these "divers and several children," including Thomas Clifton, probably were not impressed, as the deposition states, "for the acting of parts in base plays and interludes." Why would Evans and Giles seek to increase their financial liability by increasing the number of boys for whom they had to provide? They did impress them, as Henry Clifton asserted, for "mercenary gain and private commodity," but in many cases that "gain" may have been a fee for their discharge paid by their parents or masters from the trade to which they had been apprenticed. A guild artisan would be glad to pay a fee to regain his apprentice. Not only was he losing his apprentice's labor, but he also lost all the time and effort spent to train him, and the £10 fee he, or the apprentice's father, had paid the guild to register the apprentice legally. He might even lose the apprentice altogether, for guild regulations specified that an apprentice could be freed from his obligations to his master if he were "diverted to other Occupations than his own Mystery."[23]

Such a view explains the seemingly stupid arrogance Giles and Evans displayed towards Henry Clifton. The smug assertions they made "that they had authority sufficient to take any nobleman's son," that Clifton could "complain to whom he would," that Clifton's son "should be employed" as a player, and the threat made before his father's eyes that if Thomas did not "obey the said Evans, he should be surely whipped," were ploys to force Clifton to make an offer for the discharge of his son from Blackfriars. The escalation of the verbal exchanges, topped by bringing the boy into the room and threatening him with a whipping, were *meant,* as Henry Clifton asserted, "to despite and grieve" him, so that Clifton would get the hint and buy his son's discharge. Evans and Giles probably never mentioned money to Henry Clifton; they must have assumed he knew what was expected.

Clifton, however, did not take the hint. Perhaps he was unused to the sophisticated collections of fees and favors rampant in Elizabeth's London because of his Norfolk upbringing; perhaps he was so outraged he refused to play Evans' and Giles' game. In any case he was not satisfied with the release of his son. He did make the affair a "Star Chamber matter,"[24] and a year later presented his own case, and evidence he had gathered concerning other impressments and "misdemeanors and offences." By that time Evans knew he might be in for trouble. Shortly before the case went before the Star Chamber he transferred all his goods to his son-in-law Alexander Hawkins.[25]

Henry Evans had gambled and lost in the Clifton matter. His timing could not have been worse; by the end of 1600 Elizabeth's subjects had become so fed up with abuses of royal monopolies and patents of privilege that it was a major issue in the House of Commons the following year. Clifton's official complaint was accepted by the Star Chamber 15 December 1601, only four days before that Parliament ended its sessions on 19 December.[26] The Queen, in her opening address, had promised reforms; Evens' censure, and the restrictions placed upon his future involvement with the Blackfriars Boys' Company, may well have been one of the first instances in which the Council hoped to demonstrate the Queen's good faith.

Perhaps the Chamberlain's Men may have helped trip up Evans. If, as is probable, he was involved in stealing their version of *Spanish Tragedy*, and pirating *Merry Wives of Windsor* at a time when Shakespeare hurriedly was revising it for public performance, the company's ire would be aroused. Someone (or ones) knowledgeable about the London theatre must have helped Clifton gather information for his deposition concerning the other impressments Evans had carried out, and he later stated that it was the Lord Chamberlain, patron and namesake of Shakespeare's company, who ordered him to leave London for at least the space of a year. Certainly Clifton had the help of the choirmasters at Paul's, Grymes and Pierce.

Yet perhaps of even greater significance to Evans, he had reached too high up the Elizabethan social scale. Neither the seven boys Clifton specified by name in his deposition, nor the "divers and several children" unspecified, whose cases Clifton noted, were described as sons of the Gentry; later litigation described Evans' censure by the Star Chamber specifically for "takinge vp of gentlemens children." The Privy Council obviously was not concerned with, nor did it seek to stop the impressment of, children from the Commons.

Henry Clifton, Esquire, probably knew the Stanhopes, the Howards, the Bacons, the Cokes;[27] most tradesmen and artisans and schoolmasters had no such high connections at court. The Commons was used to paying its "betters" for the privilege of buying salt or drinking glasses, or anise seeds or spangles, for brewing beer for export or selling wines or keeping taverns, for demolishing gig mills or transporting ashes and old shoes, for being committed and discharged from prison, for being manacled and unmanacled in prison, for food and drink and bed in prison, for all sorts of goods and services which were licensed to individuals under the guise of royal patents of privilege.[28] One can only wonder how much money Evans may have raised "to the great oppression and wrong of divers of your Majesty's loving and faithful subjects" before he was tripped up by Henry Clifton. Man a father and master, silently and resignedly, may have "bought-out" his son's or apprentice's "contract" to help finance Henry Evans' reopening of Blackfriars Theatre.

The Clifton episode caused a minor stir in the London theatrical world, and perhaps a few smug smiles of satisfaction for Evans' enemies. Another series of episodes dating from the same time, however, had much more far-reaching impact on that world. The factionalism between the Essex camp and the Cecil camp boiled over between 1599 and 1601, and ripples of that political struggle played a role which affected the directions taken in the repertories of the theatre companies over the next ten years.

Chapter 9

Eddies of the Essex Episode
Political Ripples in the Theatre and Book Trades

The uneasy political situation in Elizabethan England between 1599 and the abortive coup d'etat attempted by the Earl of Essex and his faction in 1601 touched more than just the political scene. Uncertainties concerning what was politically acceptable or unacceptable were reflected in activities as seemingly unrelated to Court politics as the London book trade and the London theatre. Those uncertainties may have been partly responsible for a shift in the book trade, and in theatrical repertories, which ended the longstanding popularity of books and plays about English history. They also may have contributed to the turn-of-the-century change in Elizabethan playwrights' style and focus, which resulted in Greco-Roman plays like Shakespeare's *Julius Caesar* and Heywood's *The Golden Age, Bronze Age* and *Iron Age*, newer styles of tragedies like Shakespeare's *Othello*, and Heywood's *A Woman Killed with Kindness*, and developments in comedy scholars have labeled "city comedy" and the "War of the Theatres."

During the last decade and a half of the sixteenth century, playwrights in all the theatrical companies were remarkably synchronized in their patterns of production. As seen in the table and accompanying graph on the following page, plays dramatizing English history ranked as one of the most popular types of plays throughout the 1590s. On the other hand, the writing and staging of tragedies like Kyd's *The Spanish Tragedy*, and Marlowe's *The Jew of Malta* and *Doctor Faustus*, which had been popular in the 1580s and early 1590s, declined precipitously after 1592. No new tragedies appear in Henslowe's accounts or in the Stationers' Register. About 1600, however, playwrights in virtually all the theatre companies abruptly shifted away from English history plays, and began to produce dramatizations of Greco-Roman classics and various types of tragedies. Some of their "new" plays were little more than revisions of plays 20 years old, or older.[1]

205

Table 17 Known New Plays by Genre (English History, Greco-Roman, Tragedy), Various Repertories (1583-1613)				
Bench-Mark Events	Approx. Years	English History	Greco- Roman	Tragedy
Spanish Tragedy first performed to foundation of Chamberlain's Men	1583-94	14	5 (most by Lyly for Paul's Boys)	15 (53% by Marlow & Kyd, before 1592)
Swan Theatre constructed to suppression of J. Hayward's Henry IV	1595-99	14	2	1
Fortune Theatre constructed to death of Elizabeth, accession of James	1600-03	0	7	8
Gunpowder Plot to King's Men lease Blackfriars Theatre	1604-08	0	10	12
King's Men at Globe/Blackfriars to burning of the Globe	1609-13	1	9	8

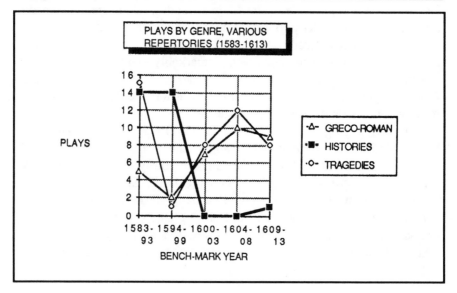

Most of the Greco-Roman plays also can be classified as tragedies. Tragedy in general, therefore, began to be produced by all theatre companies with a frequency which almost matched the previous popularity of plays about English history. Shakespeare's *Julius Caesar* and *Hamlet* were performed by the Chamberlain's Men in the Autumn of 1599 or early 1600, contemporary with Chettle's *Tragedy of Hoffman*, performed by the Admiral's Men, and Marston's *Antonio's Revenge*, performed by the Paul's Children's Company. Evidence also suggests that the Blackfriars Boys pirated, and performed, the Chamberlain's Men version of Kyd's *Spanish Tragedy*,[2] making it appear that there was an almost simultaneous revival of the genre of tragedy among almost all major London acting troupes. As the following graph illustrates, tragedies, especially Greco-Roman ones, may have been used to replace English histories in the theatrical repertories.

Comedy type changed as well. Playwrights began to produce biting satirical comedies attacking each other and rival acting companies, an episode which has been labeled the "War of the Theatres." Ben Jonson was at the center of this type of play. His *Cynthia's Revels* and *Poetaster* took snide potshots at most other playwrights and acting companies in London. They were countered by Marston's *Histriomastix*, and *Jack Drum's Entertainment*, and Dekker's *Satiromastix*, all of which attacked Jonson and his pretensions as an author. For the most part these ripostes

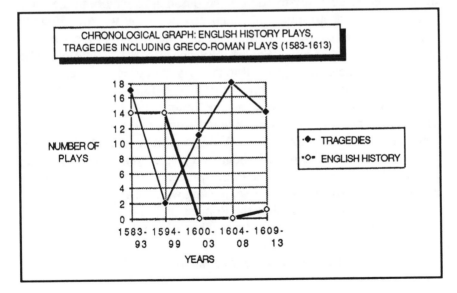

CHRONOLOGICAL GRAPH: ENGLISH HISTORY PLAYS, TRAGEDIES INCLUDING GRECO-ROMAN PLAYS (1583-1613)

were confined to the Children's companies; yet the adult companies did show some reaction to Jonson's jibes. Most likely, Shakespeare's comments about players in *Hamlet* were in answer to Jonson's attacks. His revisions of *Merry Wives of Windsor* also were part of this phenomenon, and, in one of the few examples of a play from the Children's Companies showing up on the stage of an adult playhouse, the Chamberlain's Men staged Dekker's *Satiromastix*, the most sweeping and biting counter-attack on Jonson.[3]

Playwrights also began to produce so-called "Cittie comedie." Some of these, like Jonson's *Every Man Out of His Humour*, burlesqued the greed, and social pretensions of the urban bourgeoisie. Others, like Heywood's *Four Prentices of London*, and Dekker's *Shoemaker's Holiday*, celebrated the achievements and values of that same bourgeoisie. In both cases, with few exceptions, playwrights and theatre companies ceased writing and staging romantic-type, aristocratic comedies, gently spoofing the manners of courtiers (and perhaps certain courtiers themselves), like Shakespeare's *Love's Labour's Lost* or *Midsummer Night's Dream.*[4]

Traditionally, these changes in the theatre have been viewed as artistic maturation, or the influence of "new blood," as represented by such writers as Heywood, Jonson, Marston. More recently, there has been emphasis upon a change in audience demands.[5] Yet none of these explanations seems fully to address the question of why both the book trade, and the theatre repertory, both driven by the wave of English nationalism which surfaced during and after the events of the Armada, seemed to have abandoned English histories after the middle of 1599. Both these businesses depended upon mass market tastes. Yet though English nationalism certainly did not decline suddenly at the end of the sixteenth century, nonetheless, almost no history books were printed and virtually no history plays were scripted from 1600 until 1610. To be sure, there were a few exceptions. A single printing of Stowe's *Annals*, in abbreviated form, appeared about every other year, and there were two or three printings of William Warner's *Albion's England*, a rambling, discursive work, in verse, treating with the so-called history of Britain from before the time of the Romans until the union of Scotland and England under James (but with nothing about recent English history after the defeat of the Armada).

On the other hand, suddenly, from an average of no more than one every two years before 1599, printers produced four Greco-Roman translations in 1600 and continued an average of two per year for the next 16 years. Printers, playwrights and acting companies had not paid substantial attention to Greco-Roman translations or plays based on Greco-Roman material before 1600. Publication records, and references in Henslowe's Diary show few repeat editions and few repeat performances of books or plays on those themes throughout the 1590s.[6]

One cannot dismiss completely that there were changes in reading and playgoing tastes occurring within the London market, or that authors and playwrights sought new directions. Dekker's *Shoemaker's Holiday* and Heywood's *Edward IV,* both probably written before 1598, demonstrate that certain playwrights were starting to shift to themes emphasizing city life, and the values and concerns, of the urban mercantile and tradesmen classes. So too do the increased printings, towards the end of the century, of chivalric romances, books on cosmetics and other "domestic" types of books—as well as the emphasis upon the pathos of Jane Shore in Heywood's *Edward IV*—probably reflect, more explicitly, a recognition of the increasing role of urban women in the market place as consumers.[7] Shakespeare himself, in his almost self-conscious appeals to the imaginations of his viewers in the choruses to *Henry V*, may be implicitly admitting that the London audience had now become too sophisticated to accept, as Sir Philip Sidney criticized earlier: "Asia on the one side, and Affricke of the other...two Armies file in, represented with foure swords & bucklers." Still, it strains probability to suggest that such a precipitous decline in the popularity of one type of genre, and such a steep climb in the popularity of another, occurred within the short space of one year. Though these were trends in changing audience and consumer tastes, some other factors must have accelerated the process and triggered the rapid shift of theatrical repertories and printing inventories.

It may have been political reasons which influenced the abrupt cease in the publication of English history books and the staging of English history plays. The political situation in London became extremely tense in the last few months of 1599 and continued to be so throughout the next two years. On September 27 the Earl of Essex, accompanied by a few supporters, disobeyed the Queen's orders and returned from his desultory campaign in Ireland to confront the Queen concerning his beliefs that his enemies in the Court, especially Cecil,

Raleigh, and Cobham, were conspiring his ruin—at least that was what he later said were his reasons. He surprised the Queen, bursting in on her *toilette* in her private chambers at Nonsuch Palace. Once Elizabeth regained her composure, she summoned Essex before the Privy Council. As a result, from October 1, 1599 onward, Essex was forbidden the Court and kept under close surveillance or house-arrest, first at the London residence of, and under the supervision of, the Lord Keeper, and then at his own London residence. Throughout 1600 Essex supporters brawled in taverns, started rumors and libels against his enemies in court, printed books with thinly veiled pro-Essex sympathies and alternately plotted his escape or open rebellion against the authority of the Court. Some of his supporters even attempted to encourage James to bring a Scottish army south to claim the throne and save Essex. The Privy Council seems to have been so fearful of pro-Essex sentiment that it allowed him a period of freedom to return to his country estates and cancelled plans for Star Chamber proceedings against Essex concerning charges of disobedience and sedition.[8]

Because of Privy Council jitters, the climate for books on more recent English history books may have turned cold. The printing of Sir John Hayward's *History of Henry IV*, one month after Essex's departure for Ireland in April 1599, created a stir. The book described Henry Bolingbroke's return to England, his successful deposition of King Richard II, and contained a long section describing Richard's abdication. It was a best seller, going through the first printing in a month, and was reprinted in May, when the Stationers' Guild stepped in, confiscated the new printing, and turned the run over to the Bishop of London, who had all copies burned. In July 1599, Hayward was summoned before Lords of the Council to answer questions about possible sedition. A few days later Hayward was imprisoned in the Tower. Hayward's printer, and the censor who passed the book for publication, also were grilled by the Attorney General, Sir Edward Coke. The Council saw too many obvious parallels between the Bolingbroke story and Essex's return from Ireland to "reclaim his rights." The State Papers concerning the interrogations reveal that the Council either was convinced that Essex plotted treason, or was determined to build a case against him.[9] Hayward was still in the Tower in 1601 when the Essex faction struck. After the abortive Essex uprising early in 1601, Augustine Phillips from the Chamberlain's Men was summoned before the Council to answer for staging Shakespeare's

Richard II the day before the attempted coup d'etat. Elizabeth herself, it was reported, noticed the similarities and brooded aloud that "I am Richard II."[10]

No wonder, Hayward's book, and its dedication to Essex, were not as innocent as he and his printer claimed nor as many historians have come to believe. Hayward's printer, John Wolfe, was a Protestant with a decided French Calvinist bent, who previously had printed several works by authors in the Essex circle noted for their slavish praise of the earl: Thomas Churchyard, Gabriel Harvey, Robert Greene, Barnabe Barnes. He also printed works by Machiavelli, and certain translated excerpts from the Huguenot justification for rebellion against monarchs, *Vindiciae contra tyrannous*. In a dispute with the Stationers' Company in the 1580s he stated that "Luther was but one man, and reformed all ye world for religion, and I am that one man, that must and will reforme the government in this trade." Hayward had connections to the Latin scholar, Sir Henry Savile, or at least copied certain of his phrases from his essay "The Ende of Nero and the Beginning of Galba," attached to Savile's 1591 translation of Tacitus' *Annals* and *Histories*. Savile had connections to the Essex faction and himself was jailed briefly in the aftermath of the Essex rising. The point is that the borrowings from Savile's "Ende of Nero" were phrases, the import of which justified breaking personal oaths of allegiance to a monarch, and rebellion, if the monarch's government were weak and corrupt. Hayward's use of those passages in his *Henry IV* transferred that notion from the remote Roman past, and justified it within the framework of *English history*. Its appearance and dedication to the Earl of Essex, shortly after he had raised the largest army ever mustered during the entire reign of Elizabeth, and at a time when the Essex faction, and much popular gossip, were criticizing several of Elizabeth's closest advisors (such as Robert Cecil) for corrupt and effete policies which were damaging the realm and depriving the common man, suggests some sort of collusion within the Essex circle to tap English feelings of discontent. Such feelings of discontent were there to be tapped. A year later, 2 June 1600, the Queen issued a proclamation against libels accusing the Council of corruption in grain shipments, "especially concerning the Lord High Treasurer [Robert Cecil]." It ordered "Maiors, Justices of the Peace, Balifs, Constables, Headboroughs and all other her publike officers, to be very diligent to finde out such vnnaturall vipers...and also to make knowen, That all that shall heare any such speeches, and not reueale them to the next Officer, shall be held partaker of those heinous offences."[11]

No one will ever know just what Essex planned ultimately, if indeed he had much of a plan. He, the Earl of Southampton, and most of his supporters claimed after the rising that their only purpose was to save Essex from plots on his life by his enemies Sir Walter Raleigh and Lord Cobham, and to rescue the Queen from Councillors who were ruining her government. Sir Christopher Blount, however, did say at the block that should the Queen have offered any resistance, the conspirators were ready to shed her blood. Perhaps deep down Essex planned to make himself king. Robert Cecil stated at Essex's trial that the earl's "ambitious affections inclined to usurpation," and when asked at the trial by the Earl of Southampton, "what in your conscience, you think we would have done to her Majesty if we had gained the Court?" Edward Coke replied: "I do believe she should not have lived long after she had been in your power. Note by the precedents of former ages; how long lived King Richard the Second after he was surprised in the same manner? The pretense there also was to remove certain Councillors."[12] Rumors to that affect had circulated before. In 1594, interrogations of Irish Catholic conspirators revealed that they had been told on the Continent that Essex was plotting to seize the throne. In 1595, a book entitled *A Conference on the Next Succession to the Crown of England* was smuggled into England and distributed. The book, printed on the Continent and now attributed to the Jesuit Robert Parsons, averred that blood-descent alone was not a sufficient reason for succession. The claims of all the Tudor-descended claimants, James VI of Scotland, the Spanish Infanta, the Earls of Derby, Huntingdon, and Hertford were treated with bland equality. Not only was *Succession* dedicated to Essex, but it stated that at Elizabeth's death he was apt "to have a greater part or sway in deciding of this great affair." In other words Essex might be "kingmaker" or king himself. Later, in 1600, Privy Council documents voiced suspicions that during his private conferences in Ireland with the rebel Earl of Tyrone, Essex had plotted to ally himself with Tyrone, give that earl control of Ireland, and use his support in order to gain the crown.[13]

The interrogations of all concerned, and the trial before the House of Lords, made much of Essex's seeming fascination with Henry

Bolingbroke and the deposition of Richard II. Sir Walter Raleigh wrote Cecil in 1597 that Essex had been "wonderful merry at your conceit concerning Richard II." Privy Council documents noted his frequent attendance at that play. Such a comparison of himself, and his situation, to that of Bolingbroke or Richard of York could have been on his mind, or in the minds of his followers. The succession question dominated the 1590s. Like Richard II, the childless descendant of Edward III, Elizabeth was the childless, last, direct-line representative of the Tudors. Richard's heir presumptive, the Earl of March, had died before his deposition, leaving the succession question wide open. Elizabeth, of course, steadfastly refused to name an heir, creating a similar uncertainty over her own succession. The slaughter of the Wars of the Roses, and the policies of Henry VII and Henry VIII aimed at eliminating the direct descendants of the House of York, meant that few peers could claim any direct royal descent.[14] Given that situation, Essex's descent from the daughter, and sole heir, of Edward III's youngest son, Thomas of Woodstock, *and* from a granddaughter of Richard of York, gave him as good a claim to legitimacy as any living English peer.

Elizabethans kept track of pedigrees. The State Papers contain pedigrees of obscure families sketched out by Lord Burghley himself. Essex's pedigree would have been well known. It was, in some ways, more noble than that of the Tudors. Henry VII, Elizabeth's grandfather, descended, on his father's side, from an obscure Welsh knight, Owen Tudor. His sole claim to the throne came from his mother, Margaret Beaufort, third-cousin of Henry VI, but her descent was from the Beauforts, a bastard branch of the Lancastrian family.[15] Indeed, Elizabeth herself only trusted those whose family origins were as lowly as her mother's—Knollys, Norrises, Careys, Dudleys, Cecils.[16] The Devereaux family, on the other hand, traced its ancestry back to the Norman nobility of William the Conqueror. It had gained wealth from lands on the Welsh border, and prominence during the reign of Edward III. The sixteenth-century Devereauxs could claim descent from three of the sons of Edward III, not only from the heiress of Edward's youngest son Thomas of Woodstock, but from the House of York as well, through Margaret Pole, granddaughter of Richard of York. Shakespeare's *1 Henry VI* (II, 5) and *2 Henry VI* (II, 2) shows the legal legerdemain possible in tracing a pedigree. He spells out, in detail, how Richard of York's descent from both Lionel, Duke of Clarence, and Edmund, Duke of York (second and

Table 18			
Royal Descent of English Earls, 1594-1603			
Earldom	Holder	Royal Ancestor	Remarks
Essex	Robert Devereaux	Daugh. of Thomas Woodstock, youngest son of Edward III, & Margaret Pole	Earl Marshall. Popular with aristocrats. Popular with army. Popular with people.
Hertford	Edward Seymour	Mary Tudor, Henry VIII's younger sister	Under Elizabeth's suspicion. Lived in semi-retirement.
Huntingdon	Henry Hastings	Margaret Pole, daugh. of Yorkist Duke of Clarence	Died, 1595.
Huntingdon	George Hastings	Brother to Henry (above)	No popular support, nor army support.
Northumberland	Henry Percy	Daugh. of Lionel of Clarence, 2nd son of Edward III	Powers reduced because father's treason.
Sussex	Robert Radcliffe	Beaufort (illegit.) descendants of John of Gaunt	Played little role in Court politics.
Worcester	Edward Somerset	Beaufort (illegit.) descendants of John of Gaunt	Played lesser role in Court politics. Allied to Cecil.
Oxford	Edward de Vere	no clear descent	
Shrewsbury	Gilbert Talbot	no clear descent	
Pembroke	Henry Herbert	no clear descent	
Derby	Ferdinando Stanley	no clear descent	
Derby	William Stanley	no clear descent	
Lincoln	Henry Clinton	no clear descent	
Bath	William Bourchier	no clear descent	
Bedford	Edward Russell	no clear descent	
Cumberland	George Clifford	no clear descent	
Desmond	James Fitzgerald	no clear descent	
Kent	Henry Grey	no clear descent	
Rutland	Roger Manners	no clear descent	
Nottingham	Charles Howard	no clear descent	
Southampton	Henry Wriothesley	no clear descent	

Fig. 25. Engraving: Robert Devereaux, Earl of Essex as Earl Marshall.

Fig. 26. Engraving: Henry Wriothesley, Earl of Southampton in armor.

fourth sons, respectively, of Edward III)[17] was superior to the claims of the Lancastrian King Henry VI. Since Elizabeth always avoided naming a successor, and forbade Parliament to issue any act for the succession, the only other guideline was the will of Henry VIII, but that will excluded the descendants of his elder sister Margaret, who had married the Stuart king of Scotland. It favored the claims of his younger sister, Mary, who had married the Duke of Suffolk. Elizabeth, on the other hand, throughout her reign undermined the claims of the Suffolk line.[18] Under those circumstances, the royal pedigrees of English peers might well serve to sway a Parliament to name someone other than a descendant of Henry VII.

Unlike his fellow earls with like descent from royalty, Essex was immensely popular among Londoners. Like James VI of Scotland, the most serious candidate for succession, Essex, too, was a darling not only of the Catholics because of his seeming tolerance towards them in numbering many who were Catholic sympathizers among his close associates, but also of the Puritans, because of his Puritan leanings in matters of personal religion. And, according to the terms of the will of Henry VIII, James was excluded from succession. In the unsettled period before his attempted coup, Puritan preachers delivered sermons in the courtyard of Essex House echoing John Knox's admonitions that virtuous men in authority, under certain conditions, had the right to "restrain, correct, and if necessary, depose sovereigns." Sir John Harrington, Elizabeth's godson, acting as go-between for the Queen and the earl, wrote of Essex that "ambition thwarted in its career, doth speedelie leade on to madnesse," for he had heard Essex speak "strange wordes borderinge on such strange desygns, that made me hasten forthe and leave his presence." Among other things, Essex stated that the Queen was an old woman "as crooked and distorted in mind as in body."[19] To boot, Gelly Merrick, Essex's steward, was forging networks of alliances with Welsh landlords much like Bolingbroke's alliances with Owen Glendower's Welsh forces, which were instrumental in helping Bolingbroke depose Richard II.

Like Bolingbroke too, Essex had forged strong ties with members of the high aristocracy who believed themselves excluded from power and privilege. His following included the earls of Southampton, Sussex, Bedford, and Rutland, and lords Mounteagle, Mountjoy, Cromwell, and Sandys. He also had a large, armed following of soldiers, gained from his previous exploits and his Irish campaign, and disgruntled because of poor pay and fiscal mismanagement and corruption on the part of government suppliers. His return from Ireland was couched in terms like those of Henry Bolingbroke, who ostensibly returned from exile in France to claim his "rights," and drive out "evil" councillors, and personal enemies, surrounding Richard II, and in terms like those of Richard of York, who returned from Ireland to do the same in the reign of Henry VI. Those parallels to other "overmighty subjects" who in the past two centuries had overthrown monarchs did not go unnoticed by the anti-Essex faction, as the accounts of the interrogations of John Hayward reveal.[20]

Though no official action, other than against Hayward, and an order by the Bishop of London on 1 June 1599 that "noe English historyes be printed excepte they bee allowed by some of her maiesties privie Counsell," *prohibited* printing and staging matters dealing with English history, the official climate after the middle of 1599 must have had a dampening effect. Printers and theatrical companies must have come to believe that any themes touching upon fairly recent history were too dangerous to risk. Later actions by the Privy Council certainly confirmed such beliefs. After staging *Richard II* the day before the Essex uprising, the Chamberlain's Men sent Augustine Phillips to answer angry inquiries by the Council. His excuses were that the company had demurred to stage the play on the grounds it was so old, that few remembered the lines, and that the company was cajoled by the offer of a special fee of 40 shillings, a fee which essentially would cover all production costs.[21] Given the timing of the play, the Privy Council's inquiry was understandable, and may well have reflected a view that its performance was somehow coupled with Hayward's *History of Henry IV* as part of a conspiracy designed to stir up the London populace. Scholars have noted the sympathetic tone towards Bolingbroke in Shakespeare's *Richard II*, and *1* and *2 Henry IV*, and Sir Edward Coke was almost obsessed with the Richard II parallels; he brought them up over and over again in all of his interrogations concerning the Essex rising; he made the parallel in the trial of Essex and Southampton, and he used the staging of the play as evidence of the Essex circle's attempt to arouse the populace at the trial of Essex's steward Gelly Merrick.[22]

Whether or not the performance was only designed to bolster the courage of the Essex conspirators,[23] it does seem to have served as a signal for the Court to take action. For months, Essex supporters had been gathering in London—soldiers returned from Ireland, Welsh adventurers, Puritan preachers and other malcontents. The numbers collecting at Essex House had become so great that Gelly Merrick dispossessed the tenants of a nearby house to house the overflow. It was known to the Court that Essex was making inquiries about possible supporters in London. Yet the Court did not act, except on 21 December 1600 the Queen issued a proclamation "forbidding the vse of carying and shooting in Gunnes by common and ordinary persons," which noted that some "doe in secret maner goe prouided of such meanes to doe mischiefe." Its timing cannot just have been to protect innocent citizens, as the proclamation averred. And again the Council saw the parallels to conditions under Richard II; on January 22, 1601, the author John Hayward, still locked in the Tower, was again grilled by Attorney General Coke.

Given the Court's own preoccupation with the Richard II parallels, what was it to think when it received word that Essex's supporters had commissioned a performance of Shakespeare's *Richard II*? It must have received that information. The Chamberlain's Men were approached by Essex followers Lord Mounteagle, Sirs Charles and Joscelyn Percy, Gelly Merrick, on February 6. The company had a whole evening and morning to inform its patron, the Queen's cousin, George Carey, the Lord Chamberlain, and his allies Robert Cecil and the Lord Admiral, of the performance scheduled for the afternoon of 7 February. There were government informers who hung about the theatres and other public places gathering rumors. There also is some evidence that Cecil and the Lord Admiral had informants in Essex's household, and it does seem that the performance of *Richard II* galvanized the Court into action. That same evening the Queen asked the Council to take action to force Essex's hand, and Cecil doubled the guard at Whitehall. The Council then summoned Essex to appear at Court. Upon Essex's refusal to appear, the Council, sent out calls to arms to the men of Westminster, and neighboring villages, and determined to send an official delegation to Essex House the next morning. Meantime, Cecil's agents circulated about London warning people not to become involved, invoking the dreaded word "treason." Therefore, though it sought to avoid an armed confrontation, the Court was not as ill-prepared to deal with the Essex rising of the next day as some accounts maintain. It was forewarned, by its continual intelligence gathering, and the signal sent by the performance of *Richard II*, and it went to work immediately to counter any popular support that performance might conjure up.[24]

Perhaps public opinion did not count for as much in Elizabethan England as it seems to count now in the age of television, but Elizabeth's Court always was concerned about it. Between 1581 and 1602 authorities had to deal with 35 popular uprisings and public disturbances. Individuals and groups sought public approval as a means to enhance their own positions *vis-a-vis* rivals, and to pressure those in power towards their interests. During the Wars of the Roses, London opinion favored the House of York; the city's negative attitudes toward Henry VI's wife, Queen Margaret, were, in part, a reason Edward IV was able to secure the throne in 1461, and regain it in 1471, after he had been driven from England. Within the living memory of many, London's support had guaranteed Mary's succession, Elizabeth's safety from Mary's suspicions, and her ultimate succession. Lack of support in London had doomed Lady Jane Gray, and Sir Thomas Wyatt's rebellion against Mary. On a smaller scale, popularity in London had saved one of Thomas Wyatt's followers. A London jury acquitted Sir Nicholas Throckmorton of treason.

As concerns the popularity of Essex among Londoners, Elizabeth and the Cecil-Howard faction earlier had shown concern, curtailing publicity for his part in the Cadiz expedition of 1596. In August 1600 Cockson's heroic engraving of Essex (see p. 215) was suppressed. After Essex's arraignment for treason, the Council issued proclamations denouncing his, and his confederates, "divers treasonable actions...to murder our sayd Counsellers and others...spreading divers and strange and seditious inventions, to haue drawen our people to their partie," ordering those who had no "certaine dwelling or abode with the Citie and Suburbs thereof" to "get them downe into the Countrey, upon paine of death by Marshall Lawe," and offering the stupendous reward of "the summe of one hundred pounds of current money" to anyone who reported "the Authors, Writers, or dispensers of any of the sayd Libels." Each of the proclamations specifically thanked subjects for their loyalty, "as specially or our Citizens of London." To reinforce these actions, sermons were ordered throughout London to explain Essex's ambitions and crimes against the Queen. Citizens' attendance at those sermons was made compulsory. After Essex's conviction, Robert Cecil discovered a plot by apprentices to lead an uprising and free the earl from the Tower.

Fig. 27. Engraving: Elizabethan Censorship, The hangman buring books.

Fear of negative public opinion was why Essex was executed privately inside the Tower. That fear was not misplaced; upon leaving the Tower, the executioner was mobbed, and the authorities called out the London sheriffs to see that he was escorted safely home.[25]

Save for word-of-mouth, sermons, printed broadsides and ballads, and plays presented on the stage, were the only vehicles in Elizabethan London for the dissemination of news and the shaping of public opinion. Certainly, theatrical presentations did not create revolutionaries who charged out onto the streets bearing torches and pitchforks, but obviously the authorities did not view the theatre as completely under their control, and powerless. Lord Burghley himself seems to have acknowledged that plays thinly disguised real events being brought before the Star Chamber, and other Court records concerning plays indicate they "came close to modern newspaper reportage," and, at least concerning the events surrounding the *Isle of Dogs* episode of 1597, informants were sought, and sent, to the Council with reports to confirm what was being said and done on stage.[26] Edmund Tilney, Master of the Revels, made so many demands for changes in the script of the collaborative *Sir Thomas More* ("Leave out the insurrection wholly and the cause thereof"), that the authors seem to abandoned the play altogether. The Court also tried to use the Stationers' Company to control opinion.[27] The Stationers' Wardens ordered the deposition scene in *Richard II* stricken from the copies of the play printed in 1597 and 1598, and even though his book was passed by a censor, Hayward was interrogated and jailed for publishing his *History of Henry IV*, and most of the second printing was burned by the public hangman. The fact that less than a dozen copies still survive indicates the diligence of censorship when the authorities were provoked. Such incidents certainly illustrate that the Privy Council was keeping a fairly close watch upon what was being read by, and presented to, the London audience, and that it believed books and plays were important in shaping popular opinion.

Such a climate of censorship after the burning of Hayward's book in May 1599, and his arrest in July, would have punched quite a hole in the repertories of the acting companies. Shakespeare's company, for instance, immediately must have dropped his *Richard II*. Hayward had pointedly noted in his dedication to Essex that he shared a title with Bolingbroke, one of whose titles was Earl of Hereford, just as one of Essex's was Viscount Hereford. Earlier gossip in 1595 had already noted parallels between the play's portrait of Bolingbroke doffing "his bonnet to an oyster wench" (I, 4), and Essex, who "vaileth his cap to each one he doth meet." Its printed versions already had been censored,[28] and Phillips' remarks before the Privy Council in 1601 suggest the play had been dormant for a few years, though probably only three, since the play had been printed in 1598. When, however, it became known in the summer of 1599 that John Hayward was being badgered to admit his *Henry IV* was a conscious attempt to make a parallel between Bolingbroke and Essex,[29] the Chamberlain's Men would have been fools to continue the play in their repertory.

More significant to the company's repertory than this three or four year old play, Shakespeare's brand-new *Henry V* probably became unsafe to perform within a month or two of its first staging. Veiled allusions to Essex are suggested in the parallels between Henry V's Welsh connections as "Harry of Monmouth" and the Devereaux family's long-term association with Wales. Henry's fictional Welsh captain, Fluellen, noted by critics for the individuality of his characterization,[30] looks more than a bit like Essex's real Welsh captain Gelly Merrick, whose Welsh name, *Gwyllyam*,[31] even sounds similar to Fluellen. The play's fifth act prologue praises Essex overtly. Given all that, the play must have had a truncated run, disappearing from the company's offerings soon after, or even before, the arrest of John Hayward in July. The Stationers' Register in August of 1600 listed the play specifically to block its printing, the version printed in that year may be an unauthorized one, and it omitted all the choruses and any other passages which might have been construed to be analogies to Essex.[32] Privy Council jitters over Hayward's *History of Henry IV* obviously would have killed the staging of Shakespeare's *1 and 2 Henry IV*, with their constant references to the deposition of Richard II and usurpation of Henry IV. Also unsafe would be *1, 2,* and *3 Henry VI*, and *Richard III*, stories of tangled claims to the throne, weak governments dominated by venal ministers, Yorkist pedigrees seemingly presented as superior to that of the Lancastrian ancestors of the Tudors, uprisings, usurpations, and the murders of kings.

Even *King John* could be suspect, with its tale of Prince Arthur's murder and the rebellion of the barons against John. All nine of Shakespeare's English history plays would be deemed unsafe to stage after 1599, and that accounts for the works of just *one* of the playwrights working for the Chamberlain's Men. The Admiral's Men, as seen in titles listed in Henslowe's *Diary*, would be forced to drop about twice that number from its repertory, and the new Worcester's Men, its *1* and *2 Edward IV* by Thomas Heywood. Both Heywood's *Edward IV* and Shakespeare's *Henry V* (stripped of its fifth act chorus praising Essex) appeared so quickly in print in 1600 that it appears the plays were being dumped from the repertories.

That sudden loss of repertory helps explain the heightened production of Shakespeare between 1599 and 1604, with the revising of *Merry Wives of Windsor,* and the writing of *Much Ado About Nothing, Hamlet, Twelfth Night, Julius Caesar, Troilus and Cressida, As You Like It, All's Well That Ends Well, Othello,* and *Measure for Measure.* A similar flurry of activity occurred at the same time within the Admiral's Men. Dekker seems to have turned out *The Shoemaker's Holiday* and *Old Fortunatus* between the late summer and November of 1599 with what some critics term "extraordinary speed and vigor." More than seven new plays (all non-history) were added to the Admiral's Men's repertory, and between 1600 and 1602 hurried revivals and revisions were made of old standbys like *The Jew of Malta, The Spanish Tragedy* and *Doctor Faustus.* In 1602 Middleton wrote a prologue and epilogue to Greene's *Friar Bacon and Friar Bungay,* a comedy from the late 1580s or early 1590s. For the next decade other older plays, some dating back thirty years or more were revised or rewritten. *Patient Grissell* was a collaborative rehash of a play dating back to the 1560s; in 1610 Webster and Heywood rewrote *Appius* and *Virginia,* dating from 1564.

Though we tend to forget the fact, Shakespeare did the same thing. *Hamlet,* after all, was rewritten from a play dating back to the the 1580s or early 1590s, and Shakespeare's *King Lear* turned a comedy of the same name from the 1580s into a tragedy. Many scholars have remarked upon his seeming "restlessness and experimentation," as he moved from plays as different in type as *Julius Caesar,* to *Hamlet,* to *Troilus and Cressida,* to *Measure for Measure,* to *Othello,* to *All's Well,* to *King Lear.* Others have commented upon the seeming "borrowing" taking place among playwrights. Shakespeare may have "borrowed" from Heywood's *1 Iron Age,* for *Troilus and Cressida;* Heywood "borrowed" from Shakespeare for *2 Iron Age.*

Arden of Feversham, considered one of the first of the "domestic" tragedies, was written and staged sometime before 1592. Yet there are few other examples of this type of play, that is a plot built around violence and death in a domestic household rather than on a grander, political scale, until the turn of the century. *Arden* was reprinted in 1598, and soon thereafter Thomas Heywood's *A Woman Killed with Kindness* appeared in the repertory of the Fortune Theatre. The success of Heywood's domestic tragedy there, may have served as inspiration for Shakespeare's "domestic tragedy," *Othello*, and the anonymous *Yorkshire Tragedy* at the Globe. The popularity of *Patient Grissell*, and novels featuring the long-suffering wife, may have been, in part, responsible for Shakespeare's "Grissell," Helena in *All's Well That Ends Well*. The satirical "Cittie comodies" of Jonson, such as *Every Man Out of His Humor*, of Marston, such as *The Malcontent*, of Dekker, such as *Blurt, Master Constable*, of Middleton, such as *Phoenix*, probably were influential in Shakespeare's scripting of *Measure for Measure*. This flurry of activity on the part of all the theatre companies over a very short time, suggests that all the companies were scrambling to find new additions to their repertories.

A very few plays dealing with aspects of English history were scripted, such as Dekker's and Webster's *Sir Thomas Wyatt*, and Heywood's two-part *If You Know Not Me, You Know Nobody*, but these new plays dealt not with the great political events of English history, but with Protestant martyrs and Popish plots against Elizabeth. Even the so-called "War of the Theatres" among the Boys' Companies, in which Jonson, Dekker, and others brought out plays attacking each others' acting companies, and playwriting abilities, smacks of haste. What quicker way to get witty, yet seemingly politically innocuous, new plays on the boards than to burlesque theatrical rivals, with parodies of each others' acting styles, repertories, and lines? In short, the acting companies had to fill up the holes in their repertories with plays that were politically non-controversial.[33]

The book trade displays a similar groping for titles, a shift to translations of Greco-Roman classics, books and about long-ago, far away, and *non-English* topics. Historical favorites of the 1580s and 1590s, like Grafton's and Holingshed's *Chronicles*, saw no new issues. In the 1580s, even before the political crisis of 1599, certain parts of Holingshed had been excised by order of the Privy Council because it believed them too dangerous for public consumption. The even more popular Stowe's *Chronicles*, and his *Annals*, and *Survey of London*, saw a hiatus in publishing from the turn of the century until 1603 and 1604,[34] in other words until after the death of the Queen. The printing of sermons increased, averaging about fifteen per year, and some of those were reprints of sermons by clergy like Hugh Lattimer or John Jewel, whose works dated from the middle decades of the sixteenth century, and which had last seen print in the early 1590s. Almanacs, which seem to have declined in popularity around 1590, begin to reappear in larger numbers. Songbooks, books on rhetoric, translations of Italian, French and Spanish romances, stories of Protestant martyrs under Queen Mary, and playscripts, were printed in large numbers.

Until 1600, on average, less than five playscripts per year were printed (with the notable exception of 20 in 1594 when acting troupes were in dire need of money due to three years of plague in London). In 1599 and 1600, however, 14 plays were printed, many, like *Arden of Feversham* or *Doctor Faustus*, reprints of plays ten years old or older. The annual average for the printing of plays over next ten years was 15 per year. Novels extolling the accomplishments and virtues of successful merchants, artisans and tradesmen, like the fabled Dick Whittington, became ever more frequent, and there were reprints of books not published for years, for instance: Robert Greene's *Never too late*, reprinted in 1600 after a ten-year hiatus, *Gwyndonius* in 1607, last printed in 1593, and *Pandosto* in 1609, last printed in 1595, and other older works including a treatise on the compass from 1581, a treatise on horsemanship from 1565, a treatise on navigation dating from 1561, and a reprint of the story of Sir Bevis of Southampton, dating from 1500.

The increase in Greco-Roman titles, especially reprints of translations of Plutarch's *Lives*, Sallust's and Lucan's *Histories*, Caesar's *Gallic* and *Civil Wars*, and William Caxton's translation of Lefevre's *History of Troy* (dating back to 1475, and last printed in 1591), may well represent the book trade's attempt to satisfy the public's interest in history with easily produced alternatives to the now politically dangerous English histories. These also were histories, but of times, places, and people long ago and far away, and therefore less likely to be visited by Privy Council disapproval because of seeming topicality. The reward of £100, offered, in 1601, to anyone who "make knowen...the name of any of the Authors, Writers, or dispersers of...Libels" must have given printers and players the jitters that they could be denounced for sedition. Sir Walter Raleigh, writing his *Historie of the World*, during his confinement in the Tower (1603-16), noted that it was safer to write ancient history because "whosoever, in writing a modern history, shall follow truth too near the heels, it may haply strike out his teeth."[36]

Certainly that would seem to explain the theatre's proliferation of Greco-Roman tragedies, and other tragedies like Chapman's *Bussy D'Ambois* and Shakespeare's *King Lear*. These are still chronicle type plays; they still offer the great men, the battles and spectacles, grand themes, pathos and bathos that the English history plays had offered.[37] Most attractive, no new investment need be made to stage these plays. Except for some draping about the shoulders of major characters to suggest Greco-Roman dress, all plays were done in Elizabethan "modern costume."[38] Mounting new productions was expensive, yet by utilizing Greco-Roman and other tragedies all the velvet doublets, robes gowns, crowns, swords, armor, chariots, and so on, that had been used to such good effect to dramatize the Wars of the Roses could continue to be used when dramatizing stories of the Trojan War (Shakespeare's *Troilus and Cressida*, Heywood's *Iron Age*), or the Battles of Phillipi (Shakespeare's *Julius Caesar*) and Pharsalus (Chapman's *Caesar* and *Pompey*), or the pageantry of a *Charles Duke of Byron*, or a *Tragedy of Nero*, or a *King Lear*, or a *Macbeth*.

That Shakespeare's company moved faster, somewhat, in the direction of Greco-Roman and tragedy plays (with *Julius Caesar* and *Hamlet* in 1599 and 1600) is no surprise. The connections of that company to the Essex-Southampton circle, and its occasional performance of veiled propaganda in its favor, were known; what protection that connection may have provided in the past was now negated by Essex's and Southampton's disgrace, and the ascendency at Court of the anti-Essex faction. The acting company would not wish to be seen overtly producing pro-Essex publicity. Furthermore, both its legal patron, the Lord Chamberlain, and the patrons of the the rival adult companies, the Lord Admiral, and the Earl of Worcester, were leading figures in the faction which ruined Essex. Since the legal right to exist, and perform, as an acting company depended upon that patronage, no company would risk offending, and perhaps losing, its official patron.

Even after Essex had been dead for two years, the Privy Council still displayed a watchful hostility towards any venue which smacked of praise for Essex, or the involvement of disaffected members of the aristocracy in politics, or conspiracy to overthrow monarchs. Sir Walter

Raleigh and Lord Cobham were imprisoned on the flimsiest of charges shortly after James' arrival in England. That incident may only have been internecine conflict within the Council, but the Council's concern about possible plots was, perhaps, justified. The Gunpowder Plot in 1604, which planned to blow up Parliament on its opening day, involved many of the same men who had supported Essex and survived his fall. Therefore anything which might serve to sustain, or recreate, the opposition to the dominant faction that the Essex circle had represented was suspect. The Privy Council's vigilance even extended to books or plays which were not about English history but based upon Greco-Roman stories, or any other item touching on conspiracies. In 1603 Ben Jonson was summoned before the Privy Council to answer charges that his play, *Sejanus*, staged by the King's Men, seemed seditious, and in 1604 Samuel Daniels was likewise summoned concerning his play *Philotas*. Though both plays dealt with classical Greco-Roman historical subjects, they nonetheless depicted conspiracies, and the Privy Council seemed to believe, or fear, that the plays were attempting veiled allusions to justify the Essex conspiracy, or might be construed as such by their audiences.

Other attempts to slide by that vigilance failed. The anonymously written play about Gowrie's attempt to assassinate King James in Edinburgh in 1600 was suppressed. Fulke Grenville was forbidden access to documents by Robert Cecil when he attempted to write a history of Elizabeth's reign. Most literature and plays which touched on kings and nobles, generally were romances, politically neutral, dealing with a king's inherent justice and goodness. When attempts were made to write of the Essex episode, they met with quick action. Robert Prickert, in 1604, attempted to publish a life of Essex; the printings were confiscated, and he and the printer interrogated. Ballads, such as Thomas Lodge's poetic encomium to the dead Essex, though they followed the "official" line that he had been lead astray by evil advisors, were confiscated and destroyed.[39]

Hence, the collapse of Essex's faction and his execution in 1601 did not end the climate of censorship which contributed to the changes in printing and playwriting at the turn of the seventeenth century. Nor did the accession of James I in 1603. The Cecil-Howard faction which had opposed, and destroyed, Essex, remained in power throughout the period. Lady Anne Clifford noted in her diary that people flocked to

James' court "all full of hopes, every man expecting mountains and finding molehills, excepting Sir R. Cecil and the house of the Howards." James himself was opposed to any popular material which seemed to question the policies he pursued, the personnel and functioning of his court, or the legitimacy of royal authority. It cannot be just enthusiasm for, and curiosity about, the new monarch that produced seven editions of James' treatise on kingship, *Basilikon Doron*, in 1603 and 1604, including one in *Welsh*. James was using the book trade to circulate his own propaganda. In 1604, *Eastward Ho*, Jonson's, Marston's, and Chapman's attempt to satirize James' Court was suppressed, and the playwrights, and some of the actors were jailed, and threatened by the king with the loss of noses and ears. In the following year, John Day's satire, *The Isle of Gulls*, met with similar treatment.[40]

The changing themes, new genres, and lively experimentation among playwrights at the turn of the seventeenth century, which have been noted by scholars, may well have been hastened as much by *necessity*, as by changing audience tastes, or conscious artistic choices, or increased artistic competition, or "new blood" in the theatre world. The political fallout from the Essex episode no doubt drove playwrights to explore and develop more quickly what were fledgling efforts at domestic tragedy and city comedy at the end of the sixteenth century. Forced, precipitously, to abandon themes which smacked of contemporary politics, or criticism of the Court, those writing for the commercial printers, and commercial theatres, searched for new themes and genres which would slip by the censors, but still appeal enough to popular audiences to bring in the pennies. It cannot be pure coincidence that their old standbys, books and plays about English political and dynastic history, only reappeared in 1613. Sir John Hayward's *The Lives of the III. Normans Kings of England* seems to reflect a nostalgia for an idealized past. So too does Shakespeare's and Fletcher's *Henry VIII*. That play bears little resemblance to earlier chronicle histories; it appears more like a kind of "national pageant." Its appearance was coincident with political episodes occurring in 1612-13: the death of Henry, Prince of Wales, and appearance of funeral encomiums comparing him to Henry VIII, the re-entombment of James' mother Mary Queen of Scots, *and* the eclipse of the Cecil-Howard faction at Court, caused by the Lord Admiral's decline in influence, and the death of Sir Robert Cecil.[41]

Observations

In the last two decades of the sixteenth century, the London theatre achieved autonomy from its earlier dependence upon courtly or religious patronage. It became a popular, commercial theatre, which found a place for itself within the framework of the emerging market economy of Renaissance England. Its practitioners' methods of making money were no different than those of the aspiring agricultural yeomen, artisans and entrepreneurs who were changing England from an agrarian-based, manorial system into a commodity oriented, money based economy.[1] Finding a more or less permanent base in London, they sought to sell their new commodity, entertainment, to as many people as possible. As such London theatre was more closely tied to mass market tastes than either the courtly or religious theatre which preceded it, or the upper-class, status-oriented, entertainment it was starting to become just before, and after, the English Civil War.[2]

Theatre offered men a means to make large amounts of money quickly. Investing in theatre buildings and theatrical activities could, and did, bring huge profits with little effort save the investment of capital. Despite its risks, theatre's lure for potential profits are demonstrated in the substantial investments of James Burbage, joiner and carpenter, John Brayne, grocer, Philip Henslowe, dyer, Robert Keysar, goldsmith. On a small scale, therefore, the theatre business reflects the same economic drives that created such risky overseas investments as the Virginia Company, and just as that company involved merchants and peers, such as the Grocers' Company and the Earl of Southampton, the theatre business witnessed a certain merging of groups for financial gain which traditionally had been separated by hierarchical status.

For those with less capital to invest, becoming a Sharer in a successful London-based acting company offered a means to bypass the restrictions on income imposed by the traditional economic system, and achieve, and surpass, the income of members of the country Gentry and liveried Masters within the traditional guilds. The loose form of aristocratic patronage necessary for legal existence, such as that held by

231

the Admiral's and Chamberlain's Men, or the manipulation of a Royal Patent, such as that held by Evans and Giles, gave shrewd men access to a means of making money denied the average yeoman, artisan, or craftsman. Like most other Englishmen seeking profit, theatrical personnel were bending the traditional system to make money for themselves by providing a new commodity and service, professional entertainment.

Only when it is remembered that the Elizabethan theatre was dominated by mass market audiences, and actors whose hope for income was directly tied to pleasing those audiences, does the amazing literary productivity of late sixteenth-century playwrights become understandable. Unlike a touring company which could recycle the same plays from town to town without fear of repetition, the fixed locale of the acting troupes in London meant an ever increasing need for new scripts to draw crowds.

Just as professional theatre created the new profession of professional actor, perhaps the acting companies' needs for new scripts created a new profession, that of professional writer. University graduates like George Peele, Robert Greene, Christopher Marlowe, and literate, talented middle class men like Thomas Dekker, Thomas Kyd, Michael Drayton, and Ben Jonson could now earn a living with their pens.[3] Even though playwrights who only wrote plays never made as much as actor-Sharers, like Shakespeare and Heywood who also wrote plays, nonetheless an acting company still paid its writers much more than a printer paid for a tract, a translation, a ballad, a broadside, or a novel. One play could earn a playwright as much as the average, wage-earning artisan labored a year to achieve.

Yet the plays were company assets and commodities, owned by the acting companies, not literature controlled by the author. As such they were guarded by their owners, the actors, as jealously as techniques and secrets of crafts were guarded by the Masters of the guilds. In an age when guild control over its members and products was declining, and guild members were circumventing the secrets and standards of their guilds, it is not surprising to find that Sharers' had troubles controlling their members, like Will Kempe, and that popular plays were pirated in print by those who sought to cash in on the success of this new product.

In those last two decades of the sixteenth century, the London theatre also reflected the conflicting social and political pressures and uncertainties in England at the end of Elizabeth's reign. The appearance of domestic tragedies and city comedies display the new, changing social scene in London, where traditional, rural social relationships no longer answered the concerns of an urban, wage-earning populace faced with the economic pressures of an emerging commercial and capitalist system. The affair of *The Isle of Dogs*, and the moratorium on English history books and plays during the Essex crisis, exemplify the political uncertainties, especially about just who *was*, and who *would be*, in control of the realm. Identifying who, and what, was responsible for the closing of the theatres in 1597, after the staging of *The Isle of Dogs*, is a painstaking jigsaw puzzle, which only can be pieced together by tracing relationships and parallels within theatrical personnel, aristocratic patronage, court intrigue, and economic pressures. By the same token, the probable catalysts for the extremely rapid shift in theme and focus of plays at the end of the sixteenth century and the beginning of the seventeenth are not obvious until relationships among theatrical, mercantile, and political factors are examined. Neither of these episodes initially seems to lead to the unsettling, political presence of the Earl of Essex, until his actions, conflicts, and personality seem to shimmer pervasively, and unbidden, whenever new pieces of the puzzles are uncovered. In contrast, to identify who and what was responsible for the closing of *Eastward Ho* in 1604 is transparent; the play burlesqued the actions of the king, and the orders to close the play, and arrest the playwrights and actors, came quickly and directly from King James himself.

Those political uncertainties, and the conflicting political censorship reflected by them, caused playwrights to be relatively non-specific in their satire, spoofs, and allusions to topical events. A play clearly scripting the "treachery" of Dr. Lopez would never have been allowed to be performed, at least not for many performances, but a play about a "vile Jew" which subliminally reminded audiences about the Lopez incident could be staged. Perhaps, therefore, we should thank that censorship which forced Shakespeare and his contemporaries to be very circumspect. It forced them into writing plays universal enough in themes, plots, characters, and contents that they still can be read, and played, today.

One of the ways to identify, and attempt some relationships among all these factors is to view the study of sixteenth-century English theatre as a kind of detective story. Chronology becomes extremely important, but a chronology of a kind which views a variety of things within thin slices of time, which then are then put into a composite form. Why a particular play was written when it was, *is* a significant question, if we wish to find fuller understanding of that play, its seeming perplexities, its form, and the role that theatre played within its societal context. Chronologies of play genres also need to be used for more than identification of poetic evolution or evidence of societal attitudes, tastes, and trends. Those aspects of "telling time" need to be linked to chronologies of character types in plays, and need to be aligned with other interests and events, like London gossip, Court intrigue, and above all, contemporary theatrical business sense—please the crowd, but don't cross the authorities enough to get shut down.

Sometimes, for purposes of interpretation, we need to turn to educated imagination, in order to try to place ourselves within the immediate temporal framework of those Elizabethan playwrights and audiences, so that interpretations are based on some of the things those playwrights may have meant to be seen, and what some members of those audiences could see, or feel, in a single viewing, not in a leisurely and studious reading.[4] Yet paradoxically, the fruits of leisurely and studious reading, as it appears in the works of literary and dramatic scholars and critics, are themselves one means of educating our imaginations about that very milieu of playwright, audience, and society at large. An eclectic approach to all these methods and viewpoints, societal, chronological, esthetic, linguistic, may be what is needed. Eclecticism is sometimes a "dirty word" in scholarship, for it implies, perhaps, a certain naivete in selecting and recombining elements from a variety of methods and interpretations without enough due regard for their internal integrity. But should we therefore reject, or ignore, valuable insights, methods, and new directions of thought to be found in disparate approaches, simply because we may lack full appreciation for, or disagree with, the overall structure of those methods and interpretations?

Above all, we need to remember that Shakespeare and his contemporaries, like anyone then or now, rarely were motivated by thoughts of posterity or universality of theme. They had to deal with constantly shifting, and sometimes contradictory, "physical facts, historical facts, legal and political facts, and especially, for each person, the ever approaching phalanx of practical facts," which confront a person from hour to hour and day to day.[5] Sometimes those "practical facts" were the necessity to compete with established rivals, sometimes to repay debts to powerful patrons, sometimes to avoid the ire of those in power, sometimes to meet the needs and limitations of the acting company, but *always* to meet the practical ends of keeping the company going so as to make a living, prosper, and survive in a business which was beset with the doubly volatile problems of potential audience rejection and official disapproval.

Appendix

Scholars are justly wary of attempting the conversion of monies from one age to another. Yet most of us find that sums left in the pristine form of a bygone age give little indication of their real value. Comparison to incomes and expenses of that bygone time are of some help in addressing the idea of scales of expenditures and income, but those comparisons still lack the impact and understanding that sums given in our own currency provide,even if those sums give only a crude approximation. For instance, Henslowe, Alleyn, Burbage, Heminges, Shakespeare, and the other giants of the Elizabethan theatre business earned enough money to be ranked within the top five percent income bracket of sixteenth-century England. Impressive, but still a bit vague in fixing some idea of what that meant in comparison to their contemporaries and to us. By modern American standards, however, it means at least annual incomes of between $91,750 (*Money Income & Poverty Status in the U.S., 1989*, Department of Commerce, Bureau of the Census) and $100,000 or over (*Newsweek* 4 Nov. 1991).

In 1940, Alfred Harbage (*Shakespeare's Audience*) attempted to give some meaning to a modern American reader when he estimated that in terms of proportion of income, the one-penny basic admission an average Elizabethan working man spent at the public theater was about the same as the basic price of a movie ticket to an average American working man of 1940. If we use the movie ticket price as a guide to inflation over the past 50 years, the Elizabethan penny today would equal about $5.50. At 240 pennies to the Elizabethan pound sterling, therefore, £1 in 1595 would roughly equal $1320 in the early 1990s.

Bearing in mind all of the problems involved in such conversion—questions of relative purchasing power, (for instance an average urban dweller of Shakespeare's day used 75 percent to 80 percent of income for food), differing availability of goods and services, remembering that finished goods in general were higher priced to the Elizabethan, that labor costs were lower, that the skilled craftsman today is paid proportionately higher than one of the sixteenth century—the formula

237

still offers a crude base for comparison. For instance, if £1=$1320, then the average artisan's yearly wage in sixteenth century London, £15, would roughly equal $19,800 today. That figure is remarkably close to sums given by the Bureau of Labor Statistics in 1989-90 as the average American wage. Then, as now, those in the upper ten percent bracket garnered about 40 percent of the distribution of total annual income.

The following table duplicates some of the information contained in Table 3, "Art Imitates Business," but with one exception. Substituted for the comparison to years of labor to the Elizabethan artisan, are sums in modern American currency. Please keep in mind that these are only meant to give a very, very, very crude idea of what those Elizabethan sums might mean today.

Comparison of Selected Theatre-Related Monies of the Sixteenth Century to United States Dollars (1992)		
Item	**16th-Cent.£**	**U.S. $**
Construction Costs: Burbage's "Theatre"	£666	$879,120
Construction Costs: Henslowe's "Rose"	£816	$1,077,120
Construction Costs: "The Globe"	£600	$792,000
Construction Costs: Henslowe's "Fortune"	£600	$792,000
Average Construction Costs (4 Theatres)	£673	$888,360
Land Rent, Annual: Burbage's "Theatre"	£14	$18,480
Average Play Production Costs: Annually	£900	$1,188,000
Average Maintenance Costs: Annual	£100	$132,000
Average Daily Receipts: "Globe" or "Rose"	£8.5	$11,220
Average Daily Receipts: "Blackfriars"	£15.75	$20,790
Total Daily Average: Globe/Blackfriars	£23.25	$30,690
Annual Receipts: Globe/Blackfriars	£6545	$8,639,400
Costumes/Properties: "The Swan"	£300	$396,000
Buy-In, Buy-Out Share: Acting Companies	£70-£90	$92-$118,000
Playwright's Fee Per Play	£6	$7,920
Playwright's Fee + "Benefit" Performance	£14.5	$19,140
Burbage's Landed Income (London Property)	£300	$396,000
Heminges' Minimum Income (1623)	£1000	$1,320,000
Henslowe's Theatre Expenses (1593-1603)	£2399	$3,166,680
Shakespeare's Cash Bequests (In Will)	£387	$510,840
Shakespeare's House in Blackfriar Dist.	£140	$184,800
Cooke's Cash Bequests (In Will)	£150	$198,000
Alleyn's Upkeep Costs: Dulwich Manor	£1700	$2,244,000
Purchase Price of Dulwich Manor	£10000	$132,000,000

Notes

Chapter 1

[1]A. Harbage, *Shakespeare and the Rival Traditions* (Bloomington, IN, 1970), 89. W. Ingram, "Robert Keysar, Playhouse Speculator," *Shakespeare Quarterly*, 38 (1986), 476. K.E. McLuskie's recent work: "The Poets' Royal Exchange: Patronage and Commerce in Early Modern Drama," *The Yearbook of English Studies*, 21 (1991), 62, refreshingly points out that many of the professional playwrights, like Thomas Dekker, seem to have accepted that "the theatre and the market have become one: poets provide the commodity which is dealt in by the players and purchased by the audience: patronage has become a matter of commerce and the only patrons the paying audience."

[2]For example, Harbage, *Traditions*, 5. W. Ingram, "Henry Lanman's Curtain Playhouse as an 'Eraser' to the Theatre, 1585-1592," in *The First Public Playhouse. The Theatre in Shoreditch, 1576-1598*, Ed. H. Berry (Montreal, 1979), 17-27.

[3]Much of Table 1 was compiled from information found in E. Nungezer, A *Dictionary of Actors...before 1642* (New Haven, 1929), *passim*. Nungezer's work is an invaluable starting place for information concerning figures connected with theatre and entertainment in England of the sixteenth and early seventeenth centuries. Other information garnered from: E.A. Gerrard, *Elizabethan Drama and Dramatists* (New York, 1972), 118-298; J.M. Sargeaunt, *John Ford* (New York, 1966), 6; B.H. Newdigate, *Michael Drayton and His Circle* (Oxford, 1961), 4-5; G. Price, *Thomas Dekker* (New York, 1969), 21; N. Brittin, *Thomas Middleton* (New York, 1972), 13-16; T.A.Dunn, *Philip Massinger* (Edinburgh, 1957), 5-15; A. Nicoll, ed., *The Works of Cyril Tourneur* (New York, 1963), 3-5, 23-29; A.M. Clark, *Thomas Heywood* (Oxford, 1931), 1-7; E.K. Chambers, *The Elizabethan Stage* (Oxford, 1923), v. 1, 348-50, v. 2, 81, 299-350, v. 3, 215, 249, 263, 289, 306, 314, 323, 352, 394, 418, 427, 444-50, 507; *Dictionary of National Biography* (Oxford, 1949-50), v. 4, 924, v. 9, 384, v. 18, 126, v. 20, 1031; A. Gurr, *The Shakespearean Stage* 1574-1642 (Cambridge, 1980), 216-28; S.P. Cerasano, "Revising Phillip Henslowe's Biography," *Notes and Queries. New Series*, 32 (1985), 67-72; D. Honneyman, "The Family Origins of Henry Condell," *Notes and Queries. New Series*, 32 (1985), 467-68.

[4]K. Wrightson, *English Society* 1580-1680 (New Brunswick, NJ, 1982), 30-33; R.E. Seavoy, *Famine in Peasant Societies* (New York, 1986), 31-33, 44-

45, 67-71, 76-84, 89-90; M.L. Campbell, *The English Yeoman* (New Haven, 1942), 10-11, 24-26; S.T. Bindoff, *Tudor England* (New York, 1978), 121-27, 200-01; W. Cohen, *Drama of a Nation. Public Theater in Renaissance England and Spain* (Ithaca, NY, 1985), 143-45; J.C. Agnew, *Worlds Apart: The Market and the Theatre in Anglo-American Thought, 1550-1750* (Cambridge, 1986), 57-58.

[5]M. Plant, *The English Book Trade* (London, 1965), 36; and Bindoff, *Tudor*, 100-01: both stress that the Statute of Artificers (1563) attempted to discourage the physical or social mobility of occupations. See also Agnew, *Worlds*, 51-55.

[6]Seavoy, *Famine*, 84.

[7]L. Stone, *The Crisis of the Aristocracy, 1558-1641* (Oxford, 1965), 758-67; Seavoy, *Famine*, 84.

[8]Chambers, *Stage*, vol. 1, 349-51; *DNB*, vol. 4, 924, vol. 9, 384, Nungezer, *Dictionary*, 98-99, 179, 188, 280, 315; S. Schoenbaum, *William Shakespeare: Records and Images* (New York, 1981), 57-58; A.L. Rowse, *William Shakespeare* (New York, 1963), 290, 445-46; *Henslowe Papers*, Ed. W.W. Greg (London, 1907).

[9]B. Weinreb and C. Hibbert, *The London Encyclopaedia* (London, 1983), 12-13, 67-68, 213, 338, 344, 669, 803, 829; S. Manley, *London in the Age of Shakespeare* (University Park, PA, 1986), 5-8, 10, 17-21, 38-39.

[10]Nungezer, *Dictionary*, 99, 179; Harbage, *Traditions*, 24-25; Gurr, *Stage*, 88-89; C. Bridenbaugh, *Vexed and Troubled Englishmen* (New York, 1968).

[11]W. Besant, *London in the Age of the Stuarts* (London, 1903), 374; Gurr, *Stage*, 88-90; Chambers, *Stage*, vol. 1, 349-51.

[12]See note 3 above. See also A. von Martin, *Sociology of the Renaissance* (New York, 1963), 31.

[13]I. Archer, *The Pursuit of Stability. Social Relations in Elizabethan England* (Cambridge, 1991), 100-48; H.G. Koenigsberger and G.L. Mosse, *Europe in the Sixteenth Century* (New York, 1968), 34-40; Manley, *London*, 5-8; von Martin, *Sociology*, 6-9; N. Carson, *A Companion to Henslowe's Diary* (Cambridge, 1988), 1-5; W. Ingram, *A London Life in the Brazen Age. Francis Langley, 1548-1602* (Cambridge, MA, 1978), 1-120, and his "Keysar," 479-82; Bindoff, *Tudor*, 124-27; Agnew, *Worlds*, 48-52.

[14]Chambers, *Stage*, v 1, 349; Cohen, *Drama*, 171-75; Agnew, *Worlds*, 106-07.

[15]Gurr, *Stage*, 110; A. Harbage, *Shakespeare's Audience* (New York, 1964), 15-16; Agnew, *Worlds*, 54-55; Cohen, *Drama*, 161-63.

[16]T.R. Reddaway, "London and the Court," *Shakespeare Survey*, 17 (1964), 3-12; Manley, *London*, 5-18.

[17]M. Edmunds, "The Builder of the Rose Theatre," *Theatre Notebook*, XLIV (1990), 50-54.

[18]T. Nashe, *Pierce Penilesse, His Supplicaton to the Divell*, Ed. R.B. McKerrow, *Works*, I (London, 1904), 148-49, 169-71, 212-18; S. Mullaney, *The Place of the Stage. License, Play and Power in Renaissance England* (Chicago, 1988), 7-8; S. Dickey, "Shakespeare's Mastiff Comedy," *Shakespeare Quarterly*, 42 (1991), 255-62; R. Ashton, "Popular Entertainment and Social Control in Later Elizabethan and Early Stuart London," *London Journal*, 9 (1983), 3-16; M. Byrne, *Elizabethan Life in Town and Country* (London, 1961), 240-77; A. Gurr, *Playgoing in Shakespeare's London* (Cambridge, 1-22; Harbage, *Audience*, 57-61. W. Lewis, *The Lion and the Fox. The Role of the Hero in the Plays of Shakespeare* (New York, n.d.), 35-36 discusses the playwright as "an entertainer" who sought to appeal to a broad spectrum of classes. Agnew, *Worlds*, 109-20, describes how drama reflected a self-conscious view of the new notions of a commercial, "market," economy by viewing the relationship between performance and audience almost as a "commercial contract."

[19]Harbage, *Audience*, 19-22; Gurr, *Stage*, 113-30; I. Ribner, *William Shakespeare* (Waltham, MA, 1969), 144-52; I. Smith, *Shakespeare's Blackfriars Playhouse* (New York, 1964), 130-33; M. Edmund, "The Builder of the Rose Theatre," *Theatre Notebook*, 44 (1990), 51.

[20]von Martin, *Sociology*, 16.

[21]Stone, *Crisis*, 767, and Appendix XXIII; Harbage, *Audience*, 55-62.

[22]Smith, *Blackfriars*, 127-56. Mullaney, *Stage*, 27-32, maintains that theatres and playhouses became *de facto* corporations by avoiding the jurisdiction of the city fathers.

[23]Gurr, *Stage*, 118-30; Harbage *Traditions*, 23.

[24]Stone, *Crisis*, Appendix XXIII; Harbage, *Audience*, 55-62.

[25]Henslowe's contract with Peter Street is often reproduced. See, for instance, *The Riverside Shakespeare*, Ed. G.B. Evans (Boston, 1974), 1849-50. W. Besant, *London in the Age of the Tudors* (London, 1904), 276 discusses the lavish decoration of wealthy merchant townhouses.

[26]Cohen, *Drama*, 162-68; Mullaney, *Stage*, 19-55. A.M. Nagler, *A Source Book in Theatrical History* (New York, 1952), 126-33 gives excerpts of Puritan attacks on the immorality and lawlessness of theatres, and of various spectators eye-witness accounts of audience attentiveness and decorum. See also Gurr, *Playgoing*, 44-48.

[27]Gurr, *Stage*, 116-19.

[28]Chambers, *Stage*, vol 1, 358-68; Smith, *Blackfriars*, 173-74; Gurr, *Stage*, 131-32, Ribner, *Shakespeare*, 145-47. Henslowe remarks in his Diary that he met Thomas Pope in June 1603 "consernynge the tackynge of the Leace of the

Littell Roose," but that the offer made by Pope was such that "I sayd I wold rather pulle downe the playhowse then I wold do so."

[29]G. Wickham, " ' Heavens,' Machinery and Pillars in the Theatre and Other Early Playhouses," *First Public Playouse*, 1-13; Smith, *Blackfriars*, 276-79; *Henslowe's Diary*, 6, 7, 59. Table 2 is compiled from the N. Carson's invaluable *Companion*, 102-15.

[30]*Henslowe's Diary*, 8, 13, 44, 61, 65; G.E. Bentley, *The Profession of Dramatist in Shakespeare's Time, 1590-1642* (Princeton, 1986), 152-63; Bentley, *The Profession of Player in Shakepeare's Time* (Princeton, 1986), 152-53.

[31]Stone, *Crisis*, 761; Harbage, *Audience*, 43-52; Gurr, *Stage*, 196.

[32]Smith, *Blackfriars*, 263, 274.

[33]Smith, *Blackfriars*, 274.

[34]Chambers, *Stage*, vol. 1, 372-75.

[35]Harbage, *Audience*, 43-52; Smith, *Blackfriars*, 276.

[36]C.M. Cipolla, *Before the Industrial Revolution* (New York, 1976), 12-14.

[37]Shakespeare's will is often reproduced. See, for example, *Riverside*, 1832-33. See also Smith, *Blackfriars*, 250-51; Chambers *Stage*, vol. 1, 270.

[38]Chambers, *Stage*, vol. 2, 311; Gurr, *Stage*, 88-89; Smith, *Blackfriars*, 186-88, 253-55; Nungezer, *Dictionary*, 102, 280-82, 285-86.

[39]Harbage, *Audience*, 15-16; Smith, *Blackfriars*, 264-66, 281-82.

[40]Harbage, *Audience*, 43-52.

[41]Smith, *Blackfriars*, 264-65.

[42]Harbage, *Tradition*, 104-05.

[43]For *Love's Labors' Lost* and *Cardenio* see *Riverside*, 49, 50, 55; H. Child, "Stage History of *The Taming of the Shrew*" in *New Cambridge Shakespeare* (Cambridge, 1968), 184-85. R. Fleissner, *Shakespeare and the Matter of the Crux* (Lewiston, NY, 1991) argues convincing that *Much Ado About Nothing* probably is a reworking of Meres' notation of the non-existent *Love's Labour's Won*.

[44]Plant, *Book Trade*, 241; H.S. Bennett, *English Books and Readers, 1558-1603* (Cambridge, 1965), 94, 215-17; F.S. Fussner, *Tudor History and the Historians* (New York, 1970), 261, 270, 282.

[45]Harbage, *Audience*, 146-47.

[46]J. Simon, *Education and Society in Tudor England* (Cambridge, 1967), 299-332; D. Cressy, "Educational Opportunity in Tudor and Stuart England," *History of Education Quarterly*, 16 (1976); M.H. Curtis, "Education and Apprenticeship," *Shakespeare Survey*, 17 (1964), 53-66; R.D. Pepper, ed., *Four Tudor Books on Education* (Gainesville, FL, 1966) is facsimile reproduction of four treatises dating from 1533 to 1588. See also: A. Pitt, *Shakespeare's Women*

(Totowa, NJ, 1981), 19-25; Plant, *Book Trade*, 83, 91, 240-41; Bennett, *Books*, 215-20; Fussner, *Historians*, 232, 261, 270, 282. W. Besant. *Tudors*, 377, gives the example of William Lambe, wealthy clothworker of London (d. 1577) who endowed two free schools in his native county of Kent.

⁴⁷A.W. Pollard and G.R. Redgrave, eds., *A Short-Title Catalogue of Books. Printed in England...1475-1640* (London, 1956), see especially 267-68, 543 for the numerous editions of Grafton and Stowe; *Annals of English Literature, 1475-1950* (Oxford, 1961); A. Brown, "The Printing of Books," *Shakespeare Survey*, 17 (1964), 205-13; Bennett, *Books*, 79-80, 84-89, 93, 103, 218-19; Plant, *Book Trade*, 36-39; Fussner, *Historians*, 233. B.M. Horner, "Seventeenth-Century English Songs and Songbooks," *Selected Papers. Shakespeare and Renaissance Association of West Virginia*, 13 (1988), 48-55, notes that even in the specialized area of music there were 85 songbooks published between 1588 and 1632.

⁴⁸Basic to the identification of Shakespeare's sources is G. Bullough's eight-volume *Narrative and Dramatic Sources of Shakespeare* (Boston, 1974). Table compiled from *Riverside*, 48-56, 1861-69; Bennett, *Books*, 69, 82-84, 93-97, 215-20.

⁴⁹Chambers, *Stage*, vol. 1, 352-54. E.J.A. Honigmann, *Shakespeare: the 'lost years'* (Towata, NJ, 1985), 119-21, maintains that the dates of Shakespeare's earliest plays need to be set back by at least two years. Table compiled from A. Harbage and S. Schoenbaum, eds., *Annals of English Drama, 975-1700* (Philadelphia, 1964); Pollard and Redgrave, *A Short-Title Catalogue; Annals of English Literature*; Harbage, *Rival Traditions*, 343-50; Gurr, *Stage*, 216-28; *Riverside*, "Chronology and Sources," 47-56, and "Annals," 1854-93.

⁵⁰Plant, *Book Trade*, 83, 91, 240-41; Bennett, *Books*, 215-20; Fussner, *Historians*, 231, 261, 270-82.

⁵¹Rowse, *Shakespeare*, 61. G. Mattingly, *The Armada* (Boston, 1959), 344-51, describes English nationalism burgeoning in the late sixteenth century.

⁵²E.H. Miller, *The Professional Writer in Elizabethan England* (Cambridge, MA, 1959), 4, discusses the close relationship between printers, writers, and book buyers; Bennett, *Books*, 69, 82-89, 93-97, 215-20.

⁵³Tables compiled from *Henslowe's Diary*, Eds. R.A. Foakes and R.T. Rickert (Cambridge, 1961), 16-60; Harbage and Schoenbaum, *Annals*; Pollard and Redgrave, *Short-Title Catalogue* (London, 1956); *Annals of English Literature*; Harbage, *Rival Traditions*, 343-50; Gurr, *Stage*, 216-28. Gurr, in his *Playgoing in Shakespeare's London* (Cambridge, 1987), discusses Lyly's tailoring plays to a courtly audience with tastes shaped by the Humanist education of the universities.

⁵⁴Thomas Nashe, *The Vnfortvnate Traveller*, Ed. H.F. Brett-Smith (Oxford, 1936); S. Warneke, "Educational Travellers: Popular Imagery and

Public Criticism in Early Modern England," *Journal of Popular Culture* (forthcoming); S. Clark, *The Elizabethan Phamphleteers* (London, 1983), 17-25.

[55]Gurr, *Playgoing*, 115-69.

[56]Chambers, *Stage*, vol. 1, 352-54.

[57]Smith, *Blackfriars*, 133-38; 149-56, 176-85. H.N. Hillebrand, *The Child Actors, University of Illinois Studies in Language and Literature*, XI (Urbana, IL, 1926) I; A. Shapiro, *Children of the Revels* (New York, 1977); and R. Gair, *The Children of Paul's* (Cambridge, 1982) are the most complete works on the boys' companies.

[58]Gair, *Children of Paul's*, 63-66, 167-72; Smith, *Blackfriars*, 190-93; Hillebrand, *Child Actors*, 164; Harbage, *Tradition*, 29-119, 339-42; Gurr, *Stage*, 93-97, 112, 199.

[59]Chambers, *Stage*, vol. 1, 358-68.

[60]Chambers, *Stage*, vol. 1, 353-54.

[61]M.C. Bradbrook, *The Growth and Structure of Elizabethan Comedy* (London, 1955), 74-76; J.D. Huston, "To Make a Puppet," *Shakespeare Studies*, 9 (1976), 77; Harbage, *Tradition*, 62-63.

[62]C.S. Felver, *Robert Armin, Shakespeare's Fool*, Research Series V, *Kent State University Bulletin* (Kent, OH, 1961), 12-14; Gurr, *Stage*, 102-04; Harbage, *Tradition*, 88-89; Smith, *Blackfriars*, 250-53.

[63]T.W. Baldwin, *The Organization and Personnel of the Shakespearean Company* (New York, 1961), 268-70; R. Barry, "Hamlet's Doubles," *Shakespeare Quarterly*, 37 (1986), 205; Ribner, *Shakespeare*, 48-50, 155-58.

[64]J.F. Matthews, ed., *Shaw's Dramatic Criticism from the Saturday Review (1895-98)* (New York, 1959). 12-13, 219, 281; and E. Wilson, *Shaw on Shakespeare* (New York, 1961), 5, 7, 113, 127. Various reviews and letters Shaw had written concerning Shakespearean performances stress Shaw's appreciation of Shakespeare's "word-music." In a review of 2 February 1895 Shaw wrote that Shakespeare's most famous attribute "delineation of character, owes all its magic to the turn of the line." To an actress playing Lady Macbeth he wrote: "When you play Shakespeare, don't worry out the character, but go for the music." For Elizabethans' emphasis on sound see: McLuskie, "Poets' Royal Exchange," 56-57; Harbage, *Audience*, 117-20; Gurr, *Stage*, 97, 110-11, 199-212. Professor W.T. Brown, "Shakespeare on Wheels," paper presented before the Shakespeare and Renaissance Association of West Virginia (23 April 1988), described that when presenting a travelling troupe to Nigerian audiences, often the audiences would echo aloud the most famous soliloquies when an actor began to deliver them.

[65]T.L. Berger, "Casting Henry V," *Shakespeare Studies*, XX (1988), 89-104; R. Fotheringham, "The Doubling of Roles on the Jacobean Stage," *Theatre*

Research International, 10 (1985), 18-32; J.C. Meagher, "Economy and Recognition: Thirteen Shakespearean Puzzles," *Shakespeare Quarterly*, 34 (1984), 7-22; Barry, "Doubles," 205-07; Gurr, *Stage*, 101-03.

⁶⁶R. Barnfield, *The Encomiom of Lady Pecunia: or The Praise of Money* (London, 1598). Wrightson, *Society*, 129-39. Quotation from p. 129.

⁶⁷Heywood's chiding of Jonson for considering "Playes" to be "Workes" is found in *The Jonson Allusion-book*, Ed. J.F. Bradley and J.Q. Adams, (New Haven, 1922), 175. McLuskie, "Poets' Royal Exchange," 53-62; Gurr, *Stage*, 20-21; Harbage, *Tradition*, 7-9, 70-75; 101-05.

Chapter 2

¹A.L. Rowse, *William Shakespeare* (New York, 1963), 75; see also, for example, K. Macgowan, W. Melnitz, G. Armstrong, *Golden Ages of the Theater* (Englewood Cliffs, NJ, 1979), 112-13. This essay originated as a presentation to the Shakespeare and Renaissance Association of West Virginia, 1990.

²Rowse, *Shakespeare*, 201-02; R. Speaight, *Shakespeare. The Man and His Achievement* (New York, 1977), 74; M. Chute, *Ben Jonson of Westminster* (New York, 1960), 112. Heywood's criticism of Jonson's pretensions is quoted in J.F. Bradley and J.Q. Adams, *The Jonson Allusion-book* (New Haven 1922), 175. G.E. Bentley's excellent book, *The Profession of Player in Shakespeare's Time* (Princeton, 1987) makes reference to Shakespeare approximately 47 times. Yet of those references, 27 are to him as a playwright. Of the 20 references remaining, most deal with him in the context of Sharer in the acting company. Only two specifically refer to Shakespeare as an actor, and one of those asserts he had no distinction as an actor. S. Schoenbaum, *William Shakespeare. A Compact Documentary Life* (Oxford, 1987), 184-200, notes that "...he must have done a good deal of acting, especially in the earlier years." Schoenbaum concedes, however, "Posterity, understandably enough, reserves veneration for the dramatist." E.J.A. Honigmann, *Shakespeare's Impact on His Contemporaries* (Towata, NJ, 1982), 49-52, asserts that Shakespeare was so concerned with his literary reputation that he insisted upon the publication of "Good Quartos" to correct the pirated editions of his plays. Though I agree with much of Honigmann's important and innovative work, I think here he inadvertently has succumbed to "Bardolatry." Honigmann often stresses Shakespeare's hardheadedness in money matters. In this case I believe my assertion in chapter 5, "The Mole in Shakespeare's Company," that the release of "Good Quartos" was a business decision designed to blunt the effect of the "Bad Quartos" is closer to Honigmann's own picture of Shakespeare's character.

³H. Smith, Introductions to *Venus and Adonis, The Rape of Lucrece, Sonnets, The Passionate Pilgrim, A Lover's Complaint, The Phoenix and the*

Turtle in *The Riverside Shakespeare*, Ed. G.B. Evans (Boston, 1974), 1703-04, 1720-01, 1745-46, 1781, 1795. Speaight, *Shakespeare*, 74, suggests Shakespeare wrote non-dramatic poetry "for his pleasure," especially in the lean years 1592-94.

⁴N. Carson, *A Companion to Henslowe's Diary* (Cambridge, 1988), 82-84, gives a chronological listing of all plays listed by Henslowe, and indicated those still extant. Macgowan, et. al., *Golden Ages*, 111.

⁵T.P. Morris, "Shakespeare hath given him a purge to make him bewray his credit," *Shakespeare and Renaissance Association of West Virginia. Selected Papers*, 15 (1992), discusses the burlesque of the Jonson in Shakespeare's *Merry Wives*. See *Hamlet*, Act II, scene 2, and for his swipe at Jonson in *Twelfth Night* see: A. Gurr, *Playgoing in Shakespeare's London* (Cambridge, 1988), 156; A. Hager, *Shakespeare's Political Animal* (Newark, DE, 1990), 76-87; R. McDonald, *Shakespeare & Jonson. Jonson & Shakespeare* (Lincoln, NE, 1988), 56-62,

⁶For the "War of the Theatres" see A. Gurr, *The Shakespearean Stage* (Cambridge, 1980), 26, 53, 68, 146, 174, 219-20, and his most recent work *Playgoing*, 47, 74, 84, 154-56, 163; J.R. Brown and B. Harris, eds. *Jacobean Theatre* (New York, 1967), 43-46, 54, 60, 73-78; Chute, *Jonson*, 88-90, 96-103, 109-11, 147-48, 185-86, 211-12, 339-41; A. Harbage, *Shakespeare and the Rival Traditions* (Bloomington, IN, 1953), 90-119. Gurr, "Who Strutted and Bellowed," *Shakespeare Survey*, 16 (1963), 95-102, discusses Shakespeare's comments within his scripts concerning bad performances. For the York Herald's complaint, *Ratseis Ghost* and *Willobie his Advisa*, see E.K. Chambers, *William Shakespeare. A Study of Facts and Problems*, II (Oxford, 1930), 113-18, 569-71, and Honigmann, Impact, 9-10, 51. A. Cargill, "Shakespeare as an Actor," *Scribner's Magazine*, 9 (May 1891), 613-35, raised the issue "How rarely do we think of Shakespeare as an Actor!" Though delightful reading, Cargill's article concentrates on matters such as the horse-handler anecdote, Shakespeare performing as Old Adam before the Queen, and still ends up assuming that Shakespeare acted to support his writing with the erroneous assertion that "For one thing, his work of dramatic authorship proved to be a more lucrative occupation than the actor's calling." For Greene's attack, see his *Groat's Worth of Wit* (1592), rpt. in *Elizabethan and Jacobean Pamphlets*, Ed. B. Saintsbury (New York, 1892), 156-59.

⁷Greene's attack, and Henry Chettle's famous apology for seeing to the printing of that attack in his *Kind-Hartes Dream*, are oft cited and discussed. Honigmann, *Impact*, 2-7, has an interesting discussion of the Greene attack as evidence of Shakespeare's early reputation as tight-fisted and hard-headed (and perhaps hearted) in money matters. L. Marder, *His Exits and His Entrances*.

The Story of Shakespeare's Reputation (Philadelphia, 1963), cites Thomas Nashe's 1592 acknowledgement of the success of the *Henry 6* plays, but notes that at the end of the sixteenth century "popular drama was not considered literature." After first issue of *Venus and Adonis* (1593) Shakespeare's narrative poems gained great popularity with the men of the Inns of Court and the so-called "Cambridge Circle." See pages 45-46, 87-88.

⁸Bentley, *Player*, 29-30. E.K. Chambers, *The Elizabethan Stage*, I (Oxford, 1923), 372-75.

⁹Gurr, *Stage*, 19-20; Honigmann, *Impact*, 7-8. W. Cohen, *Drama of a Nation. Public Theater in Renaissance England and Spain* (Ithaca, NY, 1985), 170-71; R.L. Knutson, "Influence of the Repertory System on Revival and Revision of the Spanish Tragedy and Dr. Faustus," *English Literary Renaissance*, 18 (1988), 257-74, notes the commercial demand of an acting company in commissioning revisions of these scripts.

¹⁰Honigmann, *Impact*, 9-10, 23.

¹¹*Calendar of State Papers, Domestic Series*, v. 3, *Elizabeth, 1591-94* (London, 1867), 290: Rowse, *Shakespeare*, 34-35, 54-56.

¹²See excerpts from the "Sharer Papers" in I. Smith, *Shakespeare's Blackfriars Playhouse* (New York, 1964), 553-59.

¹³G.E. Bentley, *The Profession of Dramatist in Shakespeare's Time* (Princeton, 1986), 197-263, gives an extensive discussion of collaboration and revision by playwrights.

¹⁴Chute, *Jonson*, 82, 111-12, 309, 326-27, 346.

¹⁵Honigmann, *Impact*, 1-14.

¹⁶T. Heywood, *An Apology for Actors* (rpt. London, 1841); Bentley, *Player*, 34-35, 40.

¹⁷Bentley, *Player*, 25-63.

¹⁸For example, in tables given in M. Spevack's *Complete and Systematic Concordance to the Works of Shakespeare*, I: Comedies (Hildesheim, 1968), for *Midsummer Night's Dream*, of a total of 504 speeches in the play, eight percent to ten percent of that total are assigned to the characters Bottom, Demetrius, Lysander, Helena, Hermia, Puck and Theseus.

¹⁹*Aubrey's Brief Lives*, ed. O.L. Dick (New York, 1972), 334.

²⁰John Davies of Hereford, *The Complete Workes*, Ed. A.B. Grosart (Private Printing, 1875), I, *Microcosmos*, 82 and *Scourge of Folly*, epigram 159. Marder, *Exits and Entrances*, 22, notes that by 1600 there were "almost three dozen references to 'honey-tongued' Shakespeare."

²¹Bentley, *Player*, 25-63.

²²Chambers, *Stage*, I, 372-75; *Henslowe's Diary*, Ed. W.W. Greg (London, 1904-08), and his supplement, *Henslowe's Papers* (London, 1907) give numerous examples throughout of payments to playwrights. Neil Carson's,

Companion to Henslowe's Diary is of invaluable help in interpreting Henslowe's accounts.

[23]A. Harbage, *Shakespeare's Audience* (New York, 1964), 23-33; Carson, *Companion*.

[24]T.W. Baldwin, *Organization and Personnel of the Shakespearean Company* (Princeton, 1927), 52; Gurr, *Stage*, 46.

[25]F. Simpson, "New Place. The Only Representation of Shakespeare's House from an Unpublished Manuscript," *Shakespeare Survey*, 5 (1952), 55-57; Smith, *Blackfriars*, 250-51; Chambers, *Stage*, I, 370.

[26]Harbage, *Audience*, 19-52; Smith, *Blackfriars*, 553-59.

[27]Smith, *Blackfriars*, 558.

[28]Speaight, *Shakespeare*, 261; Rowse, *Shakespeare*, 444-50.

[29]N. Carson, "Collaborative Playwriting," *Theatre Research International*, 14 (1989).

[30]Bentley, *Dramatist*, 123-25.

[31]Introductions to *Henry VIII* and *The Two Noble Kinsmen*, *Riverside*, 977-78, 1639-41.

[32]Bentley, *Dramatist*, 208; Gurr, *Stage*, 220.

[33]R. Flatter's short work, *Shakespeare's Producing Hand* (New York, 1948), gives some fascinating insights into metric "irregularites" as indications of actor-pauses, simultaneous speeches, or actors' characterizations.

[34]T. Cole and H.K. Chinoy, *Actors on Acting* (New York, 1970), provides examples of actors' love for Shakespearean roles from eighteenth-, nineteenth-, twentieth-century actors from Italy, France, Germany, England, the U.S.A., such as Adelaide Ristori (443-50), Sarah Bernhardt (204, 209), John Gielgud (398, 400), Lawrence Olivier (411, 413-16), Edwin Booth (562-63), Alfred Lunt (609). Angela Pitt, *Shakespeare's Women* (Totawa, NJ, 1981), provides transcripts of interviews done in 1979 (194-218) with the successful British actresses Brenda Bruce, Judi Dench, Glenda Jackson, and Janet Suzman. All comment on the depth, difficulty, and scope of such roles as Cleopatra, Juliet, Gertrude, Queen Margaret, Mistress Quickly.

[35]Each of these characters are on stage from the opening of the play until its closing, with little or no time off stage. There are several other roles one can name that are similar: Sidney in Ira Levin's *Deathtrap*, Tom in Tennessee William's *Glass Menagerie*, Rosencrantz and Guildenstern in Peter Shaffer's *Rosencrantz* and *Guildenstern Are Dead*. By contrast Hamlet appears in only 15 of the 20 scenes in the play, and in three enters only near the end of the scene; Richard III appears in only 15 of 23 scenes.

[36]L. Potter, " 'Nobody's Perfect': Actors' Memories and Shakespeare's Plays of the 1590s," *Shakespeare Survey*, 42 (1990), 85-97.

Chapter 3

[1]S. Orgel, "Nobody's Perfect: Or Why Did the English Stage Take Boys for Men," *South Atlantic Quarterly*, 88 (1989), 7-29. For interpretations of Elizabethan drama as misogynistic see, for example, D. Callaghan, *Woman and Gender in Renaissance Tragedy* (Atlantic Highlands, NJ, 1989), 39-41, 53, 109, 120-30, 140-46, 155-71; L. Jardine, *Still Harping on Daughters. Women and Drama in the Age of Shakespeare* (Totowa, NJ, 1983), 1-33; K.E. McLuskie, *Renaissance Dramatists* (Atlantic Highlands, NJ, 1989), 123-57; and the following essays in *The Woman's Part. Feminist Criticism of Shakespeare*, Eds. C.R.S. Lenz, G. Greene, C.T. Neely (Urbana, IL, 1980): P.S. Berggren, "The Woman's Part. Female Sexuality as Power in Shakespeare's Plays," 17-31; M Gohlke, " 'I wooed thee with my sword': Shakespeare's Tragic Paradigms," 150-67; C. Kahn, "Coming of Age in Verona," 171-81.

[2]G.E. Bentley, *The Jacobean and Caroline Stage*, I (Oxford, 1966), 25. S Wells, "Introduction," *A Midsummer Night's Dream, New Penguin Shakespeare* (New York, 1967), 13. W.G. Leary, *Shakespeare Plain. The Making and Performing of Shakespeare's Plays* (New York, 1977), 243: J.L. Styan, *Shakespeare's Stagecraft* (Cambridge, 1975), 40-42.

[3]G. Gordon, *Shakespearean Comedy* (Oxford, 1944), 21-25; Styan, *Stagecraft*, 40-42; Leary, 243-45. In her *Shakespeare and the Nature of Women* (New York, 1975), 5, J. Dusinberre asserts Shakespeare's sensitivity to women seems to suggest he was a "feminist." A. Pitt, *Shakespeare's Women* (Totowa, NJ, 1981), details the strong female characters who people Shakespeare's comedies, histories and tragedies, noting that even in the tragedies and histories, where men are the focus of attention, there still appear such formidable female characters as Queen Margaret, Mistress Quickly, Goneril and Regan, Cleopatra, and Volumnia. Ms. Pitt (194-218) gives transcripts of interviews conducted in 1979 with British actresses Judi Dench, Brenda Bruce, Janet Suzman, and Glenda Jackson. All attest to the depth and scope of roles for women in Shakespeare's plays. T. Cole and H.K. Chinoy, *Actors on Acting* (New York, 1970), provides examples of actors' love for Shakespearean roles from eighteenth-, nineteenth-, twentieth-century actresses such as Adelaide Ristori (443-50) and Sarah Bernhardt. (204, 209).

[4]M. Spevack, *A Complete Concordance to the Works of William Shakespeare*, I (*Comedies*), 2 (*Histories*), 3 (*Tragedies*) (Hildesheim, 1968). Percentages of lines for each characters are given at the beginning of the concordances according to character, which follow the concordances according to play. *The Riverside Shakespeare*, Ed. G.B. Evans (Boston, 1974). Scene count is my own.

[5]E.A.J. Honigmann, *Shakespeare: the "lost years,"* (Totowa, NJ, 1985), 59-76.

⁶Leary, 243-44.

⁷See, for example, N.K. Hayes, "Sexual Disguise in *As You Like It* and *Twelfth Night*" in *Shakespeare Survey*, 32 (1979), 63-72; L.S. Marcus, "Shakespeare's Comic Heroines, Elizabeth I, and the Political Uses of Androgyny," *Women in the Middle Ages and Renaissance*, Ed. M.B. Rose (Syracuse, 1986), 135-53; B.J. Bono, "Mixed Gender, Mixed Genre in Shakespeare's *As You Like It*" in *Renaissance Genres: Essays on Theory, History, and Interpretation*, Ed. B.K. Lewalski (Cambridge, MA, 1986), 189-212; J. Howard, "Crossdressing, The Theatre, and Gender Struggle in Early Modern England," *Shakespeare Quarterly*, 39 (1989), 418-40.

⁸Leary, 244.

⁹J. Dusinberre, "*King John* and Embarrassing Women," *Shakespeare Survey* 42, (1990), 37-52, notes the contiuing appearance of strong, assertive women throughout Shakespeare's repertory. Cuthbert Burbage's remarks concern moving the King's Men to Blackfriars. They are found in the famous "Sharer Papers," reproduced in part in E. Smith, *Shakespeare's Blackfriars Playhouse* (New York, 1964), 553-59.

¹⁰See, for instance, the famous *Historia Histrionica* (1699) by James Wright. See also the cast lists in G.E. Bentley, *The Professions of Dramatist and Player in Shakespeare's Time, 1590-1642* (Princeton, 1986), appendix, 247-95.

¹¹Bentley, *Dramatist*, 62-87; J.H. Forse, "Art Imitates Business," *Journal of Popular Culture*, 24 (1990), 180-97.

¹²Pitt, *Women*, 165, states "It is unclear how recruitment was organized." A. Gurr, *The Shakespearean Stage, 1574-1642* (Cambridge, 1980), 28-112, and Bentley, *Dramatist*, 62-87, *Player*, 25-146, detail the writing of plays for repertory performances and the relationships among "sharers," dramatists, "hired men," and apprentices. W.R. Davies, *Shakespeare's Boy Actors* (New York, 1939), discusses how Shakepeare scripted roles to accommodate female characterizations done by males. Though he insists on boys, drawn from he knows not where, he concedes that older female roles were probably portrayed by grown men. Leary, 246-50, stresses the clusters of similar male character types stretching throughout Shakespeare's plays. R.L. Knutson, "Influence of the Repertory System on Revival and Revision of *The Spanish Tragedy* and *Dr. Faustus*" in *English Literary Renaissance*, 18 (1988), 257-74, notes how the Admiral's Men commissioned revisions of these scripts to keep the actors of their company up to the competition being offered them by Shakespeare's "new" tragedies like *Hamlet*.

¹³*Forse*, "Business," 177-79.

¹⁴E.J.A. Honigmann, *Shakespeare's Impact on His Contemporaries* (Towata, NJ, 1982), 40-49.

[15]*Forse*, "Business," 165-74.

[16]See notes 12, 13 above, and C. Bridenbaugh, *Vexed and Troubled Englishmen, 1590-1642* (New York, 1968), 169-75.

[17]Bridenbaugh, 169-75.

[18]Forse, "Business," 189-90.

[19]F. Braudel, *The Mediterranean and the Mediterranean World in the Age of Phillip II*, 2, tr. S. Reynolds (New York, 1972), 444-46. For the substitution of women for males in the Restoration see H. Hunt, "Restoration Acting," *Restoration Theatre*, Eds. J.R. Brown and B. Harris (New York, 1967), 179-80.

[20]P.H. Parry, "The Boyhood of Skakespeare's Heroines," *Shakespeare Survey*, 42 (1990), 99-109; A. Gurr, "Who Strutted and Bellowed," *Shakespeare Survey*, 16 (1963), 95-102, discusses the seeming preference for "naturalistic" acting by Shakespeare's company.

[21]For descriptions of Elizabethan dress see M. St. C. Byrne, *Elizabethan Life in Town and Country* (London, 1961), 63-69.

[22]C. Haigh, *Elizabeth I* (London, 1988), 86-95, 146-48, discusses the various means used to disguise Elizabeth's age, including government censorship of portraits.

[23]Henry Jackson saw a King's Men performance of Othello at Oxford in 1610, and commented in a letter (reproduced in *Riverside*, 1852) that he was moved by Desdemona's performance. Parry, "Boyhood," 99-109; Leary, 244-45, and Styan, *Stagecraft*, 40-42, give examples of Shakespeare's making sure that there are allusions to the femininity of female characters on stage. Engraving of Shakespeare from H. Kokeritz, ed. *Mr. William Shakespeare's Comedies, Histories and Tragedies*. Facsimile ed. of the First Folio (New Haven, 1954). That of Elizabeth from R.C. Strong, *Gloriana. The Portraits of Queen Elizabeth I* (New York, 1987). My thanks to my good friend Mr. Terry P. Morris, who used his skills in computer enhancing and drafting in "shaving" and "crossdressing" Shakespeare.

[24]M.H. Curtis, "Education and Apprenticeship," *Shakespeare Survey*, 17 (1964), 66-70; Wright, *Historia*. E. Nungezer, *A Dictionary of Actors...before 1642* (New Haven, 1929), 135-41, 156, 196-97, 261-65, 321, 373, 380, 384-85; Bentley, *Player*, 248-50. Bentley, convinced that only boys played youngish female roles, glosses over the fact that Honeymann, Sharpe, and Trigge must have been at least 18 or 20 years old when they still were listed in female roles. His conclusion is, therefore, that the cast lists in the printed edition of *The Duchess* (1623) must be incorrect, since "especially the three boys Richard Sharpe, John Thompson, and Robert Pallant," could not have been playing the same roles for an interval of five or more years. Later on he asserts, that since John Thompson played a female role in *The Swisser* (1631), that he could not have played the Cardinal's Mistress in *The Duchess of Malfi* (1614) 17 years

earlier. First he seems to be saying that Thompson could not have been playing the same role five years later, because he no longer would be a boy; then he seems to be implying that Thompson could not have played the role at all, because he would have been at best a babe-in-arms. For Henslowe's probable age at marriage see N. Carson, *A Companion to Henslowe's Diary* (Cambridge, 1988), 1; for Venetian guild age limits see C.M. Cipolla, *Before the Industrial Revolution* (New York, 1976), 93.

[25]*Riverside, Anthony and Cleopatra*, Act 5, scene 2.

[26]T. Heywood, *Apology for Actors* (rpt. London, 1841); Pitt, *Women*, 168.

[27]R. Gair, *The Children of Paul's* (Cambridge, 1982), 170-72; A.N. Hillebrand, *The Child Actors, Illinois Studies in Language and Literature*, XI (Urbana, IL, 1926), 268-75.

[28]Gurr, *Playgoing*, Appendix 2, 205-51, presents a valuable selection of most playgoing references to be found in Elizabethan and Jacobean sources, including the Puritan attacks on the theatre.

[29]Nungezer, *Dictionary*, 102; Gurr, *Shakespearean Stage*, 38-40.

[30]Both are quoted in Nungezer, *Dictionary*: Davenant's patent, 113-14, poetic epilogue, 212-13.

[31]Bridenbaugh, 156.

[32]Honigmann, *Lost Years*, 59, 128.

[33]For the traditional role assignments see T.W. Baldwin, *The Origination and Personnel of the Shakespearean Company* (Princeton, 1927), charts between 228-29, and 254-62, and J.Q. Adams, *A Life of William Shakespeare* (Boston, 1923), 424-27. For Shakespeare's strong women see J. Dusinberre "Embarassing Women."

[34]Nungezer, *Dictionary*, 102, 375.

[35]C.T. Neely, "Shakespeare's Women: Historical Facts and Dramatic Representations," *Shakespeare's Personality*, Ed. N. Holland, S. Homan, B. Paris (Berkeley, 1989), 120-31.

[36]*Aubrey' Brief Lives*, Ed. O.L. Dick (New York, 1949), 334. Schoenbaum's *Shakespeare. The Globe and the World* (New York, 1979), 343-46, discusses Spurgeon's physical description of Shakespeare. His *William Shakespeare: Records and Images* (New York, 1981), 156-61, 166-71, gives lengthy discussions of the Droeshout engraving and the memorial bust. M. Edmond, "It was for gentle Shakespeare cut," *Shakespeare Survey*, 42 (1991), 339-44, argues convincingly that the engraving was done by Martin Droeshout the elder, an uncle of the younger Martin to whom the portrait usually is ascribed. The elder Martin was a closer contemporary of Shakespeare, and in London from the 1580s on; hence he would have better knowledge of the young Shakespeare's appearance than his younger namesake nephew who was only 15 when Shakespeare died.

[37]D.W. Foster, "Reconstructing Shakespeare 1: The Roles that Shakespeare Performed," *The Shakespeare Newsletter* (Spring/Summer, 1991), 16-17. In the same issue W. Smith ("Will the Computer Finally End Authorship Controversies?"), 15, 17, discusses difficulties with stylometric analyses.

[38]For Edmond Malone's early (1790), questions over these Old Adam anecdotes see his *The Plays and Poem of William Shakspeare*, I, 466-67, and II, 138, 285-87 (rpt. London, 1821, itself a rpt. New York, 1966). Schoenbaum, *Compact Life*, 97-108, explores the deer poaching myth.

[39]N. Rowe, "Some Account of the Life of William Shakspeare," reproduced by Malone, I, 439; John Davies of Hereford, *The Complete Workes*, I, Ed. A.B. Grosart (Private printing, 1875), "Scourge of Folly," epigram 159.

[40]Robert Greene, *Groat's Worth of Wit* (1592), rpt. in *Elizabethan & Jacobean Pamphlets*, Ed. G. Saintsbury (New York, 1892), 156-59. Honigmann, *Shakespeare's Impact*, 40-49, and *Lost Years*, 71, gives interesting and innovative discussions of Greene's attack on Shakespeare.

[41]A.W. Pollard, and G.R. Redgrave, eds., *A Short-Title Catalogue of Books Printed in England...1475-1640* (London, 1956), 339, 393, 447; N. Carson, *A Companion to Henslowe's Diary* (Cambridge, 1988), 82-84.

Chapter 4

[1]W. Winter, *Shakespeare on the Stage* (New York, 1915), 449, 506-08; G.C. Odell, *Shakespeare from Betterton to Irving*, I (New York, 1963), 230-31; B. Morris, Introduction to The Taming of the Shrew, *The Arden Shakespeare* (London, 1981), 88-97, 109. H. Child, "The Stage-history of The Taming of the Shrew," in *The Taming of the Shrew*, Ed. A. Quiller-Couch and J.D. Wison, *The New Cambridge Shakespeare* (Cambridge, 1968), 184-85.

[2]S.L. Wentworth's unpublished dissertation, *An Historical and Critical Study of Crucial Direction and Acting Problems in William Shakespeare's The Taming of the Shrew* (Bowling Green State University, Aug. 1983), surveys some of the production strategies used over the past 150 years to solve the "problems" of staging *Shrew*. It was discussions with Ms. Wentworth while serving as a reader on her dotoral committee, and after staging "Shrew" myself for the local comunity theater as an example of bad acting and bad staging, that led me to organize my thoughts concerning Shrew as a parody play. Ms. Wentworth prefers the traditional view of the play, and therefore declined my suggestion to co-author the original version. But I am indebted to her study for much material concerning the stage-history of Shrew. Of particular value is her work in consulting extant prompt books from major productions of the last 150 years.

[3]The following works serve to illustrate the poles of opinion concerning

Christopher Sly and the Induction: P. Alexander, "The Original Ending of The Taming of the Shrew" in *Shakespeare Quarterly*, 20 (Spring 1980), 111-16; T.N. Greenfield, "The Transformation of Christopher Sly," *Philological Quarterly*, 22 (Jan. 1954), 34-42; R. Hosley, "Was There a 'Dramatic Epilogue' to The Taming of the Shrew?" *Studies in English Literature*, 1 (Spring 1961), 17-34; E.P. Kuhl, "Shakespeare's Purpose in Dropping Sly," *Modern Language Notes*, 36, (June 1921), 321-29; K.P. Wentersdorf, "The Original Ending of The Taming of the Shrew: A Reconsideration," *Studies in English Literature*, 13 (Spring 1978), 201-15; J.D. Huston, "To Make a Puppet: Play and Playmaking in The Taming of the Shrew," *Shakespeare Studies*, IX (New York, 1976), 73-89; M. Webster, *Shakespeare Without Tears* (New York, 1975), 104-05.

⁴Wentworth, 14-18, surveys several performances which have omitted Sly scenes altogether, and others which sought to compensate for this omission through emphasizing the concept of strolling players, such as the famous Lunt/Fontaine production of 1935, 1940. Her discussion also includes various positive and negative reactions by theater critics.

⁵Wentworth, 24-27. R. Heilman in his introduction to *Shrew* in *Signet Classic Shakespeare* (New York, 1966), 28 voices the concern of many literary and theater critics that inclusion of the *First Folio* Sly scenes leaves "something...uncomfortably hanging."

⁶E.M.W. Tillyard, *Shakespeare's Early Comedies* (New York, 1965), 73, discusses this old view, see also pp. 74-102, and A. Leggett, *Shakespeare's Comedy of Love* (London, 1974), 48-49; M. Van Doren, *Shakespeare* (New York, 1939), 20.

⁷Wentworth, 101-02.

⁸M. Felheim, *The Theater of Augustin Daly* (Cambridge, MA, 1956), 239-40. Wentworth, 111-12.

⁹See, for example: Van Doren, *Shakespeare* (Garden City, NY, 1953), 37-38; A.L. Rowse, ed., *The Annotated Shakespeare*, 1, *The Comedies*, 23-25; R. Speaight, *Shakespeare. The Man and His Achievement* (New York, 1977), 59; M. Chute, *Stories from Shakespeare* (New York, 1956), 31-34.

¹⁰Wentworth, 116-20.

¹¹Webster, 105.

¹²Wentworth, 58-61. See, for example: Tillyard, 81-83; Webster, 105; Chute, 31-35; Speaight, 59; A. Barton, Introduction, *The Taming of the Shrew* in *Riverside Shakespeare* (Boston, 1974), 106; Van Doren, 38.

¹³Anne Barton, Introduction, *Much Ado About Nothing* in *Riverside*, 327; *The Taming of A Shrew*, in G. Bullough, *Narrative and Dramatic Sources of Shakespeare*, I, (London, 1957), 77 (scene v, lines 25-26 and 41-43). Wentworth, 2-5.

¹⁴G.W. Williams, "Kate and Petruchio: Strength and Love," *English*

Language Notes, XXIX (1991), 18-24; Barton, *Shrew*, 106; Speaight, 59; Wentworth, 72-89.

[15]Van Doren, 38.

[16]Webster, 105.

[17]Huston, 73. For *Shrew* as a source of study for gender relationships see E. Boose, "Scolding Brides and Bridling Scolds: Taming the Woman's Unruly Member, *Shakespeare Quarterly*, 42 (1991), 179-213, and her extensive bibliography given in note 5, p. 181.

[18]N. Frye, "The Argument of Comedy," *Shakespeare: Essays in Criticism*, Ed. L.F. Dean (Oxford, 1967), 79-89.

[19]A. Pitt, *Shakespeare's Women* (Totowa, NJ, 1981), 75; G. Gordon. *Shakespearean Comedy* (Oxford, 1944), 22-27; Barton, *Shrew*, 107.

[20]Rowse, *Annot. Shakespeare*, I, 21; W.G. Leary, *Shakespeare Plain* (New York, 1977), 19.

[21]Barton, *Much Ado*, 327; Speaight, 182, notes that in *Shrew* Shakespeare "is writing below his best."

[22]A. Harbage, *Shakespeare and the Rival Traditions* (Bloomington, IN, 1970), 4-5.

[23]*Henslowe's Diary*, ed. R.A. Foakes and R.T. Rickert (Cambridge, 1961), 21-22, lists the following plays for the period of 3 to 13 June, dates generally considered to be those in which the newly formed Chamberlain's Men shared the theater at Newington Butts with Henslowe's and Alleyn's Admiral's Men: 3 June—*Hester and Asheweros*, 4 June—*The Jew of Malta*, 5 June—*Andronicus*, 6 June—*Cutlack*, 7 June—*Bellendon*, 9 June—*Hamlet*, 10 June—*Hester*, 11 June—*The Tamynge of a Shrew*, 12 June—*Andronicus*, 13 June—*The Jew of Malta*. After 13 June, *Hamlet*, *Andronicus*, and *Shrew* are not listed as producing revenue for Henslowe. See M.M. Reese *Shakespeare. His Life and His Work* (London, 1980), 134-36; Rowse, *Annot. Shakespeare*, I, 12.

[24]Huston, 73-74, stresses the false beginnings leading up to the appearance of the strolling players; the notion that there is a "re-rebeginning" with the entrance of Petruchio is my own.

[25]*The Taming of the Shrew* in *Riverside*, 113 (Induction, 2, lines 130, 141).

[26]Barton, *Shrew*, 106-07; M.C. Bradbrook, *The Growth and Structure of Elizabethan Comedy* (London, 1955), 74; Barton, *Shrew*, 106-07.

[27]George Gascoigne, *Supposes*, in *Chief Pre-Shakespearean Drama*, Ed. J.Q. Adams (Boston, 1924), 536, 546.

[28]Bullough, I, 59; T.N. Greenfield, *The Induction in Elizabethan Drama* (Eugene, OR, 1969), 97-119; M.C. Hyde, *Playwriting for Elizabethans* (New York, 1949), 107-14.

[29]M.C. Bradbrook, *Elizabethan Stage Conditions* (Hamden, CT, 1962),

107; A. Gurr, "Who Strutted and Bellowed?" *Shakespeare Survey*, 16 (1963) 96; A. Gurr, *The Shakespearean Stage*: 1574-1642 (Cambridge, 1980), 97; Huston, 75.

[30]Gurr, "Who Strutted," 95-102; Huston, 75.

[31]Huston, 77; Bradbrook, *Growth*, 74-76; Harbage, *Traditions*, 62-63.

[32]J. Shaw. "The Staging of Parody and Parallels in *I Henry IV*," *Shakespeare Survey*, 20 (1967), 61-73; *Henslowe's Diary*, 21-22; Reese, 134-36; Rowse, *Annot. Shakespeare*, I, 12.

[33]Thomas Kyd, *The Spanish Tragedy*, in An Anthology of English Drama Before Shakespeare, Ed. R.B. Heilman (New York, 1952), 270-71 (Act II, scene 4).

[34]*Shrew* in *Riverside*, Act I, scene 2.

[35]Christopher Marlowe, *Tamburlaine the Great, Part II* in *Christopher Marlowe (Five Plays)*, Ed. H. Ellis (New York, 1960), Act III.

[36]Robert Greene, *Orlando Furioso*, in *The Life and Complete Works of Robert Greene*, III, Ed. A. Grosart (New York, 1964), 155. Stage directions read: "Enter Orlando attired like a mad-cap."

[37]T.P. Morris, "Shakespeare hath given him a purge to bewray his credit," *Renaissance Association of West Virginia. Selected Papers*, 15 (1992).

[38]Introductions to *The Comedy of Errors, and Titus Andronicus* in *Riverside*. Volume I, *Life of Greene* is a translation of Storojenko's work by E.A.B. Hodgetts. Greene, it is asserted (229), saw Shakespeare "not only a successful rival, but an enemy, who beat the established dramatists with their own weapons, which he had stolen from them." Later it is noted: "When Greene commenced his dramatical labours, his first productions were satirized by two unknown dramatists, one of whom was Marlowe."

[39]Harbage, *Rival Traditions*, 9-119.

[40]Child, 184-85.

[41]Barton, *Introduction to Much Ado About Nothing* in *Riverside*, 327; Child, 184-85.

[42]I. Ribner, *William Shakespeare* (Waltham, MA, 1969), 173.

Chapter 5

[1]Andrew Gurr discusses that rivalry in *Playgoing in Shakespeare's London* (Cambridge, 1987), and *The Shakespearean Stage* (Cambridge, 1980). See also Alfred Harbage, *Shakespeare and the Rival Tradition* (Bloomington, 1952), and *Shakespeare's Audience* (New York, 1941). This essay first appeared in *Shakespeare and Renaissance Association of West Virginia. Selected Papers*, 13 (1988).

[2]Shakespeare revised his plays over the years. Hence attempts to date

them by internal references to current events can be problematic.

[3]Chronology of printings in *The Riverside Shakespeare* (Boston, 1974), 48-56.

[4]H. Gray, "The Roles of William Kempe," *Modern Language Review*, 25 (1930), 261-73.

[5]C. Blagden, *The Stationers' Company. A History, 1403-1959* (Cambridge, MA, 1960), 42-43; E.K. Chambers, *The Elizabethan Stage*, v. 2 (London, 1923), 197.

[6]A. Cairncross, "Pembroke's Men and Some Shakespearean Piracies," *Shakespeare Quarterly*, 11 (1960), 335-49.

[7]A. Pollard, *Shakespeare's Fight with the Pirates* (Cambridge, 1920).

[8]Cairncross, 335-49.

[9]J.M. Nosworthy, "*Hamlet* and the Player Who Could Not Keep Counsel," *Shakespeare Survey*, 3 (1950), 74-82; I. Ribner, *William Shakespeare* (Waltham, MA, 1969), 335-49.

[10]Cairncross, 349.

[11]T. Baldwin, *Organization and Personnel of the Shakespearean Company* (New York, 1961), 311, 327.

[12]Gurr, *Stage*, 103.

[13]E.J.A. Honigmann, "The Date of Hamlet," *Shakespeare Survey*, 9 (1956), 24-34; Nosworthy, "Hamlet and the Player," 76-82; *Riverside*, 971. A. Patterson, *Shakespeare and the Popular Voice* (Oxford, 1989), 71-76, points out that many of the arguments for "Bad" Quarto appellation turn on notions of "good" and "bad" writing.

[14]Gray, 265.

[15]Gray, 267-72.

[16]R. Speaight, *Shakespeare* (New York, 1977), 211-12; J.H. Forse, "Ben Jonson's *Isle of Dogs*: Politics and Playwriting in Elizabethan England," *Selected Papers. Shakespeare and Renaissance Society of West Virginia*, 14 (1989). A. Harbage, *Audience*, 58-61, gives daily, weekly, and yearly averages for the London artisan of Shakespeare's day.

[17]Ribner, 40-50; W. Ingram, *A London Life in the Brazen Age. Francis Langley, 1548-1602* (Cambridge, MA), 168-85; C. Chermely, "Madness in Shakespearean England: An Historical Perspective," *Shakespeare and Renaissance Association of West Virginia. Selected Papers*, 12 (1987), 8.

[18]*Riverside*, 48-59; Forse, "*Isle of Dogs*."

[19]Nungezer, *Dictionary*. For free lance entertainment in London see B. Reay, "Introduction," 17-18, and P. Burke, "Popular Culture in Seventeenth Century London," 37-39, both in *Popular Culture in Seventeenth Century England*, Ed. B. Reay (New York, 1985). For the popularity of *Commedia dell'Arte* see, for instance, A.P. Royce, "The Venetian Commedia: Actors and

Masques in the Development of the *Commedia dell'Arte*," *Theatre Survey*, 27 (1986), 69-87, and A. Nicoll, *Masks, Mimes and Miracles* (New York, 1963).

²⁰E.W. Ives, "The Law and the Lawyers," *Shakespeare Survey*, 17 (1964), 73-86; Cairncross, 346-49. See also *The Diary of Philip Henslowe*, Eds. R.A. Foakes and R.T. Rickert (Cambridge, 1961). For Kempe's concern about money see his *Kempe's nine daies wonder* (London, 1600: rpt. Dereham, Norfolk, 1985), 24-25. The appendices to I. Smith's *Shakespeare's Blackfriars Theatre* (New York, 1964) reveal some of the many litigations among theatrical entrepreneurs.

²¹Gray, 266-73. Harbage, *Audience*, 23-24, 27-33. S.D. Amussen, *An Ordered Society. Gender and Class in Early Modern England* (Oxford, 1988), 78-81, notes that it was common for propertied people, yeoman status and up, to leave wills.

²²Gray, 266; Gurr, *Stage*, 46.

²³K. Macgowen, W. Meinitz, G. Armstrong, *Golden Ages of the Theatre* (Englewood Clifs, 1979), 112-13; Harbage, *Audience*, 27-32, 49-50.

²⁴Macgowan, et al., *Golden Ages*, 111-13; Smith, *Blackfriars*, 252-53; Gray, 268-71; Blagden, *Sationers*', 42-43; B. Capp, "Popular Literature," 17-18.

²⁵Gray, 266-73.

²⁶T.P. Morris, "Shakespeare hath given him a purge to make him bewray his credit," *Shakespeare and Renaissance Association of West Virginia. Selected Papers*, 15 (1992). For Shakespeare's dislike of the child companies see Hamlet, Act II, scene 2, and for his swipes at Jonson in *Twelfth Night* see: Gurr, *Playgoing*, 156; A. Hager, *Shakespeare's Political Animal* (Newark, DE, 1990), 76-87; R. McDonald, *Shakespeare & Jonson. Jonson & Shakespeare* (Lincoln, NE, 1988), 56-62, who also (31-55) discussess similarities between *Merry Wives* and *Every Man in His Humour*. For Kempe's accusations see *nine dais wonder*, 28-30.

Chapter 6

¹R.W. Kenny, *Elizabeth's Admiral. The Political Career of Charles Howard Earl of Nottingham, 1536-1624* (Baltimore, 1970), 43-44. M. Prior, "Which is the Jew that Shakespeare Drew? Shylock Among the Critics," *American Scholar*, 50 (1981), 479-98; C. Marder, *His Exits and His Entrances. The Story of Shakespeare's Reputation* (Philadelphia, 1963), 44, 58; I. Ribner, *William Shakespeare. An Introduction to His Life, Times, and Theatre* (Waltham, MA, 1969), 228-36.

²*The Complete State Papers, Domestic* (Hassocks, Sussex, 1979, microfilm), v. 225, n. 21 (henceforth *SPD*). Four letters written by Lopez are preserved in the State Papers, v. 124, n. 38 (18 June 1578), v. 225, ns. 21, 22

(12 July 1589), v. 247, n. 93 (26 February 1594). He generally signed himself Roger, once Ruy. All the letters are in Italian. This essay originally was presented before the Carolina Symposium on British Studies, October, 1990.

[3]M. Hume, "The So-called Conspiracy of Dr. Ruy Lopez," *Jewish Historical Society of England, Transactions* (sessions 1908-10), 36 (henceforth *JHSE*). Lopez first was treated as more than a minor footnote to history by S.L. Lee, "The Original of Shylock," *The Gentleman's Magazine*, 246 (1880), 185-200. Lee, in attempting to identify Shylock with Lopez, concentrates on the "racking" passage from *Merchant*, and the possibility that Richard Burbage knew Lopez through his father's (James) contacts with the Earl of Leicester as a member of Leicester's Men. Other historians picked up on the Lopez incident over the next 20 or so years. A. Dimock, "The Conspiracy of Dr. Lopez," *English Historical Review*, 9 (1894), 440-72, accepts the official Elizabethan version of Lopez's guilt as detailed in the State Papers. Hume's article (*JHSE*), making use of hitherto unavailable Spanish documents, demonstrates that Lopez was viewed by the Spanish as a possible go-between for peace negotiations. M.J. Kohler, "Dr. Rodrigo Lopez...and His Relations to America," *Publications of the American Jewish Historical Society*, 17 (1909), 9-25, reiterates much of what Lee and Hume had written, and adds the interesting little story of Lopez being given a boat load of captured Papal Indulgences by the Queen to sell in the Americas for his own profit. The most recent article on Lopez, J. Gwyer, "The Case of Dr. Lopez," *JHSE*, 15 (1952), 163-84, follows Lee's and Hume's views about Lopez's innocence. He views the doctor as a sacrifice to factionalism within the Privy Council. All these historians accept without question that Lopez secretly practiced Judaism and was persecuted because he was a Jew.

[4]Sir Francis Bacon, "A True Report of the Detestable Treason Intended by Doctor Roderigo Lopez," *Bacon's Works*, Ed. B. Montagu (Philadelphia, 1851), 216. Gabriel Harvey's comments are marginalia in his own hand found on a copy of his treatise *In iudaeorum medicastorum calumnis....* The marginalia, with some commentary about Lopez, was reproduced by F. Marcham, *Lopez the Jew. Executed 1594. An Opinion by Gabriel Harvey* (Private printing, 1927), no pagination. Records of baptism of the children of Dunstan Ames are found in *Registers of St. Olave. Hart Street London*, Ed. W.B. Bannerman (London, 1916). A.M. Hyamson, *The Sephardim of England* (London, 1951), 5 n. maintains Sarah Lopez was a sister of Jorge Anes, father of Dunstan, but cites no references.

[5]S.W. Baron, *A Social and Religious History of the Jews*, 13 (New York, 1969), 44-50. Baron's multi-volume work is invaluable, not only for content by for its exhaustive notes. Two other works on Renaissance Jewry, both by C. Roth are: *The Jews in the Renaissance* (Philadelphia, 1964) and *A History of*

the Marranos (New York, 1974).

⁶William Camden, *The History of the Most Renowned and Victorious Princess Elizabeth, Late Queen of England*, 3rd ed. (London, 1675), 484. Sir George Buck, *The History of King Richard the Third*, ed. A.N. Kincaid (Gloucester, 1979), 171.

⁷Bacon, "True Report," 217.

⁸C. Hilton, "St. Bartholomew's Hospital, London, and its Jewish Connections," *JHSE*, 30 (1987-88), 23-25; Hume, "Conspiracy," 36-37. *Calendar of Patent Rolls. Elizabeth I*, 11 (London), n. 647. The Rolls entry is quite specific, naming his predecessor, and listing Lopez's salary as £50 per year. Hume, Lee and others date Lopez's appointment in 1586, basing that date on a letter Lopez wrote in 1589 stating he had spend large sums over the past three years in the Queen's service. The three years must refer to expenses as Walsingham's agent. We therefore tentatively can set the date at which Lopez began to function in the espionage network as 1586.

⁹Baron, 51, 122-26; Hume, "Conspiracy," 37.

¹⁰*Calendar of Letters and State Papers Relating to English Affairs in the Archives of Simancas*, Ed. M.S. Hume (London), 3, ns. 122, 524 (henceforth CSPS), detail Spanish knowledge of these various expeditions. *SPD*, v. 224, n. 123, names Lopez as a member of the interrogations team, *CSPS*, 4, n. 582, details Andrada's account of the incident.

¹¹T. Birch, *Memoirs of the Reign of Queen Elizabeth* (London, 1754), 1, 99. Birch collected, edited and transcribed the papers of Anthony Bacon, Essex's "spymaster."

¹²*CSPS*, 3, n. 29.

¹³Bibliography on the factionalism of the Court is enormous. J.E. Neale, *Queen Elizabeth I* (Garden City, NJ, 1957), 313-91 details Essex's rivalries with members of the Court. G.R. Elton, *The Parliament of England* (Cambridge, 1986), 350-72 points up the vicious rivalries of the courtiers, as do S. Adams, "Eliza Enthroned? The Court and its Politics," *The Reign of Elizabeth I*, ed. C. Haigh (New York, 1984), 73-77, and D. Starkey, et al, *The English Court from the Wars of the Roses to the Civil War* (London, 1987), 174, 201 (and elsewhere).

¹⁴Bishop Godfrey Goodman, *The Court of James I*, Ed. J.S. Brewer (London, 1839), 1, 149-53. R. Lacey, *Robert, Earl of Essex* (New York, 1971), 201, and G.B. Harrison, *The Life and Death of Robert Devereaux, Earl of Essex* (New York, 1937), 80-86, discuss the Lopez affair. Neither historian believes Lopez guilty of anything more than arousing Essex's ire.

¹⁵C. Haigh, *Elizabeth I* (London, 1988), 135-39.

¹⁶M. Hume, *Treason and Plot* (London, 1901), 151-53, suggests that

Lopez may have been willing to poison Don Antonio or Antonio Perez. Gwyer, "Dr. Lopez," 169-71 believes that Lopez hoped to secure money to migrate to Constantinople and practice his ancient faith openly.

[17]Goodman, *Court*, 152-53. Using Birch's *Memoirs*, and State Papers detailing the several interrogations of Lopez, Gwyer, "Dr. Lopez," 169-72, details the actions of the Queen. See also Haigh, *Elizabeth*, 79-83, 146-52.

[18]Birch, *Memoirs*, 100, 106-08, 114, 144.

[19]L.B. Smith, *Treason in Tudor England. Politics and Paranoia* (Princeton, 1986), 4, 189-94.

[20]Goodman, *Court*, 149-53.

[21]*SPD*, v. 247, ns. 13, 19, 51, 70, 82-84; Birch, *Memoirs*, 156-59.

[22]*SPD*, v. 347, no. 51.

[23]*SPD*, v. 247, n. 13.

[24]Birch, *Memoirs*, 150

[25]Birch, *Memoirs*, 150.

[26]Birch, *Memoirs*, 152.

[27]Dimock, "Conspiracy," 448-49.

[28]*SPD*, v. 247, ns. 12, 13, 19, 51, 70, 82-84. Philip Gawdy, *Letters*, Ed. I.H. Jeanes (London, 1906), 85.

[29]*SPD*, v. 247, ns. 82-84.

[30]*SPD*, v. 248, ns. 33, 38-39, 42-47, 51-58, 60-64, 73-78, 81. The quotation is from n. 53.

[31]*SPD*, v. 248, n. 26

[32]G.K. Hunter, "Elizabethans and Foreigners," *Shakespeare Survey*, 17 (1964), 37-52, discusses Englishmen's often xenophobic reaction to the numbers of foreigners migrating to London. For Renaissance stereotypes concerning Jews see P. Burke, *Popular Culture in Early Modern Europe* (New York, 1978), 167-68. John Strype, *Annals of the Reformation*, 4 (Oxford, 1824), 296-301, reproduces the petition. *The Calendar of State Papers and Manuscripts...Venice*, 9 (London), ns. 261, 274 (henceforth *CSPV*), reflect the information circulating in London concerning Lopez's longstanding espionage for the King of Spain. Nashe's *Unfortunate Traveller* is discussed in H. Sinsheimer, *Shylock, the History of a Character* (New York, 1947), 68-71. Once Lopez's guilt became the "official" line, members of the Court jumped on Essex's bandwagon. Lord Burghley wrote, and revised, a lengthy tract concerning the supposed Lopez plot (*SPD*, v. 250, n. 10). C. Read, *Lord Burghley and Queen Elizabeth* (New York, 1960), 498-99, discusses Lord Burghley's propaganda. Robert Cecil (*SPD*, v. 247, n. 10) wrote to Thomas Windebank asking him to inform the Queen of the conviction of the "vile Jew." C.D. Bowen, *The Lion and the Throne* (Boston, 1957), 90-95, related Sir Edward Coke's inflammatory rhetoric at Lopez's trial. The quotation is from a

letter sent by Tobie Matthew, Dean of Durham Cathedral, to Lord Burghley, in Strype, *Annals*, 4, 281. William Waad, in a letter to Lord Burghley of 19 March 1594 (reproduced in Wolf, "Jews in Elizabethan England," 85-86), tells of the "discontent of the people so greate" over the Lopez matter. Haig, *Elizabeth*, 144, writes of Lopez as one of the "unfortunate individuals framed by councillors to put the frighteners on Elizabeth." See also "Ways and Means in Elizabethan Propaganda," *History*, new ser., 26 (1941).

[33]J.A. Williamson, *The Age of Drake* (Cleveland, 1965), 335-64; B. Penrose, *Travel and Discovery in the Renaissance* (Cambridge, MA, 1952), 235-58; J. H. Parry, *The Age of Reconnaissance* (New York, 1963), 212-15; G. Mattingly, *Renaissance Diplomacy* (Boston, 1971), 204-06.

[34]No record of Lopez's trial is contained in the State Trials. Accounts are found only in indictments and charges in the State Papers, v. 247, ns. 10, 99-103. For the "Stalinist" nature of treason trials see L.B. Smith, "English Treason Trials and Confessions in the Sixteenth Century," *The Elizabethan Age*, Ed. D.L. Stevenson (Greenwich, CN, 1966), 60-65. For accounts of Lopez's execution see: Goodman, *Court*, 143; Camden, *Elizabeth*, 484-85; Gawdy, *Letters*, 85; John Stow, *Annals*, continued by E. Howes (London, 1631), 768.

[35]Theatres in London had been closed because of plague; both the Admiral's Men and the Chamberlain's Men shared Henslowe's Newington Butts theatre. Henslowe' *Diary*, Ed. R.A. Foakes and R.T. Rickert (Cambridge, 1961), 21, lists no performances on 7 June 1594.

[36]Bacon, "True Report," 217-18; Goodman, *Court*, 153-54; Hume, "Conspiracy," 36, 39; *SPD*, v. 247, ns. 82-84, and v. 251, n. 50 (the grant to Lopez's widow); *Calendar of the Manuscripts of the Marquis of Salisbury* (London), 7, n. 253 (henceforth *CMMS*).

[37]A. Gurr, *Playgoing in Shakespeare's London* (Cambridge, 1987), 141-47; *Aubrey's Brief Lives*, Ed. O.L. Dick (New York, 1949), 163; L. Barroll, "A New History for Shakespeare and His Time," *Shakespeare Quarterly*, 39 (1988), 449-54. A Harbage, *Shakespeare and the Rival Traditions* (Bloomington, IN, 1970), and G.E. Bentley, *The Profession of Dramatist in Shakespeare Time* (Princeton, 1986), discuss the shaping of repertories by playwrights to suit the interests and tastes of their patrons and audiences. W. Lewis, *The Lion and the Fox. The Role of the Hero in Shakespeare's Plays* (New York, n.d.), 37-38, quotes Essex and others who complained of the portrayal of real people in Elizabethan theatres.

[38]See, for example, A. Barton, introduction to *The Merchant of Venice* in *The Riverside Shakespeare*, Ed. G.B. Evans (Boston, 1974), 251. The Lopez affair was reported in *The Fugger News-Letters*, Ed. V. von Klarwill, tr. L.S.R. Byrne (New York, 1926), 255. For Lopez in plays see: Thomas Dekker, *The Whore of Babylon*, Ed. M.G. Riely (New York, 1980), Act 4, scene

2, and Thomas Middleton, *A Game of Chess*, Ed. J. Harper (New York, 1967), Act 4, scene 3. C. Hoy, *Introductions, Notes and Commentaries to Text in the Dramatic Works of Thomas Dekker*, 2 (Cambridge, 1980) provides some valuable information about Dekker's use of Lopez as an image of the worst kind of treachery.

[39]For Shakespeare's layering of clues to develop his burlesque see T.P. Morris, "Shakespeare hat given him a purge to make him bewray his credit," *Shakespeare and Renaissance Association of West Virginia. Selected Papers*, 15 (1992). Morris convincingly shows that Shakespeare parodied Ben Jonson through the character of Abraham Slender in *Merry Wives of Windsor*. W. Clemen, *The Development of Shakespeare's Imagery* (New York, 1951), 82 notes Shakespeare's "delicate touches and hints...often enough not understood at the moment" to prepare his audience for further plot developments. A.M. Eastman, *A Short History of Shakespearean Criticism* (New York, 1968), 274-75, 282, discusses Shakespeare creating cumulative impressions through "linked images," and "image clusters." J.L. Palmer, *Comic Characters in Shakespeare* (London, 1961), 53-56, cautiously suggests Shylock may be an allusion to Dr. Lopez. B. Grebanier, *The Truth About Shylock* (New York, 1962), 8-14, discusses attempts to equate Shylock with Dr. Lopez, and points out how "racking" and Lopez to *lupus* to wolf, as such arguments have been presented by scholars, do not stand up. S. Schoenbaum, *William Shakespeare. A Compact Documentary Life* (Oxford, 1977), 199-200, warns of attempting to relate Shakespeare's characters to real Elizabethans. G. Taylor, *Reinventing Shakespeare* (New York, 1989), discusses problems which have arisen over time as a result of prejudices of later eras being applied to interpretations of Shakespeare's plays. W.G. Leary, *Shakespeare Plain. The Making and Performing of Shakespeare's Plays* (New York, 1977), 27-35, discusses the complexity of Shylock's character. A. Downer, "The Merchant of Venice," *Teaching Shakespeare*, Ed. A. Mizener (New York, 1969), 77-80, traces the various actor interpretations of Shylock.

[40]Marcham, *Lopez*, no pagination. Camden, *Elizabeth*, 485, reports Lopez's final remarks.

[41]Marcham, *Lopez*, no pagination, lists several contemporary criticisms of Lopez. Bacon, "True Report," 217, sneers at his pursuit of the wealthy and powerful. *SPD*, v. 124, n. 38, and v. 225, n. 21, are Lopez's letters concerning the collection of debts, and the request for a renewal of his monopolies for the importation of anise seed and sumac.

[42]*SPD*, v. 247, n. 84; *CMMS*, 7, n. 253. E. Withycombe, *The Oxford Dictionary of English Christian Names* (Oxford, 1977), 176, notes that Shakespeare's use of "Jessica" is the first written instance of the name. L. Dunkling and W. Gosling, *The Facts on File Dictionary of First Names*

(New York, 1983), 139, notes it was considered a Jewish name from Shakespeare's time until the twentieth century.

⁴³SPD, v. 225, n. 21.

⁴⁴Hume, "Conspiracy," 36, 39. *Leicester's Commonwealth*, Ed. D. Peck (Athens, OH, 1985), 116, calls Lopez an expert on poisons and abortion methods.

⁴⁵Hume, *Treason*, 163-64. S. Mullaney, *The Place of the Stage. Liberty, License and Power in Renaissance England* (Chicago, 1988), 116-17, describes the ritual of dragging condemned traitors through the streets so that they could be seen by citizens "as the rarest sort of monsters."

⁴⁶Bacon, "True Report," 220. On Portia's peculiar status see E. Tucker, "The Letter of the Law in Merchant of Venice," *Shakespeare Survey*, 29 (1976), 97, and D. Beauregard, "Sidney, Aristotle, and Merchant of Venice," *Shakespeare Studies*, 20 (1988), 40-47.

⁴⁷Goodman, *Court*, 152-53.

⁴⁸SPD, v. 251, n. 50. S. D'Ewes, *A Compleat Journal of the...House of Lords and House of Commons* (facs. of 1693 ed., Wilmington, DE, 1974), 599 relates Lord Egerton remarking that Elizabeth wore the Lopez ring on her girdle. For Elizabeth's parsimony see the remarks of her own courtier, Sir Robert Naunton, *Fragmentia Regalia*, Ed. J.S. Cerowski (Washington, 1985), 16-18. *The Secret History of the Most Renowned Queen Elizabeth and the Earl of Essex by a Person of Quality* (London, 1685), relates the ring legend. Schoenbaum, *Compact Life*, 97-108, explores the deer poaching myth.

⁴⁹Wolf, "Jews in Elizabethan England," 56-91, reproduces many letters from Don Solomon to England, and to Lopez, dealing with Solomon's representing English interests at the Ottoman Court, and warning Lopez of the dissolute character of the Pretender Don Antonio. For "gabardine" see *Oxford English Dictionary*, 2nd ed. (Oxford, 1989), 6, 302. For the etymology of "Leah" see Dunkling and Gosling, *Facts on File*, 162; Withycombe, *Names*, 192, and C.M. Yonge, *History of Christian Names* (London, 1884), 15.

⁵⁰W. Strunk Jr., "The Elizabethan Showman's Ape," *Modern Language Notes*, 32 (1917), 215-21; E. Nungezer, *A Dictionary of Actors...before 1642* (New Haven, 1929), 246. *Love's Labor's Lost*, Act 1, scene 2, lines 51-54, *Riverside*. See also plate 31 and commentary (between 1518 and 1519).

⁵¹H. Kokeritz, Ed., *Mr. William Shakespeare's Comedies, Histories and Tragedies* (New Haven, CN, 1954), facsimile edition of the *First Folio*; J. Allen, ed., *Shakespeare's Plays in Quarto* (Berkeley, 1981) where the final e is present throughout the speech in the "Good Quarto" edition of 1600. Burke, 167. P.G. Simonds, "Sacred and Sexual Motifs in All's Well That Ends Well," *Renaissance Quarterly*, 42, 34.

⁵²Marder, *Exits and Entrances*, 44, 58.

[53]Hume, *Treason*, 130-33; Neale, *Elizabeth*, 355. G.B. Harrison, *The Elizabethan Journals* (Garden City, NY, 1956), 1, 417, 485, gives the records from Acts of the Privy Council concerning the detained Venetian argosy.

[54]Goodman, *Court*, 152-53; Birch, *Memoirs*, 150, 152-53; Gawdy, *Letters*, 85, writes that the day Lopez was executed, the Queen was absent from London on Progress. Dimock, "Conspiracy," 468-69, discusses the vagueness of the documentation surrounding the order for Lopez's execution.

[55]For Elizabeth's travels between 1589-1603 see J. Nichols, *The Progresses and Public Processions of Queen Elizabeth*, 3 (London, 1823), Neale, *Elizabeth*, 347-50. Haigh, *Elizabeth*, 161.

[56]H. Vetter, "Faint Smile in Defeat," *Military History* (April 1991), 23-28; Neale, *Elizabeth*, 351-57.

[57]J.J. Hurwich, "Lineage and Kin in the Sixteenth-Century Aristocracy," in *The First Modern Society*, Eds. A.L Beier, D. Cannadine, J.M. Rosenheim (Cambridge, 1989), 33-64, discusses how extended kinship relationships did serve to unite interests, especially if the kinship relationship (as was the case with Southampton and Essex) was reinforced by personal friendship. E.J.A. Honigmann, *Shakespeare: the 'lost years'* (Totowa, NJ, 1985), 64-69: W. Ingram, *A London Life in the Brazen Age. Francic Langley, 1548-1602* (Cambridge, MA, 1978), 121; Barroll, "New History," 449-54, suggests that Essex's supporters were staging the play to encourage themselves to action. Neale, *Elizabeth*, 360, discusses the frustration of the Essex faction concerning his lack of recognition for the Cadiz expedition. Henslowe lists sums almost equaling £30 for the properties, costumes, etc., necessary to stage a new play he called *The Spensers*. See *Diary*, 147-48.

[58]R. Strong, *Gloriana. The Portraits of Queen Elizabeth I* (London, 1987), 12-18, discusses the censorship of the Queen's portraits. *SPD*, v. 5, ns.165, 449-51, 455, describe the actions taken against John Haywood. Kincaid, in his introduction to Buck's *Richard the Third* (xii-iv), traces the connections between the Buck, Tilney, and Howard families. Gurr, *Playgoing*, 59-79, discusses the preferences of Inns of Court gallants for the Chamberlain's Men. See also Barroll, "New History," 449-54.

[59]Neale, *Elizabeth*, 69-84, 137-56, 243-64, discusses Elizabeth's various suitors within the framework of domestic and international politics.

[60]Haigh, *Elizabeth*, 146-52; Hume, *Treason*, 139; R. Smithey, *English Seamen*, Ed. D. Hannay (London, 1904), 2, 93-109, gives a detailed account of the Cadiz expedition.

[61]Lacey, *Essex*, 120; Harrison, *Essex*, 86.

[62]E. Jenkins, *Elizabeth the Great* (New York, 1959), 272; Read, *Burghley*, 586, n. 33.

[63]Venetian dispatch, dated 15 March 1594, Prague: "The Queen is ill. She has taken a Portuguese doctor out of prison to attend her case." *CSPV*, 9, n. 258. Other historians seem to have missed this peculiar bit of information. The domestic State Papers from the same time contain a letter from Sir Thomas Egerton saying: "Doctor Lopez has kept his bed for the most part, since his trial...." "Dr. Lopez has kept to his bed" perhaps was an official reason to explain Lopez not being at the Tower. *SPD*, v. 248, n. 26.

[64]Honigmann, *lost years*, 64-69.

[65]A.L. Rowse, *Shakespeare's Southampton* (New York, 1965), 65-66; Kenny, *Admiral*, 43-44; *Diary*, 110.

[66]L. Pronko, *The World of Jean Anouilh* (Berkeley, 1968), xxi; O Brockett and R. Findley, *Century of Innovation. A History of European and American Theatre and Drama Since 1870* (Englewood Cliff, NJ, 1973), 389-90; D. Grossvogel, *20th Century French Drama* (New York, 1961), 104. J.H. Forse, "*Romeo and Juliet*: A Play for All Seasons," *Shakespeare and Renaissance Association of West Virginia. Selected Papers*, 16 (1993), 88-99, notes that where Shakespeare deviated from his source story, those deviations parallel difficulties faced by the Earl of Southamton.

[67]The entire of volume 20, *Shakespeare Studies* (1988), was devoted to problems of interpretation concerning *The Merchant of Venice*.

[68]See the following articles in *Shakespeare Studies*, 20: D.N. Beauregard, "Sidney, Aristotle, and The Merchant of Venice," 31-51; L.E. Boose, "The Comic Contract and Portia's Golden Ring," 241-54; T. Cartelli, "Shakespeare's Merchant, Marlowe's Jew: The Problem of Cultural Difference," 255-60; M.D. Perret, "Shakespeare's Jew: Preconception and Performance," 261-68; J. Shapiro, "Which is The Merchant here, and which The Jew? Shakespeare and the Economics of Influence," 269-79; see also F. Laroque, "An Analogue and Possible Secondary Source to the Pound-of-Flesh Story in The Merchant of Venice," *Notes and Queries, New Series*, 30 (1983), 117-18; J.O. Holmer, " 'When Jacob graz'd his uncle Laban's sheep': a New Source for The Merchant of Venice," *Shakespeare Quarterly*, 36 (1985), 64-65; A.N. Benston, "Portia, the Law, and the Tripartite Structure of The Merchant of Venice," *Shakespeare Quarterly*, 30 (1979), 367-85; *Marder, Exits and Entrances*, 44, 58.

[69]*SPD*, v. 124, n. 36; v. 225, ns. 21, 22; v. 247, n. 93. For Shakespeare's idiosyncratic speeches see P.S. Berggren, "The Woman's Part. Female Sexuality as Power in Shakespeare's Plays," *The Woman's Part. Feminist Criticism of Shakespeare*, Eds. C.R.S. Lenz, G. Greene, C.T. Neely (Urbana, IL, 1980), 17-18; Leary, *Shakespeare Plain*, 30. Shylock's terse speech is mentioned frequently by critics. See for example, W. Clemen, *Imagery*, 119, and Palmer *Comic Characters*, 68-70, who (p. 88) writes of "the imaginative

effort expended by Shakespeare in making his Jew a comprehensibly human figure." Bentley, *Player*, and Gurr, *Playgoing*, mention numerous instances of complaints about Elizabethan and Jacobean actors using characteristic costume, makeup, speech patterns and gestures in obvious impersonations of important, real, living people.

[70]A. Barton, Introduction to *Merchant of Venice* in *Riverside*, 251.

[71]Harbage, *Rival Traditions*, 351-58.

Chapter 7

[1]*Acts of the Privy Council*, 27, ed. J.R. Dasent (London, 1909), 313, 338. Various accounts of the incident blame the satire of the play, or a desire to close the third theatre so as to restrict the number of theatres to the already established two, or a desire to target Langley himself as a suspected dealer in stolen jewelry. See, for example, G. Wickham, *Early English Stages* 1300-1660, II, pt. 2 (London, 1972), 9-29; W. Ingram, "The Closing of the Theatres in 1597: A Dissenting View," *Modern Philology*, 69 (1971-2), 105-15, and his *A London Life in the Brazen Age. Francis Langley, 1548-1602* (Cambridge, MA, 1978), 168-89; A. Gurr, *The Shakespearean Stage* (Cambridge, 1980), 43-44.

[2]See Thomas Nashe's remarks written in 1599 in *Lenten Stuffe*; quoted in J.F. Bradley and J.Q. Adams, *The Jonson Allusion-book* (New Haven, 1922), 5. For the use of allusions to *The Isle of Dogs* to identify Jonson see T.P. Morris, "Shakespeare hath given him a purge to bewray his credit," *Shakespeare and Renaissance Association of West Virginia. Selected Papers*, 15 (1992).

[3]M. Chute, *Ben Jonson of Westminster* (New York, 1960), 51. The most recent biographies of Jonson are: R. Miles, *Ben Jonson. His Life and Work* (London, 1986) and D. Riggs, *Ben Jonson: A Life* (Cambridge, MA, 1988).

[4]*Privy Council*, 27, 338. For Thomas More see G.B. Evans, in *The Riverside Shakespeare*, Ed. G.B. Evans (Boston, 1974), 1683-85.

[5]For receipts,of Henslowe's company see *Henslowe's Diary*, ed. R.A. Foakes and R.T. Rickert (Cambridge, 1961). N. Carson, *A Companion to Henslowe's Diary* (Cambridge, 1988), organizes various sums received and disbursed according to the records contained in the *Diary*. A. Harbage, *Shakespeare's Audience* (New York, 1941), 55-62, discusses receipts and gives fifteen thousand as a "conservative" estimate of weekly attendance at both theatres. L. Stone, *The Crisis of the Aristocracy, 1558-1641* (Oxford, 1965), 758-67 and Appendix xxiii gives incomes for the Elizabethan and Jacobean aristocratic classes.

[6]Gurr, *Stage*, 118-30; Ingram, *London Life*, 185-89.

[7]D. Starkey, et. al., *The English Court from the Wars of the Roses to the Civil War* (London, 1987), 149-70); O.J. Campbell and E.G. Quinn, *The Reader's Encyclopedia of Shakespeare* (New York, 1966), 39, 448. Langley's

position supposedly certified the measurements and quality of woolen cloth sent to the Court.

⁸Starkey, *Court*, 162-3, discusses £100 as an "opening" offer for favors.

⁹Ingram, *London Life*, 107-22, 141-56. See also: A. Cairncross, "Pembroke's Men and Some Shakespearean Piracies," *Shakespeare Quarterly*, 11 (1960), 335-49; I. Smith, *Shakespeare's Blackfriars Playhouse* (New York, 1964), 276-79; M. Byrne, *Elizabethan Life in Town and Country* (London, 1961), 267-69.

¹⁰Harbage, *Audience*, 55-62.

¹¹Ingram, *London Life*, 120-21; *Diary*, 54-60; Carson, *Companion*, 138.

¹²F.G. Fleay, *A Chronicle History of the London Stage* (London, 1890), 98-101; *Diary*, 54-60; Byrne, *Life*, 267-68.

¹³M.C. Cipolla, *Before the Industrial Revolution* (New York, 1976), 23, 30-31; S. Mullaney, *The Place of the Stage. Liberty, License and Power in Renaissance England* (Chicago, 1988), 70-71; Fleay, *Chronicle*, 101; *Diary*, 58.

¹⁴Campbell/Quinn, *Encyclopedia*, 506, 873. Byrne, *Life*, 269-70; Gurr, *Stage*, 72-74. The Ordinance of 1559 specified censorship in "matters of the governaunce of the estate of the commonweal."

¹⁵Starkey, *Court*, 15, 149-72, 196, 211; Byrne, *Life*, 76; Campbell/Quinn, *Encyclopedia*, 39, 86, 122, 373-74, 448, 506; Gurr, *Stage*, 72-76.

¹⁶J. E. Neale's *Queen Elizabeth I* (Garden City, NY, 1957) remains one of the best accounts of her reign. For the Essex rivalries see pages 313-91. See also E. Jenkins, *Elizabeth the Great* (New York, 1959), 290-319; C. Haigh, *Elizabeth I* (London, 1988), 98-104; Starkey, *Court*, 164-65, 170-71; A. Collins, ed., *Letters and Memorials of State...from Originals at Penshurst*, 1 (London, 1746), 370-72.

¹⁷*Calendar of the Manuscripts of the Marquis of Salisbury*, 7 (London, 1899), 343; Ingram, *London Life*, 122-38; Chute, *Jonson*, 48-52, 56-57; 73, 80, 152-63; E. Nungezer, *A Dictionary of Actors...in England before 1642* (New Haven, 1929), 63, 118, 323, 331; D.H. Brock, *A Ben Jonson Companion* (Bloomington, IN, 1983), 242.

¹⁸G.R. Elton, *The Parliament of England* (Cambridge, 1986), 350-72; S. Adams, "Eliza Enthroned?" *The Reign of Elizabeth I*, ed. C. Haigh (New York, 1984), 73-74. Neale, *Elizabeth*, 347-49; Ingram, London Life, 161-62.

¹⁹J. Manningham, *The Diary of John Manningham*, 1602-03, ed. R.P. Sorlien (Hanover, NH, 1976), 119; R.F. Patterson, ed., *Ben Jonson's Conversations with William Drummond* (Norwood Editions, 1977), 31. See L. Barroll, "A New History for Shakespeare and His Time," *Shakespeare Quarterly*, 39 (1988), 449-54, suggests Essex's supporters may have perceived the theatre as more potent in affecting public opinion than it really was. Neale,

Elizabeth, 313-91, gives a detailed picture of the Essex rivalry with virtually every other faction at the Court. W. Lewis, *The Lion and the Fox. The Role of the Hero in Shakespeare's Plays* (New York, n.d.), 37, quotes Essex's fears he would be the butt of stage jokes.

[20]Ingram, *London Life*, 128-38; Bradley/Adams, *Allusion-book*, 278; Harbage, *Traditions*, 53; Gurr, *Stage*, 44; Chute, *Jonson*, 192-95, 289.

[21]L. Barroll, "New History," 448-53.

[22]Patterson, *Conversations*, 24-25; Neale, *Elizabeth*, 342-43; Ingram, *London Life*, 183-85; Campbell/Quinn, *Encyclopedia*, 86, 122, 506.

[23]Starkey, *Court*, 170-72; Haigh, *Elizabeth*, 133-38; Neale, *Elizabeth*, 313-91; Ingram, *London Life*, 135-38.

[24]N. Carson, "Collaborative Playwriting," *Theatre Research International*, 14 (1989), describes the methods of collaboration probably used by Elizabethan playwrights. Quotation from Nashe in Bradley and Adams, *Allusion-book*, 5.

[25]C.F. Wheeler, *Classical Mythology in the Plays, Masques, and Poems of Ben Jonson* (Princeton, 1938), 90, 132, 142, 166. Wheeler identifies allusions to *Frogs, Wasps, Wealth, Ecclesiazusae, Themophoriazusae*, and *Theogany*; Bradley/Adams, *Allusion-book*, 141.

[26]D.J. Geanakoplos, *Greek Scholars in Venice* (Cambridge, MA, 1962), 275-78; P.O. Kristeller, *Renaissance Thought* (New York, 1961), 15-17; R. Marius, *Thomas More* (New York, 1985), 72-97; M. Phillips, *Erasmus and the Northern Renaissance* (New York, 1965), 76-80, 100-01; K.J. Dover, *Aristophanic Comedy* (Berkeley, 1972), 2, 228-29; Aristophanes, *Complete Plays*, Ed. M. Hadas (New York, 1962), references to Aristophanes' plays will be from this edition. R. Dutton, *Ben Jonson: The First Folio* (Cambridge, 1983), 25, notes that Jonson patterned his comedies after the Roman comedies of Plautus and Terence. In his prologue to *Bartholomew Fair*, Jonson wrote that the audiences' ignorance of the classics meant that he must present the Hero and Leander story in such a way as to "make it a little easie, and moderne for the times." See also J.R. Brown and B. Harris, eds., *Jacobean Theatre* (New York, 1967), 73-77, 87; Riggs, *Jonson*, 28-29; Gurr, *Stage*, 222; Chute, *Jonson*, 22-33.

[27]B. Weinreb and C. Hibbert, eds., *The London Encyclopedia* (London, 1983), 411-12, 550. F.C. Chalfant, *Ben Jonson's London: A Jacobean Placename Dictionary* (Athens, GA, 1978), 106-07. Chalfant notes that when playwrights made reference to the real Isle of Dogs, they always used it for associations with canine qualities.

[28]R. Lacey, *Robert, Earl of Essex* (New York, 1971), 305

[29]Neale, *Elizabeth*, 293-359; Haigh, *Elizabeth*, 124-42; Weeler, *Classical*, 90, 132, 143, 166.

[30]Aristophanes, *Knights*, 89; *Wasps*, 167-71; Dover, *Comedy*, 122-29.

[31]Brown/Harris, *Jacobean*, 73-77; Chute, *Jonson*, 32-33, 65-75, 180-82, 210-16; Bradley/Adams, *Allusion-book*, 33.

[32]G.E. Bentley, *The Profession of Dramatist in Shakespeare's Time* (Princeton, 1987), 188-89; A. Gurr, *Playgoing in Shakespeare's London* (Cambridge, 1988), 145; O.L. Dick, ed., *Aubrey' s Brief Lives* (New York, 1987), 163; Chute, *Jonson*, 150-54, 196-97. On the rivalry between English and Scots and James' "Frenchyfied" court see M. Lee, *Great Britain's Solomon: James VI and I in His Three Kingdoms* (Urbana, IL, 1990), 109-11, 117-18, 143-46, and Starkey, *Court*, 173-225. Cecil may have been the source of rumors that appropriations to the King would not fall into the "bottomless pockets of the the Scots courtiers." The offending scene, which put playwrights Jonson, Marston, and Chapman, and several of the boy actors into prison, see *Eastward Ho*, in *Ben Jonson*, IV, eds. C.H. Herford and P. Simpson (Oxford, 1932), 581. Perhaps Jonson's epigram number xliii, dedicated to Robert Cecil, opens with a touch of irony as well as self-depreciation: "What need hast thou of me? or of my muse?" in Herford/Simpson *Jonson*, VIII, 40.

[33]Aristophanes, *Wealth*, 494-98.

[34]W. Besant, *London in the Time of the Tudors* (London, 1904), 66, quotes the Venetian ambassador. See Strong, *Gloriana*, for numerous example of Elizabeth's portraits. Haigh, *Elizabeth*, 86-95, 146-48. In 1596, the Privy Council ordered all unflattering (that is any which showed aging) portraits of the Queen to be destroyed. David Norbrook, in a review (*The New Republic*) of Riggs' biography of Jonson, notes that Jonson always had an "element of innovative risk," and an "equation of art with intrigue."

[35]Gurr, *Stage*, 26, calls *Cataline* a veiled allusion to the Gunpowder Plot. Drummond wrote Jonson preferred to lose a friend than lose a joke. Dekker's line, *Satiro-mastix*, is cited in Bradley/Adams, *Allusion-book*, 17. Jonson probably was commenting on his own career and controversiality in epigram lxviii, "On Play-Wright" (Herford, *Jonson*, VIII, 49).

> Play-wright convict of publike wrongs to me,
> Takes private beatins, and begins againe.

Chapter 8

[1]I. Smith, *Shakespeare's Blackfriars Playhouse* (New York, 1964) reproduced the lease to Richard Farrant for Blackfriars' first use as a theatre and litigations among various leaseholders after his death (463-68; 505-08). For the boys companies in the 1570s and 1580s see Smith, *Blackfriars*, 130-52; G.E. Bentley, *The Profession of Player in Shakespeare's Time* (Princeton, 1986), 136-45; A. Gurr, *The Shakespearean Stage* (Cambridge, 1980), 33, 93-97; and his Playgoing in *Shakespeare's London* (Cambridge, 1988), 129-32. The fullest accounts of the boys' companies are H.N.

Hillebrand, *The Child Actors, University of Illinois Studies in Language and Literature*, 11 (Urbana, IL, 1926), and M. Shapiro, *Children of the Revels* (New York, 1977). This chapter appeared in somewhat shorter form in *Theatre Survey*, 31 (1990).

[2]Most recent on Paul's Boys is R. Gair, *The Children of Paul's* (Cambridge, 1982). For the Westcote era and aftermath see pp. 13-76. See also, Hillebrand, *Child Actors*, 117-50. In an appendix (pp. 327-30), Hillebrand prints Westcote's will. Smith, *Blackfriars*, 463-68, 505-08, details the battles of Evans with Sir William More, primary landlord of Blackfriars.

[3]Terms of the lease are found in litigations involving Evans: see Smith, *Blackfriars*, 509-46, and 175-90. Lawsuits often refer to the supposed use of Blackfriars as a school. For example, the landlord, Sir William More, asserted, "Farrant pretended unto me to use the house only for the teaching of the Children of the Chapel." Frequently there is mention of a separate area at Blackfriars called "the schoolhouse."

[4]Clifton's deposition is reproduced in Smith, *Blackfriars*, 484-86. Later litigation over Blackfriars recounts Evans' censure and subsequent absence from London (544).

[5]For Burghley's pedigree see *Complete State Papers Domestic* (Hassocks, Sussex, 1979,.microfilm), 260, n. 85. For Clifton's genealogy and Coat of Arms see *The visitacion of Norfolk, Anno 1563 and Anno 1613.* Harleian Society, 32 (London, 1891), 75 and *The Visitation of Norfolk, Anno 1664.* Harleian Society, 85 (London, 1933), 50. F. Blomefield, *An Essay towards a Topographical History of the County of Norfolk* (London, 1810), v. I, 375-78, v. II, 380, v. V, 406. See also T. Fuller, *The Worthies of England*, 2 (New York, 1965), 469. Clifton's will is recorded in M.A. Farrow, ed., *Index of Wills Proved in the Consistory Court of Norwich 1604-86* (Norfolk Record Society, 1958), 51.

[6]A.H. Smith, *County and Court: Government and Politics in Norfolk, 1558-1603* (Oxford, 1974), 52-58, 167-73, 363. W.T. MacCaffrey, "Place and Patronage in Elizabethan Politics," *Elizabethan Government and Society* (London, 1961), 106-07, 112-13; Blomefield, *Norfolk*, v. VI, 261, v. VII, 203-04; J.F. Williams, ed. *Diocese of Norwich. Bishop Redman's Visitation, 1597* (Norfolk Record Society, 1946), 51-54; *Burke's Genealogical and Heraldic History of Peerage, Baronetage and Knightage*, ed. P. Townend (London, 1967), 2360, 2496; *Ordinance Service of Great Britain*, Quarter Inch Fifth Series, sheet 14 (Crown copywright, 1966); *The Times Index Gazeteer of the World* (Boston, 1966), 547, 855.

[7]Smith, *Blackfriars*, 463-68, 505-08.

[8]Smith, *Blackfriars*, 485-86; Hillebrand, *Child Actors*, 160-69, J. Simon, *Education and Society in Tudor England* (Cambridge, 1967), 365.

⁹Burbage's terms to Evans appear in litigations in Smith, *Blackfriars*, 509-46.

¹⁰E.K. Chambers, *The Elizabethan Stage*, 2 (Oxford, 1923), 40-41; Bentley, *Player*, 32-33, 47-48, 165-66, 176-77.

¹¹*Henslowe's Diary*, ed. R.A. Foalkes and R.T. Rickert (Cambridge, 1961), and *Henslowe's Papers*, ed. W.W. Gregg (London, 1907), are replete with references to advances paid to playwrights and their chronic pleas of poverty. Gurr, *The Shakespearean Stage* (Cambridge, 1980), 217, 222, notes that Jonson's *Cynthia's Revels* and Chapman's *May-Day* were the first known plays produced at the new Blackfriars, sometime in 1601.

¹²Bentley, *Player*, 152-53, discusses "gifts" to the Master of the Revels. D. Starkey, et. al., *The English Court from The Wars of the Roses to the Civil War* (London, 1987), 162-65, discusses the custom of bestowing "gifts" for favors from those in authority or with influence. The starting price seems to have been £100.

¹³Smith, *Blackfriars*, 528-29.

¹⁴Hunnis' petition is reproduced in Smith, *Blackfriars*, 478-79. Also reproduced there are excerpts from the diary of the Duke of Stettin-Pomerania, and from the license for the Children of the Queen's Revels, both of which describe the keeping and training of boys attached to the Chapel Choir (488, 551-52).

¹⁵M. S. Byrne, *Elizabethan Life in Town and Country* (London, 1961), 203-04.

¹⁶Byrne, *Life*, 205.

¹⁷Byrne, *Life*, 204-05, 308-12.

¹⁸A court interluder in Elizabeth's time was paid no larger stipend that that paid one in the reign of her father. See E. Nungezer, *A Dictionary of Actors...before 1642* (New Haven, 1929), 250, 333, 403. Elizabeth's courtier Sir Robert Naunton (1563-1635) described her frugality, even with her favorites, in *Fragmenta Regalia*, ed. J.S. Cerovski (Washington, 1985), 16-18. C. Haigh, *Elizabeth I* (London, 1988), 89-93, 132-33, 141-42, discusses Elizabeth's bestowal of wardships, leases, and licenses as rewares, and her attempts to hold down military costs. J.E. Neale, *Queen Elizabeth I* (Garden City, NJ, 1957) often stresses Elizabeth's parsimony.

¹⁹A. Harbage, *Shakespeare and the Rival Traditions* (Bloomington, IN, 1970), 339-42.

²⁰Quotation from Clifton's deposition, in Smith, *Blackfriars*, 484-86.

²¹G.B. Harrison, *The Elizabethan Journals*, 2 (Garden City, NJ, 1965), 283-94, gathers references from Acts of the Privy Council, State Papers, memoirs, letters, and other sources, which tell of various legal and illegal abuses of authority. See also Naunton, *Regalia*, 16-18, Neale, *Elizabeth*, 399-402.

[22]Giles' commission reproduced in Smith, *Blackfriars*, 482-83.

[23]J. Strype, *Annals of the Reformation*, II (Oxford, 1824), 455-58. W. Besant, *London in the Time of the Tudors* (London, 1904), 328-32 discusses apprenticeships, and the regulation of apprentices.

[24]See T.P. Morris, "Shakespeare hath given him a purge to bewray his credit," *Shakespeare and Renaissance Association of West Virginia. Selected Papers*, 15 (1992). Morris suggests that Justice Shallow's opening line in the *First Folio* version of *The Merry Wives of Windsor*, "Sir Hugh [Evans, a Welsh parson], persuade me not; I will make a Star Chamber matter of it," may be a topical allusion to the Clifton incident.

[25]Gurr, Stage, 50-51, Smith, *Blackfriars*, 185.

[26]The Parliament of 1601 sat from 27 October to 19 December 1601: See A. Kinney, *Titled Elizabethans* (New York, 1973), 9.

[27]Haigh, *Elizabeth*, 48-49, 66-68, 87-91, 97-99, describes the relationships between local gentry and the nobility, and the importance of having the ear of someone with influence at court, especially someone like Sir John Fortescue or Lord Admiral Charles Howard who were in constant attendance at the Privy Council.

[28]E. Lodge, *Illustrations of British History...in the Reigns of Henry VIII, Edward VI, Mary, Elizabeth*, 3 (London, 1791), 6-10, lists several of Elizabeth's grants of monopolies gleaned from the papers of the Earl of Shrewsbury. S. and B. Webb, *History of English Local Government*, 6: *English Prisons under Local Government* (Hamden, CT, 1963), 1-12, and C. Dobb, "London's Prisons," *Shakespeare Survey*, 17 (1964), 93-99, describe the collection of fees by prison wardens for virtually everything.

Chapter 9

[1]Table compiled from: A. Harbage, *Shakespeare and the Rival Traditions* (Bloomington, IN, 1970), 343-50; A. Gurr, *The Shakespearean Stage* (Cambridge, 1980), 216-28; Henslowe's *Diary*, ed. R.A. Foakes and R.T. Rickert (Cambridge, 1961), 16-60. Neil Carson's *A Companion to Henslowe's Diary* (Cambridge, 1988), 82-84, gives a chronological listing of plays included in the Diary, noting those scripts that are extant.

[2]A. Mizener, *Teaching Shakespeare* (New York, 1969), 49, observes that the Greco-Roman plays like *Julius Caesar* differ from those classified in the *First Folio* as the "Histories" only in not being written about English history. R. Gair, *The Children of Paul's* (Cambridge, 1982), 170-72; H.N. Hillebrand, *The Child Actors, Illinois Studies in Language and Literature*, XI (Urbana, IL, 1926), 268-75.

[3]A. Gurr, *Playgoing in Shakespeare's London* (Cambridge, 1988), 153-58; Harbage, *Traditions*, 90-119; D. Farley-Hills, *Shakespeare and the Rival*

Playwrights, 1600-06 (London, 1990), 7-12; T.P. Morris, "Shakespeare hath given him a purge to bewray his credit," *Shakespeare and Renaissance Association of West Virginia. Selected Papers*, 15 (1992), 51-59.

⁴W. Cohen, *Drama of a Nation. Public Theater in Renaissance England and Spain* (Ithaca, 1985), 292-316; B. Gibbon, *Jacobean City Comedy* (London, 1980), 1-17; T.B. Leinwand, *The City Staged. Jacobean Comedy, 1603-13* (Madison, WI, 1986), 3-20, 44-80; Harbage, *Rival Traditions*, 58-119; Gurr, *Playgoing*, 141-69.

⁵H. Craig, "Motivation in Shakespeare's Choice of Materials," *Shakespeare Survey*, 4 (1951), 26-34; A.C. Bradley, *Shakespearean Tragedy* (Greenwich, CT, n.d.), 71-73; Gurr, *Playgoing*, 141-69; Farley-Hills, *Rival Playwrights*, 7-24.

⁶F.S. Fussner, *Tudor History and the Historians* (New York, 1970), 231, 261, 270-82; M. Plant, *The English Book Trade* (London, 1965), 36-39, 83, 91, 240-41; H.S. Bennett, *English Books and Readers, 1558-1603* (Cambridge, 1965), 69, 82-89, 93-97, 215-20; Gurr, *Playgoing*, 115-69. A.L. Rowse, *William Shakespeare* (New York, 1963), 61, calls Shakespeare the "mouthpiece" of English Nationalism. G. Mattingly, *The Armada* (Boston, 1959), 344-51 describes the nationalism of the late sixteenth century.

⁷R.L. Smallwood, and S. Wells, eds., "Introduction," *The Shoemaker's Holiday* (Manchester, 1979); B. Field, ed., *The First and Second Parts of King Edward IV*. Histories by Thomas Hewoood (London, 1842).

⁸J. Hurstfield, *Freedom, Corruption and Government in Elizabethan England* (Cambridge, MA, 1973), 126-30; G.V.P. Akrigg, *Shakespeare and the Earl of Southampton* (London, 1968), 92-133.

⁹*Complete State Papers Domestic* (Hassocks, Sussex, 1979, microfilm), v. 274, nos. 58-61; v. 275, nos. 25, 28, 31-33, 35 (henceforth SPD).

¹⁰J. Nichols, *The Progresses and Public Processions of Queen Elizabeth, III* (New York, rpt. of 1823 ed.), 552-53; S. Greenblatt, *The Power of Forms in the English Renaissance* (Norman, OK, 1982), 4; L. Barroll, "A New History for Shakespeare and His Time," *Shakespeare Quarterly*, 39 (1988), 443-53, discusses the possibility that it was the Haywood book, and not the staging of Richard II which called forth the Privy Council questioning of Augustine Phillips.

¹¹D. Womersley, "Sir John Hayward's tacitism," *Renaissance Studies*, 6 (1992), 46-59, is a brilliant textual reading, and analysis of the context, of Hayward's *Henry IV*. His "*3 Henry VI*: Shakespeare, Tacitus and parricide," *Notes and Queries*. New Series, 32 (1985), 468-73, traces Savile's connections to Essex. Proclamation in H. Dyson, *A Booke containing all svch Proclamations, As were published dvring the Raigne of the late Queene Elizabeth* (London, 1618), v. II, n. 374.

[12]G.B. Harrison, *The Life and Death of Robert Devereaux Earl of Essex* (New York, 1937), 307.

[13]SPD, v. 248, nos. 33, 38-39, 42-37, 51-58, 60-64, 73-78, 81; Harrison, *Essex*, 314; R. Lacey, *Robert Earl of Essex* (New York, 1971), 127-28.

[14]M. Lee, *Great Britain's Solomon: James VI and I in His Three Kingdoms* (Urbana, IL, 1990), 99, 106; E. Edwards, *The Life of Sir Walter Raleigh*, 2 (London, 1868), 169; Hurstfield, *Freedom, Corruption*, 104-34; C. Ross, *The Wars of the Roses* (New York, 1977), 93-94.

[15]A.F. Kinney, *Titled Elizabethans* (Hamden, CT, 1973), lists 19 legitimate earldoms in the period 1594 to the end of Elizabeth's reign: Nottingham, Essex, Oxford, Shrewsbury, Pembroke, Derby, Lincoln, Bath, Bedford, Cumberland, Desmond, Hertford, Huntingdon, Kent, Northumberland, Rutland, Southampton, Sussex Worcester. There were no dukes after the execution of the duke of Norfolk in 1572. The table compiled from information given in the *Dictionary of National Biography* (London, 1949-50), under the surnames of the peers and their ancestors. A.R. Myers, *England in the Late Middle Ages* (Baltimore, 1966), 202-04; Ross, Roses, 93-94.

[16]Nichols, *Progresses*, 420-23.

[17]J.A. Matter, *My Lords and Lady of Essex: Their State Trials* (Chicago, 1969), 1. For the complicated genealogies of the descendants of Edward III who, after the usurpation of Henry IV, became referred to as the Houses of York and Lancaster see genealogical tables in P. M. Kendall, Richard III (New York, 1956) and C. Ross, *The Wars of the Roses*.

[18]Hurstfield, *Freedom, Corruption*, 104-34; Lee, *Solomon*, 99.

[19]Nichols, *Progresses*, 444; Lacey, *Essex*, 277; Harrison, *Essex*, 276-77.

[20]Lacey, *Essex*, 206, 274-75, 298-09, 315-16; Akrigg, *Southampton*, 128. For examples of pedigrees drawn in Burghley's own hand see SPD, v. 274, n. 85. For Bolingbroke's return and subsequent usurpation see C.W. Hollister, *The Making of England* (Lexington, MA, 1992), 298-303, and for York's return from Ireland and the beginning of the Wars of the Roses see C. Ross, *The Wars of the Roses*, 24-29.

[21]Barroll, "New History," 443-53.

[22]E.M. Taft, "Henry Bolingbroke's England," *Shakespeare and Renaissance Association of West Virginia. Selected Papers*, 15 (1992), 61-66.

[23]Barroll, "New History," 443-53.

[24]A. Haynes, *Robert Cecil, Earl of Salisbury* (London, 1989), 62-64; R.W. Kenny, *Elizabeth's Admiral. The Political Career of Charles Howard, Earl of Nottingham* (Baltimore, 1970), 234-39; Harrison, Essex, 276-93.

[25]SPD, 278, nos. 63, 112, 114; Haynes, *Cecil*, 66-67. For attempts to deny Essex favorable publicity for the Cadiz expedition, see below, chapter 6.

[26]S.T. Bindoff, *Tudor England* (New York, 1978) 166, 173-74; J.E. Neale, *Queen Elizabeth I* (Garden City, NY, 1957), 325-27; Gurr, *Playgoing*, 142-45; Ross, *Roses*, 47, 51-54, 90.

[27]E.J.A. Honigmann, "The Play of Sir Thomas More and Contemporary Events," *Shakespeare Survey*, 42 (1990), 77-83: I Ribner, *William Shakespeare. An Introduction to His Life, Times, and Theatre* (Waltham, MA, 1969), 163-66.

[28]Lacey, *Essex*, 128, 209; A.W. Pollard and G.R. Redgrave, eds., *A Short-Title Catalogue of Books Printed in England...1475-1640* (London, 1956), 519.

[29]SPD, v. 274, nos. 58-61; v. 275, nos. 25, 28, 31-33, 35

[30]P. Saccio, *Shakespeare's English Kings* (Oxford, 1979), 70.

[31]Lacey, *Essex*, 21-22, 206, 275-76.

[32]Ribner, *Shakespeare*, 166, 171.

[33]P. Alexander, *Shakespeare's Life and Art* (New York, 1967), 158-67, 191-93; Farley-Hills, *Rival Playwrights*, 12-27, 41-51, 104-31, 136-45; Cohen, *Drama*, 292-316; Barroll, "New History," 443-53; R.L. Knutson, "The Influence of the Repertory System on Revival and Revision of The Spanish Tragedy and Dr. Faustus," *English Literary Renaissance*, 18 (1988).

[34]*Short-Title*, 267, 302, 543.

[35]B. Capp, "Popular Literature," *Popular Culture in Seventheenth-Century England* (New York, 1985), ed. B. Reay, 209-12, and *Short-Title*, passim.

[36]G.E. Hadrow, ed., *Sir Walter Raleigh, Selections from His Historie of the World* (Oxford, 1917), 61. Lee, *Solomon*, 152-53 notes the obliqueness of theatrical fare in dealing with political issues.

[37]A. Mizener, *Teaching Shakespeare* (New York, 1969), 49-50; K. Muir, *Shakespeare's Tragic Sequence* (New York, 1979), 42.

[38]R. Speaight, *Shakespeare. The Man and His Achievement* (New York, 1977), 212-14.

[39]N.E. McClure, ed., *The Letters of John Chamberlain*, I (Philadelphia, 1939), 199; Cohen, *Drama*, 301-16; M. Chute, *Ben Jonson of Westminster* (New York, 1960), 142; Akrigg, *Southampton*, 139; Capp, "Popular Literature," 209-12, 227-29. Lee, *Solomon*, 103, 108-10, discusses the firm hold the Cecil-Howard faction held on the Court in the first years of James' reign in England.

[40]S. Mullaney, *The Place of the Stage. Liberty, License and Power in Renaissance England* (Chicago, 1988), 135-37; Haynes, *Cecil*, 146-55: *Short-Title*, 321.

[41]Kenny, *Elizabeth's Admiral*, 287-318; Haynes, *Cecil*, 210-12: J.M. Davis, "The Problems of Henry VIII: History and National Pageant in the Tragicomic Mode," *Shakespeare and Renaissance Association of West Virginia. Selected Papers*, 14 (1989-90), 44-59.

Observations

[1] W. Cohen, *Drama of a Nation. Public Theater in Renaissance England and Spain* (Ithaca, NY, 1985), 143-45, 161-68, 171-75; J.C. Agnew, *Worlds Apart: The Market and the Theatre in Anglo-American Thought, 1550-1750* (Cambridge, 1986), 48-55, 106-20.

[2] S. Mullaney, *The Place of the Stage. License, Play, and Power in Renaissance England* (Chicago, 1988), 132-34, discussed Jacobean absolutism and the theatre.

[3] D.E. Wayne, "The 'Exchange of Letters': Early Modern Contradictions and Postmodern Conundrums," *The Consumption of Culture in the Early Modern Period*, ed. A. Bermingham and J. Brewer (London, forthcoming from Routledge): K.E. McLuskie, "The Poets' Royal Exchange: Patronage and Commerce in Early Modern Drama," *The Yearbook of English Studies*, 21 (1991), 62.

[4] R. Gross, *Understanding Playscripts. Theory and Method* (Bowling Green, OH 1974), 43-44, 123, 193.

[5] S.K. Langer, *Philosophical Sketches* (New York, 1964), 127.

Works Cited and Consulted

Sixteenth- and Seventeenth-Century Works

Adams, J.Q., ed. *The Dramatic Records of Sir Henry Herbert.* New Haven, 1917.

Allen, J. ed. *Shakespeare's Plays in Quarto.* Berkeley, 1981.

Bacon, Sir Francis. "A True Report of the Detestable Treason Intended by Doctor Roderigo Lopez." *Works.* Ed. B. Montagu. Philadelphia, 1851.

Bannerman, W.B., ed. *The Registers of St. Olave.* London, 1916.

Barnfield, R. *The Encomiom of Lady Pecunia: or The Praise of Money.* London, 1598.

Birch, T. *Memoirs of the Reign of Queen Elizabeth I.* London, 1754.

Brooke, R. (York Herald). *A Catalogue and Succession of the Kings, Dukes, Marquesses, Earles, and Viscounts of this Realme of England, since the Norman Conquest, to this present year, 1619.* London, 1619.

Buck, George. *The History of King Richard III.* Ed. A. Kincaid. Gloucester, 1979.

Burgoyne, F.J., ed. *Collotype Facsimile and Type Transcript of an Elizabethan Manuscript Preserved at Alnwick Castle, Northumberland.* London, 1904.

Calendar of Letters and State papers Relating to English Affairs in the Archives of Simancas. Vol. 3. Ed. M.S. Hume. London.

Calendar of the Manuscripts of the Marquis of Salisbury. Vol. 7. London.

Calendar of Patent Rolls. Elizabeth. Vol. 11. London.

Calendar of State Papers, domestic Series, of the Reigns of Edward VI, Mary, Elizabeth. London.

Calendar of State Papers and Manuscripts...Venice. Vol. 9. London.

Camden, W. *The History of the Most Renowned and Victorious Princess Elizabeth, Late Queen of England.* 3rd ed. London, 1675.

Carleton, G. *A Thankfull Remembrance of Gods Mercy.* London, 1630.

Clapham, J. *Elizabeth of England: Certain Observations Concerning the Life and Reign of Queen Elizabeth.* Eds. E. Plummer and C. Reed. Philadelphia, 1951.

Clement, F. *The Petie Schole.* Leeds, 1967, facsimile of 1587 ed.

Collier, J.P. *Memoirs of Edward Alleyn, Founder of Dulwich College.* London, 1841.

Collins, A., ed. *Letters and Memorials of State...from Originals at Penshurst.* 2 vols. London, 1746.

Complete State Papers Domestic. Hassocks, Sussex, 1979, microfilm.

Coote, E. *The English Schoole-Maister.* Leeds, 1968, facsimile of 1596 ed.

D'Ewes, S. *A Compleat Journal of the Votes, Speeches and Debates, Both of the House of Lords and House of Commons throughout the whole Reign of Queen Elizabeth.* Wilmington, DE, 1974, facsimile of 1693 ed.

Daniel, S. *The Civil Wars.* Ed. L. Michel. New Haven, 1958.

_____. *The Tragedy of Philotas.* Ed. L. Michel. New Haven, 1949.

Dasent, J.R., ed. *Acts of the Privy Council.* London, 1909.

Davies, John (Hereford). *The Complete Workes.* Ed. A. Grosart. Private printing, 1875.

Dekker, T. *Satiromastix,* in *The Dramatic Works of Thomas Dekker.* Ed. F. Bowers. Cambridge, 1953.

_____. and T. Middleton. *The Roaring Girl.* Ed. A. Gomme. London, 1976.

Drummond, W. *Ben Jonson's Conversations with William Drummond of Hawthorneden.* Ed. R.F. Patterson. Norwood, PA, 1977.

Dyson, H. *A Booke containing all svch Proclamations, As were published dvring the Raigne of the late Queen Elizabeth.* London, 1618.

Foakes, R.A. and R.T. Rickert, eds. *Henslowe's Diary.* Cambridge, 1961.

Fuller, T. *The Worthies of England.* 2 vols. New York, 1965.

Gawdy, P. *Letters.* Ed. I.H. Jeanes. London, 1906.

Goodman, Bishop Godfrey. *The Court of King James I.* Vol. 1. Ed. J.S. Brewer. London, 1839.

Greene, R. *A Groat's Worth of Wit.* Ed. G. Saintsbury, in *Elizabethan and Jacobean Pamphlets.* New York, 1892.

Greg, W.W., ed. *Henslowe Papers.* New York, 1975, rpt. of London, 1907 ed.

_____*Henslowe's Diary.* London, 1904-08.

Hadow, G.E., ed. *Sir Walter Raleigh, Selections from His Historie of the World* Oxford, 1917.

Harrington, J. *Letters and Epigrams.* Ed. N.E. McClure. Philadelphia, 1930.

Hayward, J. *The First Part of the Life and Raigne of King Henrie III.* London, 1599.

Heywood, T. *An Apology for Actors.* Rpt. London, 1841.

_____. *Englands Elizabeth.* Amsterdam, 1973, rpt. of London, 1631 ed.

_____. *King Edward IV* parts 1 and 2. Ed. B. Field. London, 1842.

_____. *Troia Britanica.* Amsterdam, 1974, rpt. of London, 1609 ed.

Hughes, C. *Shakespeare's Europe. Unpublished Chapters of Fynes Moryson's Itinerary.* London, 1903.

Ionsonus Virbius. Or, The Memorie of Ben Johnson. Revived by the Friends of the Muses. Amsterdam, 1970, rpt. of London, 1638 ed.

Jonson, B. *Bartholomew Fair,* in *The Selected Plays of Ben Jonson.* Vol. 2. Ed. M. Butler. Cambridge, 1989.

_____. *Cynthia's Revels*, in *The Complete Plays of Ben Jonson*. Vol. 2. Ed. G. Wilkes. Oxford, 1981.

_____. *Poetaster*, in *The Complete Plays of Ben Jonson*. Vol. 2. Ed. G. Wilkes. Oxford, 1981.

_____. Chapman, G., Marston. *Eastward Ho* in *The Complete Plays of Ben Jonson*. Vol. 2. Ed. G. Wilkes. Oxford, 1981.

Kempe, W. *Kemps Nine Daies Wonder. Performed in a Daunce from London to Norwich.* Dereham, 1985, rpt. of London, 1600 ed.

Kokeritz, H., ed. *Mr. William Shakespeare's Comedies, Histories and Tragedies.* New Haven, 1954, facsimile of the *First Folio*.

Kyd, T. *The Spanish Tragedy*. Ed. P. Edwards. Cambridge, MA, 1959.

Leishman, J.B., ed. *The Three Parnassus Plays*. London, 1949.

Lodge, E. *Illustrations of British History in the Reigns of Henry VIII, Edward VI, Mary, Elizabeth.* 3 vols. London, 1791.

Mares, F.E., ed. *The Memoirs of Sir Robert Carey*. Oxford, 1972.

Marston, J. *Historio-mastix*, in *The Plays of John Marston*. Vol. 3. Ed. H.H. Wood. Edinburgh, 1934-39.

_____. *Jack Drums Entertainment*, in *The Plays of John Marston*. Vol. 3. Ed. H.H. Wood. Edinburgh, 1934-39.

McClure, N.E., ed. *The Letters of John Chamberlain*. 2 vols. Philadelphia, 1939.

Middleton, T. *A Game of Chess*. Ed. J. Harper. New York, 1967.

Nashe, T. *Pierce Penilesse, His Supplication to the Divell*. Ed. R.B. McKerrow, *Works*. Vol. 1. London, 1904.

_____. *The Vnforvnate Traveller*. Ed. H.F. Brett-Smith. Oxford, 1936.

Naunton, Sir Robert. *Fragmentia Regalia*, Ed. J.S. Cerowski. Washington, 1985.

Nichols, J. *The Progresses and Public Processions of Queen Elizabeth.* 3 vols. London, 1823.

Osborne, F. *Historical memoires on the reigns of Queen Elizabeth, and King James.* London, 1658.

Peck, E., ed. *Leicester's Commonwealth*. Athens, OH, 1985.

Pepper, R. ed. *Four Tudor Books on Education*. Gainesville, FL, 1966.

Sackville-West, V., ed. *The Diary of the Lady Anne Clifford*. London, 1923.

The Secret History of the Most Renowned Queen Elizabeth and the Earl of Essex by a Person of Quality. London, 1695.

Sorlien, R.P., ed. *The Diary of John Manningham of the Middle Temple, 1602-1603.* Hanover, NH, 1976.

Stow, J. *Annals*, continued by E. Howes. London, 1631.

_____. *Survey of London, 1598, 1603*, Ed. C.L. Kingsford. London, 1908.

The Visitacion of Norfolk, Anno 1563 and Anno 1613. Harleian Society 32. London, 1891.

The Visitation of Norfolk, Anno 1664. Harleian Society 85. London, 1933.

von Klarwill, V., ed. *The Fugger News-Letters.* Tr. L.S. Byrne. New York, 1926.

Warner, W. *Albions England. A Continued Historie of the same Kingdome, from the Originals of the first Inhabitants thereof...vnto the happie Raigne of our now most gracious Soueraigne Queene Elizabeth...* London, 1602, another edition in 1606.

Wentworth. P. *A Pithie Exhortation on to Her Maiestie for Establishing Her Successor to the Crowne.* Amsterdam: 1973, facsimile of 1598 ed.

Williams, C., tr. *Thomas Platter's Travels in England, 1599.* London, 1937.

Williams, J.F., ed. *Diocese of Norwich. Bishop Redman's Visitation, 1597.* Norfolk Record Society, 1946.

Williams, S., ed. *Letters Written by John Chamberlain.* Vol. 79. London: Camden Society, 1861.

Wright, J. *Historia Histrionica.* London, 1699.

Modern Works

Adams, J.Q. *A Life of William Shakespeare.* Boston, 1923.

Adkins, J.F. " 'Unpath'd Waters, undream'd shors': Art and Artifice in *The Winter's Tale.*" *Shakespeare and Renaissance Association of West Virginia. Selected Papers* 13 (1988).

Agnew, J.C. *Worlds Apart: The Market and the Theater in Anglo-American Thought, 1550-1750.* Cambridge, 1986.

Alexander, P. *Shakespeare's Life and Art.* New York, 1967.

_____. "The Original Ending of *The Taming of the Shrew.*" *Shakespeare Quarterly* 20 (1980).

Alter, I. " 'To Reform and Make Fitt': *Henry VIII* and the Making of 'Bad' Shakespeare." *"Bad" Shakespeare: Reevaluations of the Shakespeare Canon.* Ed. M. Charney. Rutherford, NJ, 1988.

Altman, J. *The Tudor Play of Mind.* Berkeley, 1978.

Amussen, S.D. *An Ordered Society. Gender and Class in Early Modern England.* Oxford, 1988.

Andresen-Thom, M. "Thinking About Women and Their Prosperous Art: a Reply to Juliet Dusinberre's 'Shakespeare and the Nature of Women'." *Shakespeare Studies* 11 (1978).

_____. "Shrew-taming and Other Rituals of Aggression: Baiting and Bonding on the Stage and in the Wild." *Women's Studies* 9 (1982).

Anglin, J.P. *The Third University: a survey of schools and schoolmasters in the Elizabethan Diocese of London.* Norwood, PA, 1985.

Archer, I. *The Pursuit of Stability. Social Relations in Elizabethan England.* Cambridge, 1991.

Armstrong, W.A. "Actors and Theatres." *Shakespeare Survey* 17 (1964).

Ashton, R. "Popular Entertainment and Social Control In Later Elizabethan and Early Stuart London. *London Journal* 9 (1983).

Baines, B. J. *Thomas Heywood.* Boston, 1984.

Baldwin, T.W. *Organization and Personnel of the Shakespearean Company.* Princeton, 1927.

Barber, C. L. *Shakespeare's Festive Comedy: A Study of Dramatic Form and Its Relation to Social Custom.* Princeton, 1959.

Baron, S. *A Social and Religious History of the Jews.* Vol. 13. New York, 1969.

Barroll, J.L. "A New History for Shakespeare and His Time." *Shakespeare Quarterly* 39 (1988).

_____. *Shakespearean Tragedy.* Washington, D.C., 1984.

_____. A. Leggatt, R. Hosely, A. Kernan, eds. *The Revels History of the Drama in English, 1576-1603.* Vol. 3. London, 1975.

Barry, R. "Hamlet's Doubles." *Shakespeare Quarterly* 37 (1986).

Bassnett, S. *Elizabeth I: a Feminist Perspective.* New York, 1988.

Bean, J.C. "Comic Structure and the Humanizing of Kate in *The Taming of the Shrew," The Woman's Part. Feminist Criticism of Shakespeare.* Eds. C.R.S. Lenz, G. Greene, C.T. Neely. Urbana, IL, 1980.

Beauregard, D.N. "Sidney, Aristotle, and *The Merchant of Venice." Shakespeare Studies* 20 (1988).

Beier, A.L. and R. Finlay, eds. *London 1500-1700: the Making of the Metropolis.* London, 1986.

Belsey, C. *The Subject of Tragedy.* London, 1985.

Bennett, H.S. *English Books and Their Readers, 1558-1603.* Cambridge, 1965.

Benston, A.N. "Portia, the Law, and the Tripartite Structure of *The Merchant of Venice. Shakespeare Quarterly* 30 (1979).

Bentley, G.E. *The Jacobean and Caroline Stage.* 7 vols. Oxford, 1941-1968.

_____. *The Profession of Dramatist in Shakespeare's Time,* and *The Profession of Player in Shakespeare's Time.* Princeton, 1987.

Berek, P. "Text, Gender, and Genre in *The Taming of the Shrew." "Bad" Shakespeare: Reevaluations of the Shakespeare Canon.* Ed. M. Charney. Rutherford, NJ, 1988.

Berger, T.L. "Casting Henry V." *Shakespeare Studies* 20 (1988).

Bergeron, D. "The Patronage of Dramatists: The Case of Thomas Heywood." *English Literary Renaissance* 18 (1988).

Berggren, P.S. "The Woman's Part. Female Sexuality as Power in Shakespeare's Plays." *The Woman's Part. Feminist Criticism of Shakespeare.* Eds. C.R.S. Lenz, G. Greene, C.T. Neely. Urbana, IL, 1980.

Berry, H. *The Boar's Head Playhouse.* Washington, D.C., 1986.

_____. "The First Public Playhouses, Especially the Red Lion." *Shakespeare Quarterly* 40 (1989).

_____., ed. *The First Public Playhouse. The Theatre in Shoreditch, 1576-1596.* Montreal, 1979.

Bertram, P. "What Shakespeare Looked Like: the Spielmann Position and the Alternatives." *Journal of the Rutgers University Libraries* 41 (1979).

Besant, W. *London in the Time of the Stuarts.* London, 1903.

_____. *London in the Time of the Tudors.* London, 1904.

Bindoff, S.T. *Tudor England.* New York, 1978.

_____., J. Hurstfield, C.H. Williams, eds. *Elizabethan Government and Society. Essays presented to Sir John Neale.* London, 1961.

Blagden, C. *The Stationers' Company, 1403-1959.* Cambridge, MA, 1960.

Blomefield, F. *An Essay towards a Topographical History of the County of Norfolk.* 11 vols. London, 1810.

Boas, F.S. *Thomas Heywood.* London, 1950.

Bohannon, "Shakespeare in the Bush." *Natural History* 75 (1966).

Bono, B.J. "Mixed Gender, Mixed Genre in Shakespeare's *As You Like It.*" *Renaissance Genres: Essays on Theory, History, and Interpretation.* Ed. B.K. Lewalski. Cambridge, MA, 1986.

Boose, L.E. "Scolding Brides and Bridling Scolds: Taming the Woman's Unruly Member." *Shakespeare Quarterly* 42 (1991).

_____. "The Comic Contract and Portia's Golden Ring." *Shakespeare Studies* 20 (1988).

Bowen, C.D. *The Lion and the Throne.* Boston, 1957.

Bradbrook, M. *Elizabethan Stage Conditions.* Hamden, CT, 1962.

_____. *The Growth and Structure of Elizabethan Comedy.* London, 1955.

_____. *The Rise of the Common Player: A Study of Actor and Society in Shakespeare's England.* Cambridge, 1962.

Bradley, J.F. and J.Q. Adams. *The Jonson Allusion-book.* New Haven, 1922.

Braudel, F. *The Mediterranean and the Mediterranean World in the Age of Philip II.* 2 vols. Tr. S. Reynolds. New York, 1972.

Bray, A. *Homosexuality in Renaissance England.* London, 1982.

Bredbeck, G.W. *Sodomy and Interpretation. Marlowe to Milton.* Ithaca, NY, 1991.

Bridenbaugh, C. *Vexed and Troubled Englishmen, 1590-1642.* New York, 1968.

Bristol, M. *Carnival and Theatre: Plebeian Culture and the Structure of Authority in Renaissance England.* London, 1985.

Brittin, N. *Thomas Middleton.* New York, 1972.

Brockett, O. *History of the Theatre.* Boston, 1968.

Brockett, O. and R. Findley, *Century of Innovation. A History of European and American Theatre and Drama Since 1870.* Englewood Cliffs, NJ, 1973.

Brown, A. "The Printing of Books." *Shakespeare Survey* 17 (1964).

Brown, J.R. "The Realization of Shylock: A Theatrical Criticism." *Early Shakespeare.* Eds. J.R. Brown and B. Harris. New York, 1961.

Brown, J.R. and B. Harris, eds. *Restoration Theatre.* New York, 1967.

_____., eds. *The Jacobean Stage.* New York, 1967.

Buck, George. *The History of King Richard III.* Ed. A. Kincaid. Gloucester, 1979.

Bullough, G. *Narrative and Dramatic Sources of Shakespeare.* 8 vols. Boston, 1974.

Burke, P. *Popular Culture in Early Modern Europe.* New York, 1978.

Burley, A. "Courtly Personages: The Lady Masquers in Ben Jonson's *Masque of Blackness." Shakespeare and Renaissance Association of West Virginia. Selected Papers* 10 (1985).

Callaghan, D. *Woman and Gender in Renaissance Tragedy.* Atlantic Highlands, NJ, 1989.

Camden, W. *The History of the Most Renowned and Victorious Princess Elizabeth, Late Queen of England.* 3rd ed. London, 1675.

Campbell, M. L. *The English Yeoman.* New Haven, 1942.

Cargill, A. "Shakespeare as an Actor." *Scribner's Magazine* 9 (May 1891).

Carson, N. *A Companion to Henslowe's Diary.* Cambridge, 1988.

_____. "Collaborative Playwriting." *Theatre Research International* 14 (1989).

Cartelli, T. "Shakespeare's *Merchant*, Marlowe's *Jew*: The Problem of Cultural Difference." *Shakespeare Studies* 20 (1988).

Cerasano, S.P. "Revising Philip Henslowe's Biography." *Notes and Queries. New Series* 32 (1985).

Chambers, D. *The Imperial Age of Venice 1380-1580.* New York, 1970.

Chambers, E.K. *The Elizabethan Stage.* 4 vols. Oxford, 1923.

Chapman, W., ed. *Annals of English Literature, 1475-1950.* Oxford, 1961.

Cecil, D. *The Cecils of Hatfield House: An English Ruling Family.* Boston, 1973.

Child, H. "The Stage-history of *The Taming of the Shrew." The New Cambridge Shakespeare.* Cambridge, 1968.

Chute, M. *Ben Jonson of Westminster.* New York, 1960.

_____. *Stories from Shakespeare.* New York, 1956.

Cipolla, C.M. *Before the Industrial Revolution.* New York, 1976.

Clark, A.M. *Thomas Heywood.* Oxford, 1931.

Clemen, W. *The Development of Shakespeare's Imagery.* New York, 1951.

Cohen, D.M. "The Jew and Shylock." *Shakespeare Quarterly* 31 (1980).

Cohen, W. *Drama of a Nation. Public Theatre in Renaissance England and Spain.* Ithaca, NY, 1985.

_____. "*The Merchant of Venice* and the Possibilities of Historical Criticism." *ELH* 49 (1982).

Cole, T. and H.K. Chinoy, eds. *Actors on Acting.* New York, 1970.

Coleman, E.D. *The Jew in English Drama. An Annotated Bibliography.* New York, 1943.

Collinson, P. *The Birth Pangs of Protestant England: Religious and Cultural Change in the Sixteenth and Seventeenth Century.* London, 1989.

Cook, A.J. *The Privileged Playgoers of Shakespeare's London 1576-1642.* Princeton, 1981.

Cressy, D. "Educational Opportunity in Tudor and Stuart England." *History of Education Quarterly* 16 (1976).

Cromwell, O. *Thomas Heywood, Dramatist.* New Haven, 1928.

Curtis, M.H. "Education and Apprenticeship." *Shakespeare Survey* 17 (1964).

Daalder, J. "Senecan Influence in Shylock's 'Hath not a Jew eyes?' " *English Studies* 65 (1984).

Daniell, D. "The Good Marriage of Catherine and Petruchio." *Shakespeare Survey* 37 (1984).

Davies, W.R. *Shakespeare's Boy Actors.* New York, 1939.

Davis, J.M. "The Problems of *Henry VIII*: History and national Pageant in the Tragicomic Mode." *Shakespeare and Renaissance Association of West Virginia. Selected Papers* 14 (1989-90).

_____. and S.L.F. Richards. "The Merchant and the Jew: a Fourteenth-Century French Analogue to *The Merchant of Venice*." *Shakespeare Quarterly* 36 (1985).

Dean, L.F., ed. *Shakespeare. Modern Essays in Criticism.* Oxford, 1967.

DeBord, B. "The Stage as Mirror of Society: The Widow in Two Seventeenth Century Comedies." *Shakespeare and Renaissance Association of West Virginia. Selected Papers* 10 (1985).

Dickey, S. "Shakespeare's Mastiff Comedy." *Shakespeare Quarterly* 42 (1991).

Dimock, A. "The Conspiracy of Dr. Lopez." *English Historical Review* 9 (1894).

Dobb, C. "London's Prisons." *Shakespeare Survey* 17 (1964).

Dolan, F.E. "Home-Rebels and House-Traitors: Murderous Wives in Early Modern England." *Yale Journal of Law and the Humanities* 4 (1992).

Dunn, T.A. *Philip Massinger.* Edinburgh, 1957.

Dusinberre, J. "*King John* and Embarrassing Women." *Shakespeare Survey* 42 (1990).

_____. *Shakespeare and the Nature of Women.* New York, 1975.

Eagleton, T. *William Shakespeare*. Oxford, 1986.

Eastman, A.M. *A Short History of Shakespearean Criticism*. New York, 1968.

Edmond, M. "It was for gentle Shakespeare cut." *Shakespeare Survey* 42 (1991).

Edmunds, M. "The Builder of the Rose Theatre." *Theatre Notebook* 44 (1990).

Elton, G.R. *The Parliament of England*. Cambridge, 1986.

Ergang, R. *The Renaissance*. Princeton, 1967.

Erikson, P. *Patriarchal Structures in Shakespeare's Drama*. Berkeley, 1985.

Evans, G.B., ed. *The Riverside Shakespeare*. Boston, 1974.

Evans, R.C. *Ben Jonson and the Poetics of Patronage*. Lewisburg, PA, 1989.

Farrow, M.A., ed. *Index of Wills Proved in the Consistory Court of Norwich 1604-86*. Norfolk Record Society, 1958.

Feldheim, M. *The Theatre of Augustin Daly*. Cambridge, MA, 1956.

Fellow, R.B.L. "More about the Moor: Redefining *Othello*." *Selected Papers. Shakespeare and Renaissance Association of West Virginia* 13 (1988).

Felver, C.S. *Robert Armin, Shakespeare's Fool*. Kent, OH, 1961.

Flatter, R. *Shakespeare's Producing Hand: A Study of his Marks of Expression to be found in the First Folio*. New York, 1948.

Fleissner, R. *Shakespeare and the Matter of the Crux*. Lewiston, NY, 1991.

Forse, J.H. "Art Imitates Business: Profit and Business Practices as Forces in the Elizabethan Theater." *Journal of Popular Culture* 24 (1990).

_____. "Ben Jonson's *The Isle of Dogs*. Politics and Playwriting in Elizabethan England." *Shakespeare and Renaissance Association of West Virginia. Selected Papers* 14 (1989-90).

_____. "Extortion in the Name of Art." *Theatre Survey* 31 (1990).

_____. "*Romeo and Juliet*: A Play for All Seasons or How to Please Patron, Pass the Censor, and Pack the Theatre." *Shakespeare and Renaissance Association of West Virginia. Selected Papers* 16 (1993).

Foster, D.W. "Reconstructing Shakespeare: New Directions in Textual Analysis and Stage History." *The Shakespeare Newsletter* (Winter 1991).

_____. "Reconstructing Shakespeare: The Roles that Shakespeare Performed." *The Shakespeare Newsletter* (Spring/Summer 1991).

_____. "Reconstructing Shakespeare: The Sonnets." *The Shakespeare Newsletter* (Fall 1991).

Fotheringham, R. "The Doubling of Roles on the Jacobean Stage." *Theatre Research International* 10 (1985).

Fraser, A. *The Weaker Vessel. Woman's Lot in Seventeenth-Century England*. London, 1989.

Fussner, F.S. *Tudor History and the Historians*. New York, 1970.

Gair, R. *The Children of Paul's, 1553-1608*. Cambridge, 1982.

Garner, S.N. *"The Taming of the Shrew.* Inside or Outside of the Joke?" *"Bad" Shakespeare: Reevaluations of the Shakespeare Canon.* Ed. M. Charney. Rutherford, NJ, 1988.

Gerrard, E.A. *Elizabethan Drama and Dramatists.* New York, 1972.

Gibbon, B. *Jacobean City Comedy.* London, 1980.

Gildersleeve, V. *Government Regulation of the Elizabethan Drama.* Westport, CT, 1975, rpt. of 1908 ed.

Gohlke, M. " 'I wooed thee with my sword': Shakespeare's Tragic Paradigms." *The Woman's Part. Feminist Criticism of Shakespeare.* Eds. C.R.S. Lenz, G. Greene, C.T. Neely. Urbana, IL, 1980.

Goodman, J.R. *British Drama Before 1660. A Critical History.* Boston, 1991.

Gordon, G. *Shakespearean Comedy.* Oxford, 1944.

Grebanier, B. *Playwriting.* New York, 1961.

_____. *The Truth About Shylock.* New York, 1962.

Greenblatt, S. *Learning to Curse: Essays in Early Modern Culture.* London, 1990.

_____. *Shakespearean Negotiations: The Circulation of Social Energy in Renaissance England.* Oxford, 1988.

Greenfield, T.N. *The Induction in Elizabethan Drama.* Eugene, OR, 1969.

_____. "The Transformation of Christopher Sly." *Philological Quarterly* 22 (1954).

Greg, W.W. *A Bibliography of the English Printed Drama to the Restoration.* Vol. 1. *Stationers' Records. Plays to 1616.* London, 1962.

Gross, R. *Understanding Playscripts.* Bowling Green, OH, 1974.

Grossvogel, D. *Twentieth Century French Drama.* New York, 1961.

Guicciardini, F. *The History of Italy.* Tr. S. Alexander. New York, 1969.

Gum, C. *The Aristophanic Comedies of Ben Jonson. A Comparative Study of Jonson and Aristophanes.* The Hague, 1969.

Gurr, A. *Playgoing in Shakespeare's London.* Cambridge, 1988.

_____. *The Shakespearean Stage.* Cambridge, 1980.

_____. "Who Strutted and Bellowed." *Shakespeare Survey* 16 (1963).

Gwyer, J. "The Case of Dr. Lopez." *Jewish Historical Society of England. Transactions* 16 (1952).

Hager, A. *Shakespeare's Political Animal.* Newark, DE, 1990.

Haigh, C. *Elizabeth I.* London, 1988.

_____., ed. *The Reign of Elizabeth I.* New York, 1984.

Halpern, R. *The Poetics of Primitive Accumulation: English Renaissance Culture and the Genealogy of Culture.* Ithaca, NY, 1991.

Harbage, A. and S. Schoenbaum, eds. *Annals of English Drama, 975-1700.* Philadelphia, 1964.

_____. *Shakespeare and the Rival Traditions*. Bloomington, IN, 1952.

_____. *Shakespeare's Audience*. New York, 1964.

Harris, B. "Dissent and Satire." *Shakespeare Survey* 17 (1964).

Harrison, G.B. *The Elizabethan Journals*. 2 vols. Garden City, NY, 1965, rpt. of 1938 ed.

_____. *The Life and Death of Robert Devereaux, Earl of Essex*. New York, 1937.

Hartwig, J. "Horses and Women in *The Taming of the Shrew*." *Huntington Library Quarterly* 45 (1982).

Hayes, T. *The Birth of Popular Culture. Ben Jonson, Maid Marian and Robin Hood*. Pittsburgh, 1992.

Hayles, N.K. "Sexual Disguise in *As You Like It* and *Twelfth Night*." *Shakespeare Survey* 32 (1979).

Haynes, A. *Robert Cecil. Earl of Salisbury, 1563-1612*. London, 1989.

Heffernan, C.F. "*The Taming of the Shrew*: the Bourgeoisie in Love." *Essays in Literature* 12 (1985).

Hill, R.F. "*The Merchant of Venice* and the Pattern of Romantic Comedy." *Shakespeare Survey* 28 (1975).

Hillebrand, H.N. *The Child Actors. University of Illinois Studies in Language and Literature* 11. Urbana, IL, 1926.

Hollister, C.W. *The Making of England*. Lexington, MA, 1992.

Holmer, J.O. " 'When Jacob graz'd his uncle Laban's sheep': a New Source for *The Merchant of Venice*." *Shakespeare Quarterly* 36 (1985).

Honigmann, E.J.A. *Shakespeare's Impact on His Contemporaries*. Towata, NJ, 1982.

_____. *Shakespeare. The lost years*. Towata, NJ, 1985.

_____. "The Date of Hamlet." *Shakespeare Survey* 9 (1956).

Honneyman, D. "The Family Origins of Henry Condell." *Notes and Queries. New Series* 32 (1985).

Hopkins, L. *Elizabeth I and Her Court*. New York, 1990.

Horner, B.M. "Seventeenth-Century English Songs and Songbooks." *Shakespeare and Renaissance Association of West Virginia. Selected Papers* 13 (1988).

Hoskins, W.G. "Provincial Life." *Shakespeare Survey* 17 (1964).

Hosley, R. "The Discovery of Space in Shakespeare's Globe." *Shakespeare Survey* 12 (1959).

_____. "Was There a Dramatic Epilogue to *The Taming of the Shrew*?" *Studies in English Literature* 1 (1961).

_____. "The Playhouses and the Stage." *A New Companion to Shakespeare Studies*. Eds. K. Muir and S. Schoenbaum. Cambridge, 1971.

Hotson, L. *Shakespeare's Motley*. New York, 1952.

Howard, J.E. and M.F.O'Connor. "New Historicism in Renaissance Studies." *English Literary Renaissance* 16 (1986).

_____. "Crossdressing, The Theatre, and Gender Struggle in Early Modern England." *Shakespeare Quarterly* 39 (1988).

_____. *Shakespeare's Art of Orchestration: Stage Techniques and Audience Response.* London, 1984.

Hoy, C. *Introductions, Notes, and Commentaries to Texts in the Dramatic Works of Thomas Dekker.* Vol. 2. Cambridge, 1980.

Hull, S.W. *Silent and Obedient. English Books for Women 1475-1640.* San Marino, CA, 1982.

Hume, M. "The So-called Conspiracy of Dr. Ruy Lopez." *Jewish Historical Society of England. Transactions* (sessions 1908-10).

_____. *Treason and Plot.* London, 1901.

Hunter, G.K. "Elizabethans and Foreigners." *Shakespeare Survey* 17 (1964).

Hurstfield, J. *Freedom, Corruption and Government in Elizabethan England.* Cambridge, MA, 1973.

Hurwich, J.J. "Lineage and Kin in the Sixteenth-Century Aristocracy" in *The First Modern Society.* Eds. A.L Beier, D. Cannadine, J.M. Rosenheim. Cambridge, 1989.

Huston, J.D. "To Make a Puppit: Play and Playmaking in *The Taming of the Shrew.*" *Shakespeare Studies* 10 (1976).

Hyamson, A.M. *The Sephardim of England.* London, 1951.

Hyde, M.C. *Playwriting for Elizabethans.* New York, 1949.

Ingleby, C.M., L. Toulmin, F.J. Furnivall. *The Shakespeare Allusion-Book.* 2 vols. Oxford, 1932.

Ingram, W. *A London Life in the Brazen Age. Francis Langley, 1548-1602.* Cambridge, MA, 1978.

_____. "Robert Keysar, Playhouse Speculator." *Shakespeare Quarterly* 38 (1986).

Ingramm, M. *Church Courts, Sex and Marriage in England, 1570-1640.* Cambridge, 1987.

Ives, E.W. "The Law and Lawyers." *Shakespeare Survey* 17 (1964).

James, M. "At a Crossroads of the Political Culture: The Essex Revolt, 1601." *Society, Politics and Culture.* Cambridge, 1986.

Jardine, L. *Still Harping on Daughters. Women and Drama in the Age of Shakespeare.* Totowa, NJ, 1983.

Jenkins, E. *Elizabeth the Great.* New York, 1959.

Kahn, C. "Coming of Age in Verona." *The Woman's Part. Feminist Criticism of Shakespeare.* Eds. C.R.S. Lenz, G. Greene, C.T. Neely. Urbana, IL, 1980.

Karras, R.M. "The Regulation of Brothels in Later Medieval England." *Signs* 14 (1989).

Katz, J. *Exclusiveness and Tolerance: Studies in Jewish-Gentile Relations in Medieval and Modern Times*. London, 1961.

Kawachi, Y. *Calendar of English Renaissance Drama 1558-1642*. New York, 1986.

Kendall, P.M. *Richard III*. New York, 1956.

Kenny, R.W. *Elizabeth's Admiral. The Political Career of Charles Howard Earl of Nottingham, 1536-1624*. Baltimore, 1970.

Kinney, A. *Titled Elizabethans*. New York, 1973.

Knapp, R.S. *Shakespeare—The Theater and the Book*. Princeton, 1989.

Knights, L.C. *Drama and Society in the Age of Jonson*. London, 1937.

Knutson, R.L. "Influence of the Repertory System on Revival and Revision of *The Spanish Tragedy* and *Dr. Faustus*." *English Literary Renaissance* 18 (1988).

Koenigsberger, H.G. and G.L. Mosse. *Europe in the Sixteenth Century*. New York, 1968.

Kohler, M.J. "Dr. Rodrigo Lopez...and His Relations to America." *Publications of the American Jewish Historical Society* 17 (1909).

Kuhl, E.P. "Shakespeare's Purpose in Dropping Sly." *Modern Language Notes* 36 (1921).

Lacey, R. *Robert, Earl of Essex*. New York, 1971.

Langer, S.K. *Philosophical Sketches*. New York, 1964.

Lanier, G.W. "From Windsor to London: The Destruction of Monarchial Authority in *Richard II*." *Shakespeare and Renaissance Association of West Virginia. Selected Papers* 13 (1988).

Laroque, F. "An Analogue and Possible Secondary Source to the Pound-of-Flesh Story in *The Merchant of Venice*." *Notes and Queries. New Series* 30 (1983).

Leary, W.G. *Shakespeare Plain. The Making and Performing of Shakespeare's Plays*. New York, 1977.

Lee, M., Jr. *Great Britain's Solomon: James VI and I in His Three Kingdoms*. Urbana, IL, 1990.

Lee, S.L. "The Original of Shylock." *The Gentleman's Magazine* 246 (1880).

Leggatt, A. *Shakespeare's Political Drama*. London, 1988.

_____. *Shakespeare's Comedy of Love*. London, 1974.

Leinwand, T.B. *The City Staged. Jacobean Comedy, 1603-1613*. Madison, WI, 1986.

Lell, G. " 'Ganymede' on the Elizabethan Stage: Homosexual Implications of the Use of Boy-Actors." *Aegis* 1 (1973).

Levin, R. "Women in the Renaissance Theatre Audience." *Shakespeare Quarterly* 40 (1989).

Lewis, W. *The Lion and the Fox. The Role of the Hero in Shakespeare's Plays*. New York, n.d.

Lindenberger, H. *Historical Drama: The Relation of Literature to Reality.* Chicago, 1975.

Loengard, J.S. "An Elizabethan Lawsuit: John Brayne, his Carpenter, and the Building of the Red Lion Theatre." *Shakespeare Quarterly* 35 (1984).

Logan, O. *Culture and Society in Venice 1470-1790.* New York, 1972.

Luke, M. M. *Gloriana, the Years of Elizabeth I.* New York, 1973.

Macgowan, K., and W. Melnitz, and G. Armstrong. *Golden Ages of the Theater.* Englewood Cliffs, NJ, 1979.

Malone, E. *The Plays and Poems of William Shakspeare.* Vols.1, 2. New York, 1966, rpt. of 1821 ed.

Mann, D. *The Elizabethan Player.* London, 1991.

Manning, B. *Village Revolts: Social Protest and Popular Disturbances in England, 1509-1640.* Oxford, 1988.

Marcham, F. *Lopez the Jew. Executed 1594. An Opinion by Gabriel Harvey.* Private printing, 1927.

Marcus, L.S. "Levelling Shakespeare: Local Customs and Local Texts." *Shakespeare Quarterly* 42 (1991).

———. *Puzzling Shakespeare.* Berkeley, 1988.

———. "Shakespeare's Comic Heroines, Elizabeth I, and the Political Uses of Androgyny." *Women in the Middle Ages and Renaissance.* Ed. M.B. Rose Syracuse, 1986.

Marder, L. *His Exits and His Entrances. The Story of Shakespeare's Reputation.* Philadelphia, 1963.

Matter, J.A. *My Lords and Lady of Essex: Their State Trials.* Chicago, 1969.

Matthews, J.F., ed. *Shaw's Dramatic Criticism from the Saturday Review (1895-98).* New York, 1959.

Mattingly, G. *Renaissance Diplomacy.* Boston, 1971.

McAlindon, T. *English Renaissance Tragedy.* Vancouver, 1986.

McNeill, W. *Venice: The Hinge of Europe 1081-1797.* Chicago, 1974.

McCoy, R. " 'A Dangerous Image': the Earl of Essex and Elizabethan Chivalry." *Journal of Medieval and Renaissance Studies* 13 (1983).

McDonald, R. *Shakespeare & Jonson. Jonson & Shakespeare.* Lincoln, NE, 1988.

McLuskie, K.E. *Renaissance Dramatists.* Atlantic Highlands, NJ, 1989.

———. "The Poets' Royal Exchange: Patronage and Commerce in Early Modern Drama." *The Yearbook of English Studies* 21 (1991).

Meagher, J.C. "Economy and Recognition: Thirteen Shakespearean Puzzles." *Shakespeare Quarterly* 34 (1984).

Miklashevskii, K. *La Commedia dell'Arte.* Paris, 1927.

Miller, E.H. *The Professional Writer in Elizabethan England.* Cambridge, MA, 1959.

Mizener, A., ed. *Teaching Shakespeare.* New York, 1969.

Moisan, T. " 'Knock me here soundly': Comic Misprision and Class Consciousness in Shakespeare." *Shakespeare Quarterly* 42 (1991).

Morris, B. "Introduction." *The Taming of the Shrew.* London, 1981.

Morris, T.P. "Shakespeare hath given him a purge to make him bewray his credit." *Shakespeare and Renaissance Association of West Virginia. Selected Papers* 15 (1992).

Muir, K. *Shakespeare. Contrasts and Controversies.* Norman, OK, 1985.

Mullaney, S. *The Place of the Stage. License, Play and Power in Renaissance England.* Chicago, 1988.

Myers, A.R. *England in the Late Middle Ages.* Baltimore, 1966.

Neale, J.E. *Queen Elizabeth.* Garden City, NY, 1957.

Neely, C.T. " 'Documents in Madness': Reading Madness and Gender in Shakespeare's Tragedies and Early Modern Culture." *Shakespeare Quarterly* 42 (1991).

Neill, M. "Unproper Beds: Race, Adultery, and the Hideous in Othello." *Shakespeare Quarterly* 40 (1989).

Nelson, B. *The Idea of Usury: From Tribal Brotherhood to Universal Otherhood.* Chicago, 1969.

Newdigate, B.H. *Michael Drayton and His Circle.* Oxford, 1961.

Newman, K. "Portia's Ring: Unruly Women and Structures of Exchange in *The Merchant of Venice.*" *Shakespeare Quarterly* 38 (1987).

_____. "Renaissance Family Politics and Shakespeare's *The Taming of the Shrew.*" *English Literary Renaissance* 16 (1986).

Nicoll, A. *Masks, Mimes, and Miracles.* New York, 1963.

_____, ed. *The Works of Cyril Tourneur.* New York, 1963.

Nosworthy, J.M. "*Hamlet* and the Player Who Could Not Keep Counsel." *Shakespeare Survey* 3 (1950).

Novy, M.L. "Patriarchy and Play in *The Taming of the Shrew.*" *English Literary Renaissance* 9 (1979).

Nungezer. E. *A Dictionary of Actors...until 1642.* New Haven, 1929.

O'Hara, J. "Shakespeare's *The Merchant of Venice.*" *Explicator* 37 (1979).

Odell, G.C. *Shakespeare from Betterton to Irving.* New York, 1963.

Orlin, L.C. *Private Matters in Post-Reformation England.* Ithaca, NY, forthcoming from Cornell UP.

Orrell, J. "Peter Street at the Fortune and the Globe." *Shakespeare Survey* 33 (1980).

Owen, T. "Twenty Questions on Shakespeare's *Troilus and Cressida.*" *Selected Papers. Shakespeare and Renaissance Association of West Virginia* 13 (1988).

Palmer, J.L. *Comic Characters in Shakespeare*. London, 1961.

Parry, J.H. *The Age of Reconnaissance*. New York, 1963.

Parry, P.H. "The Boyhood of Shakespeare's Heroines." *Shakespeare Survey* 42 (1990).

Patterson, A. *Shakespeare and the Popular Voice*. Oxford, 1989.

Penrose, B. *Travel and Discovery in the Renaissance*. Cambridge, MA, 1952.

Perret, M.D. "Shakespeare's Jew: Preconception and Performance." *Shakespeare Studies* 20 (1988).

Pitt, A. *Shakespeare's Women*. Totowa, NJ, 1981.

Plant, M. *The English Book Trade*. London, 1965.

Plowden, A. *The Elizabethan Secret Service*. New York, 1991.

Pollard, A.W. and G.R. Redgrave, eds. *A Short-Title Catalogue of Books. Printed in England...1475-1640*. London, 1956.

Popkin, R.H. "A Jewish Merchant of Venice." *Shakespeare Quarterly* 40 (1989).

Potter, L. " 'Nobody's Perfect': Actors' Memories and Shakespeare's Plays of the 1590s." *Shakespeare Survey* 42 (1990).

Price, G. *Thomas Dekker*. New York, 1969.

Prior, M. "Which is the Jew that Shakespeare Drew? Shylock Among the Critics." *American Scholar* 50 (1981).

Pronko, L. *The World of Jean Anouilh*. Berkeley, 1968.

Pye, C. *The Regal Phantasm. Shakespeare and the Politics of Spectacle*. London, 1990.

Quinn, D.B. "Sailors and the Sea." *Shakespeare Survey* 17 (1964).

Rackin, P. *Shakespeare's Tragedies*. New York, 1978.

_____. *Stages of History: Shakespeare's English Chronicles*. Ithaca, NY, 1990.

Rappaport, S. *World within Worlds: Structures of Life in Sixteenth-Century London*. Cambridge, 1989.

Read, C. *Lord Burghley and Queen Elizabeth*. New York, 1960.

Reay, B., ed. *Popular Culture in Seventeenth Century England*. New York, 1985.

Reddaway, T.F. "London and the Court." *Shakespeare Survey* 17 (1964).

Reese, M.M. *Shakespeare. His Life and His Work*. London, 1980.

Ribner, I. *The English History Play in the Age of Shakespeare*. London, 1965.

Ridley, J. *Elizabeth I*. New York, 1988.

Riggs, D. *Ben Jonson: a Life*. Cambridge, MA, 1989.

Roberts, J.A. "Horses and Hermaphrodites: Metamorphoses in *The Taming of the Shrew*." *Shakespeare Quarterly* 34 (1983).

Robertson, J., ed. *A Calendar of Dramatic Records in the Livery Companies of London, 1485-1640*. London, 1954.

Rose, M.B. *The Expense of Spirit: Love and Sexuality in English Renaissance Drama.* Ithaca, NY, 1988.

_____. "Where Are the Mothers in Shakespeare? Options for Gender Representation in the English Renaissance." *Shakespeare Quarterly* 42 (1991).

Rosenberg, E. *From Shylock to Svengali. Jewish Stereotypes in English Fiction.* Stanford, CA, 1960.

Ross, C. *The Wars of the Roses.* New York, 1986.

Roth, C. *Magna bibliotheca anglo-judaica: a bibliographical guide to Anglo-Jewish history.* London, 1937.

_____. *The Jews in the Renaissance.* New York, 1964.

_____. *A History of the Marranos.* New York, 1974.

Rowse, A.L. *Shakespeare's Southampton.* New York, 1965.

_____. *William Shakespeare.* New York, 1963.

Royce, A. "The Venetian Commedia: Actors and Masques in the Development of the *Commedia dell'Arte.*" *Theatre Survey* 28 (1986).

Rudnytsky, P. L. "Henry VIII and the Deconstruction of History." *Shakespeare Survey* 43 (1990).

Rye, W., ed. *Norfolk Records.* Norwich, 1892.

Saccio, P. *Shakespeare's English Kings.* Oxford, 1979.

_____. "Shrewd and Kindly Farce." *Shakespeare Survey* 37 (1984).

Sams, E. "The Timing of the *Shrews.*" *Notes and Queries. New Series* 32 (1985).

_____. "Thompson, A., (ed.), *The Taming of the Shrew.*" *Notes and Queries. New Series* 33 (1986).

Sargeaunt, J.M. *John Ford.* New York, 1966.

Schoenbaum, S. *Shakespeare: The Globe and the World.* New York, 1979.

_____. *William Shakespeare. A Compact Documentary Life.* Oxford, 1987.

_____. *William Shakespeare: Records and Images.* New York, 1981.

Schonfeld, S.J. "A Hebrew Source for *The Merchant of Venice.*" *Shakespeare Survey* 32 (1979).

Schwarz, M.L. "Sir Edward Coke and 'This scept'red Isle': a Case of Borrowing." *Notes and Queries. New Series* 35 (1988).

Seavoy, R.E. *Famine in Peasant Societies.* New York, 1986.

Seltzer, "The Actors and Staging." *A New Companion to Shakespeare Studies.* Eds. K. Muir and S. Schoenbaum. Cambridge, 1971.

Shaheen, N. "*A Warning for Fair Women* and *Hamlet.*" *Notes and Queries. New Series* 30 (1983).

Shapiro, B.J. "Which is The Merchant here, and which The Jew?: Shakespeare and the Economics of Influence." *Shakespeare Studies* 20 (1988).

Shapiro, M. *Children of the Revels.* New York, 1977.

Sharpe, K. and S.N. Zwicker. *Politics of Discourse. The Literature and History of Seventeenth-Century England.* Berkeley, 1987.

Sharpe, R.B. *The Real War of the Theatres.* New York, 1935.

Shaw, J. "The Staging of Parody and Parallels in *I Henry IV.*" *Shakespeare Survey* 20 (1967).

Simon, J. *Education and Society in Tudor England.* Cambridge, 1967.

Simonds, P.G. "Sacred and Sexual Motifs in All's Well That Ends Well." *Renaissance Quarterly* 17 (1989).

Simpson, F. "New Place. The Only Representation of Shakespeare's House from an Unpublished Manuscript." *Shakespeare Survey* 5 (1952).

Sinsheimer, H. *Shylock. The History of a Character.* New York, 1947.

Sisson, C.J. *The Boar's Head Theatre. An Inn-yard Theatre of the Elizabethan Age.* Ed. S. Wells. London, 1972.

Smidt, K. *Unconformities in Shakespeare's Tragedies.* New York, 1990.

Smith, A.H. *County and Court: Government and Politics in Norfolk, 1558-1603.* Oxford, 1974.

Smith, B.R. *Homosexual Desire in Shakespeare's England.* Chicago, 1991.

Smith, I. *Shakespeare's Blackfriars Playhouse.* New York, 1964.

Smith, L.B. *Elizabeth Tudor: Portrait of a Queen.* Boston, 1975.

_____. "English Treason Trials and Confessions in the Sixteenth Century." *The Elizabethan Age.* Ed. D.L. Stevenson. Greenwich, CT, 1966.

_____. *Treason in Tudor England. Politics and Paranoia.* Princeton, 1986.

Smith, W. *Italian Actors of the Renaissance.* New York, 1930.

Smithey, R. *English Seamen.* 2 vols. Ed. D. Hannay. London, 1904.

Snyder, S. *The Comic Matrix of Shakespeare's Tragedies.* Princeton, 1979.

Somerset A. *Elizabeth I.* New York, 1991.

Southern, R. *The Seven Ages of Theatre.* New York, 1963.

Speaight, R. *Shakespeare. The Man and His Achievement.* New York, 1977.

Spevack, M. *A Complete and Systematic Concordance to the Works of Shakespeare.* 5 vols. Hildesheim, 1968.

Spikes, J.D. "The Jacobean History Play and the Myth of the Elect Nation." *Renaissance Drama. New Series* 8 (1977).

Starkey, D., et. al. *The English Court from the Wars of the Roses to the Civil War.* London, 1987.

Sternfeld, F.W. "Music and Ballads." *Shakespeare Survey* 17 (1964).

Stone, L. *Family and Fortune: Studies in Aristocratic Finance in the Sixteenth and Seventeenth Centuries.* Oxford, 1973.

_____. *The Crisis of the Aristocracy, 1558-1641.* Oxford, 1965.

_____. *The Family, Sex and Marriage in England, 1500-1800.* New York, 1979.

Stopes, C.C. *Burbage and Shakespeare's Stage.* London, 1913.

Strachey, L. *Elizabeth and Essex.* New York, 1928.

Strong, R. *Gloriana. The Portraits of Queen Elizabeth I.* London, 1987.

Strunk, W., Jr., "The Elizabethan Showman's Ape." *Modern Language Notes* 32 (1917).

Strype, J. *Annals of the Reformation.* Vols. 2, 4. Oxford, 1824.

Styan, J.L. *Shakespeare's Stagecraft.* Cambridge, 1975.

Taft, E.M. "Henry Bolingbroke's England." *Shakespeare and Renaissance Association of West Virginia. Selected Papers* 15 (1992).

Taylor, G. *Reinventing Shakespeare.* New York, 1989.

Tennenhouse, L. *Power on Display. The Politics of Shakespeare's Genres.* New York, 1986.

The Oxford English Dictionary. 2nd ed. Oxford, 1989.

Thirsk, J. *Economic Policy and Projects. The Development of a Consumer Society in Early Modern England.* Oxford, 1978.

Thompson A. "Dating Evidence for *The Taming of the Shrew.*" *Notes and Queries. New Series* 29 (1982).

Tillyard, E.M.W. *Shakespeare's Early Comedies.* New York, 1965.

Townend, P., ed. *Burke's Genealogical and Heraldic History of the Peerage Baronetage and Knightage.* 104th ed. London, 1967.

Tucker, E. "The Letter of the Law in *Merchant of Venice.*" *Shakespeare Survey* 29 (1976).

Underdown, D. *Revel, Riot, and Rebellion. Popular Politics and Culture in England. 1603-1660.* Oxford, 1985.

Van Doren, M. *Shakespeare.* New York, 1939.

Vetter, H. "Faint Smile in Defeat." *Military History* (April 1991).

von Martin, A. *Sociology of the Renaissance.* New York, 1963.

Warneke, S. "Educational Travellers: Popular Imagery and Public Criticism in Early Modern England." *Journal of Popular Culture* (forthcoming).

Wayne, D.E. "Drama and Society in the Age of Jonson." *Renaissance Drama* 13 (1982).

_____. "The 'Exchange of Letters': Early Modern Contradictions and Postmodern Conundrums." *The Consumption of Culture in the Early Modern Period.* Eds. A. Bermingham and J. Brewer. London, forthcoming from Routledge.

Webb, S. and B. *History of English Local Government.* Vol. 6. *English Prisons under Local Government.* Hamden, CT, 1963.

Webster, M. *Shakespeare Without Tears.* New York, 1975.

Weinreb B. and C. Hibbert. *The London Encyclopaedia.* London, 1983.

Wells, R.H. *Shakespeare: Politics and the State.* London, 1986.

Wells, S. "*The Taming of the Shrew* and *King Lear*: A Structural Comparison. *Shakespeare Survey* 33 (1980).

Wentersdorf, K.P. "The Original Ending of *The Taming of the Shrew*: A Reconsideration." *Studies in English Literature* 13 (1978).

Wentworth, S.L. *An Historical and Critical Study of Crucial Directing and Acting Problems in William Shakespeare's The Taming of the Shrew.* Dissertation, Bowling Green State University, 1983.

Wheeler, C.F. *Classical Mythology in the Plays, Masques, and Poems of Ben Jonson.* Princeton, 1938.

Wickham, G. *Early English Stages, 1300 to 1660.* 3 vols. New York, 1963.

Williams, G.W. "Kate and Petruchio: Strength and Love." *English Language Notes* 24 (1991).

Williamson, J.A. *The Age of Drake.* Cleveland, 1965.

Williamson, M. *The Patriarchy of Shakespeare's Comedies.* Detroit, 1986.

Wilson, E. *Shaw on Shakespeare.* New York, 1961.

Wilson, E. and A. Goldfarb. *Living Theater.* New York, 1983.

Wilson, R. " 'A Mingle Yarn': Shakespeare and the Cloth Workers." *Literature and History* 12 (1986).

Winter, W. *Shakespeare on the Stage.* New York, 1915.

Withycombe, E. *The Oxford Dictionary of English Christian Names.* 3rd ed.

Woodbridge, L. *Women and the English Renaissance.* Urbana, IL, 1984.

Womersley, D. "*3 Henry VI*: Shakespeare, Tacitus and parricide." *Notes and Queries. New Series* 32 (1985).

_____. "Sir John Hayward's tacitism." *Renaissance Studies* 6 (1992).

Wrightson, K. *English Society 1580-1680.* New Brunswick, NJ, 1982.

Yachnin, P. "The Powerless Theater." *English Literary Renaissance* 21 (1991).

Yonge, C.M. *History of Christian Names.* London, 1884.